Globalization under Construction

Globalization under Construction

Governmentality, Law, and Identity

Richard Warren Perry and Bill Maurer, Editors

University of Minnesota Press
Minneapolis • London

Published by the University of Minnesota Press
111 Third Avenue South, Suite 290
Minneapolis, MN 55401-2520
http://www.upress.umn.edu

Printed in the United States of America on acid-free paper

Library of Congress Cataloging-in-Publication Data

Globalization under construction : governmentality, law, and identity /
Richard Warren Perry and Bill Maurer, editors.
    p. cm.
Includes bibliographical references and index.
    ISBN 0-8166-3965-5 (hardcover : alk. paper) — ISBN 0-8166-3966-3
(pbk. : alk. paper)
    1. Globalization. I. Perry, Richard Warren. II. Maurer, Bill, 1968–
JZ1318 .G6792 2003
303.48′2—dc21
                                        2003008777

The University of Minnesota is an equal-opportunity educator and employer.

12 11 10 09 08 07 06 05 04 03   10 9 8 7 6 5 4 3 2 1

Contents

Acknowledgments

The essays in this volume derive from the conference "New World Orders? The Contested Terrains of Globalization," held at the University of California, Irvine, in 1998. This event was funded by conference grants from the University of California's systemwide Institute on Global Conflict and Cooperation, from the UC Irvine Center for Global Peace and Conflict Studies, and from the UC Irvine School of Social Ecology. The preparation of this manuscript has been supported in part by a research grant from Irvine's Center for Global Peace and Conflict Studies ("Alternative Globalizations," awarded to Paula Garb, Bill Maurer, and Richard Perry).

In addition to the contributors to this volume, other participants in the conference included David Smith, John Torpey, James Ferguson, Kathleen McAfee, Nikolai Ssorin-Chaikov, Kate Sullivan, Joachim Blatter, Helen Ingram, Ruth Buchanan, Suzana Sawyer, Iain Boal, David McDermott Hughes, Pamela Doughman, Roger Rouse, Victoria Bernal, Vladimir Bobrovnikov, Paula Garb, Nahum Chandler, Alison Brysk, and Barbara Yngvesson. Many of the conference papers specifically on transnational environmental issues were published as the book *Reflections on Water: New Approaches to Transboundary Environmental Cooperation and Conflict*, edited by Helen Ingram and Joachim Blatter (Cambridge: MIT Press, 2001).

This volume and the conference from which it derives are both elements of a several-year collaboration of UC Irvine faculty, visiting faculty, and graduate students. In 1996, Richard Perry submitted a grant proposal titled "Law as Regimes of Culture in the Global Era" to fund a cluster of visiting faculty. This grant brought Rosemary Coombe, Nahum Chandler, and Susan Coutin to the Irvine campus as Chancellor's Visiting Faculty in the spring of 1997 (Coutin has since become a permanent member of the Irvine faculty). At the same time, Perry also submitted a conference proposal, "The End of History and the Governmentality of Space." The following year, this proposal was revised in collaboration with Bill Maurer, Rosemary Coombe, Susan Coutin, Helen Ingram, and John Whiteley and was ultimately awarded the funding that made the "New World Orders?" conference possible. For crucial advice and support, the editors offer special thanks to Helen Ingram, John Whiteley, James Ferguson, Liisa Malkki, and Kitty Calavita.

This book benefited greatly from the help of a number of other colleagues, coworkers, and student assistants. We are grateful for the efforts of Judy Omiya, Barbara Atwell, Andrea Denish, Norma Mendoza, Mirela Marinelli, Melanie Craig, Padraic McCoy, Scott Kaminski, Tamara Teghillo Campbell, and Dimitri Bogazianos.

Globalization and Governmentality: An Introduction

Richard Warren Perry and Bill Maurer

Global Positionings

In this volume, scholars from a variety of disciplines not only question the exorbitant popular hype around "globalization," but also seek to build upon the pioneering global theorizing of the 1990s (represented by David Harvey, Saskia Sassen, Arjun Appadurai, Manuel Castells, and Anthony Giddens, among numerous others). Much of that theoretical work has focused on epistemic shifts of recent decades, shifts described in terms of a causal relation between globalization phenomena and the "postmodern condition."

This is marked by a new economy made possible by its "informational mode of production" that has created a new global "space of flows" (Castells 1998), "an economy with the capacity to work in real time on a planetary scale" (Castells 1996, 92). This global space is distinguished by flexible production, flexible political identities, porous borders, and an accompanying general fragmentation or fluidity (an ongoing process of disaggregation or "unbundling") of modernity's foundational concepts—the territorial nation-state, and its national society, economy, and *raison d'état*.

"Globalization" is also a discursive topos; it is a space of debate, both popular and academic, that has emerged as the "successor to the debates on modernity and postmodernity in the understanding of sociocultural change and as the central problematic for social theory"

(Featherstone, Lash, and Robertson 1995, 1). It is a space of debate about alternative visions of humankind's future—a magic kingdom that is alternately utopian and dystopian. To quote the introduction of a recent volume on globalization:

> "Globalization" has become an increasingly influential paradigm in the human sciences since the beginning of the 1990s. It has in a very important sense been the successor to the debates on modernity and post-modernity in the understanding of sociocultural change and as the central problematic for social theory . . . [G]lobalization should be seen as now no longer emergent, but as a more fully "emerged" theory in the social sciences . . . [Where] Marxist predecessors focused on a temporal meta-narrative about the various transitions from feudalism to capitalism to socialism . . . for some theorists of postmodernity, history is to be conceived as a parallel set of temporal transitions from tradition to modernity to postmodernity. Here postmodernity is in effect accorded the status of being the latest stage in a master logic of development, notwithstanding all the obligatory homilies paid to the critique of development. In this context, the concept of globalization represents an important shift in transmuting this temporality into a spatial framework. (Ibid., 1)

"Globalization," then, is less the name of a generally agreed-upon set of technological, economic, sociocultural, or political developments than it is an ensemble of intersecting arguments about the history of the present, and about the nature of the particular future that the quite specific present portends.

The aspiration of this volume is not to resolve an ultimate semantic or philosophical or ontological debate over what "globalization" is or is not, nor is it to decide between what Pierre Bourdieu has called "the 'globalization' myth" and a definitive historical truth of globalization (Bourdieu 1998; see also Sadowski 1998); for, as Nikolas Rose pointedly observes, the "truth effects" of globalization discourses are "somewhat independent of the veracity of the analysis" (Rose 1996,

354). Instead, this volume approaches globalization discourses as "an intellectual framework for rendering reality thinkable as a site of practical activity [because] 'it is through language that governmental fields are composed, rendered thinkable and manageable'" (O'Malley 1996, 311, quoting Miller and Rose 1990, 7).

Therefore, rather than a quest for some transhistorical "why" of globalization, this volume addresses globalization as an ensemble of quite specific governmental "hows," as a "range of rationalities and techniques" (Valverde 1996, 358; Rose 1996, 328), as a disparate array of practices and their effects, as metapragmatic discursive mediations of order and disorder, as effects of government and ungovernment. Its goal is to discern in the disparateness of contemporary events the precipitation of emerging patterns of global governmentality.

The following chapters seek to draw connections among aspects of globalization that are too often treated in isolation from one another—when they are not ignored altogether—because of academic divides and disciplinary vanishing points. This project is not so much a recuperating as a reframing of a debate already in progress. The contributors to this volume represent various academic disciplines and perspectives—anthropology, sociology, law, geography, history—as well as "rootless" scholars thoroughly committed to spaces of interdisciplinarity. All, however, are interested in the bringing together of globalization and governmentality—fraught conceptual frames through which to approach fraught phenomena, yet frameworks of analysis that, as the volume makes clear, need to be brought into productive tension if we are to apprehend the epochal changes of the present. The scholars who have contributed to this volume give particular attention to the nature of novel transnational flows of capital, information, commodities, and people that are thought to distinguish globalization, at least in the standard view, from other world-girdling linkages of the past. They do so, however, not to quantify these flows as new independent variables that have effects on familiar sociological structures, in a narrowly positivist, causal social-scientific mode, but rather to query the dynamics of the "flow" metaphor itself, and to question how its dynamics are imagined such that they can be presumed, by analysts and policy makers, elites and everyday folk, to be so magically causal in the first place.

What in fact emerges in these chapters are even more complicated ensembles of relations than expected and, indeed, discourses and practices of relationality itself, that structure the globalist epistemic field and the forms of scholarly inquiry that have developed around it. Although each of the directions of research on contemporary global questions that is represented in this volume surely carries along its own disciplinary baggage and blind spots, we find that placing them in dialogue with one another provides a useful juxtaposition of vantage points from which to consider contemporary global trends. To address "globalization" requires a heterogeneity of perspectives that encompasses not just different disciplinary objects of study, but also diverse knowledge practices of disciplinarity, both academic and governmental. This volume is intended to offer precisely that.

Why Global Governmentality?

Much of the existing literature on globalization (to the extent that there already exists a "globalization canon") has been preoccupied with the status of the territorial nation-state form and the ongoing corrosive effects on it of the global economic regimes of the late twentieth century. Proliferating transnational media soberly report with each passing news cycle that global markets in capital, services, commodities, labor, natural resources, pollution rights, intellectual and other property rights, as well as human rights and similar transnational fields and flows of interest and action, are all busily eroding the sovereign territorial powers of nation-states. In the United States, the unheralded coming together of trade unionists, neocommunitarians, paleoconservatives, and environmentalists that opposed the North American Free Trade Agreement and defeated the "fast-track" authorization of trade agreements is simply one striking example of an abiding national sensibility asserted against the disintegrative effects of global market flows.

Still, what one finds in the studies presented here is that the

nation-state, its territoriality, and its sovereignty are not so much eroding as transforming into overlapping and hierarchically nested jurisdictions, interpenetrated transnational fields of interest, and graduated
sovereignties (see Ong in this volume). From this angle, globalization
appears as a "refiguring of the territory of government" (Rose 1996,
308), as a transformation in the spatiotemporal regimes of modern governmentality, and as proliferating strategies for the management of
individuals and populations that operate in concert with, but that are
not reducible to, the structures of the liberal nation-state. The nation-
state form, we find, is not evaporating, but rather is transforming itself
into a frame of scalar reference against which the directionality and
velocity of these movements and flows become legible.

In its broadest outlines, this transformation has been variously described as a "reterritorialization" of grids of power (Gupta and Ferguson
1992), as "rezoning sovereignty" (Ong 1998), and as the "unbundling"
of national territoriality and the "de-nationalizing of sovereignty"
(Slaughter 1997; Sassen 1999). This widely noted trend toward "perfo-
rated," "graduated," "dispersed," "distributed," "leaking," or postmodern sovereignties in the global "space of flows" (Macklem 1993; Mezey
1996; Ong 1998; Lipschutz 1992; Soja 1989; Castells 1998) has been
accompanied by an emergence of other sorts of spatial frontiers. In
terms borrowed from Benedict Anderson's foundational work on "imagined communities," one could describe what is taking place as a reconfiguration of the "modular" elements of the "grammar" of "nation-ness"
(1991, xiv, 4). This reconfiguration has similarly implied a shift in the
meaning of fundamental concepts such as state, market, civil society,
family–kin networks, tribes, ethnoracial groups, nation-states, risk, space,
and time. Theories and practices of governance increasingly incorporate
social, cultural, and private managerial logics as new arts of governmentality emerge.

Today's new world orders, even as they rest on sedimented configurations of spatial difference inherited from the ethnoracial and colonial/
imperial systems of the past (see Kalpagam 2000, 2002; Moore 1998),
are constructed of novel regimes of spatial and temporal segregation,

innovations of enclosure and exclusion. To comprehend the mutually contingent relations of state and market (as well as the very categories "state" and "market" themselves—not to mention "local" and "global" and the other constitutive binaries of globalization discourses) requires close attention to particular times and places. One ought not therefore obsess over whether the state is withering away or that it is being reempowered, or whether the market is either all-pervasive or is still in service to the nation-state. Rather, as the essays that follow show, *state* and *market* themselves are being reconfigured in novel ways (just as are the scholarly understandings of them). Indeed, one finds new regimes of translocal or transnational governmentality—"unbundled" nation-state functions being networked into "transgovernmental" world orders, in Anne-Marie Slaughter's useful terminology (1997)—distinguishing the current moment of globalization.

Attending to Anna Tsing's cautions about research on "the global situation" (Tsing 2000), rather than attempt to isolate the "local" and the "global" as distinct phenomenal scales, we suggest that it is necessary to question scalarity itself, those ideologies that rely on stable and stabilizing assumptions about place, region, globality as well as movement, stasis, circulation, flow. We note the "rhetorics of scale as well as contests over what will count as relevant scales" (Tsing 2000, 347). And, rather than simply assuming global epochal shifts, as the first wave of global theorizing has tended to do, we instead look for "projects of governance" (Valverde 1996, 358), for "bundles of ideas and practices as [they are] realized in particular times and places" (Tsing 2000, 347). The particular sort of projects we have in mind in this volume are global-governmental ones.

Consider briefly the example of Africa—the example routinely, all but obligatorily, cited in globalist discourse as the paradigm case of failed state-political governance, of multiethnic "pandemonium," and so on (Moynihan 1993). At the conference from which this volume derives, James Ferguson, a leading scholar of development in Africa, considered the question of how and by whom Africa is in fact governed now. He suggested that the state regimes of African countries operate within a larger fabric of governance composed of multinational corporations, multinational nongovernmental organizations, as well as organs of the World Bank, the International Monetary Fund, and other supranational entities. This is what some commentators have termed, more generally, the "quango-ization of the State"—where "quango" is a professional term of art, an acronym for "quasi-autonomous nongovernmental organization" (Rose 1996, 350, 354). The specific governmental rationalities at work in Africa include resource extraction, public health, and religious proselytization. The point is that this governance of Africa is not in fact anomalous in kind—it is simply a salient case of the more general pattern of overlapping and interpenetrated forms and rationalities of governance found elsewhere in the world. The Enlightenment vision of state, market, and civil society as distinct fields of action and domains of rationality—to the extent that it might ever have been accurate—is now no more adequately descriptive of Europe or Asia or the Americas than it is of Africa.

In this connection, the close attention to particular times and places that Tsing recommends need not devolve into the positivism that has burdened Anglophone social science since its contemporary disciplinary formulation after World War II. The chapters collected here attempt to strike a balance between grounded empirical research and a questioning of the theoretical presuppositions that have undergirded positivist social inquiry. More specifically, to recognize the convergence of academic theories of globalization and the discourses and practices of global elites—along with the unarticulated legitimating effects of that convergence—requires attention to the metapragmatics of "globalization." This is to ask how accounts of global phenomena, academic, managerial, and other, are deployed to varied ends, in different contexts, and still to perceive the convergent implications of globalizing epistemics. This is to acknowledge the channeling strictures of academic as well as governmental disciplines.

The very fact that globalization commentary has remained so mired in a debate over the primacy of the nation-state or the global economy demonstrates that this writing remains within reified models inherited from early-modern sociopolitical theory (specifically, the opposition in political theory between left and right Hegelians over the rationality of the state versus that of the market and civil society; see Fukuyama 1992). It is precisely here that we have found heuristic value in Michel Foucault's notion of "governmentality." Less a theory than an analytics, "governmentality" helps to articulate the specific dynamic rationalities intrinsic to the modern arts of government—this is the study of "actually existing, often unsystematic assemblages of technologies and rationalities" (Valverde 1996, 358) and "the imbrication of resistance and rule, the contradictions and tensions, . . . and the subterranean practices of government consequently required to stabilize rule" (O'Malley 1996, 311).

Taken together, a number of recent readings of Foucault's (1991) essay "Governmentality" (mostly Anglophone readings, and readings that are far from entirely congruent with one another) have helped to reinvigorate and to sharpen critical sociolegal responses to Foucault's supposed "expulsion of the law" (Colin Gordon in Burchell, Gordon, and Miller 1991; O'Malley 1994; Simon 1999). A confluence of interest between scholars of governmentalities, on the one hand, and globalizations, on the other, has resulted in a productive rethinking of the relationships among power, discipline, governance, and law.

The essays collected here are, we believe, the clearest expression to date of this confluence. As Aihwa Ong argues (in this volume), "globalization has induced governments to think up new ways of governing and valuing different categories of their subject populations," that is, to new arts and rationalities of government, or governmentalities. On the figuring of sovereignty in globalization discourse, Ong reconsiders "sovereignty as 'an effect of practices' associated with law and other forms of regulation that construct relations between the state, its population, and the market." It is in just this fashion, by attending to the effects of the practices of globalization and of global discourses, that the studies presented here distinguish themselves from the broad trend of globalization commentary. As Foucault observed in another context, "People know what they do, they frequently know why they do what they do; but what they don't know is what what they do does" (Foucault quoted in Dreyfus and Rabinow 1983, 187; see also the discussion in Michaels 1987, 179).

In this volume, then, we worry less over the question of what globalization is than we focus on the metapragmatics of what doing "globalization" does. Rather than setting out either to bless globalization or to condemn it, our project is to explore the forms and practices and effects of governmentality that are integral to global modernity's architecture of flows and freedoms. We ask what are the rationalities of government implicit within the globalist project of reconfiguring scale and mobilizing space, time, and difference.

The essays in this volume seek both to look behind the magic acts for the governmental rationalities/technologies that make "globalization" possible and to recognize that, by framing questions the way they have been framed, global theorizing has never not been under the spell of the globalization mythos. It is our view that, as Diane Nelson has suggested referring to commodity fetishism, "Playing detective and getting down to how the fetish 'really' works completely misses the magic act" (1999, 77). To focus on the forms, as it were, of globalization—looking for the real behind the global hype or the global hope—misses the crucial question of why the global should assume such forms in the first place. We do not seek simply to demythologize Bourdieu's "myth of globalization," or to "unmask" globalization, or to "de-dupe" those "blinded" by its wonders. We also seek to understand these wonders and their effects.

The implicit and explicit emphasis on governmentality gives the essays collected here their analytic punch. If the tactics and strategies of governance characterizing new world orders operate on a market model, could assessments of those tactics and strategies hold state and market separate as analytic categories? Or do critical analysts of globalization need a new conceptual repertoire? This volume argues the latter, and these essays provide good examples of how to develop that perspective. They interrogate the terms and the metaphysics implicit and explicit in globalization theorizing: the market, the nation-state, sovereignty, space, time, movement, capital, and labor. Regarded from one angle, they argue that the nation-state and its sovereignty ought not be considered prefabricated forms into which history and geography are poured; rather, they are being reconfigured, rearticulated, reinvented, rerationalized in distinctive ways (Ong, Perry, Calavita and Suárez-Navaz, Coutin, Merry).

Viewed from another angle, these essays argue that the market, the economy, the domain of private interest in civil society are likewise not a transparent field of free rational choice and action, but complicated constellations of practice and knowledge whose effects are never known in advance (Roberts, Maurer, Coombe, Perry, Coutin, Leonard).

To understand these reconfigurations of state and market entails exploring cosmological dimensions of space, time, and risk, the new media of governance in disjunctive jurisdictions (Maurer, Perry, Sanchez). The reformulation proposed in these essays calls for a new look at some old problems in globalization theory, such as international migration and labor flows (Coutin, Leonard), as well as the imaging of the nation (Merry, Calavita and Suárez-Navaz).

Ultimately, the focus on governmentalities carries the debate beyond the now-belabored stumbling point of the "effects of globalization" on the state, and beyond the historical quandaries of distinguishing contemporary global economies from earlier ones. Governmentality helps us bring to view the constellations of knowledge and techniques that mediate between individual subjects and the imagined monoliths of the modern state and the market. It is this focus on forms of knowledge and intervention that helps us to see that neither the state nor the economy could be a unified, homogeneous entity. Rather, governmentality enables us to disaggregate both state and economy in ways that can contribute considerable analytic purchase to contemporary globalization debates.

References

Anderson, Benedict. 1991. *Imagined Communities: Reflections on the Origins and Spread of Nationalism*. 2d ed. New York: Verso.

Appadurai, Arjun. 1996. *Modernity at Large: Cultural Dimensions of Globalization*. Minneapolis: University of Minnesota Press.

Barry, Andrew, Thomas Osborne, and Nikolas Rose, eds. 1996. *Foucault and Political Reason: Liberalism, Neo-Liberalism, and Rationalities of Government*. Chicago: University of Chicago Press.

Bourdieu, Pierre. 1998. *Acts of Resistance: Against the New Myths of Our Time*. Trans. Richard Nice. Cambridge: Polity Press.

Burchell, Graham, Colin Gordon, and Peter Miller, eds. 1991. *The Foucault Effect: Studies in Governmentality with Two Lectures and an Interview with Michel Foucault*. Chicago: University of Chicago Press.

Castells, Manuel. 1996. *The Rise of the Network Society*. Cambridge: Blackwell Press.

———. 1998. *The Information Age: Economy, Society and Culture*, vol. 1, *The Rise of the Network Society*. Malden, Mass.: Blackwell Publishers.

Dean, Mitchell. 1999. *Governmentality: Power and Rule in Modern Society*. London: Sage.

Dreyfus, Hubert, and Paul Rabinow. 1983. *Michel Foucault: Beyond Structuralism and Hermeneutics*. Chicago: University of Chicago Press.

Featherstone, Mike, Scott Lash, and Roland Robertson, eds. 1995. *Global Modernities*. London: Sage Publications.

Foucault, Michel. 1991. "Governmentality." In *The Foucault Effect: Studies in Governmentality*, ed. Graham Burchell, Colin Gordon, and Peter Miller. Chicago: University of Chicago Press. 87–105.

Fukuyama, Francis. 1992. *The End of History and the Last Man*. New York: Free Press.

Giddens, Anthony. 1990. *The Consequences of Modernity*. Stanford, Calif.: Stanford University Press.

Goldman, Michael. 2001. "Constructing an Environmental State: Eco-governmentality and Other Practices of a 'Green' World Bank." *Social Problems* 48(4) (November): 499–524.

Gupta, Akhil, and James Ferguson. 1992. "Beyond 'Culture': Space, Identity and the Politics of Difference." *Cultural Anthropology* 7(1) (February): 6–23.

Harvey, David. 1989. *The Condition of Postmodernity: An Enquiry into the Origins of Cultural Change*. Cambridge: Blackwell Publishers.

Kalpagam, U. 2000. "Colonial Governmentality and the 'Economy' (India)." *Economy and Society* 29(3) (August): 418–39.

————. 2002. "Colonial Governmentality and the Public Sphere in India." *Journal of Historical Sociology* 15(1) (March): 35–49.

Lipschutz, Ronnie. 1992. "Reconstructing World Politics: The Emergence of Global Civil Society." *Millennium: Journal of International Studies* 21(3): 399.

Macklem, Patrick. 1993. "Distributing Sovereignty: Indian Nations and Equality of Peoples." *Stanford Law Review* 45: 1311.

Maurer, Bill. 1998. "Cyberspatial Sovereignties: Offshore Finance, Digital Cash, and the Limits of Liberalism." *Indiana Journal of Global Legal Studies* 5(2): 493–519.

Merry, Sally Engle. 2001. "Spatial Governmentality and the New Urban Social Order: Controlling Gender Violence through Law." *American Anthropologist* 103(1) (March): 16.

Mezey, Naomi. 1996. "The Distribution of Wealth, Sovereignty, and Culture through Indian Gaming." *Stanford Law Review* 48: 711.

Michaels, Walter Benn. 1987. *The Gold Standard and the Logic of Naturalism.* Berkeley: University of California Press.

Miller, Peter, and Nikolas Rose. 1990. "Governing Economic Life." *Economy and Society* 19(1): 1–27.

Moore, Donald S. 1998. "Subaltern Struggles and the Politics of Place: Remapping Resistance in Zimbabwe's Eastern Highlands." *Cultural Anthropology* 13(3) (August): 344–82.

Moynihan, Daniel Patrick. 1993. *Pandemonium: Ethnicity in International Politics.* New York: Oxford University Press.

Nelson, Diane M. 1999. *A Finger in the Wound: Body Politics in Quincentennial Guatemala.* Berkeley: University of California Press.

O'Malley, Pat. 1994. "Gentle Genocide: The Government of Aboriginal Peoples in Central Australia." *Social Justice* 21.4 (winter): 46–66.

————. 1996. "Indigenous Governance." *Economy and Society* 25(3): 310–26.

Ong, Aihwa. 1998. *Flexible Citizenship: The Cultural Logics of Transnationality.* Durham, N.C.: Duke University Press.

Rose, Nikolas. 1990. *Governing the Soul: The Shaping of the Private Self.* New York: Routledge.

————. 1996. "The Death of the Social? Refiguring the Territory of Government." *Economy and Society* 25(3): 327–56.

Sadowski, Yahya. 1998. *The Myth of Global Chaos.* Washington: Brookings Institution Press.

Sassen, Saskia. 1995. *Losing Control: Sovereignty in an Age of Globalization*. New York: Columbia University Press.

———. 1999. "De-nationalization: Some Conceptual and Empirical Elements." *PoLAR: Political and Legal Anthropology Review* 22(2): 1–17.

Simon, Jonathan. 1999. "Law after Society." *Law and Social Inquiry* 24: 143–94.

Slaughter, Anne-Marie. 1997. "The Real New World Order." *Foreign Affairs* 76(5) (September/October): 183–97.

Soja, Edward. 1989. *Postmodern Geographies*. New York: Verso.

Tsing, Anna. 2000. "The Global Situation." *Cultural Anthropology* 15(3): 327–64.

Valverde, Mariana. 1996. "'Despotism' and Ethical Liberal Governance." *Economy and Society* 25(3): 357–72.

———. 1998. *Diseases of the Will: Alcohol and the Dilemmas of Freedom*. New York: Cambridge University Press.

CHAPTER 1

Global Strategic Vision: Managing the World

Susan Roberts

This essay presents some aspects of a bigger project investigating transnational corporate spatial practices within the context of the problematique of globalization. Specifically, the focus is on ways in which the ideal types of *the* global corporation and the subject of *the* global manager are made up or constructed in the discourse of global management. Source material is drawn from the Anglo-American field of management: management textbooks, management theory books and articles, popular and how-to management books, and business school materials (course descriptions, publicity material, etc.). I am not claiming that representations of *the* global corporation or *the* global manager are translated directly into the actual practices of managers in transnational or global corporations. However, I do argue that the ways these representations are set up are important as they have effects as key elements in a discourse of global management.

This discourse is itself just one element in the larger "discursive constellation" identified as globalization. This constellation includes other key discourses such as those of neoliberal economics (and associated discourses of structural adjustment, devaluation, trade liberalization, and austerity); development; deregulation; and new world orders. This constellation powerfully defines collective political and spatial imaginations. The discursive constellation that is globalization is notorious for depicting globalization as a set of imperatives, often portrayed as extrasocial (and extraterritorial) in origin (by treating the economy as a separate and originary sphere or by treating technology in the same way), leaving places and populations no choice but to "compete" on its terms. It is important, therefore, to think through how the discursive constellation that is globalization serves to create (or at least enable) the very circumstances it appears to be describing. It is also important to recall that the discursive is fully social (and vice versa) and as such is never a fixed or totally sutured set of social practices. Rather, it is a set of practices that is in flux at the same time that it is structured by power geometries (see Massey 1993). Thus, although the discursive constellation that is globalization might appear as a completed or even hegemonic set of imperatives, it is the (temporary) result of struggles over material and representational practices between different people and groups of people. By taking a closer look at some of the actors that are presumed most powerful in the discursive constellation of globalization, I explore (in a preliminary way) the uncertainties and anxieties at the heart of globalization.

The discourse of global management that is central to globalization may be seen, following Foucault, as a strategy of power. Like any other strategy of power, this one works by being deployed spatially: it is one element in a bundle of significant strategies of power that at once discursively and materially produce space. The idea of "producing space" signals a poststructuralist theorization of space, drawn largely from the ideas of Henri Lefebvre (1991), in which space is seen as a fully social "thing" that is in no sense prediscursive (cf. Harvey 1989; Natter and Jones 1993). Societies, through spatial practices, "secrete" their spaces. Following Lefebvre, spatial practices may be seen as including "production and reproduction, and entailing the daily routines and flows that secrete communications and transport networks, produce urban hierarchies, and differentiate public and private spaces" (Roberts and Schein 1995, 172). Spatial practices are themselves partly defined by (and work to define) what Lefebvre identifies as representations of space (maps, charts, and any ways of laying out or "knowing" space in an instrumental way) and representational spaces (more "imaginative" spaces reliant on nonverbal symbols and signs, for example, art and film). Representational practices, then, are spatial; and spatial practices are representational (see Lefebvre 1991, 1–67; Harvey 1989, 256–78; Roberts and Schein 1993).

Specifically, in the case of global management, as well as in globalization more broadly, scalar restructuring is depicted as a set of imperatives in which the global is demarcated as the domain of capital in a simplified representation of the world that seems to cast most persons, places, and institutions into unambiguous and largely reactive roles (cf. Appadurai 1990; Smith 1993; Swyngedouw 1997 on scale). In contradistinction, the global corporation and the global manager are constructed as strategic actors and shapers of world space. As Lefebvre noted with regard to what he termed "political ideologies,"

> such ideologies relate to space in a most significant way, because they intervene in space in the form of *strategies*. Their effectiveness in this role—and especially a new development, the fact that worldwide strategies are now seeking to generate global space, their *own* space, and to set it up as absolute—is another reason, and by no means an insignificant one, for developing a new concept of space. (1991,105; emphasis in original)

This essay aims to contribute to an intervention in these sorts of ideological scriptings of world space and politics (cf. Gibson-Graham 1996). It is an examination of a few of the threads in the discourse of global management. First, the ideal type of the *global corporation* is investigated. Barnet and Cavanagh have called global corporations "the midwives of the new world economy" (1994, 15). In the management discourse, this supposedly new organizational form is seen as at once driven by the (extrasocial, etc.) imperatives of globalization, and as driving that process. In management discourse, the global corporation is seen as so different from its predecessors that it requires new techniques of management. The field of *global strategic management* has arisen to address this issue and focuses on how the volatile and risky world economy can be controlled and "managed." As such, global strategic management is a part of contemporary attempts at government in the broadest sense (see Foucault 1991). Changing styles and techniques of government/ management can only be realized through the creation of a new type of manager—the *new global manager*. This is the supposedly new and different subject who can enact global strategic management and lead the global corporation in its drive for competitive advantage. I will argue that this new person is a key subject in the discursive constellation of globalization. The new global manager may be seen, however, as a product more of the desire to manage an unruly world and anxieties about that challenge than of a surefooted and certain hegemonic thing called globalization or even "capitalism" (see Gibson-Graham 1996). In management discourse, the desire to manage is depicted as realized through *global strategic vision*—an essential and distinguishing attribute of the true global manager. What exactly this vision might mean will be addressed—particularly as it entails representations of space and spatial practices.

Through these beginnings, then, "globalization" might be rendered less steady. I join J. K. Gibson-Graham in rejecting "globalization as the inevitable inscription of capitalism" (ibid., 139).

The Global Corporation

In the light of what has just been sketched out, it should seem reasonable not to present an empirical assessment of the validity of the corporate claims to globality. Let me note, however, that I am sympathetic to those who point out that there are not that many really global corporations—that the purported "global reach" is, more often than not, not actually global; that a firm might be "globalized" yet not do business in any part of Africa save perhaps South Africa; that although a firm might have the majority of its workers outside its home country, it still is identified as a corporate citizen of that homebase, and so on and so forth. Here, however, I am mostly concerned with how the business literature represents, and to a degree invents, the global corporation.

It would be wrong to claim that in the business literature there is an agreed-upon single idea of what the global corporation is. The defining features of the global corporation remain under discussion in business schools and management literatures. Sometimes a stage-like model is implied. Such a developmental model would have the firm progress or develop through stages—national, international, then multinational to transnational—ending up at the highest stage: global. However, there is actually little agreement on nomenclature and there are many characterizations of emerging organizational forms. Nonetheless, it is possible to identify some recurrent themes in the business literature concerning key necessary or desirable attributes of the global firm. These include the following:

1. The ability to manage spatially strung-out production/consumption (or value-adding) chains. From raw materials sources to final merchandising and servicing can be a chain that has links in all corners of the globe.

2. This ability is often portrayed as involving a certain commitment to a supranational strategy. Sylvia Ostry notes: "the idea of a global firm is one operating on a world scale and on the basis of a worldwide, rather than a multicountry strategy" (1990, 97). A world-scale strategy is difficult to execute with multicountry organizational structures, so a global corporation is depicted as having a different sort of structure. Percy Barnevik, president and CEO of ABB (Asea Brown Boveri), explains the decentering and denationalization of his company:

> ABB is a company with no geographic center, no national ax to grind. We are a federation of national companies with a global coordination center. Are we a Swiss company? Our headquarters is in Zurich, but only 100 professionals work at headquarters and we will not increase that number. Are we a Swedish company? I'm the CEO, and I was born and educated in Sweden. But our headquarters is not in Sweden, and only two of the eight members of the board of directors are Swedes. Perhaps we are an American

company. We report our financial results in US dollars, and English is ABB's official language. We conduct all high-level meetings in English.

My point is that ABB is none of those things—and all of those things. We are not homeless. We are a company with many homes. (In Taylor 1992, 69)

The corporate structure of the (flexible) global firm is often represented pictorially as the result of an organizational shift from *hierarchy* to *network* or *web*, and from *verticality* to *horizontality*. Terms to describe, and pictorial representations of, the supposedly emergent network organizational form of global corporations have multiplied. For example: Malone and Rockart (1993) write of new "adhocracies" and "answer networks"; Eccles and Nolan (1993) of "informal networks floating on formal hierarchies"; and Konsynski and Karimi (1993) of "integrated-network organizational structure." A typical example of the shift, in this case from hierarchy to the amoeba model of Kazuo Inamori, is shown in Figure 1.1 taken from Nelson's book *Managing Globally* (1994). This shift in corporate form may be seen in the context of longer-term and broader shifts in the organization and representation of economic systems in general (hierarchy to network). Such a shift was appraised by Susan Buck-Morss (1995) as part of her broader project on the invention of "the economy."

3. Such networks or horizontal organizational structures are built around communications infrastructure. Massive investments in the machinery and personnel to organize, process, and transmit huge quantities of information—to generate various sorts of knowledges—are a key feature of the global corporation (cf. Thrift 1998).

4. The "many homes" claimed by ABB in the quotation above signal an additional important attribute of the global firm. This one has attained the status of a mantra in the business school literature; it is the ability to be simultaneously global and local. Preston Townley, president and CEO of the Conference Board, stated

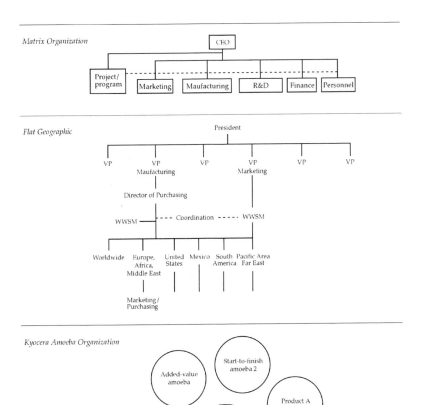

Figure 1.1. Hierarchy to amoeba. Reprinted with permission from Dr. Carl A. Nelson, author of *Managing Globally: A Complete Guide to Competing Worldwide,* and from the Global Manager series by Thompson Learning.

bluntly, "'global' thinks about the world in total *and* about its parts in particular" (1991, 5; emphasis added). This ability of global firms to know the particularities of local markets, to be able to "act like an insider" when doing business in the various markets around the globe, is what Akio Morita, chairman of Sony Corporation, meant by his oft-quoted "global localization." This means creating a structure that can be flexible and responsive to changing circumstances—be they global or local.

5. Flexibility is not just a strategy in the face of changes across space. Flexibility is seen as the essential attribute in a world economy of tremendous uncertainty. In operating and managing strung-out production chains, the global firm faces a host of risks and volatilities that make flexibility essential. Temporal as well as spatial variations have been very significant factors in the emergence of flexibility as the key to success for, and the quintessential characteristic of, the global firm. Bruce Kogut of the University of Pennsylvania's Wharton School noted in an early paper on global management strategies:

> the unique content of a *global* versus a purely domestic strategy lies less in the methods to design long-term strategic plans than in the construction of flexibility which permits a firm to exploit the uncertainty over future changes in exchange rates, competitive moves, or government policy. This flexibility can be attained, for example, by building excess capacity into dispersed sourcing platforms or by arbitraging between different tax regimes. In short, flexibility may be gained by decreasing the firm's dependence on assets already in place. (Kogut 1985, 27; emphasis in original)

Indeed, the rise of strategic management theory as a subdiscipline coincides with the increasing volatility in the world economy faced by U.S. corporations pursuing multinationalization. Flexibility is a term almost as "catchall" as globalization and, as Andrew Sayer and Richard Walker note, this term should also be approached critically as it is slippery, "double-edged and value-laden," and denotes processes with "different political interests at stake" (Sayer and Walker 1992, 198). In the case here, flexibility may be seen as an often vague strategic goal.

Most writers agree that global firms do not have to be huge. Walter Wriston, former CEO of Citicorp, for example, notes: "[s]cale alone is not enough. You have to combine financial strength, market position, and technology leadership with an organizational focus on speed, agility, and simplicity" (Wriston 1992, 8).

So, this decentered organizational structure—flexible enough to be able to take advantage of the uneven topographies of all sorts and of the volatility in the key variables—is crucial. It should be noted, of course, that this is not all brand new, and that what Doreen Massey (1993) calls the "power geometry" underlying these changing representations may be coalescing in quite familiar ways. In his book *Company Man*, Anthony Sampson quotes Bertil Nordquist, an ABB engineer, as saying of Barnevik's corporation: "ABB is not as decentralized as it may appear. Responsibility has been decentralized—but not power" (Sampson 1995, 312).

Global Strategic Management

Rethinking the structure of the multinational firm as it has become the "global corporation" has entailed a concomitant rethinking of the practices of management best suited to running such an organization.

Ideas and practices of management are produced in popular, everyday, corporate, and academic contexts (to name but a few). Nigel Thrift has done some work delineating elements in what he calls the "cultural circuit of capital" that is "responsible for the production and distribution of managerial knowledge to managers" (1998, 42). Thrift identifies three key loci for the production and distribution of "business knowledge": academia (especially business schools), management consultants, and management gurus. These institutional categories are actually very interrelated. For example, 30 percent of Wharton's graduating class of 1997 gained employment in consulting (slightly ahead of the 24.5

percent who ended up in investment banking) (see Wharton 2000). Faculty at business schools are often also consultants (independent or for one of the big and growing firms such as Accenture [formerly Anderson], McKinsey, or PricewaterhouseCoopers [see Ramsay 1996], and even gurus (e.g., Rosabeth Moss Kanter holds an endowed chair at the Harvard Business School). Furthermore, business schools enter into corporate partnerships and corporations establish their own universities (Prahalad 1990; cf. Thrift 1998).

Motorola University was established in 1989. It is described as

the strategic learning organization of the corporation, complementing the training that takes place in Motorola's business groups. Motorola University is organized into regions and colleges with design teams to serve its customer base efficiently. The University manages 7 learning facilities around the world and has 20 offices in 13 countries on 5 continents.

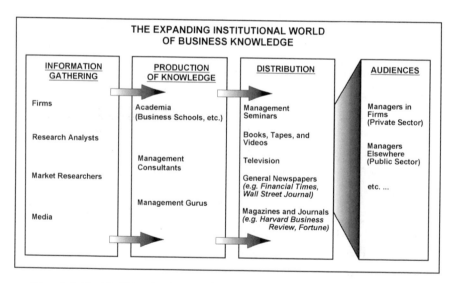

Figure 1.2. Nigel Thrift's cultural circuit of capital. Originally published in *An Unruly World? Globalization, Governance, and Geography*, edited by Andrew Herod, Gearóid Ó Tuathail, and Susan M. Roberts (New York: Routledge, 1998). Reprinted with permission from Routledge/Taylor and Francis.

Motorola University is staffed with a workforce of 400 profession-als. A flex force of 700 writers, developers, translators, and instructors provide service on an as-needed basis. (Motorola 1997)

Motorola University has its own museum and runs the Motorola University Bookstore and administers the Motorola University Press.

University business schools, like corporations, read their environments and recognize shifts in their context. In the 1990s, in the United States and Europe (at least) the top business schools regeared their popular MBA programs in an attempt to cater to the perceived demand for the skills of global management demanded by the global corporation. For example, in 1990 the University of Michigan's Business School's Professor Noel Tichy noted that just as corporations have to undergo massive restructuring to compete in the new globalized world of volatility and uncertainty, so do business schools: "The unfreezing of the faculty from old ways of doing research and teaching will be no easy task and the requirements for global transformational leadership in our business schools is as serious an agenda as for business" (Tichy 1990, 3). Michigan's Business School has developed a Global Leadership Program designed to meet the requirements of graduates who "will require new and diverse skills to facilitate their professional roles as members of *management teams* operating in a virtually *borderless world*" (Barnett 1990, 19; emphasis in original). The dean of Stanford's Graduate School of Business noted in a 1997 letter:

> At the moment, neither we nor any other business school has developed a body of research or a curriculum that we feel provides adequate conceptual frameworks or teaching materials on global management. We are working to remedy this . . . a distinguished group of our faculty are currently developing a new course—Managing in the Global Economy—that will become a required part of the MBA program next year. (Spence 1997)

Conceptualizing the skills presumed to be needed to run and lead a global corporation has become a central task for many business schools as the international MBA gains currency in Europe and other regions outside the United States, and even as hot new management topics such as e-commerce and knowledge economies arrive on the curriculum. In addition, U.S. business schools have been forming alliances with business schools in Europe and Asia (typically). For example, through an alliance between the Wharton School and INSEAD, MBA students can take courses at any of four campuses in Philadelphia, San Francisco, Fontainebleau, and Singapore (Wharton 2000).

Managing the global corporation requires a set of global management skills. In general, managing the global corporation requires vast amounts of information of different sorts, processed efficiently and transmitted effectively. Information and informations and communications technologies have become crucial in the assessment and "management" of risks of all sorts (Ewald 1991). Countering, and even profiting from, risk management is a major way in which today's global corporations outcompete one another—a game that has been so highly developed as to have become the underlying premise for international finance today.

The key skills and knowledges seen as central to the tasks of global management are taught and encoded under the label global strategic management (GSM). GSM is now a very significant subfield of management studies. For example, it is a core required course in the MBA program of the University of Pennsylvania's Wharton School (Wharton 2000).

GSM has grown out of strategic management more generally. Although strategy in management discourse has deep roots (see Knights 1992), contemporary strategic management theory may be seen as arising out of quantitative exercises in "strategic planning" developed in business and management schools in the postwar years (Ansoff 1991). As the 1970s world economy became more volatile and risky, planning and forecasting became at once more important and considerably more difficult. Strategic planning, by corporations and states, is a technique embedded in the whole complex of practices that seek to manage spheres (such as the economy, the population) that Foucault captures in the

Figure 1.3. Business school advertisements from the *Economist*.

term *governmentality* (Foucault 1991; see also Knights 1992). Joseph A. Maciariello notes that "management control is the process of ensuring that the human, physical, and technological resources are allocated so as to achieve the overall purpose of an organization" (quoted in Wilson 1991, 119). It is possible to see how an imperative to control may be linked to historically and socially constructed notions of masculinity— a point to which I shall return (cf. Barry and Hazen 1996, 147).

Strategic management theory grew out of strategic planning theory. However, although the two fields share a future orientation, strategic management entails a definitively relational stance for the corporation as it seeks to investigate how a firm can outcompete its rivals in a volatile and risky world economy. There has been a shift away from planning per se and from the strictly quantitative business of modeling and forecasting toward a more "fuzzy" and broader sense of what strategic management is—a shift that one text characterizes as from "planning" to "coping with the unexpected" (Brake, Walker, and Walker 1995, 7). Nonetheless, strategic management is still about attempts to control.

An additional important aspect of strategy is that it is all about gaining "competitive advantage" (an idea of Michael Porter's [e.g., 1980] that seems to have become almost universally accepted). Thus the concept of "strategy" is relational in an adversarial way—an observation that points toward the military connotations of this practice. More particularly, GSM can be seen to be about devising and enacting spatial strategy, and as such is an intensely geopolitical discourse and practice (cf. Schoenberger 2000). It is not uncommon for their critics to depict transnational corporations as geopolitical actors—specifically as (neo)-imperialists (e.g., Barnet and Cavanagh 1994)—but geopolitics and the trope of imperialism also figure within management discourse itself. Indeed, the Wharton School's MBA students may take MGMT 715, a course titled "Geopolitics" (Wharton 2000).

Imperial conquerors are often approvingly invoked as role models for the would-be global manager. For example, in their 1993 article in the *International Review of Strategic Management*, Jagdish Parikh and

Fred Neubauer approvingly invoke both Napoleon and Sir Stamford Raffles, commending their abilities to create and communicate "strategic visions." (I will return to this idea of strategic vision.) Both imperialists are held up as exemplars for the contemporary global manager (Parikh and Neubauer 1993, 110; see also Bennis 1995, 57 on Napoleon). Not only imperialistic but also militaristic, it is a small step from the skills of the "playing field" to those of the battlefield. Indeed, management texts are replete with the vocabulary of warfare. "Weapons," "strategic arsenals," and their "deployment" are regular elements of management advice for the corporate executive (Bartlett and Ghoshal 1989, 32). Global strategic management skills are often compared to those of the army commander in chief who plans and executes strategy in conditions of warfare.

Reflecting the 1980s and 1990s U.S. fascination with Japanese management techniques—embedded in a world economy wherein Japanese firms were outcompeting U.S. firms in key markets—Sun Tzu's military manual has become *The Art of War for Executives* found in airport newsstands and offering, according to the blurb on the cover, "the ancient wisdom of Sun Tzu's classic text—interpreted for today's business reader" (Krause 1995).

So, despite the New Age-y rhetoric and the purported shift in management as a practice, GSM—a bundle of ideas, concepts, and practices—which stands at the core of global management, remains uncompromisingly militaristic. As already noted, management is all about control—or at least the desire for control. As Clegg and Palmer put it:

> Management, ideally, in so many of its own representations, confers order, reduces uncertainty: it is the capacity to render the uncertain manageable, to conquer space and time with strategic discretion, that marks out the manager. (Clegg and Palmer 1996, 3–4)

Despite the amazing succession of fads in management discourse (leading to some complaints of sensory overload and accusations of "fad surfing"), and their history of poor results, management theories and

The ancient wisdom
of Sun Tzu's classic text—
interpreted for
today's business reader

"Krause puts *The Art of War*
and its concepts in context with today's
business world…easy to read and understand."
—W.C. Keppen,
International Vice President, B.L.E.

THE ART
OF WAR
FOR
EXECUTIVES

Donald G.
Krause

Figure 1.4. Book cover: *The Art of War for Executives.*

techniques, such as those under the label GSM, become popular, in large part, because they offer tools for control. Knights has examined the ways Michael Porter's ideas about strategy and competitive advantage have been adopted despite the severe contradictions and failures associated with them:

> his [Porter's] work is attractive to management also because it contributes to the transformation of management practice into an expertise that is supported by knowledge. As a rational basis for managerial prerogative, this expertise provides some illusion of control, legitimacy, and security in the face of uncertainty. It feeds on the representations of reason and rationality, fact and truth that reflect and reproduce particular "masculine" conceptions of reality. (Knights 1992, 527)

We can, then, see management as a strategy of power. As Clegg and Palmer point out, the rhetoric of management theory "provides not just a legitimation but the *raison d'être* for what it is that some people are able to do to some other people" (1996, 3). On the basis of her empirical studies of corporate culture, Erica Schoenberger takes this point a step further when she observes that "the identities of top managers are intimately caught up in the fact and the sense of power" (1997, 138). However, in considering exactly what *kinds* of power top managers enjoy, Schoenberger notes that

> one conventional candidate would be immediate power over other people: the ability to tell others what to do, what their status and position in the division of labor are, what their rights and responsibilities are. But I would like to suggest that, for the highest levels of management, this power of being the boss is less vital than others of a more conceptual and strategic nature.
>
> More centrally involved is the exercise of a strategic imagination. By this I mean the power to envision how the world should be and to establish the processes of valuation by which both the manager himself and all others are measured. (Ibid., 142)

Thus, the adoption of GSM or any type of management knowledge-practice bundle by managers is not just a matter of how a corporation is run. It is also a matter of the relative position of, and very definitions of, those managers themselves and, hence, of others. GSM is not just about techniques a manager can adopt; rather, GSM entails the global manager acting in a distinct way—indeed, being a distinct type of manager, a distinct type of person. Knights pointed out that when managers at all levels participate in implementing a particular management strategy, they at the same time "collaborate in the constitution, or *self-formation*, of their own identity as *subjects of strategy*" (1992, 528; emphasis added). Schoenberger sees changes in the strategic directions of firms as necessarily entailing difficult changes in the nature of top managers—in her words, a "rethinking" of "their own identities" (1997, 145; see also 147). GSM is about "reimagining the manager" and is thus a project of "constituting certain sorts of persons" (du Gay 1996, 21). As business schools, management gurus, consultancies, and other institutional sites are engaged in (re)producing the discourse of global (strategic) management, so too are they engaged in the fashioning of new subjects—global managers.

The Global Manager

The discourses of the global corporation as an innovative organizational form and of GSM as the appropriate way to run a competitive global corporation are moments in the circuits constituting new types of subjects. The most obvious new subject is the "global manager" himself. McKinsey management consultant Kenichi Ohmae (1990) argues that by "decentering" the global firm, "the headquarters mentality" will be got rid of. He claims that a corporation that has "decomposed its center" is best staffed by neutral "equidistant managers." The neutrality is a denationalization of corporate structure, but also of the mentality of personnel. "You really have to believe, deep down, that people may work 'in' different national environments but are not 'of' them. What they are 'of' is the global corporation" (Ohmae 1990, 96). Here, one can see clearly the way in which this discourse and its associated practices imply (or demand) the creation of new subjects via a thorough deconstruction of citizenship and national-identity categories.

In his landmark article "Who Is Them?" in the *Harvard Business Review* Robert Reich described the new global manager and his context:

> Gone are the company town, the huge local labor force, the monolithic factory, and the giant, vertically integrated corporation that dominated the entire region. Vanishing too are the paternalistic corporate heads who used to feel a sense of responsibility for their local community. Emerging in their place is the *new global manager*, driven by the irrefutable logic of global capitalism to seek higher profits, enhanced market leadership and an improved stock price. *The playing field is the world.* (Reich 1991, 80; emphasis added)

This "new global manager" who is a supercapitalist, unfettered by "a sense of responsibility," plays the global management game on a sports field that is the world. It is clear, however, from a perusal of the business section of any bookstore that many difficulties are encountered in actually playing the global game. Many works are devoted to assisting the global manager to become a successful member of the transnational cosmopolitan business elite—at home in different cultures and able to think globally and at the same time to act appropriately locally. There is a mini-industry helping managers avoid cultural gaffes and "bridge cultural gaps." One contributor to this mini-industry observes that "[d]espite the sophistication that managers call on in dealing with people, many of them still make cultural mistakes in conducting business" (Dickson 1983, 7).

However, this new global manager is meant to be able to recognize cultural difference (or more likely diversity), but also to rise above such difficulties. He (and it is a he) is a new man. The sorts of stark dualistic depictions of old and new that characterize management texts on corporate form and management practices also animate the discursive construction of the new global manager, who is depicted as an entirely different sort of person than an old-style traditional manager. For example, the Training Management Corporation offers a course called "The Effective Global Manager" in which the table in Figure 1.5 is used to highlight the differences between the traditional manager and the global manager. The defining qualities of the new subject the "global manager" have been summed up by two of the most influential academics writing on this topic in their article in the *Harvard Business Review* titled "What Is a Global Manager?" They call the global manager a "global business manager" and say that there are three roles "at the core" of such a person's job. The global manager is to be "the *strategist* for his or her organization, the *architect* of its worldwide asset and resource configuration, and the *coordinator* of transactions across national borders" (Bartlett and Ghoshal 1992, 125). They note that although there are only a few such persons needed by each corporation, "the particular qualities necessary for such positions remain in short supply" (ibid., 131).

Both Bartlett and Ghoshal are employed by business schools (Harvard and INSEAD)—key institutional nodes in the discursive circuits that coproduce global management and global managers. The imperative for business schools to "produce" or "develop" a new sort of manager is directly acknowledged. Barnett of Michigan's Business School, for example, notes that

> managing global organizations demands a brand of leadership, imagination, determination, and sense of duty that most MBAs have not been taught before . . . The MBAs of the 1990s must have a different vision and a new set of values, skills, and abilities than earlier generations of students. (Barnett 1990, 22)

Thomas P. Gerrity, dean of the Wharton School, promotes his school's MBA program as "designed to develop renaissance leaders." The context for the school's efforts is depicted thus:

> It is clear that the old models of producing either general managers or functional specialists are no longer adequate in today's environment. What is needed is truly broad-gauged leaders. These are individuals who can

discuss the nuts and bolts of operations with an employee on the line and a few hours later talk corporate strategy with the board of directors. They can review European marketing plans over breakfast in Paris and hold their own with a product design team in Chicago over dinner. They have simultaneously mastered both the art and the science, the detail and the big picture, the local culture and the global context. They are true "renaissance leaders." (Gerrity 1998)

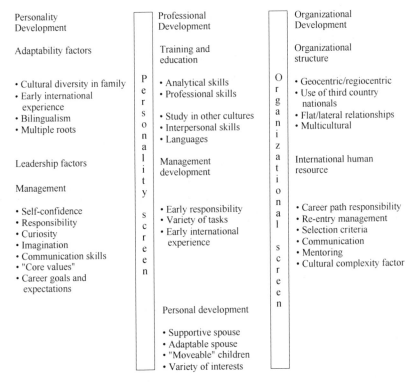

Figure 1.5. Factors contributing to development of global managers. Reprinted from *Doing Business Internationally* by Terence Brake, Daniella Medina Walker, and Thomas Walker (Burr Ridge, Ill.: Irwin Professional Publishers, 1995), by permission of The McGraw-Hill Companies. Adapted from Spyros G. Makridakis and Associates, *Single Market Europe: Opportunities and Challenges for Businesses* (San Francisco: Jossey-Bass, 1991).

These are renaissance leaders who can aspire to "run the world." "The attribute of leadership is so central to the identity of the global manager that management and leadership are often treated as the same thing" (Sashkin 1992, 156). Thus, for example, the Wharton School notes a "Global Perspective" as one of the five necessary features of a person prepared "for leadership" (Wharton 2000).

A genealogy of the concept of leadership as it is deployed in the management discourse would likely entail considering the emphasis on its analysis in military training institutes such as West Point. The leadership concept is balanced precariously between nature and nurture in the management discourse. Many of the best-sellers by successful businessmen/managers (Lee Iaccoca, Donald Trump, etc.) insist on the inborn, often intangible, personal qualities of the successful manager-leader, whereas business schools must insist that such qualities can, at least if not be "produced," be "developed" in their human students.

Global Strategic Vision

The "art" of GSM rests on specific geopolitical skills: being able to think and see globally. The global manager must, then, be able to see and think globally. Business consultant and writer Lawrence Tuller states un-equivocally: "Any company expecting to survive in the intensely competitive environment of the 21st century must become global. The starting point is to . . . develop a *global mentality*" (1991, 23; emphasis added). Other writers employ the term *global mind-set*. For example, Brake, Walker, and Walker state, "The fundamental corporate challenge is to develop and transform the collective and individual mindset in the management ranks by *broadening the manager's view of the world* and business (1995, 231; emphasis added). They define the global mind-set as "to constantly scan and interpret the world from a broad perspective, looking for unexpected trends and opportunities. The capacity to envision the future direction in an increasingly complex environment" (ibid., 232). Noel M. Tichy ranks the possession of a "global mind-set" first among the four attributes he identifies as necessary in the "global business leader" (Tichy 1990, 2).

It's a big world.
Somebody has to run it.

ANNOUNCING THE NEW TRIUM EMBA — *an alliance of*

NEW YORK UNIVERSITY STERN SCHOOL OF BUSINESS
LONDON SCHOOL OF ECONOMICS AND POLITICAL SCIENCE
HEC PARIS, GRADUATE BUSINESS SCHOOL

TRIUM is the only truly integrated, truly global Executive MBA. Participants earn a joint degree in 16 months by attending concentrated two-week study modules at the three flagship schools, plus one week each in São Paulo and Hong Kong. Distance learning and team projects occur between class sessions. It's visionary, focused and unique. Kind of like you.

For more information, call +33 1 39 67 70 94 in Europe or +1 212 998 0442 in the United States. Visit www.triumemba.org or e-mail info@triumemba.org.

Figure 1.6. Advertisement from the *Economist*.

The adoption of a global mind-set is, in the literature, bound up in (indeed often equated with) the development of a particular "worldview" (Garten 2000). This worldview is purportedly one that is "broad" (Gerritty 1998), able to take in the world. This is the precondition for being able to dream global dreams (Barnet and Cavanagh 1994) and, importantly, to enact those dreams. The global mind-set acts as a corporate (re)framing of the world. This is a strategy that entails visualization of world space. It is salutary to recall that in their now-classic 1974 study of multinational corporations, *Global Reach*, Richard Barnet and Ronald Müller recognized that "the most revolutionary aspect of the planetary enterprise is not its size but its *worldview*" (1974, 15; emphasis added).

Traditional Manager Mind-set	*Global Manager Mind-set*
Perspective	
• Narrow	• Broad
• Functional	• Cross-functional
• Specialized	• Cross-cultural
Organizational Life	
• Forces to be prioritized	• Contradictions to be balanced
• Eliminate conflict	• Conflict as opportunity
Dealing with Unexpected	
• Trust hierarchical structures	• Trust networked processes
Working Style	
• Personal self-awareness	• Cultural self-awareness
• Individual mastery	• Teamwork
Change	
• Avoid surprises	• Create change
• Change as threat	• Change as opportunity
Learning	
• Master specific knowledge/skills	• Lifelong learning

Figure 1.7. Traditional versus global mind-sets. Reprinted from *Doing Business Internationally* by Terence Brake, Daniella Medina Walker, and Thomas Walker (Burr Ridge, Ill.: Irwin Professional Publishers, 1995), by permission of The McGraw-Hill Companies. Copyright Training Management Corporation (TMC); originally published in *The Effective Global Manager* seminar and course book (Princeton, N.J.: TMC, 1993).

The idea of vision is absolutely central to the discourse of global management and the person of the global manager. Vision is meant in several ways. It implies an ability to see, to envision, global space. It also connotes an ability to see far ahead into the future, so a global manager is expected to have in his head a picture of the future of the corporation—an ideal future and a clear sense of direction for the corporation. This is to be differentiated from mere strategic planning; according to one article, "a vision is: *a future to be created*, and *not* a forecast" (Parikh and Neubauer 1993, 105; emphasis in original). Vision also has associations with being visionary: the idea of being able to see something that most people cannot—some sort of supernatural experience only a few have access to. All these connotations are played with in the business literature. And it is through this last—about vision being the property of a select few—that depictions of the new global manager connect with the business literature on leadership.

Leadership is an essential quality of the global manager because not only does he have a strategic vision, he absolutely *must* be able to communicate it (see Bennis 1995). The American Graduate School of International Management—known as Thunderbird—in Arizona notes, in publicity materials for its Global Leadership Certificate, that the required introductory course on leadership "covers the key components of leadership, including *development and communication of vision, the translation of vision into action* and the need for leaders to learn" (Thunderbird 1997; emphasis added).

In some treatments, the "vision thing" (the specter of George Bush Sr. perhaps) goes through Rostowian stages of development as it becomes a part of a corporation's organizational culture. In one account, for example, stage 1 is "the creation of a vision"; stage 2 is the "infusion" of this vision into the "corporate culture"; stage 3 involves the "mobilization of commitment"; and stage 4 is the "institutionalization of change" (Hitt and Keats 1992, 58). Jagdish Parikh and Fred Neubauer have developed a model based on a similar series of stages (Figure 1.8).

Tom Peters, management guru of gurus, noted that "*these devices— vision, symbolic action, recognition—are a control system, in the truest sense of*

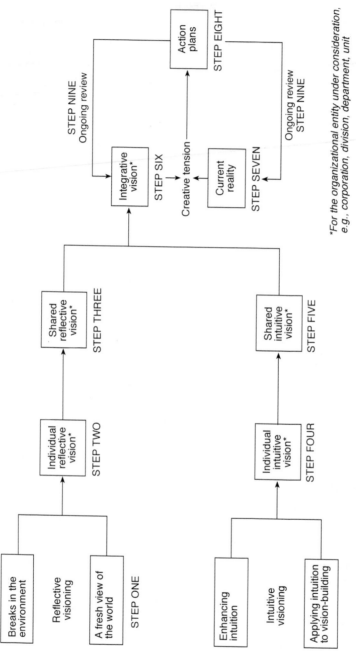

Figure 1.8. The vision-building process (Parikh–Neubauer model). Originally published in *Beyond Leadership: Balancing Economics, Ethics, and Ecology* by Warren G. Bennis, Jagdish Parikh, and Ronnie Lessem (Cambridge, Mass.: Blackwell Business, 1996). Reprinted with permission from Blackwell Publishers.

the term. The manager's task is to conceive of them as such, and to consciously use them" (cited in Roberts 1996, 64; emphasis in original).

I have stated that discourses work through space, but let me ask the more simple questions: What is the vision of global space held by the global manager? How does the new global manager view the earth and himself in relation to it?

Two examples from business books present an answer in stark terms. They represent the ideal global manager as defined by a peculiar occularity: the possession of an extraterrestrial strategic gaze.

The first is from Carl A. Nelson's 1994 book *Managing Globally: A Complete Guide to Competing Worldwide*, and depicts the position of the "equidistant global manager" argued for by Ohmae in *The Borderless World* (1990). In this example, the anthropomorphized global firm is a huge, disembodied eyeball staring at the globe. Under this figure, Nelson notes: "Figure 1-1 shows this concept [equidistance] as if the firm had its eye suspended in space looking at the earth and all its country markets. The global firm no longer sees only a home market, rather

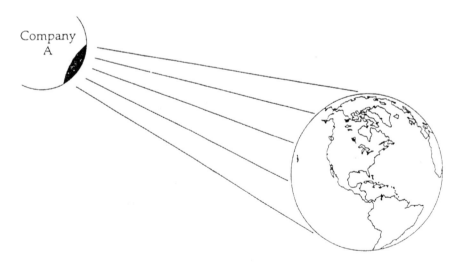

Figure 1.9. Equidistant global strategic vision. Reprinted with permission from Dr. Carl A. Nelson, author of *Managing Globally: A Complete Guide to Competing Worldwide,* and from the Global Manager series by Thompson Learning.

it sees economic denationalization and multiple opportunities" (1994, 4). By situating the disembodied eye outside that which is looked at, a series of claims are being made. The view from apart and above is one that situates the viewer outside the world—and the world (and its contents) become so many things to be managed and controlled. The gaze is strategic. It also demonstrates the "culturally pervasive association between objectivity and masculinity" and the construction of "objectivism" as a "masculine goal" that Evelyn Fox Keller (1985, 71), among others, has theorized and documented. In this case, the entire human world, the feminized other, is laid out before the eyeball of masculinized transnational capital. According to one management writer, in a successful vision, "the world becomes a theater for your visionary script" (Kevin Kingsland, quoted in Lessem 1996, 95). Donna Haraway's observation about the "god-trick of seeing everywhere from nowhere" is apposite (1991, 189). Identifying such positions as a god's-eye view is given some reinforcement by the pretensions of Hamish Maxwell, CEO of Philip Morris, who is reported to have said, after the takeover of Kraft in 1988, "You never get to where you can just sit back and say, 'Okay, I've now created the world, I'll rest'" (quoted in Barnet and Cavanagh 1994, 219).

A second example of a pictorial representation of global strategic management also highlights the intensely geopolitical view of the whole earth that is stated as a prerequisite for global managers. This illustration is taken from a book "intended to provide both practical answers and a broad theoretical perspective on the issues and trends shaping the globalization of work—specifically, the problems and opportunities of distance and diversity and the strategic implication of technology and team process" (O'Hara-Devereaux and Johansen 1994, xvii–xviii) and written to "help all the managers and teams . . . who are having to come to grips with new ways of working in the global workplace" (ibid., xiii). California-based business consultants Mary O'Hara-Devereaux and Robert Johansen illustrate their arguments in their book *Globalwork: Bridging Distance, Culture, and Time* with many flow charts, diagrams, and pictures. One of the more extraordinary illustrations is titled

"Navigating the Global Workspace" (Figure 1.10). In the accompanying text, the successful global manager is compared to a pilot who must "navigate through the different cultural weather patterns" (ibid., 104). However, in the picture the pilot is more of a spaceman cocooned in a hypertechnologized cockpit steering a "course" aimed right at the earth. It is common to see the global manager compared to an astronaut (see, for example, Hamel and Prahalad 1993, 84). In this illustration the pilot/spaceman flies beyond the horizon over a(nother) world literally inscribed with science—with a grid. This is a representation of space that exemplifies Lefebvre's conceptualization of it as motivated

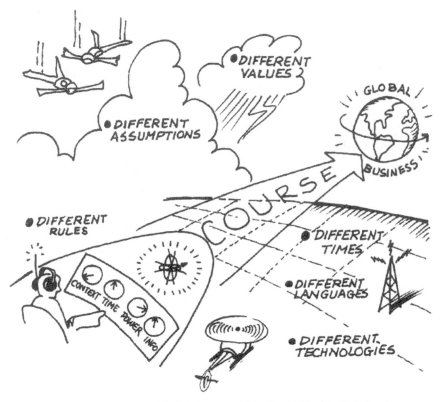

Figure 1.10. Navigating the global workspace. Originally published in *Globalwork: Bridging Distance, Culture, and Time* by Mary O'Hara-Devereaux and Robert Johansen (San Francisco: Jossey-Bass, 1994); copyright 1994 Jossey-Bass, Inc. Reprinted by permission of Jossey-Bass, Inc., a subsidiary of John Wiley and Sons, Inc.

by instrumental rationality. This extraterrestrial position is a fantasy of instrumental rationality and power made possible by what Haraway (1991) identifies as the "informatics of domination" (to be read in the pilot's gauges). Don Beck and Chris Cowan described the visual abilities of the new global manager (one of a breed of what they call "new-paradigm thinkers") as follows:

> Their sensory systems are constantly open to the flow of data from all possible sources. They disdain political games, territorial defensiveness, or other forms of information distortion and blockage. They have the capacity to navigate on past, present, and future timelines—in all directions—to obtain a sense of perspective, continuity, and receptiveness to new ideas. (Beck and Cowan 1996, 23)

It is perhaps chilling to note that this global manager appears to be an archetype nomad of the type conceptualized by Gilles Deleuze and Félix Guattari (1987, 480). He is able to escape "striated" or "gridded (state) space" because a nomad constantly deterritorializes (ibid., 380–81). Indeed, Deleuze and Guattari note that ". . . multinationals fabricate a kind of deterritorialized smooth space" *through* the very striated space of territories and states (ibid., 492; cf. Harvey 1989).

The development of global vision is not separate from the making of the new subject—the global manager. The most successful visions are those that are bound up in remaking the visionary leader as well as those who are expected to follow. Parikh, Neubauer, and Lank note at the end of a detailed explication of how to develop a vision:

> It is also important to note that this process of intuitive visioning, if pursued on a continuing basis, does lift you from the stage of "having" a vision to a level of intensely getting absorbed and identified with it or, shall we say, "*becoming*" your vision. (1996, 83; emphasis added)

Advising managers on how to convert vision into action, Ronnie Lessem cautions:

> Whatever ideas you pick up intellectually you have to develop the emotional commitment to put both them and yourself to the test. In the process you may become a *different person*, disassembled and reassembled, as a result of the emotional wrangles you have undergone. (Lessem 1996, 94; emphasis added)

The global manager as visionary leader is an ideal and rare type. He is born out of and, apparently, *through* a great deal of anxiety about self. Indeed, a professor of management, after reflecting on the structure and content of many MBA programs, concludes:

> a great deal of management education still seems to play on the insecurities and greed that wish to believe in the possibility of such managerial omnipotence, and the enormous amounts of energy and suffering are generated in the attempt to make an organizational reality out of such illusions. (Roberts 1996, 73)

Thus, the pretensions of the global manager can be seen as rooted in quotidian gendered, racialized, and otherwise differentiating sociospatial practices. The global manager, then, is far from the disembodied eyeball or the spaceman, far from the complete, whole, singular, and coherent subject the management discourse aims to "make up." We might, instead, think about the global manager as a subjectivity that is contingent, an object of (subject of) desire—a gendered desire to command and control in a world of unprecedented risk and change (cf. Huczynski 1996, especially 190–213, on the appeal of management gurus). The global manager is born out of a huge anxiety about vulnerability. Perhaps it is true that at the heart of the so-often-assumed-to-be-hegemonic discursive constellation that is globalization lies an imperative—but maybe that imperative is not some abstract competitive drive or logic of capitalism. Ordinary human politics springing from fear and doubt may instead be imperatives. Or, maybe there are no imperatives, just moments in ongoing struggles over meaning and power in which fear and doubt are enmeshed.

Conclusions

Of course, the discourse of global management is so full of hubris and arrogance that it can be seen as simply ridiculous. It is humorous, to be sure, and the empirical work aimed at finding out how elements of the discourse are enacted in management practices remains to be completed. Indeed, in an article titled "Strategic Vision or Strategic Con? Rhetoric or Reality?" management consultant Colin Coulson-Thomas notes that surveys of corporations showed that, in many cases, attempts to articulate and implement "strategic vision" had failed utterly—often resulting in an atmosphere of skepticism and distrust (Coulson-Thomas 1992). However, I am convinced that the claims of global management are of interest and import not despite, but precisely because of, their failure and their often pompous nature. As Christopher Grey and Robert French put it: "whether or not the pretensions of management to be able to manage the world are defensible, the consequences of the belief that they *are* remains an irreducible social fact" (1996, 2).

In describing a world of risks that are knowable, manageable, and controllable only by a few global managers in global corporations, the discourse of global management is an important element of the discursive constellation that is globalization. The discourse of global management participates in constituting the very conditions it purports to describe (cf. Gibson-Graham 1996, 77).

References

Ansoff, H. Igor. 1991. "Strategic Management in a Historical Perspective." In *International Review of Strategic Management*, vol. 2, ed. D. E. Hussey. New York: John Wiley and Sons. 3–69.

Appadurai, Arjun. 1990. "Disjuncture and Difference in the Global Cultural Economy." In *Global Culture: Nationalism, Globalization and Modernity*, ed. Mike Featherstone. Newbury Park, Calif.: Sage. 295–310.

Barnet, Richard J., and John Cavanagh. 1994. *Global Dreams: Imperial Corporations and the New World Order*. New York: Simon and Schuster.

Barnet, Richard J., and Ronald E. Müller. 1974. *Global Reach: The Power of the Multinational Corporations*. New York: Simon and Schuster.

Barnett, Carole K. 1990. "The Michigan Global Agenda: Research and Teaching in the 1990s." *Human Resource Management* 29(1): 5–26.

Barry, David, and Mary Ann Hazen. 1996. "Do You Take Your Body to Work?" In *Postmodern Management and Organization Theory*, ed. David M. Boje, Robert P. Gephart Jr., and Tojo Joseph Thatchenkery. Thousand Oaks, Calif.: Sage.

Bartlett, Christopher, and Sumantra Ghoshal. 1989. *Managing across Borders: The Transnational Solution*. Boston: Harvard Business School Press.

———. 1992. "What Is a Global Manager?" *Harvard Business Review* (September/October): 124–32.

Beck, Don, and Chris Cowan. 1996. "New Paradigm Thinking." In *Beyond Leadership: Balancing Economics, Ethics, and Ecology*, ed. Warren G. Bennis, Jagdish Parikh, and Ronnie Lessem. Cambridge, Mass.: Blackwell Publishers.

Bennis, Warren. 1995. "Opening Remarks: Leadership in Tomorrow's Corporation." (http://www.fed.org/conf.tomorrow95/).

Bennis, Warren G., Jagdish Parikh, and Ronnie Lessem, eds. 1996. *Beyond Leadership: Balancing Economics, Ethics, and Ecology*. Cambridge, Mass: Blackwell Business.

Brake, Terence, Daniella Medina Walker, and Thomas Walker. 1995. *Doing Business Internationally: The Guide to Cross-Cultural Success*. Burr Ridge, Ill.: Irwin Professional Publishers.

Brecher, John, John Brown Childs, and Jill Cutler, eds. 1993. *Global Visions: Beyond the New World Order*. Boston: South End Press.

Brecher, Jeremy, and Tim Costello. 1994. *Global Village or Global Pillage: Economic Reconstruction from the Bottom Up*. Boston: South End Press.

Buck-Morss, Susan. 1995. "Envisioning Capital: Political Economy on Display." *Critical Inquiry* 21(2): 434–67.

Clegg, Stewart R., and Gill Palmer. 1996. "Introduction: Producing Management Knowledge." In *The Politics of Management Knowledge*, ed. Stewart R. Clegg and Gill Palmer. London: Sage. 1–18.

Coulson-Thomas, Colin. 1992. "Strategic Vision or Strategic Con? Rhetoric or Reality?" In *International Review of Strategic Management*, vol. 4, ed. D. E. Hussey. New York: John Wiley and Sons. 87–103.

Deleuze, Gilles, and Félix Guattari. 1987. *A Thousand Plateaus: Capitalism and Schizophrenia*. Trans. Brian Massumi. Minneapolis: University of Minnesota Press.

Dickson, Douglas N. 1983. "Introduction." In *Managing Effectively in the World Marketplace*, ed. Douglas N. Dickson. New York: John Wiley and Sons. 1–16.

du Gay, Paul. 1996. "Making up Managers: Enterprise and the Ethos of Bureaucracy." In *The Politics of Management Knowledge*, ed. Stewart R. Clegg and Gill Palmer. London: Sage. 19–35.

Eccles, R. G., and R. L. Nolan. 1993. "A Framework for the Design of the Emerging Global Organizational Structure." In *Globalization, Technology, and Competition*, ed. Stephen P. Bradley, Jerry A. Hausman, and Richard L. Nolan. Boston: Harvard Business School Press. 57–80.

Economist. 1996. Advertisements. April 6, 96.

Ewald, François. 1991. "Insurance and Risk." In *The Foucault Effect: Studies in Governmentality*, ed. Graham Burchell, Colin Gordon, and Peter Miller. Chicago: University of Chicago Press. 197–210.

Foucault, Michel. 1991. "Governmentality." In *The Foucault Effect: Studies in Governmentality*, ed. Graham Burchell, Colin Gordon, and Peter Miller. Chicago: University of Chicago Press. 87–104.

Garten, Jeffrey E. 2000. *Worldview: Global Strategies for the New Economy*. Cambridge: Harvard Business School Press.

Gerrity, Thomas P. 1998. "Message from the Dean: Renaissance Leadership." Wharton School Web page (http://www.wharton.upenn.edu/mba).

Gibson-Graham, J. K. 1996. *The End of Capitalism (as We Knew It): A Feminist Critique of Political Economy*. Cambridge, Mass.: Blackwell.

Grey, Christopher, and Robert French. 1996. "Rethinking Management Education." In *Rethinking Management Education*, ed. Robert French and Christopher Grey. London: Sage. 1–16.

Hamel, Gary, and C. K. Prahald. 1993. "Strategic Intent." In *International Review of Strategic Management*, vol. 4, ed. D. E. Hussey. New York: John Wiley and Sons. 63–86.

Haraway, Donna. 1991. *Simians, Cyborgs, and Women: The Reinvention of Nature*. New York: Routledge.

Harvey, David. 1989. *The Condition of Postmodernity*. Cambridge, Mass.: Blackwell.

Hitt, Michael A., and Barbara W. Keats. 1992. "Strategic Leadership and Restructuring: A Reciprocal Interdependence." In *Strategic Leadership: A Multiorganizational-Level Perspective*, ed. Robert L. Phillips and James G. Hunt. Westport, Conn.: Quorum Books. 45–62.

Huczynski, Andrzej A. 1996. *Management Gurus: What Makes Them and How to Become One*. New York: International Thomson Business Press.

Keller, Evelyn Fox. 1985. *Reflections on Gender and Science*. New Haven: Yale University Press.

Knights, David. 1992. "Changing Spaces: The Disruptive Impact of a New Epistemology of Location for the Study of Management." *Academy of Management Review* 17(3): 514–36.

Kogut, Bruce. 1985. "Designing Global Strategies: Profiting from Organizational Flexibility." *Sloan Management Review* (fall): 27–38.

Konsynski, Benn R., and J. Karimi. 1993. "On the Design of Global Information Systems." In *Globalization, Technology, and Competition*, ed. Stephen P. Bradley, Jerry A. Hausman, and Richard L. Nolan. Boston: Harvard Business School Press. 81–108.

Korten, David C. 1995. *When Corporations Rule the World*. West Hartford, Conn.: Kumarian Press.

Krause, Donald G. 1995. *The Art of War for Executives*. New York: Perigree Books.

Lefebvre, Henri. 1991. *The Production of Space*. Trans. Donald Nicholson-Smith. Cambridge, Mass.: Blackwell.

Lessem, Ronnie. 1996. "From Vision to Action." In *Beyond Leadership: Balancing Economics, Ethics, and Ecology*, ed. Warren G. Bennis, Jagdish Parikh, and Ronnie Lessem. Cambridge, Mass.: Blackwell Publishers. 87–112.

Malone, T. W., and J. F. Rockart. 1993. "How Will Information Technology Reshape Organizations?" In *Globalization, Technology, and Competition*, ed. Stephen P. Bradley, Jerry A. Hausman, and Richard L. Nolan. Boston: Harvard Business School Press. 37–56.

Massey, Doreen. 1993. "Power Geometry and a Progressive Sense of Place." In *Mapping the Futures: Local Cultures, Global Change*, ed. Jon Bird, Barry Curtis, Tim Putnam, George Robertson, and Lisa Tickner. New York: Routledge. 59–69.

Motorola. 1997. "About Motorola University." In Motorola University Web page. Updated August 1997 (http://www.mot.com/MU/).

Natter, Wolfgang, and John Paul Jones III. 1993. "Signposts toward a Poststructuralist Geography." In *Postmodern Contentions: Epochs, Politics, Space*, ed. John Paul Jones III, Wolfgang Natter, and Theodore R. Schatzki. New York: Guilford Press. 165–203.

Nelson, Carl A. 1994. *Managing Globally: A Complete Guide to Competing Worldwide*. New York: Irwin.

O'Hara-Devereaux, Mary, and Robert Johansen. 1994. *Globalwork: Bridging Distance, Culture, Time*. San Francisco: Jossey-Bass.

Ohmae, Kenichi. 1990. *The Borderless World: Power and Strategy in the Interlinked Economy*. New York: HarperBusiness.

Ostry, Sylvia. 1990. *Governments and Corporations in a Shrinking World: Trade and Innovation Policies in the United States, Europe and Japan*. New York: Council on Foreign Relations Press.

Parikh, Jagdish, and Fred Neubauer. 1993. "Corporate Visioning." In *International Review of Strategic Management*, vol. 4, ed. D. E. Hussey. New York: John Wiley and Sons. 105–16.

Parikh, Jagdish, Fred Neubauer, and Alden G. Lank. 1994. "Developing a Vision." In *Beyond Leadership: Balancing Economics, Ethics, and Ecology*, ed. Warren G. Bennis, Jagdish Parikh, and Ronnie Lessem. Cambridge, Mass.: Blackwell Publishers.

Porter, Michael. 1980. *Competitive Strategy*. New York: Free Press.

Prahalad, C. K. 1990. "Globalization: The Intellectual and Managerial Challenges." *Human Resource Management*. 29(1): 27–37.

Ramsay, Harvie. 1996. "Managing Sceptically: A Critique of Organizational Fashion." In *The Politics of Management Knowledge*, ed. Stewart R. Clegg and Gill Palmer. London: Sage. 155–72.

Reich, Robert B. 1991. "Who Is Them?" *Harvard Business Review* 69(2): 77–94.

Roberts, John. 1996. "Management Education and the Limits of Technical Rationality: The Conditions and Consequences of Management Practice." In *Rethinking Management Education*, ed. Robert French and Christopher Grey. London: Sage. 54–75.

Roberts, Susan M., and Richard H. Schein. 1993. "The Entrepreneurial City: Fabricating Urban Development in Syracuse, New York." *Professional Geographer* 45(1): 21–33.

———. 1995. "Earth Shattering: Global Imagery and GIS." In *Ground Truth: The Social Implications of Geographic Information Systems*, ed. John Pickles. New York: Guilford Press. 171–95.

Sampson, Anthony. 1995. *Company Man: The Rise and Fall of Corporate Life*. New York: Random House.

Sashkin, Marshall. 1992. "Strategic Leadership Competencies." In *Strategic Leadership: A Multiorganizational-Level Perspective*, ed. Robert L. Phillips and James G. Hunt. Westport, Conn.: Quorum Books. 139–60.

Sayer, Andrew, and Richard Walker. 1992. *The New Social Economy: Reworking the Division of Labor*. Cambridge, Mass.: Blackwell.

Schoenberger, Erica. 1997. *The Cultural Crisis of the Firm*. Cambridge, Mass.: Blackwell.

———. 2000. "The Management of Time and Space." In *The Oxford Handbook of Economic Geography*, ed. Gordon L. Clark, Maryann P. Feldman and Meric S. Gertler. Oxford: Oxford University Press. 317–32.

Smith, Neil. 1993. "Homeless/Global: Scaling Places." In *Mapping the Futures: Local Cultures, Global Change*, ed. Jon Bird, Barry Curtis, Tim Putnam, George Robertson, and Lisa Tickner. New York: Routledge. 87–119.

Spence, A. Michael. 1997. "Letter from the Dean." Stanford Graduate School of Business Web page (http://www-gsb.stanford.edu).

Swyngedouw, Eric. 1997. "Neither Global nor Local: 'Glocalisation' and the Politics of Scale."In *Spaces of Globalization: Reasserting the Power of the Local*, ed. Kevin Cox. New York: Guilford Press. 137–66.

Taylor, William. 1992. "The Logic of Global Business: An Interview with ABB's Percy Barnevik." In *Leaders on Leadership*. Boston: Harvard Business School Press. 67–90.

Thrift, Nigel. 1998. "The Rise of Soft Capitalism." In *An Unruly World? Globalization, Governance and Geography*, ed. Andrew Herod, Gearóid Ó Tuathail, and Susan M. Roberts. New York: Routledge. 25–71.

Thunderbird. 1997. Global Leadership Certificate. University of Arizona Web page. (http://www.t-bird.edu).

Tichy, Noel M. 1990. "Editor's Note: The Global Challenge for Business Schools." *Human Resource Management* 29(1): 1–4.

Townley, Preston. 1991. "From the President." In *Managing Globally: Key Perspectives*. Report number 972. New York: Conference Board. 5.

Tuller, Lawrence W. 1991. *Going Global: New Opportunities for Growing Companies to Compete in World Markets*. Homewood, Ill.: Business One Irwin.

Wharton. 2000. Wharton School, University of Pennsylvania, MBA Program Web pages (http://www.wharton.upenn.edu/mba/curriculum/curriculum.html).

Wilson, Richard M. S. 1991. "Corporate Strategy and Management Control." In *International Review of Strategic Management*, vol. 2, ed. D. E. Hussey. New York: John Wiley and Sons. 115–66.

Wriston, Walter B. 1992. "The State of American Management." In *Leaders on Leadership*. Boston: Harvard Business School Press. 3–12.

CHAPTER 2

Zones of New Sovereignty
in Southeast Asia

Aihwa Ong

Rezoning Sovereignty

I have used the concept of "flexible citizenship" to describe the practices of refugees and business migrants who conduct businesses in one
location while their families are lodged in "safe havens" elsewhere.
Leading up to and beyond the reunification with China, Hong Kong
Chinese, for instance, prepared escape pods by sending businesses abroad
and accumulating foreign passports, second homes, and overseas bank
accounts. The strategies of mobility and relocation are constrained, however, by the cultural regimes and the market conditions in host countries (Ong 1998, 134–62). In this essay, I turn the question around, and
look at how the art of government, which is constrained by the condition of transnationality, has to further stretch the bounds of political
economy. I will argue that industrializing states in Southeast Asia have
responded to the challenges of globalization by also becoming more
flexible in their management of sovereignty.

There is a growing literature on the effects of globalization, much
of it framed in terms of a state retreat in the face of inroads by global
capital that have resulted in the expansion of transnational social orders.
Manuel Castells, for instance, proposes that there is "a new spatial form
characteristic of social practices that shape network society: the space
of flows" (1996, 412–18). By "flows" he refers to the sequences of interaction enabled by electronic circuits, communication networks, and the

social organization of globe-trotting managerial elites. Akhil Gupta and James Ferguson point to the structures of "reterritorialization" brought about by global capital and transstatal agencies that create "grids" of spatial power that discriminate by class, gender, race, and sexuality (Gupta 1992; Gupta and Ferguson 1992; Malkki 1994). Neither model pays much attention to the role of the nation-state, because both are concerned largely with emerging forms of spatial power that do not depend on governments. In contrast, I maintain that the nation-state— with its supposed monopoly over sovereignty (Latham 1998)—remains a key institution in structuring spatial order.

Despite frequent assertions about the demise of the state, the issue of state action remains central when it comes to the rearrangements of global spaces, and the restructuring of social and political relations. But Saskia Sassen (1995), for instance, maintains that global markets and supranational entities such as GATT (the General Agreement on Tariffs and Trade) and NAFTA (the North American Free Trade Agreement) have made serious inroads into state control of sovereignty. She argues that a form of "economic citizenship" has emerged that demands accountability not from governments, but from global firms and markets, or planetary organizations such as the United Nations. Yet, if we consider state power as a positive agency, the issue is no longer one of the state "losing control," but rather of its active role in refashioning sovereignty to meet the challenges of global markets and supranational organizations.

I argue that in an era of globalization, sovereignty—"the existence of a final, highest, or supreme power over a set of people, things, or places" (Latham 1998)[1]—remains key to our understanding the shifting relations between state, market, and society. Rather than accept claims about the end of sovereignty, we need to explore mutations in the ways in which localized political and social organizations set the terms and are constitutive of a domain of social existence. I maintain that in Southeast Asia, governments seeking to accommodate corporate strategies of location have become flexible in their management of sovereignty, so that different production sites often become institutional domains that vary in their mix of legal protections, controls, and disciplinary regimes. Anthony Giddens has usefully described civil, political, and economic rights as "arenas of *contestations or conflicts*, each linked to a distinctive type of surveillance, where that surveillance is both necessary to the power of superordinate groups and an axis for the operation of the dialectic of control" (1987, 205). But whereas European states have confronted these contestations sequentially over decades, postcolonial Asian states have had to deal with them simultaneously, mostly in an era of globalization. Newly industrializing regimes, eager to meet capitalist requirements, have evolved what I call a system of "graduated sovereignty," whereby citizens in zones that are differently articulated to global production and financial circuits are subjected to different kinds of surveillance and in practice enjoy different sets of civil, political, and economic rights. By thus calibrating its control over sovereignty to the challenges of global capital, the so-called tiger state develops a system of graduated zones that also protects against pockets of political unrest.

In this essay, I will discuss the model of graduated sovereignty and the ideological constructions of an Islamic normativity that have emerged in Southeast Asia. In the postcolonial era, the term *strong states* has been applied to the Southeast Asian regimes to describe their dominant role in directing the capitalist development of their economies, mainly through a powerful bureaucracy, public enterprises, and state monopolies.[2] Since the end of the Cold War, countries in the Association of Southeast Asian Nations (ASEAN) have evolved a state strategy that I refer to as "postdevelopmental." While the typical ASEAN state continues to control a (diminishing) nationalized sector of its economy, an expanding multinational sector is dominated by global capital. The postdevelopmental strategy relies on two mechanisms for attracting foreign investments and technology transfers: (1) the proliferation of strategic alliances with corporate actors (e.g., Akyuzand and Gore 1996; Evans 1997); and (2) the provision of sites that are linked to global "commodity chains" for the production of a variety of low- and high-tech goods.[3] In Malaysia, this mixed strategy requires the state to focus more and more on developing so-called smart partnerships with the private sector and foreign corporate interests. The state seeks diverse links with global capital to "maximize and balance benefits for both and for all, even if the contribution towards the partnerships may not be equal" (*Straits Times* 1997b, 1). This strategy makes more flexible the relationship between state and capital, so that enterprises enjoy greater leverage in regulating labor and trade relations within the state's territory, and legal and social forms of control can be negotiable on a case-by-case basis. Malaysia is promoting this smart partnership scheme with countries in Africa, Latin America, and Oceania. For instance, South African leaders now consider smart partnerships with foreign capital to be a strategy that will produce an "African renaissance" (ibid., 8).

Under the postdevelopmental strategy, new state–capital alliances also signal a shift in relations between state and society, as the state focuses more on producing and managing populations that are attractive to global capital. Before discussing this, we need to widen our notion of sovereignty to include other forms of power that are not strictly juridical. Whereas others view the relationship between the state and its citizens strictly in terms of political power over legal subjects, I wish to consider sovereignty as "an effect of practices" associated with law and other forms of regulation that construct relations between the state, its population, and the market.[4] Increasingly, as Asian tiger states seek to maintain their economic competitiveness and political stability, they are no longer interested in securing uniform regulatory authority over all their citizens. One can distinguish zones of graduated sovereignty in which the legal controls predominate in some places, and some state functions are outsourced to private enterprises in others. Through the differential deployment of state power, populations in different zones are variously subjected to political control and to social regulation by state and nonstate agencies.

The concept of governmentality is useful in describing regimes for constituting and maintaining social relations and practices within these domains. For instance, just as biotechnology has led to new ways of governing and valuing human life, globalization has induced governments to think up new ways of governing and valuing different categories of their subject populations (Agamben 1998).[5] Michel Foucault (1979, 143) uses the term *biopower* to refer to a central concern of the modern state in fostering of life, growth, and care of the population.[6] I argue that to remain globally competitive, the typical ASEAN state makes different kinds of "biopolitical" investments in different subject populations, privileging one gender over the other, and in certain kinds of human skills, talents, and ethnicities; it thus subjects different sectors of the population to different regimes of valuation and control. This unequal biopolitical investment in different categories of the population results in the uneven distribution of services, care, and protection; while some subjects are invested with rights and resources, others are neglected outright. Thus, globalization has induced a situation of graduated sovereignty, whereby even as the state maintains control over its territory, it is also willing in some cases to let corporate entities set the terms for constituting and regulating some domains. Sometimes, weaker and less desirable groups are given over to the regulation of supranational entities. What results is a system of variegated citizenship in which populations subjected to different regimes of value enjoy different kinds of rights, discipline, caring, and security.

There are good reasons for using Malaysia as an illustrative example of a state that is developing a system of graduated sovereignty. Since its political independence from Great Britain in 1957, the country has favored the political rights of Malays on grounds of their status as an "indigenous" majority population and their general economic backwardness when compared with the ethnic Chinese and Indians who are descended from immigrant populations. But one can argue that from the early 1970s onward, an extensive system of graduated sovereignty has come into effect as the government has put more investment into the biopolitical improvement of the Malays, or *bumiputra* ("princes of the soil," or original inhabitants), awarding them rights and benefits largely denied to the Chinese and Indian minorities. Special programs have awarded shares in state-held trusts, government contracts, business credit, scholarships, business licenses, university admissions, civil employment, and jobs in large firms to Malay subjects. This, in effect, has created the world's first affirmative-action system tied exclusively to ethnicity. The pastoral power that has been employed on behalf of the Malays has unevenly favored the middle and upper classes, and Malays as a community enjoy more rights, benefits, and claims than non-Malays. Ethnic Chinese are disciplined especially in the realms of cultural expression and economic activities (Nonini 1997, 207–8), while most ethnic Indians have remained plantation proletarians.

But this system of ethnic-based governmentality has been further elaborated into at least six zones of graduated sovereignty for the entire population: the low-wage manufacturing sector, the illegal labor market, the aboriginal periphery, the refugee camp, the cyber corridor, and the growth triangle. The multinational sector, which is based on a low-skill, industrial labor, produces most of the manufactured goods for export. Its workforce is governed by a mix of disciplining and repressive measures that ensure the social stability desired by foreign companies. Disciplinary mechanisms permit, but limit, the activities of trade unions, and policemen are quickly mobilized whenever workers engage in strikes. At the same time, state social policy ensures that the firms employ a majority of Malays in their workforce, as well as minimal wages and cost-of-living allowances to avoid charges of exploitation (Ong 1986). The workers' freedom to pray during work hours also contributes to general norms that promote self-discipline and low levels of dissent.

An immigrant labor market—that draws workers from Indonesia, Bangladesh, the Philippines, and Myanmar—has grown in response to labor shortages in the plantation and construction industries. Almost one-third of Malaysia's eight million workers are immigrant workers (*San Francisco Chronicle* 1998). They are subjected to stringent laws of employment, residence, and termination. Legal immigrants employed in domestic service, construction, and plantations enjoy limited rights of employment, but they cannot apply for citizenship. There are no labor rights for "illegals" who slip into the country. Although Muslim illegals might be more tolerated or better treated, and can often blend into the larger population by passing as Malays, non-Muslim workers when exposed are deported, with no rights of appeal. In the 1997–98 economic crisis, anti-immigrant sentiment mounted, and ridding the country of illegal migrants was considered a patriotic duty. In a cost-saving measure, the government selected female domestics from the Philippines as the first foreign workers to be expelled. But as the currency crisis worsened in Indonesia, and millions of refugees were poised to enter Malaysia, tens of thousands of Indonesian workers were expelled. Thailand evicted about one million workers from Myanmar and South Asia.

In contrast to the limited or nonexistent social rights afforded most locals and foreigners, a zone of superior privileges serves a largely Malay entrepreneurial elite. The grandly named Multimedia Super Corridor (MSC) is projected to become a "springboard to serve the regional and world markets for multimedia products and services" (Mimos 1998). The corridor, which will link Kuala Lumpur to a new technological research center and a new international airport, is designed to facilitate the creation of another Silicon Valley in Malaysia. Besides favoring the Malay elite, the MSC is a high-tech project of Islamic governmentality that is intended to offset ethnic Chinese concentrated in Penang. Special cyberlaws, policies, and practices encourage investment in a new kind of Malay subject who will be fully at home in a multimedia world. Affirmative-action employment policies are suspended to free up the flow of capital, talent, and information that will ultimately favor the Malay corporate elite. Bill Gates, of Microsoft, and other high-technology industry executives from the United States and Japan have set up enterprises in the zone. Visas will be readily issued to foreigners identified as "knowledge workers," who represent the "best minds." Students trained in "smart" (high-tech) schools and a new multimedia university will supply the labor market. New practices include residents having access to distance-learning technology, telemedical services, and an electronic government. The MSC is thus a project that involves an enormous state investment, and is intended to breed and nurture a new kind of Malay computer-literate culture. Names such as Leonardo da Vinci, Ernest Hemingway, and Stephen Spielberg are invoked as models of creativity (*New Straits Times* 1997b, 6). By focusing on high-technology knowledge production and technological innovation, the project provides an alternative to the national dependence on low-wage subcontracting industries, and offers Malaysia an opportunity to link up with the transnational "research and development" community. Although the official explanation for the MSC is that it is a "test bed" to safely experiment with "modernization without undermining . . . traditional values" (Wysocki 1997), in reality it will be a superprivileged zone where the Malay elite plugs into the world of high-technology industry.

For Southeast Asian states then, ethnicity often becomes a sorting mechanism for defining the meaning of and the claims on sovereignty. For instance, the flood of boat people in the aftermath of the Indochina war brought Vietnamese (in 1975) and later Cambodian (in 1979) refugees to camps throughout Southeast Asia. Vietnamese boat people, most of whom were ethnic Chinese, were kept in isolated camps in Malaysia, Indonesia, and the Philippines under the jurisdiction of the United Nations High Commission for Refugees (UNHCR). Along the Thai border, Cambodians in refugee camps had no political claims on the Thai government, and only the humanitarian norm of *nonrefoulement*— the right not to be returned to a country in which they would suffer persecution—allowed them to remain in "temporary" camps while awaiting resettlement, mainly in the United States and France (e.g., Levy and Sussott 1992; Tollefson 1989). In Southeast Asia, as in most Western countries receiving refugees, the prevailing practice was not to offer asylum, but to emphasize state policies of control and deterrence, so that "refugee law has become immigration law, emphasizing the protection of borders rather than the protection of persons" (Aleinikoff 1995, 263). By and large, the receiving countries refused to extend asylum to refugees (ethnic Chinese, Vietnamese, Cambodians, and Laotians) in ways that would make them citizens. The only exception was the Chams, from Cambodia, whom the Malaysian state considers part of the Malay-Muslim diaspora, and thus are acceptable as citizens. This selective reception of refugees was an expression of how sovereignty is shaped by a dominant ethnicity, and by the nation-state's definition of its desired ethnic composition. Refugees and citizens of undesirable ethnicities are frequently given over to the regulatory power of supranational agencies.

Also in the margins of mainstream sovereignty are the aboriginal areas where a mix of disciplining and civilizing powers seek to lure the aborigines away from their nomadic life in the jungles and persuade them to become settlers like the Malay peasants. Although aboriginal groups are also considered *bumiputra* (native sons of the soil) and, like the Malays, enjoy special affirmative-action rights, in practice they have access to these rights only if they abandon the aboriginal way of life and become absorbed into the larger Malay population. Jungle dwellers who resist the civilizing mission of schools, sedentary agriculture, markets, and Islam are left to their own devices in the midst of destruction caused by the encroaching logging companies. Generally, scattered and neglected nomads are made to adapt to development by becoming agricultural producers. Aboriginal groups in practice enjoy very limited rights vis-à-vis their territory, their livelihood, or their cultural identity. The Penan foragers of Sarawak have developed two different responses to territorial encroachment, each of which is shaped by a different sense of the Malaysian government's sovereignty. The Eastern Penan have actively blockaded logging activities and thus won international attention, whereas the Western Penan have acquiesced to logging as part of their acceptance of Malaysian rule (Brosius 1997).

Even as differentiated zones of sovereignty proliferate within national borders, there are also moves toward forming multinational zones of sovereignty. One modality is the development of growth triangles (GTs), which straddle the borders between neighboring states so as to maximize the locational advantages and attract global capital. GTs are determined by "economic geometry," in which location, the accessibility of cheap labor, the possibility of exploitation of complementary resources, and the proximity of a regional hub such as Singapore enhance the competitive advantage of the region in the global economy. So far, three GTs have formed by linking contiguous parts of neighboring countries. The country configurations are Indonesia-Malaysia-Singapore (Sijori); Indonesia-Malaysia-Thailand; and Brunei-Indonesia-Malaysia-Philippines. Sijori is a massive industrial park that sits astride the Riau archipelago and draws on complementary labor and technical resources of the three countries to enhance investment opportunities. From the Singaporean perspective, this growth triangle allows Singapore to retain command/control functions at home, while moving "low-end" jobs offshore. It takes advantage of cheap Indonesian labor, and it also ameliorates tensions over the presence of too many guest workers within the city-state. Sijori thus represents a zone of low-cost production in which Singapore capital and expertise can be used for training and managing regional workers. It represents the low end of a system of zones in which the city-state is the site of continuously upgrading human capital (Macleod and McGee 1996, 440, 442, 449).

Thus, growth triangles are zones of special sovereignty that are arranged through a multinational network of partnerships that exploits the cheap labor that exists within the orbit of a global hub such as Singapore. It appears that GT workers are subjected less to the rules of their home country, and more to the rules of companies, and to the competitive conditions set by other growth triangles in the region. More research needs to be done to discover the kinds of "conducive regulatory environment" and labor discipline that prevail under foreign management (*New Straits Times* 1997e, 19). It is the foreign management that defines the "business environment," that is, the rules of inclusion and exclusion and the rights and privileges of workers from different countries. To help foreign enterprises exploit the advantages of their location and their setup vis-à-vis the other growth triangles, the Sijori triangle established a graded system of labor and material conditions in each of the triangle's nodes: in Singapore, one finds skilled labor and sophisticated business and control services; in Johore (Malaysia), skilled and semiskilled labor, recreation, and land; and in Batam and Riau (Indonesia), "low-cost, controlled" labor and some natural amenities (beaches) (Macleod and McGee 1996, 443). By collecting different mixes of manpower, natural resources, and regulatory conditions in graded zones, the growth-triangle model transforms previously rural or "unproductive" hinterlands into what have been called "extended metropolitan regions" (EMRs). As dense production and distribution nodes, where the cross-border flows of capital, people, and information are intensified, EMRs further refine the time-space coordinates of "flexible production" through the regional reorganization of economic activities and social sovereignty.

Indonesia represents an interesting case of a so-called emerging tiger nation where there is a less coherent postdevelopmental strategy, and much of the manufacturing is dominated by low-skilled labor working in export-oriented industries, and where citizens enjoy different degrees of state investment and legal social protection. Like Malaysia, Indonesia over the past two decades has transformed itself into an industrializing power. It has an industrial labor force of seven million workers (Goozner and Schmetzer 1994). Large export-oriented industrial zones are located in Sumatra and Java; they depend on cheap labor to manufacture furniture, watches, clothing, shoes, toys, and plastic goods. Millions of young women have left their rice fields to work for less than a living wage in factories operated by Koreans that subcontract for brand-name companies such as Nike, Reebok, and the Gap. But besides making Indonesia part of the global production system, these industrial estates are institutional contexts of limited citizenship: workers are rarely protected by the state, are in fact frequently harassed by the military, and are left to adjust as well as they can to the exigencies of the market.

Indonesian workers are among the lowest paid in Asia, and the majority are young women who seem to lack the most basic human rights. In 1994, women working twelve-hour days sewing GAP outfits, made less than two dollars a day, including overtime. In the Tangerang zone outside Jakarta, thousands of young women employed by Adidas and Nike took home much less. That year, the Indonesian Prosperity Trade Union (SBSI), calculating that the average worker needed to earn at least $2.50 a day, broke "the taboo on labor strikes" and called a national strike to protest low wages (Goozner 1994). After a long struggle, the government agreed to a minimum wage of two dollars a day, but this was unevenly enforced, and came into effect only in some urban factories. When I visited the area in mid-1996, workers claimed they needed at least five dollars a day to survive.

The feminization of "low-end" manufacturing work depends on gendered forms of labor control and harassment. Widespread surveillance and much of the daily control of female workers center on their bodies, for instance, in the provision of food, in the granting or withholding of permission for menstrual leave, in the pressure for family planning, and in the physical confinement imposed during work hours. Examples of sexual harassment include timing visits to the toilet, and using the excuse of having to verify requests for menstrual leaves to conduct body searches. Workers are crammed into dormitories above or next to warehouses, thus creating firetraps. Managers punish the tardy by making them stand under the sun for hours, and are quick to fire those who demand basic survival wages (ibid.). Whenever there is a strike, the army is deployed against the workers, no matter how peaceful they are (Wallace 1994). In my visit to the Tangerang zone, I noticed that military barracks are often adjacent to factory sites, and army personnel mingle freely with security guards outside the factory gates.[7] I was told that the army could reach any factory within twenty minutes of an outbreak of worker insurrection. Indonesians think it is normal for the army to keep industrial cities secure for factories, and factory bosses routinely make "donations" to local commanders to help meet their costs (Borsuk 1998). In practice, these free-trade zones often operate as sovereignty-free zones, where workers are denied the most basic social protection and are generally unshielded from the onslaught of capital, while remaining vulnerable to the state's repressive apparatus.

Aboriginal peoples in jungle communities also experience limited civil rights and frequent neglect by the state. Indigenous groups are labeled *orang terasing* ("isolated peoples") on account of their isolation from mainstream society, nomadic culture, and their imputed primitivity (e.g., Li 1997; Peluso 1995). In West Kalimantan, Borneo, the indigenous Dayaks, who are not represented in the local government, are denied legal protection against crimes committed by Muslim migrants from Madura. The Dayaks are also fighting a larger battle against timber companies that are grabbing their lands. Security forces are routinely used to destroy Dayak crops and jungle resources, to enforce land theft, and to torture people into accepting "compensation" for land taken to develop plantations. The Dayaks are practicing self-defense in accordance with their customary law (which permits them to attack Madurese migrants and timber-estate developers). These clashes have produced killing fields in the jungle (Samydori 1997, 5–7, 29). As in the industrial zones, the aboriginal enclaves are subject to two regulatory authorities, namely, private enterprise and the army. Citizens are exploited and controlled in such a way that capital appears to hold local sovereignty, and this sovereignty is enforced by state troops. In the market domains where capital reigns supreme, the state function seems reduced to that of night watchman.

I have identified what might be called a system of graduated sovereignty that is superimposed on the conventional arrangement of nation-states in Southeast Asia. In varying degrees, Southeast Asian states have responded to globalization by assigning "different social destinies" to their populations according to the roles those populations play in making their countries competitive and profitable.[8] The MSC, in which Malaysia's elite has invested heavily, is shielded by the government, while the inhabitants of the free-trade zones that are the links in global commodity chains are often stripped of their right to state protection and subjected instead to severe corporate discipline, backed by the army. Aboriginal enclaves are usually places to dump unprofitable commodities or zones to be cleared for new investment ventures. But this fragmentation of sovereignty across a range of locations has required the state to assert its ideological power to build up national legitimacy and thereby to sustain economic growth, social stability, and regional interdependency. How do these new styles of governmentality, in which different categories of citizens are treated according to their ability to serve market competitiveness, take normative expression at the national and transnational levels?[9]

The New Islam as Corporate Normativity

Kuala Lumpur, its old Moorish buildings now overshadowed by twin towers that pierce the tropical sky (and that are currently enjoying fame as the world's tallest buildings), is a global city and a showcase for Islamic corporate power. On a palm-fringed hillock stands the Kuala Lumpur Hilton, where attendants in white suits and batik sarongs rush forward to greet well-groomed Malay executives wielding cellular phones as they step out of limousines. Women in silk *baju kurong* (the loose Malay tunic and sarong), dripping jewelry from their ears and necks, saunter in on their way to fancy receptions. These members of the corporate elite are the "preferred Malays" (as they are called by the Malaysian public)—the lucky, but not always talented, few who have been favored by the New Economic Policy, *and* by the patronage of powerful politicians.[10] But with regional economic integration, the horizons of new professionals have stretched beyond Malaysia. These new professionals are joining a segregated stratosphere—one created by the corporate networks, political parties, professional groupings, clubs and golf courses, think tanks, and universities—that has increased cultural commonality among elite citizens of ASEAN countries while the gulf between them and ordinary citizens in the region has widened. What we see is a revamped Islam that has come to infuse Malaysian society as well as influence ASEAN corporate culture.

The outward symbols and forms of Malaysian corporate and professional culture are shaped more by Madison Avenue and Hollywood than by local culture. For instance, Kuala Lumpur has caught up with Singapore as a city of shopping malls; it now boasts the world's largest swimming pool with man-made waves, which is located in a mall decorated like Las Vegas. American pop music blasts forth from shopping malls filled with boutiques featuring Calvin Klein, DKNY, and Ralph Lauren. Young people are increasingly educated in Western universities through an economical "twinning" arrangement in which the first two years of a foreign curriculum are completed in Malaysia before students attend an American, Australian, or British university. A new class of superficially Westernized Malay professionals now runs the country according to American management principles, although there is substantial room left for increased efficiency and imagination. As in the United States, public universities are being downsized and corporatized, while the social sciences—for example, anthropology—are being replaced by "social administration" studies. The American corporate presence in Kuala Lumpur is so pervasive that the city seems like an economic and cultural extension of California.

Perhaps not surprisingly, the headlong rush toward globalized culture has stimulated the desire for rediscovering local roots and reasserting a distinctive regional identity. New narratives about a wider religious commonality that is linked to powerful states have emerged to counter the worst excesses of flexible citizenship and consumerism. The revival of the term *civilization* by Samuel Huntington has encouraged Asian leaders to articulate a cultural logic that can guide and justify their burgeoning sense of economic power and cosmopolitanism.[11] Although local scholars question Huntington's knowledge of Asian civilizations, and his hawkish stance toward the East, they appreciate his validation of "enduring" Asian civilizations.

Alongside other "Asian values" discourses circulating in insular Southeast Asia, an Islam-infused nationalism has emerged in Malaysia. This new Islamic ethos weds a religious reflowering to an unswerving allegiance to the state; it uses religion to promote a cultural kinship that can help integrate the national project into the region.[12] In recent years, the Mahathir regime has taken steps to modernize Islam through a range of strategies. First, the state has taken away some of the more abusive personal powers of the sultans and reduced their overall role as the key symbol of (an older social order of) Islam. Second, the government is trying to regulate another bastion of traditional Islamic power— the network of Islamic courts that shape the local understandings of Islamic laws. Ulamas associated with these courts often issue arbitrary *fatwas* and other Islamic injunctions, especially against certain changes in social behavior that come with secularization. The official explanation for curbing the Islamic courts is that the national standardization of Islamic law will ensure that women are not disproportionately prosecuted for violating codes governing dress and sexual behavior (Ong forthcoming). The larger goal appears to be state control over Islamic law as an instrument of and a rationale for national growth and security.

Third, the government is claiming Islam as a force in a broader front of nationalism and state power. Political leaders argue that "an Islamic country must first ensure security and economic prosperity before getting into the details of implementing Islamic principles on the people" (*New Straits Times* 1997a). Islam should be used to turn Malaysia into a "model state," but what the politicians have in mind is not another Iran, but rather a state in which a moderate and reasonable Islam helps to strengthen the state by working and meshing smoothly with global capitalism.

The fourth strategy is a transformation of the cultural sensibility of Malaysian Islam, by emphasizing the conjunction of Islam and capitalist modernity. Prime Minister Mahathir Mohamad has declared that "Islam wants its followers to be self-sufficient, independent, and progressive" (Teik 1995, 165). During the decades when the government wanted to create a large Malay middle class and a corporate elite, Mahathir had sought to demonstrate that "there is no reason why the Islamic faith, properly interpreted, cannot achieve spiritual well-being as well as material success for the Malays" (ibid., 179). A Malaysian scholar notes:

> The values listed in the *Mid-Term Review of the Fourth Malaysia Plan* were exactly the kinds of values to raise productivity at home, increase competitiveness abroad, and ensure political stability always. Among them were "better discipline, more self-reliance and striving for excellence" which together with "thriftiness" and "a more rational and scientific approach in overcoming problems" were "values which are progressive and consistent with the needs of a modernizing and industrializing plural society." (Ibid., 181)

In insular Southeast Asia, this new role as a productive force for tolerance, inclusiveness, and economic development has culminated in claims about an "Asian renaissance." For Anwar Ibrahim, the former deputy prime minister of Malaysia, a new era of Asian cultural vitality and autonomy has dawned: "The Renaissance of Asia entails the growth, development, and flowering of Asian societies based on a certain vision of perfection; societies imbued with truth and the love of learning, justice and compassion, mutual respect and forbearance, and freedom and responsibility. It is the transformation of its cultures and societies from its capitulation to Atlantic powers to the position of self-confidence and its reflowering at the dawn of a new millennium" (Ibrahim 1997). The optimism of this quote is ironic, to say the least, in view of Anwar Ibrahim's jailing on retrograde charges.

These strong claims suggest a pan-Islamic nationalism that is built on the common Islamic links between Malaysia, Indonesia, and other Southeast Asian countries; they also recall the precolonial era (from the fourteenth to the eighteenth centuries), when Islam was the force that brought commerce and splendor to Southeast Asian trading empires (Reid 1985). Anwar Ibrahim notes that the grounds for identifying an Asian renaissance are religious revivalism, the end of socialism, and the vibrant economic transformation of the region. He claims that "centuries ago Muslim thinkers conceived and expounded the concept of *ahadiyyat a-kathra*, which presupposes the essential oneness and transcendent connectedness of the apparent diversity on the surface. Asians firmly rooted in their cultural and spiritual traditions do possess the intellectual capacity to perceive the cultural unity of Asia, its meta-culture" (*Far Eastern Economic Review* 1996, 187). But this notion of an Asian renaissance is mainly an Islamic one; Anwar cites "attempts by Muslim thinkers such as Al-Afghani, Syed Ahmad Khan and Iqbal, among others, to re-discover and re-articulate their Islamic heritage as an Islamic renaissance" (*New Straits Times* 1997f, 10). He goes on to say that the values to be cherished and disseminated "include spirituality, family cohesion, and a sense of community which are still real in many Asian societies but less meaningful in the West." Anwar's views have been disseminated in scholarly forums and through publication; they provide a framework for shaping elite thinking about Malaysian modernity. The only public dissenting voice is that of local anthropologist Shamsul A. Baharuddin, who argues that the Asian-renaissance discourse is a "kind of ideology" that is linked to the interests of the ruling class.

It seeks social order and should not be confused with the Western notion of renaissance, which implies revolt against institutionalized religion, according to Shamsul (ibid., 11).

But the Asian renaissance is precisely about deinstitutionalizing an older form of religious order by imposing from above a reformed Islam that positions the ruling elite and develops their moral power in a renewed nationalism. In sharp contrast, then, to the images of Islamic radicalism in the Middle East and in the recent past in Southeast Asia, the new Islam promotes new normativities in cultural behavior, technical expertise, and regional cooperation.[13] Political leaders claim that the new Islam not only flourishes in the multiethnic milieus of Southeast Asia, but also fosters "economic progress in partnership with others" (*Time* 1996, 18). Under the new Islam, society is exposed to the flexible operation of market principles, which includes the mass employment of young Muslim women who are frequently transported to distant workplaces where their bosses are non-Muslim South Korean or ethnic Chinese managers. This new Islamic governmentality thus deploys gender in a way that subjects working-class Malay women to disciplinary power from another ethnic group, while "civilizing" Malay male professionals are considered to be equals of the economically successful diasporan Chinese.

Muslims are encouraged to work with fewer constraints in Chinese-dominated and Westernized cities such as Singapore, Hong Kong, and Taipei. Muslim schoolchildren and businessmen are learning Mandarin to work more effectively with the Chinese communities that control commerce throughout the region. Corporate networking has tempered the more austere Islamic practices, and Southeast Asian Muslim yuppies are eager to be the new model of how a moderate and reasonable Islam can work successfully with global capital. For instance, in the world-class hotels that cater to the every whim of patrons, rooms come equipped with both minibars and a Qur'an. An arrow on the ceiling points toward Mecca to guide Muslims in prayer. Muslim movers and shakers are at home in settings where Muslim women wearing veils rub shoulders with Westerners in swimsuits and Muslims dine alongside non-Muslims eating pork and drinking brandy. The new ease that the religiously correct, self-made new Malay expresses in mingling with international players and an international clientele has been endorsed by the new Islam, which encourages both wealth accumulation and cosmopolitan worldliness that recalls an earlier era of Islamic trading empires, and the cultural syncretism of peoples across the Malay archipelago. The new Islam also defines the acceptable and unacceptable forms of "liberalism" that underlie the concept of "ASEAN solidarity"; it encourages economic liberalism and allows the presence of the legal liberalism that is associated with "Western decadence and excessive freedom"— as long as Muslims are not participants. Thus, by promoting Muslim professional and investor classes who can participate confidently in the globalized contexts of capitalism, the rise of Islamic governmentality operates as a foil to "Chinese" economic power in the region.

"Civilizational Dialogue" and Internal Colonies

Under state sponsorship, a Center for Civilizational Dialogue has been set up at the University of Malaya to produce a new moral vision of Southeast Asian regionalism. In an obvious response to Huntington's "clash of civilizations," "civilizational dialogue" focuses on civilizational differences as well as "the affinities that exist between civilizations," according to a brochure published by the center. Disavowing Huntington's paradigm, which assumes an inevitable competition between global powers, the brochure maintains that only when one "celebrates both the similarities and the differences between civilizations" can one "evolve a truly just, humane and compassionate world civilization where there is neither the dominant nor the dominated." Nevertheless, the brochure identifies a conflict—one generated by "the globalization process, propelled as it is by powerful economic and technological forces, [which] threatens to create a hegemonic, homogenous, materialistic civilization that is antagonistic to spiritually and ethically based civilizations" (Center for Civilizational Dialogue n.d.). This suggests an alternative hierarchy of civilizations that turns Huntington's model of a supremacist Western civilization on its head. From the (official) Malaysian

perspective, Asian civilizations are ethically based and therefore superior to, but threatened by, the soulless and overweening power of Western civilization. As the center of and host to such civilizational exchanges,
Malaysia prides itself on being "a nation where civilizations converge."
In rather immoderate language, the brochure claims that "there is perhaps no other nation on earth where substantial numbers of Muslims,
Buddhists, Confucianists, Taoists, Hindus, Christians, and Sikhs live
together in relative peace and harmony. What is equally remarkable
is that [in Malaysia] civilizational communities have for decades been
exposed to, and interacted with, Western civilization." The center will
be the promoter and disseminator of civilizational discourse; it has
held international conferences titled "Islam and Confucianism," "Islam,
Japan, and the West," and "Civilizational Dialogue: Present Realities;
Future Possibilities." The official, ideological nature of civilizational
language is spelled out clearly when it is linked directly to regional and
national interests: "Shared values, derived through inter-civilizational
dialogue, it is hoped, will help to mold the ASEAN identity of tomorrow" (ibid.).

Civilizational discourse that directly engages globalization processes also aids in the articulation of an enlightened set of Asian values that is friendly to economic liberalism, a concept that is redefined
as "democracy with Asian flavor and characteristics." Invoking Adam
Smith, Malaysian prime minister Mahathir talks about the "reasonable
enlightened self-interest coming from a rationality" based on multilateral cooperation, so that ASEAN countries are helping all boats to
rise "with the rising East Asian economic tide" (*New Straits Times* 1996,
12, 15). This Asian liberalism resonates with a loose sense of cultural
kinship that stresses Islam and the historical legacy of trading empires.
Perhaps nowhere else in the world has the sense of cultural kinship, combined with shared authoritarian values of state power, been deployed
more effectively to generate an elite sense of collective dignity, one that
is based on geopolitical location and common regional trade interests. As
Anthony D. Smith has pointed out, interstate groupings such as ASEAN
"only help to perpetuate, if they do not inflame, the hold of national

identities and nationalist aspirations, as do the new classes of international capitalism" (1993, 169).

The use of "civilization" as an overarching set of core values that are common to the "diverse cultures and communities" in Southeast Asia allows politicians to frame national and regional problems in stark East–West terms. Such talk about regional civilizational commonalities is also convenient for suppressing discussions about the class, cultural, regional, and political differences that are endemic throughout the region. Civilizational discourse maintains that ASEAN is the most "multi-religious and multi-cultural" regional grouping in the world (Center for Civilizational Dialogue). As the Asian tigers' growth rates have risen dramatically since the early 1990s, the rhetoric of "ASEAN solidarity" has served to present a relatively unified position within the Asia-Pacific Economic Conference (APEC), as well as a counterweight to the challenge represented by China's giant economy.

But the discourse defining an ASEAN civilizational world also lends spiritual authority to the practices of individual regimes in managing and suppressing profane others who are excluded by such discourses. Seeking to expand its economic muscle, ASEAN admitted Vietnam and Myanmar, making ASEAN an interstatal system that tolerates or is silent about human-rights violations in a network of "internal colonies."[14] Each Southeast Asian state has its own irredentist groups: the East Timorese and Acehnese in Indonesia, Shans and Karens in Myanmar, Patani Malays in Thailand, Dayaks in Malaysia and Indonesia, and the Moros in the Philippines. In a policy of scratching each other's back, governments silence debates about and criticisms of human-rights violations in their ASEAN neighbors. For instance, pro-democracy activists in Malaysia who demonstrated against Indonesia's occupation of East Timor were suppressed by the Malaysian government, which used the excuse that such activities damaged state-level relations within the region. Protests in Malaysia, Thailand, and the Philippines against the admission of the Burmese regime into ASEAN are barely reported in local media.[15] George J. Aditjondro (1996) notes that because "all ASEAN governments have their own 'East Timors' in their backyard," ASEAN has become "a conspiracy of repressive regimes, busy protecting each other's behinds." These colonies, then, are places where sovereign power is imposed with overwhelming coercion (East Timor), or is simply absent, so that a kind of low-grade struggle continues to fester (Patani in Thailand). Thus, processes of regional cooperation and modern state-endorsed subjectivity proceed alongside processes of fragmentation that seek to elude centralized power.

The galaxy of differentiated zones is thus unevenly integrated into the structures of state power and global capital. Technology zones and growth triangles are plugged tightly into globalization processes, while aboriginal and ethnic-minority reserves are often disarticulated from national and regional centers of power. In short, the structural logic of globalization has not resulted in the solidification of differences between civilizations, but rather in the proliferation of differentiated sovereignty within and across borders. The moral regulation of the state both homogenizes and individualizes its subjects, so that while unifying images and forms associated with Islam emphasize uniformity, the cultural definition of jungle dwellers, "illegals," and ethnic minorities makes them less legitimate in the social order. These zones of graduated sovereignty thus call into question the uniformity of citizenship, and the kinds of political or moral claims that subjects can make on state power. More and more, the state's authority as legitimized power depends on modes of regulation that are morally justified in terms of a hegemonic cultural model that defines normal and deviant subjects, even as it conceals relations of inequality between the ruler and the ruled.

For the middle classes who are vested in the structure of the state, moralizing discourses about national unity and ASEAN solidarity continue to sustain their claims on state protection. For instance, whereas the international press attributes the wave of currency devaluation in 1997 to reckless borrowing and lending, the building of megaprojects, and the lack of market controls in the tiger economies, local politicians blame outsiders, who are viewed as having the antithesis of Asian civilizational values.[16] Urging "ASEAN unity," Mahathir blamed international financier George Soros, whom he demonized as anti-Asia, and "anti-poor countries": "We are told that we must open up, that trade and commerce must be totally free. Free, for whom? For rogue speculators. For anarchists wishing to destroy weak countries in their crusade for open societies, to force us to submit to the dictatorship of international manipulators. We want to embrace borderlessness but we still need to protect ourselves from self-serving rogues and international brigandage" (e.g., *New Straits Times* 1997f, 29; 1997d, 1). As the crisis spread across the region and local currencies continued to slide, other Asians saw a larger conspiracy that was motivated by Western jealousy. Expressed first through attacks on local currencies, and then through regulations imposed by the International Monetary Fund (IMF), this larger conspiracy seeks to intimidate relatively healthy economies. Culture and economics become entangled as ordinary people try to understand the fiscal crisis in terms of a profound crisis in East–West civilizational values. Such a cultural understanding helps to sustain the social contract even under circumstances in which the state is increasingly unable to deliver the goods in their accustomed quantities, or to plan its economy in a world of unruly financial markets. Will the postdevelopmental strategy protecting the interests of the middle classes become undermined, and must the tiger states once again resort to repressive measures to control social unrest?

Conclusion

As the fiscal crisis gathered momentum throughout Southeast Asia, the postdevelopmental strategy that has worked so well since the 1970s appears to be unraveling. In what Stephen Gill calls "the new constitutionalism," new rules of market efficiency are imposed—through such agencies as the International Monetary Fund—on third-world politicians, further limiting their ability to use a broad range of policies to defend national or local interests from world market forces (Gill 1995, 216). As governments in Singapore, Malaysia, and Thailand struggled to secure the interests of society by making loans to domestic banks, the stiff IMF requirements for a multibillion bailout intensified rioting and toppled the Suharto government.

Attacks on merchants became inseparable from anti-Chinese rioting that spread to small and large cities throughout the archipelago.
Hundreds of Chinese-owned shops, nightclubs, churches, and even
homes were looted and destroyed.[17] To many indigenous Indonesians,
ethnic Chinese, who control much of the economy, are considered the
direct causes of economic hardship. Although a few tycoons, such as
Liem Sioe Liong, Bob Hasan, and Mocthar Riady, became exceedingly
rich working closely with the Suharto government, the majority of ethnic Chinese are small shopkeepers, traders, and professionals. But, as
the financial crisis intensifies, anti-Chinese attacks have spread as army
leaders accuse Chinese of food hoarding and disloyalty, and call on them
to bring back billions of dollars invested overseas. Muslim leaders had
called for a jihad against those suspected of pushing up food prices.
Middle-class Chinese have joined the affluent in pulling up stakes fleeing to Singapore, Australia, and the United States. The country is in
danger of losing its relatively small class of well-trained professionals
and entrepreneurs who have been crucial for running most of its modern industries. It appears that export enclaves and zones of differentiated
sovereignty, as economic and political centerpieces of tiger economies,
have not been sufficient innovations to protect them from the anarchy
of global financial markets.

Indonesia aside, the postdevelopmental strategy is a manifesta-
tion of the flexible yet stabilizing role of Asian tiger states, honed by the
challenges of global restructuring, global commodity chains, and international financial markets. Contrary to claims about the demise of the
state, I have argued that postdevelopmental Asian states have responded
positively to global capital, either by proliferating transnational linkages
to capital and multilateral agencies, or by experimenting with differentiated sovereignty as a way to make their societies more attractive
and responsive to the demands of global capital.[18] It remains to be seen
whether the system of flexible sovereignty can be sustained in the era
of a disciplinary neoliberalism, where market forces constrain the ability of states to protect their societies. My analysis of the dialectical relations between the industrializing states and global forces shows that

state-centralized forms of capital accumulation are being superseded by indirect, economic forms of a global market system. At the same time, the state is caught on the tightrope of pursuing capital while protecting society. In what Karl Polayni calls the "double movement" of history, tiger economies are merely particular examples of how middle-range states meet the challenges of globalization.[19]

The question remains: does the spread of social sovereignty—in the sense of codes, rules, and practices—mean that the state is undermined as a locus of sovereignty? The answer is no; the political space within which the nominal citizens dwell, work, and are subjectivized remains significant. The state has to will a piece of territory to be put outside the normal juridical order (as in the setting aside of free-trade zones), and to agree to outsource state functions (as in the control of particular populations) to other regulatory agencies. The social terms, codes, and norms that constitute zones of new sovereignty are the interface between the techniques of biopower and juridical rules. As Giorgio Agamben has argued, "states of exception" such as refugee camps are enabled by the modern state; more and more they are part of its normalized system of political arrangements" (Agamben 1998, 169–70). In an era of transnationality, the state deployment of disciplinary and pastoral forms of biopower has enlarged the space of the political. This politicization of life, whereby subject populations are included or excluded under different forms of sovereignty, has enabled the growth and triumph of capitalism across the globe.

Indeed, as this book is published, the economic typhoon unleashed by unruly capital markets has shattered the Indonesian economy. In contrast, Asian tiger countries have responded by strengthening the hand of the state against capital flows. The Hong Kong government, in an unprecedented move, has intervened to protect the property sector from foreign speculators. In Malaysia, Mahathir has imposed even more rigid controls on capital flows; he has also moved decisively against his political rivals. Such revolts of the Asian states (and Russia) to protect society against what has been called "Anglo-Saxon capitalism" refute Western axioms about globalization, and its inevitable weakening of the state.

Notes

1. Robert Latham (1998) defines sovereignty in terms of the legal and social forms constituting a domain of ruling, against the agency-focus model. He maintains that sovereignty "should refer to the construction and maintenance of structures of relations that set the terms for—or are constitutitive of—a domain of social existence."

2. Ruth McVey (1992, 3–34) discusses the concept of "the strong state" applied to Southeast Asian regimes that play a dominant role in controlling the developmental project of their countries, mainly through a powerful bureaucracy, public enterprises, and state monopolies. Although such state-centered institutions continue to exist in all Southeast Asian countries, new strategies focus more and more on producing and managing the middle classes.

3. The phrase "commodity chains" refers to the global production networks through which commodities are designed, produced, and marketed in a multiplicity of national sites (Gereffi 1992).

4. The phrase "an effect of practices" is from Bill Maurer, who argues that the coconstruction of state, sovereignty, market, and subject "throws into relief the *moral* claims subjects make in any momentary configuration of these power effects. Such moral claims tend to hide or naturalize the very terms—sovereignty, the market, the rule of law—from which they draw their moral force" (1998; emphasis in original).

5. I thank Paul Rabinow for alerting me to this reference.

6. Biopower "brought life and its mechanisms into the realm of explicit calculations and made knowledge-power an agent of transformation of human life" (Foucault 1979, 143).

7. In 1993, a young worker at a watch factory in Surabaya was abducted, gang-raped, and murdered for leading a strike to demand that a twenty-five-cent (U.S.) meal allowance be added to the eighty-four-cent (U.S.) daily wage. The murder provoked a national outcry, which led to the arrests of some people. There was widespread belief that the military was implicated.

8. Robert Castel observes the emergence, in neoliberal states, of "differential modes of treatment of populations, which aim to maximize the returns on doing what is profitable and to marginalize the unprofitable" ("From Dangerousness to Risk," in *The Foucault Effect*, ed. Graham Burchell, Colin Gordon, and Peter Miller [(Chicago: University of Chicago Press, 1999], 294). Although Indonesia and the tiger countries are not neoliberal economies, the strategy of

differentiation among populations in relation to market forces has produced the system of graduated sovereignty.

9. It might be added that the European states played this role of favoring corporate elites even more blatantly during their period of consolidation.

10. Affirmative-action policies that favored Malay citizens were instituted under the New Economic Policy introduced in the early 1970s. Despite having themselves benefited from this policy, there is growing resentment among Malay professionals against these "preferred Malays" for gaining power not entirely on their own merits but through even more exclusive political favors than they themselves have enjoyed.

11. Samuel Huntington's *The Clash of Civilizations* (New York: Simon and Schuster, 1996) is widely displayed in Southeast Asian bookstores.

12. Tu Wei-ming has been the proponent of a Confucian version of universalism that is also closely linked to corporate capitalism. He has lectured Singaporeans that Confucianism is not the possession of any single nation but is rather a "transvaluated" values system. With globalization, Confucianism has not rejected Enlightenment values but rather absorbed "instrumental rationality, material progress, social engineering, empiricism, pragmatism, scientism, and competitiveness." He notes that the "Confucian personality" can be realized more fully in a liberal-democratic society than in an authoritarian one. By redefining Confucianism as an ethos that has absorbed the Western rationalities of competition, technical efficiency, and economic progress, he frames the moral choices and self-actualization encouraged by Confucianism within an instrumentalist, market-oriented framework, but not the framework of human rights. See Tu, *A Confucian Perspective on Human Rights*, the Inaugural Wu The Yao Memorial Lectures, 1995 (Singapore: Center for the Arts, National University of Singapore, 1995), 27, 29.

13. For Islamic radicalism in Malaysia, see Clive Kesler, *Politics and Islam in a Malay State* (Ithaca, N.Y.: Cornell University Press, 1976).

14. See George J. Aditjondro (1996), who suggests that only a globally condemned military coup in Phnom Penh made the ASEAN leadership hesitate about including Cambodia in the new lineup.

15. For an exception, see *Aliran Monthly* 17(2) (1997): 29–40.

16. An article in the *Wall Street Journal* (August 5, 1997, 1) blamed "a grave lack of economic discipline" for the financial storm sweeping through the region, and predicted a decline in growth rates from 9 percent to 4 percent.

17. "Recent Anti-Chinese Violence," *Indonesian Archives Digest*, February 19, 1998, gives a pretty comprehensive list of all anti-Chinese incidents in Indonesia since the beginning of that year. The point made is that the attacks began for economic and not political reasons, but the violence was increasingly tinged by ethnic and religious (most Chinese are Christian) overtones.

18. See Evans (1997) for a critique of claims about the demise of the state. Evans argues that neoliberalism has middle-range and advanced states to focus on a leaner and meaner narrow set of functions focused on benefiting private interests and global capital.

19. In *The Great Transformation: The Political and Economic Origins of Our Time* (Boston: Beacon Press, 1957), Karl Polyani maintains that in the unruly conditions produced by global markets in the 1930s, new forms of state arose to assert social control over apparently natural laws of economic forces.

References

Aditjondro, George J. 1996. "All in the Name of 'ASEAN Solidarity.'" *Sydney Morning Herald*, November 14.

Agamben, Giorgio. 1998. *Homo Sacer: Sovereign Power and Bare Life*. Trans. Daniel Heller-Roazen. Stanford, Calif.: Stanford University Press.

Akyuzand, Yilmaz, and Charles Gore. 1996. "The Investment-Profits Nexus in East Asian Industrialization." *World Development* 24(2): 461–70.

Aleinikoff, Alexander T. 1995. "State-Centered Refugee Law: From Resettlement to Containment." In *Mistrusting, Refugees*, ed. E. Valentine Daniel and John C. Knudsen. Berkeley: University of California Press.

Borsuk, Richard. 1998. "Fear of Unrest Grows in Indonesian City." *Wall Street Journal*, February 20.

Brosius, Peter. 1997. "Prior Transcripts, Divergent Paths: Resistance and Acquiescence to Logging in Sarawak, East Malaysia." *Comparative Studies in Society and History* 39: 468–510.

Castells, Manuel. 1996. *The Information Age*, vol. 1, *The Rise of the Network Society*. Oxford: Blackwell.

Center for Civilizational Dialogue. N.d. *The Center for Civilizational Dialogue*. Kuala Lumpur: University of Malaya.

Evans, Peter. 1997. "The Eclipse of the State? Reflections on Stateness in an Era of Globalization." *World Politics* 50 (October): 66.

Far Eastern Economic Review. 1996. Fiftieth-anniversary Issue. Hong Kong.

Foucault, Michel. 1979. *The History of Sexuality*, vol. 1, *An Introduction*. Trans. Robert Hurley. New York: Vintage Books.

Gereffi, Gary. 1992. "New Realities of Industrial Development in East Asia and Latin America: Global, Regional, and National Trends." In *States and Development in the Asian Pacific Rim*, ed. Richard P. Appelbaum and Jeffrey Henderson. Newbury Park, Calif.: Sage. 85–112.

Giddens, Anthony. 1987. *The Nation-State and Violence*, vol. 2, *A Contemporary Critique of Historical Materialism*. Berkeley: University of California Press.

Gill, Stephen. 1995. "Globalization, Democratization, and the Politics of Indifference." In *Globalization: Critical Reflections*, ed. James H. Mittelman. Boulder, Colo., London: Lynne Rienner Publishers.

Goozner, Merril. 1994. "Western Firms Exploit Working Conditions." *Buffalo News*, November 20.

Goozner, Merril, and Uli Schmetzer. 1994. "Asian Workers Fighting Back Low Wages. Terrible Working Conditions Foster Strikes." *Chicago Tribune*, November 7.

Gupta, Akhil. 1992. "The Song of the Non-Aligned World: Transnational Identities and the Reinscription of Space in Late Capitalism." *Cultural Anthropology* 7(1): 63–79.

Gupta, Akhil, and James Ferguson. 1992. "Beyond 'Culture': Space, Identity, and the Politics of Difference." *Cultural Anthropology* 7(1): 23.

Ibrahim, Anwar. 1997. *The Asian Renaissance*. Kuala Lumpur: Times Publications. Back cover.

Latham, Robert. 1998. "States, Global Markets, and Social Sovereignty." Paper presented at the Social Science Research Council Conference "Sovereignty and Security," Notre Dame, Indiana, April 18–20.

Levy, Barry S., and Daniel C. Sussott. 1992. *Years of Horror, Days of Hope: Responding to the Cambodian Refugee Crisis*. Millwood, N.Y.: Associated Faculty Press.

Li, Tania. 1997. "Constituting Tribal Space: Indigenous Identity and Resource Politics in Indonesia." Paper presented at the University of California, Berkeley, October 17.

Macleod, Scott, and T. G. McGee. 1996. "The Singapore-Johore-Riau Growth Triangle: An Emerging Extended Metropolitan Region." In *Emerging World Cities in the Asia Pacific*, ed. Fu-chen Lo and Yue-man Yeung. Tokyo: United Nations University Press.

Malkki, Liisa. 1994. "Citizens of Humanity: Internationalism and the Imagined Community of Nations." *Diaspora* 3(1): 41–68.

Maurer, Bill. 1998. "Cyberspatial Sovereignties: Offshore Finance, Digital Cash, and the Limits of Liberalism." *Indiana Journal of Global Legal Studies* 5(2): 493–519.

McVey, Ruth. 1992. "The Materialization of the Southeast Asian Entrepreneur." In *Southeast Asian Capitalists*, ed. Ruth McVey. Ithaca, N.Y.: Southeast Asia Program, Cornell University.

Mimos. 1998. "Malaysia's Multimedia Super Corridor." http://www.jaring.my.

New Straits Times. 1996. "Future Belongs to All of Mankind." December 4.

———. 1997a. "Anwar: Carry Out Islamic Laws Wisely, Objectively." July 27.

———. 1997b. "Conduit to Fully Tap Creativity." July 30.

———. 1997c. "Currency Speculators Out to Undermine 'Asian Economies'." July 25.

———. 1997d. "Dr. M: It's Soros." July 27.

———. 1997e. "Project ASEAN As Closely-Linked: Don." February 25.

———. 1997f. "When Asia Awakes." July 29.

Nonini, Donald M. 1997. "Shifting Identities, Positioned Imaginaries—Transnational Traversals and Reversals by Malaysian Chinese." In *Ungrounded Empires: The Cultural Politics of Modern Chinese Transnationalism*, ed. Aihwa Ong and Donald M. Nonini. New York: Routledge.

Ong, Aihwa. 1986. *Spirits of Resistance and Capitalist Discipline: Factory Women in Malaysia*. Albany: State University of New York Press.

———. 1998. "Flexible Citizenship among Chinese Cosmopolitans." In *Cosmopolitics: Thinking and Feeling beyond the Nation*, ed. Pheng Cheah and Bruce Robbins. Minneapolis: University of Minnesota Press.

———. Forthcoming. "Muslim Feminists in the Shelter of Corporate Islam." *Citizenship Studies*.

Peluso, Nancy. 1995. *Rich Land, Poor People: Resource Control and Resistance in Java*. Berkeley and Los Angeles: University of California Press.

Reid, Anthony. 1985. *The Land below the Wind*, vol. 1, *Southeast Asia in an Age of Commerce*. New Haven: Yale University Press.

Samydorai, Sinapan. 1997. "The Killing Fields of West Kalimantan." *Human Rights Solidarity* (Hong Kong) 7(2) (April–July). *Human Rights Solidarity* is the newsletter of the Asian Human Rights Commission.

San Francisco Chronicle. 1998. "Malaysia Arms Its Borders against Flood of Refugees." March 31, sec. B2.

Sassen, Saskia. 1995. *Losing Control? Sovereignty in an Age of Globalization.* New York: Columbia University Press.

Smith, Anthony D. 1993. *National Identity.* Reno: University of Nevada Press.

Straits Times. 1997a. "Third Langkawi International Dialogue: Now It's How to Make It Work." July 27.

———. 1997b. "Work towards Tangible Gains, Dr. M. Tells Participants." July 29.

Teik, Khoo Boo. 1995. *Paradoxes of Mahathirism.* Kuala Lumpur: Oxford University Press.

Time. 1996. "The New Face of Islam." September 23, international ed.

Tollefson, J. W. 1989. *Alien Winds: The Reeducation of America's Indochinese Refugees.* New York: Praeger.

Wallace, Charles. 1994. "Relief Elusive for Asia's Labor Pains." *Los Angeles Times,* December 13.

Wysocki, Bernard, Jr. 1997. "Malaysia Is Gambling on a Costly Plunge into a Cyber Future." *Wall Street Journal,* June 10.

CHAPTER 3

International Political
Economy as a Cultural Practice:
The Metaphysics of Capital Mobility

Bill Maurer

Recent discussions of globalization are founded on an assumption about
the movement of capital, goods, people, and images—that movement
generates change, and that movement is a self-evident phenomenon.
Cultural approaches to globalization, such as Appadurai's (1996) and
Hannerz's (1996), tend to posit that *increasing* mobility characterizes
the contemporary era. Critics of these approaches note that capital,
goods, labor, and ideas have been moving from place to place ever since
the rise of capitalism, if not before, through trading routes and ancient
empires (e.g., Abu-Lughod 1989; Friedman 1995). Within political science, "international political economy" (IPE) scholars, while not dip-
ping quite so far back into history, do make the point that the sorts of
economic relationships that cultural critics point to as harbingers of a
new era—flexible financing, foreign direct investment, floating exchange
rates, paper trading and securitization, and all the other ancillary features of contemporary global finance (Harvey 1989)—also characterized
the heyday of nineteenth-century industrial capitalism, only to wither
away after the world wars. In the late twentieth century, as one IPE
reviewer puts it, the "phoenix" of international finance, a dead duck
after World War II, had "risen" again (Cohen 1996).

An orthodox Marxist approach to the world economy might
find resonances with the recent line in IPE that views global finance
as a "resurgence," and not a new phenomenon (e.g., Helleiner 1994;

Kindleberger 1987; Kapstein 1994). Indeed, the world described by contemporary IPE scholars sounds very much like that described by early-twentieth-century Marxists such as Rosa Luxemburg (1951), V. I. Lenin (1989), and Rudolf Hilferding (1981). These authors were writing in the aftermath of the nineteenth-century era of "free trade." It was a time of financial speculation, technological advance, especially in transport and communications, and vast movements of money, goods, people, and ideas. Even earlier, Karl Marx, writing of the role of finance in nineteenth-century British imperialism, often reads like David Harvey, writing of the role of finance in late-twentieth-century geographies of wealth and inequality. And Rosa Luxemburg, writing of the financialization of the world economy in the 1910s, makes arguments and uses rhetoric similar to those of Charles Kindleberger, an IPE authority, writing of the "resurgence of global finance" in the 1980s and 1990s. Notice how easily the following quotations can be made to follow each other in a consistent, and by now quite familiar, narrative:

> Primitive accumulation proceeded without the advance of even a shilling . . . As with the stroke of an enchanter's wand, [debt] endows unproductive money with the power of creation and thus turns it into capital, without forcing it to expose itself to the troubles and risks inseparable from its employment in industry or even in usury . . . [Debt] has given rise to joint-stock companies, to dealings in negotiable effects of all kinds, and to speculation: in a word, it has given rise to stock-exchange gambling and the modern bankocracy. (Marx 1977, 917, 919)

> This "bewildering" world of high finance encloses an equally bewildering variety of cross-cutting activities, in which banks borrow massively short-term from other banks, insurance companies and pension funds assemble such vast pools of investment funds as to function as dominant "market makers," while industrial, merchant, and landed capital become so integrated into financial operations and structures that it becomes increasingly difficult to tell where commercial and industrial interests begin and where strictly financial interests end. (Harvey 1989, 161)

These operations of capital, at first sight, seem to reach the height of madness. One loan followed hard on the other, the interest on old loans was defrayed by new loans, and capital borrowed from the British and French paid for the large orders placed with British and French industrial capital. While the whole of Europe sighed and shrugged its shoulders at [Egypt's] crazy economy, European capital was in fact doing business in Egypt on a unique and fantastic scale—in incredible modern version of the biblical legend about the fat kine which remains unparalleled in capitalist history. (Luxemburg 1951, 434)

The last decades have seen the development of . . . currency swaps, interest swaps, repos—a device for selling a security with a contract to buy it back later at a set price to gain short-term liquidity—a bewildering panoply of options and futures contracts on government bonds, interest rates, stock-market indexes and the like, packaged loans in which mortgages, automobile installment paper and credit-card debt are grouped and participants in the total sold, . . . etc. etc. (Kindleberger 1987, 65)

Such quotations might give ammunition to the argument that, where globalization (and here, specifically, capital mobility) is concerned, there is nothing new under the sun, that global movements of money, goods, people, and ideas are as old as modernity, if not older. Perhaps it is analysts who have changed more than the objective conditions, or at least structuring logics, of modern capitalism (Friedman 1995; cf. Lash and Urry 1994).

Although it does force analysts of the current era to examine closely their own claims about the novelty of recent financial operations, and to dig back into past financial systems before making any such claims, this perspective is fundamentally flawed. It assumes that the nature of the movement described by authors from Marx to Kindleberger is identical, and that such movements, and the objects being moved, are comparable. In short, it leaves unasked the questions that most need answering: What counts as capital, and what counts as movement, in discussions of capital mobility? How do certain practices and processes constitute "capital" such that it can "move"? How do they also structure its "movements" so that they can have the sorts of effects that cultural analysts of globalization ascribe to them?

In this chapter, I argue that the problem with theoretical approaches to globalization that leave movement and the objects moved relatively unanalyzed can be analogized to the problem of classical kinship studies in anthropology. In his pathbreaking critique of the anthropological study of kinship, David Schneider (1984) argued that anthropologists had sought to explain kinship systems in different societies without first understanding the metaphysical assumptions that went into their own construction of "kinship" itself. These assumptions were about both the persons related by kinship and the notion of relationship implied in the anthropological construct of "kinship systems." In discovering systems of "kinship" wherever they looked, anthropologists blinded themselves to alternative modes of relationship and affiliation, and alternative modes of personhood and identity not captured by their own kinship thinking.

Similarly, when IPE scholars and others engaged in debates over globalization look for either disjunctures or continuities in processes of capital mobility, they miss the construction of both "capital" and "mobility" in their own analyses and in the practices of the persons who create the phenomena they study. Neglecting the practices that create the objects and processes of mobility leads analysts to miss alternative constructions that seriously challenge neat narratives of globalization. In this essay, I discuss two curiously interlinked examples of such possible alternatives: the offshore financial services sector, consisting of a chain of tax-haven jurisdictions spanning the globe, each attempting to push the limits and contradictions of "capital mobility" as it is currently constructed; and the Islamic banking industry, which uses offshore financial centers, together with the moral doctrines of the Qur'an and Islamic law, to devise alternative "financial" operations and instruments. These alternative operations and instruments, in turn, challenge definitions of finance and economics and concoct alternative "globalized" modernities.

Securitization and the Meaning of Kinship

My contribution comes out of a concern with the unexamined assumptions of the IPE literature, a literature that I have found incredibly helpful to my anthropological pursuits in attempting to write a cultural study of finance. While the IPE literature in political science contains the kind of specificity on the nature of global finance that the sociology and anthropology literature often lacks, it also effects interesting metaphysical sleights of hand in its accounts of capital mobility. A leading IPE scholar, for example, attempts a definition of financial globalization that is admirable for its comprehensiveness yet peculiar—from an anthropological perspective—in the sorts of unexamined equivalencies it draws between different sorts of financial and proprietary entities:

> For our purposes, global finance is assumed to encompass all types of cross-border portfolio-type transactions—borrowing and lending, trading of currencies or other financial claims, and the provision of commercial banking or other financial services. It also includes capital flows associated with foreign direct investment . . . Financial globalization . . . refers to the broad integration of national markets associated with both innovation and deregulation in the postwar era and is manifested by increasing movements of capital across national frontiers. The more alternative assets are closely regarded as substitutes for one another, the higher the degree of capital mobility. (Cohen 1996, 269)

This definition, while breathlessly all-encompassing, depends on the ultimate convertibility of different forms of property into one another. Indeed, convertibility and substitution form the cornerstone of his measure of capital mobility: "The more alternative assets are closely regarded as substitutes for one another, the higher the degree of capital mobility." But what are the processes that make the objects of property at issue able to be converted into one another, or able to be converted at all?

At one level, this is an obvious question with an obvious answer. The most important process enabling convertibility is securitization. Securitization refers to the abstract division of objects of property into intangible "shares" represented by pieces of paper or ledger ticks. Elsewhere, I have discussed the history of securitization and the securities clearance process in terms of a shift from metaphors of substance to metaphors of risk in the construction of property (Maurer 1999). Here, however, I want to emphasize that securitization and securities clearance, which allow the kind of convertibility that Cohen identifies as integral to capital mobility, involve a set of technical and procedural norms that make equivalencies among objects of property possible by rendering these objects into the same kind of thing—abstractions of value embodied in imaginary shares.

To people familiar with the division of property into abstract shares, the process of securitization may seem as commonsensical as their belief in paternity or maternity—that a child "belongs" to or is "related to" the woman who bears and the man who begets it. Yet these are cultural conceptions of relatedness (and are closely linked to cultural conceptions of property), and there are myriad ways that people can, and have, imagined the relationship between a child and the men and women who have had a role in its creation (Delaney 1986; Strathern 1988). As post-Schneiderian kinship scholars have argued, we cannot study something called "kinship" without automatically assuming a meaning of kinship that may very well be alien to the cultural worlds we study. The language of bearing and begetting, for example, betrays a host of cultural assumptions about the relationship between a child and its parents and the notions of fatherhood and motherhood that have been central to Western kinship thinking. It assumes that a woman who "bears" a child passively "carries" it, while a man who begets provides the spark of life that animates inert matter to take form into a child. The vision of procreation and relationship entails a vision of cosmology as well, linking intimate conceptions of procreation to ultimate conceptions of a divinely created world order (Delaney 1986).

Although the extrapolation of abstract shares from physical or intangible objects may, like the "facts" of procreation, seem natural and commonsense, it is anything but. The conceptual, technical, and procedural norms of securitization are difficult to grasp, if not utterly alien, in other cultural contexts. This fact can even be deduced from the publications of institutions most invested in the idea that securitization is as natural as bipedalism. The World Bank reports that a main difficulty of financing businesses in so-called transitioning economies stems from lenders' unwillingness to accept certain kinds of collateral from potential borrowers—specifically, movable property held by the prospective borrower such as factory machinery or inventories. "Rather," the Bank writes, "lenders require that the moveable property be placed under their direct control—as if they were valuables in a bank vault or goods in a bonded warehouse" (World Bank 1996, 89). The World Bank then asks, incredulously, "Why is real estate or merchandise in a vault acceptable as collateral, but not livestock, machinery, and inventories?" In spite of people's difficulties with the logic of securitization, however, the Bank proposes the development of legal regimes that permit the "creation of security interests for any person over any thing" (ibid.). Securitization, thus, is simply not obvious or self-evident, and must be imposed.

Systems of securities also generally require sets of institutions to support them, such as a central registry or clearinghouse. "In Bulgaria," the Bank notes, "the priority of a security interest is determined by the date it is agreed to; without a central registry, this can only be uncovered by searching through hundreds of scattered notarial records" (ibid.). Teaching people proper "market-related skills and business know-how"—like "international accounting standards"—is, according to the World Bank, the key to resolving such problems and to strengthening trust and credibility (ibid., 139). What are deeply culturally specific requirements of capitalist societies with political consequences—convertibility into one scale of value, double-entry bookkeeping, accounting as a practice of knowledge, and so on—are here written as universally applicable, rational, commonsense "know-how."

It is this character of securitization and convertibility as commonsense know-how that I want to open up for questioning, for it is these processes that create the objects of global finance and render them capable of a kind of movement. The convertibility of forms of property made possible by securitization and accounting procedures recalls a classic problem in the anthropological theory of kinship, first posed by Edward Tylor (1889) in the late nineteenth century, on the nature of exogamous marriage in so-called primitive societies. Tylor and others after him were perplexed by the system of marriage exchanges they termed "circulating connubium," in which men seemed to exchange their sisters with other men for the purpose of marriage. Claude Lévi-Strauss's famous book *The Elementary Structures of Kinship* (1969) claimed to "solve" the problem of circulating connubium by positing a neat and parsimonious explanation for the process, rooting it in the universality of the incest taboo and, rather explicitly, in the presumed universality of classical economics:

> Generalized exchange establishes a system of operations conducted "on credit." A surrenders a daughter or a sister to B, who surrenders one to C, who, in turn, will surrender one to A . . . Consequently, generalized exchange always contains an element of trust . . . There must be the confidence that the cycle will close again, and that after a period of time a woman will eventually be received in compensation for the woman initially surrendered. The belief is the basis of trust, and confidence opens up credit. In the final analysis, the whole system exists only because the group adopting it is prepared, in the broadest meaning of the term, *to speculate*. (Lévi-Strauss 1969, 265; emphasis in original)

As feminist anthropologists have argued, Lévi-Strauss took for granted the following suppositions: that the value of any woman is identical to the value of any other woman; that the value of any woman inheres in the woman and is not a product of the exchange; and that women can be objectified as pieces of property (Rubin 1975; Collier 1988, 227). On what does that equivalency, inherent value, and objectification rest? Jane Collier writes:

> Lévi-Strauss alludes only to women's sexual attractiveness and to their performance of necessary tasks in societies where labor is divided by sex

(Lévi-Strauss 1969, 37–41). But the question is not What are women good for? Women—and men—do useful work and are sexually desirable . . . Rather, we should ask why, given their . . . attractiveness and usefulness, men and women do not just get together and live happily ever after. (Collier 1988, 227)

They do not, because men have rights in women that women do not enjoy in men or in other women. The question becomes, then, why do men come to have those rights in their female kin? (ibid.). As Collier summarizes, Lévi-Strauss "takes for granted what is most perplexing: that people can have rights to objects or objectified others in the first place" (ibid.).

Just as Lévi-Strauss (1969) wrote elaborate algebraic analyses of the wandering wombs in the "circulating connubium" of marriage exchanges without interrogating the categories of exchange, woman, and marriage his analysis rested upon, so analysts of globalization seek to explain the impacts of global movements of money, goods, people, and ideas without interrogating the metaphysics of "movement" and of the "objects" being moved.

Another assumption of Lévi-Strauss's analysis is that persons precede relationships. Marilyn Strathern and Michelle Rosaldo have gone to great lengths to demonstrate how the Western liberal logic that posits individuals first and social relationships second simply does not hold for people who imagine themselves as constituted through their relationships with past and present others (Strathern 1988; Rosaldo 1983, 1984; cf. Leenhardt 1979). As Strathern writes:

Far from being regarded as unique entities, Melanesian persons are as dividually as they are individually conceived. They contain a generalized sociality within. Indeed, persons are frequently constructed as the plural and composite site of the relationships that produced them. The singular person can be imagined as a social microcosm. (Strathern 1988, 13)

Similarly, in his 1947 ethnography, Maurice Leenhardt remarks that a Melanesian "knows himself only by the relationships he maintains with others. He exists only insofar as he acts his role in the course of his relationships" (Leenhardt 1979, 153). Leenhardt depicts the person of New Caledonia as a series of lines (a——b) representing relationships, radiating out from a central space, which he characterized as "empty":

> Their social reality is not in their body but in this empty place where they have their names and which corresponds to a relationship . . . But no name can cover the whole person. The Canaque [Caledonian] is obliged to have a different name for every domain which involves his person in various relationships and participations. In all this, he is unaware of himself; he is the empty space enclosed by the circle of a's. (Leenhardt 1979, 154, 156; quoted in Strathern 1988, 269)

Strathern argues that Leenhardt's only mistake was to worry over that empty space at the center:

> [H]is mistake was to conceive of a center at all. The center is where twentieth-century Western imagination puts the self, the personality, the ego. For the "person" in this latter day Western view is an agent, a subject, the author of thought and action, and thus "at the center" of relationships. (Strathern 1988, 269)

The IPE literature on capital mobility, like practitioners at the World Bank, employees of security firms, and, indeed, anyone who operates in a world where the logic of securitization makes sense, begins from a similar unstated assumption: the objects of property come first, and the shares (and their convertibility) second. The parallel to the kinship literature leads me to ask whether it is the process of securitization itself that creates the objects of property, and not the "givenness" of the objects of property that allows them to be rendered partible into abstract securities.

Constituting the Objects of Property:
Transparency and Trust

How does securitization create the objects of property? Answering this question involves asking another, about the accounting practices that go into securitization itself. When the World Bank touts securitization as the only available route to business financing, what does the World Bank say it wants? A key term picked up by policy makers in places subjected to World Bank programs is "transparency." Transparency is that quality of accountability embodied in keeping good books and in devising clear, complete, annual reports. Transparency is the goal of double-entry bookkeeping. It allows any observer, supposedly, to "see" credits and debits, transfers and purchases—in short, the movements of capital—that facilitate capitalist business practices.

A number of accounting scholars point out, however, that the presentation of the annual report is rarely as transparent as it seems. There is now a sizable literature on the politics of "seeing" in the presentation of the annual report and the annual budget (see Hopwood 1996). Trevor Gambling argues for a reassessment of the ritual dimension of the accounting profession and the business practices it purports to audit. Gambling wonders why people seem so willing to accept entities such as money, bonds, shares, and the like as "'worth something,' intrinsically" and how an act of belief makes the "magic" of money work (Gambling 1987, 321; cf. Taussig 1980). He is also interested in the logic of "legitimate" tax avoidance and other corporate accounting schemes whose validity gets assessed (and often endorsed) by accountants in charge of corporate audits. He concludes that "it is only when the schemes 'go over the top' . . . or 'come unstuck' . . . that their validity is seen as questionable" (Gambling 1987, 326). What is the role of accountants? According to Gambling, "society wants its accounting profession to . . . certify that a whole range of 'magical' transactions is somehow 'ritually valid'" (ibid., 327). In other words, accounting practices create the "transparency" demanded by economic institutions, underwrite the "credibility" of markets and market transactions, and ultimately constitute the "objects" of property.

"Transparency" is also a key word in contemporary political rhetoric of democratization, and usually entails little more than the notion of free and fair elections and a clear separation of powers. Confidence, trust, and credibility are bound up in and expected outcomes of transparent political processes and institutions. And confidence, trust, and credibility are the goals of transparent economic practices. The interconnection between political and economic transparency was brought home in a speech given by Aburizal Bakrie, the chairman of the Indonesian Bakrie Group conglomerate, during that country's financial crisis in the late 1990s. As reported in an article in the *Jakarta Post* titled "Transparency Vital to Restore Trust," Bakrie, discussing the restructuring of his own company, stated:

> There are many questions from foreign fund managers about political transparency. And I believe the government can accommodate such concerns . . . And I also believe that, in the future, transparency at the economic and corporate level will also improve because the current crisis will teach all of us about the importance of it . . . This crisis is a blessing in disguise. (*Jakarta Post*, December 20, 1997, 12)

Other newspaper articles from this period of financial crisis echo this theme, with headlines such as: "A New Crisis in Asia: Now It's Confidence" (*International Herald Tribune*, Singapore edition, December 22, 1997, 1). In Indonesia (and elsewhere) transparency has meant confidence and trust, and more specifically, the idea that confidence and trust in a government will result in confidence and trust in a national currency or national economy, and vice versa. The daughter of Indonesia's former president, Suharto, initiated a "grassroots" movement to restore trust and faith in the Indonesian currency, the rupiah, through an act of love:

> The head of the Golkar party, Haji Siti Hariyanti Rukmana [oldest daughter of Suharto], who is known more intimately as Mbak [big sister] Tutut, has said that she is prepared to begin a "love the rupiah movement" to help the government overcome the monetary crisis.

"If you say that society needs an example, well, I am ready to start this movement. Okay, let's begin!" said Mbak Tutut in the People's Representatives Hall, Thursday, January 8, 1998.

Supported by her husband, businessman Indra Rukmana, the oldest daughter of Suharto also said that it is proper for the whole Indonesian nation to follow this pioneering action of the "love the rupiah movement," in a sincere, desiring, and free manner, so that the people will exchange their dollars for rupiah as soon as possible.

There is no excuse for all the people and civil servants, businessmen, and reporters not to follow this action of the "love the rupiah movement." Businessmen must pay for their entire stocks in rupiah, officals should set an example of loving the rupiah, and reporters should write so that the people will love the rupiah, she said.

What is the concrete form of this "love the rupiah movement"?

"Well, to invite society so that within their own awareness they will choose to use the rupiah over the dollar. So whoever really has dollars, right away change them into rupiah. I guess that's what's meant by the 'love the rupiah movement,'" she said. (*Surya*, January 9, 1998, trans. Tom Boellstorff)

The link between accounting transparency and political transparency is specific only to certain places, and contains implicit narratives of origin. These origin narratives, which differentially evaluate political and economic practices based on their presumed starting point, validate some places but not others, setting up a world in which some places need more transparency (or more love) than others, for good credit ratings and hence loan eligibility, because their creditability is always already suspect. These narratives of origin put a spin on the objects of property that, like the spin of an electron, introduces instability, randomness, unpredictability, and risk. This is the risk of instability inherent in a world where all "development" means is securitization and accounting transparency, and where all "democracy" means is elections.

Offshore Finance: Pushing the Metaphysics of Mobility

Thus far, I have been outlining an official discourse of transparency, risk, and stability in international finance that, to many, and certainly to readers of the financial press, is simply common sense. I do so, however, to highlight its specificity and peculiarity. There is more to capital mobility than convertibility; there is, first of all, the magic of accountancy that renders certain activities, like securitization, "transparent." There is also the odd configuration of transparency itself, an interesting metaphor for a practice that supposedly produces a seeable, verifiable economy, yet one guided by an "invisible" hand. Finally, there is the link between economic and political transparency confirmed by such technical, bureaucratic practices as bookkeeping and ballot counting (see Coles 1997), which, in their own magic act, create confidence and trust and ensure future credibility. What happens, however, when the procedural norms and techniques of confidence, trust, and credibility are put to new purposes? What happens when they are rejected entirely, or reformulated, or redefined and given new origin points?

The offshore financial services sector provides one case of putting procedural norms and accountancy techniques to new purposes. Offshore finance points up the limits of the accounting rituals by so nicely demonstrating that the line between shady and sound dealings is incredibly difficult to draw. It also highlights an extreme logical extension of capital mobility that IPE scholars and others involved in globalization research have not really grappled with, and which seems to make the world today quite different from the world of Rosa Luxemburg.

Offshore finance trade publications list a number of Caribbean jurisdictions as tax havens (see Ginsberg 1991; Cornez 1996; see also Maurer 1995a, 126–27 for a comprehensive list of world offshore financial service centers). Many of these jurisdictions, of course, are not full-fledged "service centers," with accountancy, legal, and financial offices and workers ready to help businesses and individuals conduct their affairs "offshore." Rather, most are simply jurisdictions with tax codes that favor foreign investment. Some do so merely by offering lower corporate tax rates than the United States, the United Kingdom, and other countries, and so are true "tax havens." Others market themselves as offshore financial service centers and have encouraged banks and accountancy firms to set up shop within their territories. They have also crafted legal and regulatory apparatuses to enable certain kinds of specialized services unavailable "onshore," or to enable special kinds of "investment entities" such as offshore trusts and "international business companies"—mostly of the "brass-plate" variety.

Mainstream economists tend to evaluate offshore finance in terms of its benefits to the tax revenue base of offshore jurisdictions and its harm to onshore jurisdictions (see Hines and Rice 1994). They do this, however, based on the erroneous assumption that offshore financial service centers make money from foreign direct investment, or from taxes on corporate earnings. Economists also measure the impact that offshore financial services have on tax revenues "at home," in the onshore jurisdiction from which offshore money originates. They rarely examine the phenomenon of offshore finance from the point of view of the countries offering the services, or ask what it means to a country to be a tax haven.

Many Caribbean governments make money from the fees that they charge for their services, not from taxes they collect. In the British Virgin Islands, for example, individuals or corporations can create an "international business company" (IBC) domiciled there for a onetime incorporation fee of U.S. $300 and an annual licensing fee of U.S. $300. Such IBCs usually exist for a short time only, generally for the duration of a particular transaction a company wishes to conduct "offshore," and are then dissolved. Dissolutions are announced in the local newspapers, whose back three or four pages are always full of "voluntary liquidation" notices. Many IBCs come into and go out of existence during the course of a week, and so the revenue generated from fees can become considerable. In 1992, out of a total British Virgin Islands government revenue of U.S. $54 million, the offshore financial services sector contributed

U.S. $21 million, outstripping tourism for the first time in the islands' history (Meyers 1993; Maurer 1995b, 227).

Although it is frequently cast as marginal and shady, offshore finance is an integral part of financial globalization. The period from 1970 to 1990 has been characterized as a period of competitive deregulation in the world's financial markets (Cerny 1994). It is the same period to which David Harvey (1989) and others trace post-Fordist production strategies and niche marketing, just-in-time production, and flexible specialization. This is also the period during which many states set themselves up as offshore financial centers, rewriting their banking and finance regulations to cater to flexible accumulation strategies and to the Eurocurrency markets. At the same time, deregulation in the United States in the 1970s and in the United Kingdom in the 1980s led to new kinds of financial instruments. In the 1970s, for example, the United States ended rules governing stock brokers' commissions; this led to increased competition among brokers, who attempted more speculative and innovative investment mechanisms. In 1986, the United States Federal Reserve Board enacted Regulation Q to prohibit U.S. banks from paying interest on short-term deposits (Roberts 1994). Regulation Q made securities more attractive than loans against bank deposits, and so boosted the securities market. It also made the Eurocurrency market more attractive. Because tax haven jurisdictions are spread across the globe, in between the major onshore financial centers, offshore financial service centers could function as intermediary stepping-stones for companies interested in investing in the Eurocurrency markets, and for any company or individual interested in keeping money "moving" from time zone to time zone throughout the day (ibid.). Deregulation in the 1980s and 1990s, meanwhile, expanded finance to consumer markets through credit cards (issued by banks as well as nonbank entities and corporations), mutual funds, and retirement accounts.

As Susan Roberts argues, "changes in the international financial system cannot be understood except as operating through . . . distinct spaces" such as offshore financial services centers (ibid., 237; see Leyshon and Thrift 1997). Post-Fordist flexible production strategies have gone hand in hand with flexible financing, made possible by regulatory change in the major banking centers, the rise of nonbank financial entities, and the development of offshore centers as nodes in capital networks necessary to the financing of multinational production and business. These capital networks have expanded as a result of increasing disparities of wealth around the world. Extremely wealthy individuals seek out private banking services, corporations seek out means of getting capital to transnational arms of their operations quickly and efficiently to finance just-in-time production strategies, and individuals and corporations alike seek out means of insulating profits and assets from taxation, nationalization, or sudden exchange rate changes. (In describing these networks of capital, one must also mention the contribution of capital from illicit trade in drugs, arms, microchips, compact disks, and more mundane goods; see Maingot 1995.)

In a world where "capital" can be "mobile," offshore finance represents an example of pushing the limits of the standard procedures that create "capital mobility." In doing so, it troubles the boundary between licit and illicit practice, and highlights the contingency and instability of contemporary configurations of "capital" and "mobility" themselves. It also, of course, obscures the "transparency" that accountants are looking for and producing in the act of corporate accounting. After all, muddying transparency is the point of offshore finance in the first place. And yet, as Roberts has argued, offshore finance is vital to the "normal" functioning of the international financial system, whose hallmark is supposed to be its seeability, its transparency.

Islamic Banking: Redrawing the Objects of Property

Islamic banking is my second example of alternative financial operations. It provides a case of rejecting and redefining the technical procedures that produce "transparency." It does so by stating, essentially, "Those practices of transparency are actually rather opaque, and we've got better, more transparent, more self-evident practices to offer." Islamic banking arose during the same time period that offshore finance took off, and, indeed, the two are interrelated, for Islamic banks at first found few places with the legal apparatus that would allow them to incorporate, and so many incorporated in such offshore jurisdictions as Luxembourg and the Bahamas (Khan 1987). Their growth was aided by the fact that several jurisdictions with a majority Muslim population had also become offshore centers in their own right, such as the United Arab Emirates, Bahrain, and Brunei (Montgomery 1997).

Islamic banking proceeds from the Qur'anic injunctions against usury and interest, or *riba*, and from specific conceptualizations of uncertainty and risk. Because, according to religious doctrine, "risk and uncertainty are inherent in the Universe in which God has placed us, it is immoral to off-load any part of your personal share of risk onto someone else" (Gambling 1987, 324; Gambling and Karim 1986). Islamic banking also proceeds from precepts about social responsibility and an imagined community of Muslims who act for the betterment of the *umma* (world community of Muslims). Commitment to the *umma* is enforced through the practice of religiously mandated almsgiving (*Zakah*).

Although its roots can be found in modernist movements within Islam and a small number of key texts written as the postwar international financial system was being crafted (Qureshi 1945), Islamic banking boomed immediately after the 1973 OPEC oil price rise, and found form in a number of very diverse efforts on the part of religious leaders, financiers, and politicians from North Africa to Indonesia (see Khan 1987; Siddiqi 1983; Meenai 1989). One of the earliest and most successful Islamic financial ventures took the form of the Islamic Development Bank (IDB), which sought to compete with the International Monetary Fund in providing funds for development projects in the Muslim third world (Meenai 1989; Wilson 1990). Several Islamic republics have attempted to Islamize their banking systems completely (Iran, Pakistan, the Sudan, Brunei), with varying degrees of success. Because world Islam is characterized by debates among numerous schools of Islamic law, Islamic banking practices are quite diverse. But the underlying principles about *riba* and the *umma* are constant across these different endeavors, and Islamic bankers have devised a common tool kit of procedures, accounting practices, and investment instruments across various jurisdictions.

Two aspects of Islamic banking bear on the argument at hand. First, accounting scholars involved in Islamic banking have created an origin narrative for their practices that challenges the historiography of double-entry bookkeeping. In so doing, they have authored an alternative history for Western capitalism, and a justification for a global Islamic capitalist system. They do not appeal to "tradition" but rather to an alternate modernity, one that developed from modern, rational precepts of an ever-evolving Islamic law (Ray 1995; Hameed 1997). In essence, these accounting scholars call the bluff of the magic of Western double entry by stating that the Western "inventors" of double entry, such as Luca Pacioli (see, e.g., Littleton and Yamey 1956), got it wrong by ignoring the moral aspects of accounting practice and masking their own norma-tivity (Hameed 1997; Gambling and Karim 1986, 1991; Khan 1994).

The cornerstone of Islamic banking is the Qur'anic injunction against interest, or *riba*, embodied in various verses of the Qur'an:

Those that live on usury [*riba*] shall rise up before God like men whom Satan has demented by his touch; for they claim that trading is no differ-ent from usury. But God has permitted trading and made usury unlawful. He that has received an admonition from his Lord and minded his ways may keep his previous gains; God will be his judge. Those that turn back shall be the inmates of the Fire, wherein they shall abide for ever. (2:275)

God has laid His curse on usury and blessed almsgiving with increase. God bears no love for the impious and the sinful. (2:276)

Believers, have fear of God and waive what is still due to you from usury, if your faith be true, or war shall be declared against you by God and his apostle. (2:278)

Believers, do not live on usury, doubling your wealth many times over. Have fear of God, that you may prosper. (3:130)

> That which you seek to increase by usury will not be blessed by God; but the alms you give for His sake shall be repaid to you many times over. (30:39)

Scholars also cite a story from the Hadith about cost accounting when loans are made in kind: "Should a measure of wheat be paid back as a measure of wheat, or should one pay the market-equivalent of what was borrowed?" (Gambling 1987, 323). Muhammad's answer, and Islamic banking practice, confirms "measure for measure" as the appropriate and ethical course of action.

Measure for measure suggests two problems for Islamic banking: First, how to account for the time value of money? And second, how to make Islamic banking profitable? The time value of money turns out to be a nonissue. It only makes sense in a world where people believe that the charging of interest is, first of all, possible, and second, of no moral consequence. It hinges on the belief that the historical cost, from which interest is calculated, has meaning in and of itself. Gambling thus wonders "whether the pure time-value of money exists as a real phenomenon" or is "simply an anthropocentric device which 'explains' the ritual of taking usury." As he puts it, "we are able to make our concept of interest operational because we have the necessary sacramental machinery" (ibid., 324). As anthropological "natives" and Western historical figures such as Aristotle and Martin Luther have pointed out, those sacraments are mysterious indeed (Taussig 1980). Islamic bankers, for their part, argue that Western rituals of interest are obscure and difficult to see, whereas a system based in the "measure-for-measure" dictate of the Prophet is easy to see. Islamic banking is thus "more" transparent than Western banking.

What of profitability, for Islamic bankers are not just in the business for their souls? Islamic banking has invented new instruments for economic and moral purposes. They are not "financial" instruments in the Western capitalist sense, or in the sense that IPE scholars mean when they talk about capital mobility. Again, although practices vary widely across jurisdictions in accordance with disputes in Islamic law, there are about five alternative instruments that span the global Islamic financial markets. These provide alternatives to interest in order to mobilize funds for productive and other economic activities. *Musharaka* is a profit-and-loss sharing (PLS) system in which the financing bank is a partner and shares in management, with profits being divided according to a preset, agreed-upon ratio. Losses are shared, too, based on equity participation (Khan 1987). *Mudaraba* is a similar PLS agreement, in which one party provides finance and the other provides management. Here, profits are also shared according to a pre-agreed ratio, but losses are borne by the capital provider. *Murabaha* is a "cost plus margin of profit" agreement (Karim and Abdel 1990, 299) in which a bank purchases goods desired by a client who resells them at a markup so that both parties can profit (Martin 1997). *Ijara* is a leasing agreement in which the financing partner purchases equipment and leases it to the productive partner. Ownership is retained by the bank, and the lease duration and fees are agreed to in advance (ibid.). Finally, *Ijara-wa-igtina* is a lease/hire agreement in which the client is committed to purchasing the equipment financed by the bank at a pre-agreed price after the lease has expired.

The incommensurability between Islamic banking practices and the capital accounting required by institutions that charge interest provides the main reason that Islamic banking cannot easily incorporate in most Western jurisdictions. For such institutions, as Bank of England governor Robin Leigh-Pemberton put it, Islamic banking violates the principle that depositors have "capital certainty as to their original deposit, or certainty as to the return on it" (quoted in Rudnick 1992, 24). But, as partisans of Islamic banking maintain:

> Those accustomed to the Western approach to such matters may find it difficult to appreciate that matters of income recognition and the valuation of assets and liabilities can be moral and hence essentially theological issues. Western-style accounting standards assume the existence of a common (utilitarian) ground for all economic decisions, expressed in terms of economic theory. In fact, economic theory is an atheistic and

amoral 'faith,' which demands the same quality of belief in its own particular assumptions about the nature of the Man and the Universe, as
other religions demand for contrary propositions. (Gambling, Jones, and
Karim 1993, 200)

Furthermore, they write, "The latter 'revealed' propositions can
be made the basis for an accounting theory" (ibid.). Indeed, in 1990,
Islamic banks established the Financial Accounting Organization for
Islamic Banks and Financial Institutions (FAOIBFI) to create a set of
accountancy standards and procedural norms for Islamic financial operations accounting (ibid.; see also Karim and Abdel 1990). The FAOIBFI
works together with the Sharia Supervisory Board (SSB) of each Islamic
financial institution, which consists of religious advisers who evaluate
everything from investment decisions to the proper calculation of *Zakah*
(Karim and Abdel 1990). Karim and Abdel note that, at first glance,
the apparent laissez-faire approach to accounting practice—with each
SSB coming up with its own procedures in accordance with its own
interpretation of Islamic law, all under the rubric of the FAOIBFI—
might appear similar to accounting policy in the United States during
the period of deregulation in the 1970s and 1980s. However, because
the "SSB is supposed to make sure that accounting practices do not
violate the Sharia," "neither the management nor the auditor has the
freedom to choose the accounting procedures which they prefer in
preparing the financial statement of the bank. Rather, these accounting
practices have to be *chosen* from and *justified* with reference to the
Sharia" (ibid., 301; emphasis in original).

By now, there is a host of material on various means of accounting for Islamic finance (e.g., Harahap 1997; Hameed 1997; Khan 1994;
Pomeranz 1997; Badawi 1986). In a system based on complicated PLS
and leasing systems, whole budget lines must be added to banks' ledgers,
such as inventories and leasing agreements, and, in addition, an account
must be made for determining the "social cost and benefit" of any financial venture to the *umma* for the purposes of levying *Zakah*. Some advocate more "narrative accounts" and a move away from the balance sheet,

again, rendering accounting practice in Islamic banking "more transparent," and more accessible to those lacking the specialist's knowledge, than "Western" accounting.

Conclusion

My purpose is not to trumpet the cause or hold Islamic banking up as some kind of wonderful and morally acceptable alternative to the sort of rapacious free-market capitalism that characterizes the early twenty-first century. It bears repeating that Islamic banking and the offshore financial sector share more than a place in my analysis; they are also interlinked practices operating apart from, but also deeply within, the international financial order. And, as the Bank of Credit and Commerce International (BCCI) scandal in the early 1990s should remind us, implicated as it was in offshore and Islamic practices (Temple 1992), these practices have serious criminal potential, whether criminality is defined in terms of financial fraud and white-collar crime or as an abrogation of responsibility to the social good.

However, in pushing the limits of capital mobility, on the one hand, and rewriting the script from the ground up, on the other, offshore finance and Islamic banking cast a shadow on IPE and other globalization literature. They should lead anyone invested in globalization—as active and happy participants in the expansion of "free" markets, or as academics making a living from their critique—to examine critically their own assumptions. They should cause us to highlight the practices and norms that go into the concoction of the objects of property and mobility we often take for granted, and to which we often grant their own ontological status to guide and move us like an invisible hand transparently traversing new terrains of globalization.

References

Abu-Lughod, Janet. 1989. *Before European Hegemony: The World-System AD 1250–1350*. New York: Oxford University Press.

Apparudai, Arjun. 1996. *Modernity at Large: Cultural Dimensions of Globalization*. Minneapolis: University of Minnesota Press.

Badawi, Samir. 1986. "Accounting Practices and Procedures." In *Islamic Banking and Finance*, ed. Butterworths Editorial Staff. London: Butterworths. 86–100.

Cerny, Philip. 1994. "The Dynamics of Financial Globalization: Technology, Market Structure, and Policy Response." *Policy Sciences* 27(4): 319–42.

Cohen, Benjamin. 1996. "Phoenix Risen: The Resurrection of Global Finance." *World Politics* 48: 268–96.

Coles, Kimberly. 1997. "Bosnian Elections: Selling Democracy." Manuscript, Department of Anthropology, University of California, Irvine.

Collier, Jane F. 1988. *Marriage and Inequality in Classless Societies*. Stanford, Calif.: Stanford University Press.

Cornez, Arnold. 1996. *The Offshore Money Book*. Chicago: International Publishing.

Delaney, Carol. 1986. "The Meaning of Paternity and the Virgin Birth Debate." *Man* (n.s.) 21: 494–513.

———. 1990. *The Seed and the Soil: Gender and Cosmology in Turkish Village Society*. Berkeley: University of California Press.

Friedman, Jonathan. 1995. "Global System, Globalization and the Parameters of Modernity." In *Global Modernities*, ed. Mike Featherstone, Scott Lash, and Roland Robertson. London: Sage. 69–90.

Gambling, Trevor. 1987. "Accounting for Rituals." *Accounting, Organizations and Society* 12(4): 319–29.

Gambling, Trevor, and Rifaat Ahmed Abdel Karim. 1986. "Islam and 'Social Accounting.'" *Journal of Business and Finance Accounting* 13(1): 39–50.

———. 1991. *Business and Accounting Ethics in Islam*. London: Mansell.

Gambling, Trevor, Rowan Jones, and Rifaat Ahmed Abdel Karim. 1993. "Credible Organizations: Self-Regulation v. External Standard-Setting in Islamic Banks and British Charities." *Financial Accountability and Management* 9(3): 195–207.

Ginsberg, Anthony. 1991. *International Tax Havens*. New York: New York Institute of Finance.

Hameed, Shahul. 1997. "From Conventional Accounting to Islamic Accounting." Department of Accounting, University of Dundee, Scotland. Available at http://www.dundee.ac.uk/accountancy/phd/3fr1exte.html.

Hannerz, Ulf. 1996. *Transnational Connections: Culture, People, Places*. New York: Routledge.

Harahap, Sofyan Syafri. 1997. *Akuntansi Islam*. Jakarta: Bumi Aksara.

Harvey, David. 1989. *The Condition of Postmodernity*. Baltimore: Johns Hopkins University Press.

Helleiner, Eric. 1994. *States and the Re-Emergence of Global Finance: From Bretton Woods to the 1990s*. Ithaca, N.Y.: Cornell University Press.

Hilferding, Rudolf. 1981 [1923]. *Finance Capital: A Study of the Latest Phase of Capitalist Development*. Trans. Tom Bottomore. Reprint. London: Routledge and Kegan Paul.

Hines, James, and Eric Rice. 1994. "Fiscal Paradise: Foreign Tax Havens and American Business." *Quarterly Journal of Economics* 109(1): 149–82.

Hopwood, Anthony. 1996. "Making Visible and the Construction of Visibilities: Shifting Agendas in the Design of the Corporate Report." *Accounting Organizations and Society* 21(1): 55–56.

Kapstein, Ethan. 1994. *Governing the Global Economy: International Finance and the State*. Cambridge: Harvard University Press.

Karim, Rifaat, and Ahmed Abdel. 1990. "Standard Setting for the Financial Reporting of Religious Business Organisations: The Case of Islamic Banks." *Accounting and Business Research* 20(80): 299–305.

Khan, M. A. 1994. "Accounting Issues and Concepts for Islamic Banking." In *Development of an Accounting System for Islamic Banking*. London: Institute of Islamic Banking and Insurance.

Khan, Shahrukh Rafi. 1987. *Profit and Loss Sharing: An Islamic Experiment in Finance and Banking*. Oxford: Oxford University Press.

Kindleberger, Charles. 1987. *International Capital Movements*. New York: Cambridge University Press.

The Koran, with Parallel Arabic Text. 2000. Trans. N. J. Dawood. London: Penguin Books.

Lash, Scott, and John Urry. 1994. *Economies of Signs and Space*. London: Sage.

Leenhardt, Maurice. 1979. *Do Kamo: Person and Myth in the Melanesian World*. Chicago: University of Chicago Press.

Lenin, Vladimir. [1916] 1989. *Imperialism: The Highest Stage of Capitalism*. Reprint. New York: International Publishers.

Lévi-Strauss, Claude. [1949] 1969. *The Elementary Structures of Kinship*. Trans. James Harle Bell, John Richard von Sturmer, and Rodney Needham. Reprint. Boston: Beacon Press.

Leyshon, Andrew, and Nigel Thrift. 1997. *Money/Space: Geographies of Monetary Transformation*. New York: Routledge.

Littleton, Ananias Charles, and Basil S. Yamey, eds. 1956. *Studies in the History of Accounting*. Homewood, Ill.: Richard D. Irwin.

Luxemburg, Rosa. [1914] 1951. *The Accumulation of Capital*. Trans. Agnes Schwarzchild. Reprint. London: Routledge and Kegan Paul.

Maingot, Anthony. 1995. "Offshore Secrecy Centers and the Necessary Role of States: Bucking the Trend." *Journal of Interamerican Studies and World Affairs* 37(4): 1–24.

Martin, Josh. 1997. "Islamic Banking Raises Interest." *Management Review* 86(10): 25–29.

Marx, Karl. [1861] 1977. *Capital*, vol. 1. Trans. Ben Fowkes. Reprint. New York: Vintage Books.

Maurer, Bill. 1995a. "Complex Subjects: Offshore Finance, Complexity Theory, and the Dispersion of the Modern." *Socialist Review* 25(3–4): 113–45.

———. 1995b. "Writing Law, Making a 'Nation': History, Modernity, and Paradoxes of Self-Rule in the British Virgin Islands." *Law and Society Review* 29(2): 255–86.

———. 1999. "Forget Locke? Dematerializing Property in Financial Services." *Public Culture* 11(2): 365–85.

Meenai, S. A. 1989. *The Islamic Development Bank: A Case Study of Islamic Co-Operation*. London: Kegan Paul International.

Meyers, Jeffrey. 1993. "IBC Numbers Growing Fast." *BVI Beacon*, April 8, 8.

Montgomery, Gavin. 1997. "The Foundation for Islamic Banking." AsiaMoney 8(6): 46–52.

Pomeranz, Felix. 1997. "The Accounting and Auditing Organization for Islamic Financial Institutions: An Important Regulatory Debut." *Journal of International Accounting, Auditing and Taxation* 6(1): 123–30.

Qureshi, Anwar Iqbal. 1945. *Islam and the Theory of Interest*. Lahore: Shaikh Muhammad Ashraf.

Ray, Nicholas Dylan. 1995. *Arab Islamic Banking and the Renewal of Islamic Law*. London: Graham and Trotman.

Roberts, Susan. 1994. "Fictitious Capital, Fictitious Spaces: The Geography of Offshore Financial Flows." In *Money, Power and Space*, ed. Stuart Corbridge, Ron Martin, and Nigel Thrift. Oxford: Blackwell. 91–115.

Rosaldo, Michelle. 1983. "The Shame of Headhunters and the Autonomy of Self." *Ethos* 11(3): 135–51.

———. 1984. "Toward an Anthropology of Self and Feeling." In *Culture Theory:*

Essays on Mind, Self and Emotion, ed. Richard Schweder and Robert LeVine. Cambridge: Cambridge University Press. 137–57.

Rubin, Gayle. 1975. "The Traffic in Women." In *Toward An Anthropology of Women*, ed. Rayna Reiter. New York: Monthly Review Press. 157–210.

Rudnick, David. 1992. "Islamic Banking: Praying for Profit." *Euromoney* (November 1992): 23–25.

Schneider, David. 1984. *A Critique of the Study of Kinship*. Ann Arbor: University of Michigan Press.

Siddiqi, Muhammad Nejatullah. 1983. *Banking Without Interest*. London: Islamic Foundation.

Strathern, Marilyn. 1988. *The Gender of the Gift*. Berkeley: University of California Press.

Taussig, Michael. 1980. *The Devil and Commodity Fetishism in South America*. Chapel Hill: University of North Carolina Press.

Temple, Peter. 1992. "Islamic Banking: Principles as Well as Roots." *Accountancy* 110 (1187): 46–47.

Tylor, Edward Burnett. 1889. "On a Method of Investigating the Development of Institutions; Applied to the Laws of Marriage and Descent." *Journal of the Royal Anthropological Institute of Great Britain and Northern Ireland* 18: 245–72.

Wilson, Rodney, ed. 1990. *Islamic Financial Markets*. London: Routledge.

World Bank. 1996. *From Plan to Market: World Development Report, 1996*. Oxford: Oxford University Press.

CHAPTER 4

Spanish Immigration Law and the Construction of Difference: Citizens and "Illegals" on Europe's Southern Border

Kitty Calavita and Liliana Suárez-Navaz

On July 1, 1985, Spain enacted its first comprehensive immigration law, the Alien Law (Ley Orgánica de Extranjería, LOE), which spelled out the rights and duties of noncitizens living in Spain.[1] With this law, Spain for the first time made clear distinctions between types of aliens and their corresponding rights, with particularly sharp lines being drawn between European Community members and citizens of third-world countries, with most of this latter group now having to carry visas to enter the country.

Within days of enacting the LOE, Spain signed the treaty for entry into the European Community (Boletín Oficial del Estado 1985, 20824–29). Later that month, Belgium, France, Germany, Luxembourg, and the Netherlands signed the Schengen Agreement designed to dismantle internal borders inside the European Community (EC), and to establish more rigorous control of its external borders. Spain signed on to the Schengen Agreement in June 1990.

Many observers have noted that these two developments are not independent of each other, and that Spain's first immigration law—and the accompanying rhetorical focus on border control and the dangers of the immigrant "invasion"—were the consequence of pressure from the EC. Thus, if Spain wanted to join the EC, it had to control its external borders—which were now the critical southern wall of the European fortress (de Lucas 1996; Pugliese 1995; den Boer 1995; Borrás 1995, 21; Casey 1997, 24).

There is little doubt that Spain's entrance into the EC was contingent on its passing restrictive immigration policies, and more generally, agreeing to its new role as Europe's de facto border patrol. But, we will argue that these two developments—Spain's entry into the EC and the legislative and rhetorical construction of third-world immigrants as alien "others"—are connected in a more profound way at the level of national identity formation. In brief, the Alien Law of 1985 and its subsequent regulations and amendments, with their discourse of immigrant otherness and their policies of exclusion, have contributed to the symbolic creation of Spain as a national community; furthermore, this construction of community through the exclusion of third-world others is made possible at least in part through Spain's newfound identity as an advanced capitalist democracy and its status-affirming inclusion in the European Community. Thus, inclusion and exclusion move *in tandem* here, with new images of citizenship and belonging being created in the process.

In this essay, we look at a striking example of these dual processes of inclusion and exclusion as we explore the simultaneous transformation of conceptions of citizenship among Andalusian peasants in the south of Spain and their shifting orientation to the African immigrants with whom they had formerly worked side by side and had shared not only class solidarity, but also a long history of cultural amalgamation. As we will see, the increasing hostility expressed by Andalusian peasants for their African immigrant counterparts, and the outsider status now assigned the latter, cannot be explained by recourse to static models of cultural difference, nor to economistic discussions of immigrant labor competition. Instead, there have been fundamental shifts in the parameters of belonging, which can be traced to the exclusionist rhetoric of the new immigration law, on the one hand, and the inclusionist discourse of welfare state capitalism and EC membership, on the other.

The data for this essay come from a wide variety of sources. The first coauthor spent six months doing fieldwork on immigration policy in Spain during 1997. The data she gathered include information culled from an exhaustive survey of secondary sources (academic and journalistic), government reports, parliamentary discussions, official statistics, public opinion surveys, and interviews with academics and union officials. The primary data on Andalusian conceptions of African immigrants, and the transformation of the latter from integrated members of the local culture and economy to marginalized "illegals" and "others," were drawn from the second coauthor's dissertation fieldwork in the Alfaya Valley in Andalusia from 1992 to 1995. No doubt there are gaps in these data, and the story we are telling might be told differently. Nonetheless, the scope and diversity of the data we have independently gathered, and their internal consistency, give us confidence in the integrity of our argument.

We have organized the paper in the following way. The next section provides a general theoretical overview of several of the central concepts, including a discussion of the sense of national community as fluid and shifting; ethnic identity and culture as relational processes; and exclusion of others and community identity formation as interrelated dynamics. Following that, we briefly provide some general background on the political and socioeconomic changes in Spain over the last half century. Next, we examine the specifics of the Alien Law of 1985, focusing on how, despite substantial rhetoric about immigrants' rights and integration, the law systematically marginalizes and illegalizes third-world immigrants. The remainder of the essay explores the transformation of immigrant workers in Alfaya, Andalusia, from integral members of the local culture to shunned outsiders, and the relationship between this exclusionary process and the simultaneous shift in national identity among Andalusia's peasant population.

Theoretical Overview

Current theory and research are reviving attention to issues relating to citizenship and the nation-state (Hammar 1990; Yuval-Davis 1990; Brubaker 1992; Conway 1994; Delbruck 1994; Zolberg 1994; Torpey 2000; Beiner 1995; Falk 2000; Schuck 1998). T. H. Marshall, in his seminal work on class and citizenship in modern England, argued that the historical expansion of the rights (civil, political, and social) granted to full members of a political community served as an equalizing mechanism for the social classes displaced by capitalist relations of production. Over time, citizenship has produced not only formal rights, but social entitlements, including

> the whole range from the right to a modicum of economic welfare and security to the right to share . . . in the social heritage and to live the life of a civilized being according to the standards prevailing in society. (Marshall 1950, 11)

This definition of citizenship is increasingly being challenged by major transformations in national and world-level institutional frameworks and processes, and by the contesting of long-held assumptions about the nation, the state, and social identities as unified and bounded entities.

One criticism of Marshall's work relates to his definition of citizenship as a fixed status bestowed upon all members of a national community. As one critic put it, he

> assumes a given collectivity . . . [not] as an ideological and material construction, whose boundaries, structures and norms are a result of constant processes of struggles and negotiations, or more general social developments. Any dynamic notion of citizenship must start from the processes which construct the collectivity. (Yuval-Davis 1990, 3)

The present examination of shifting national identities among Andalusian peasants, and their relationship to African immigrants in the post–Alien Law period, allows us to pay close attention to these "processes which construct the collectivity."

It allows us also to question essentialist notions of social and cultural unity implicit in some discussions of national community building. We argue that the national political community whose borders are marked out as a sociocultural construct is a product of hegemonic processes through which the nation-state reproduces itself as the "natural embodiment of history, territory and society" (Cohn and Dirks 1988, 2; see also Anderson 1991; Hobsbawm and Ranger 1983; Hobsbawm 1990). The representation of the nation as a community of shared blood, heritage, and destiny is starkly at odds with the more complex realities of Spanish history, particularly the centuries-long cultural and political integration of, and struggles between, Spanish Catholics and the "Moors." The limitations of essentialist explanations of the national community is all the more striking as the ancient opposition between Spanish Catholics and other European Christians dissolves and is replaced by the new cultural antagonism between Western European secularized Christianity and Islam.

Even if (or, perhaps more accurately, precisely because) membership in the national political community is detached from a homogeneous cultural heritage, the model of modern citizenship relies on the mythical character of the universalist project. Further, law is central to this unifying project of modern nationalism. As Fitzpatrick (1992, 117) has argued, "As for that supra-national or universal dimension of nationalism, law in Weberian terms is the very figure of the 'legal-rational' authority characteristic of modernity." As we will see, the new legal culture in Spain that is embedded in the liberal model of citizenship has broad ramifications for the drawing of cultural boundaries between native Spaniards and African immigrants.

Just as the nation-state and citizenship are moral and cultural *projects*, not entities, so ethnic identity and culture are fluid and shifting over time and place. Omi and Winant's (1986: x) overview of contemporary racial formation in the United States is prefaced, "[R]ace is not an essence. It is not 'something fixed, concrete, and objective.'" Rather, it is "a set of social meanings." Ignatiev (1995) similarly highlights the ambiguity of race in his study of Irish immigrants to the United States, entitled *How the Irish Became White*. As Ignatiev (1995, 1) points out, "No biologist has ever been able to provide a satisfactory definition of 'race'—that is, a definition that includes all members of a given race and excludes all others." Noting that Catholics in nineteenth-century Ireland were treated as a distinct race ("Celts" or "Gaels"), and that Irish immigrants to America were called "niggers turned inside out" (and African-Americans were sometimes referred to as "smoked Irish"), Ignatiev traces Irish immigrants' simultaneous social and racial upward mobility.

Tonkin, McDonald, and Chapman's (1989) edited volume *History and Ethnicity* similarly unsettles the concept of ethnicity, with empirical studies from a variety of national and historical contexts. Focusing on the construction of ethnic identities in Iran and Afghanistan, for example, Tapper (1989, 239) notes that ethnic and racial identities "are essentially negotiable and subject to strategic manipulations." Contributors to Danielsen and Engle's (1995) anthology focus on the role of law in this identity formation process, focusing specifically on the roaming boundaries of ethnic and racial identity.

This study of African immigrants to Andalusia and the unstable racial and ethnic assignations of both the immigrants and their Andalusian coworkers follows in this line of theory and research. Until recently, Andalusian peasants and Arab immigrants to southern Spain were drawn together in a shared understanding of their common cultural heritage, a shared identity as members of a "darker" race relative to northern Europeans, and a common class position, both in the local economy where they were poor farmworkers and as citizens of relatively underdeveloped regions in the larger world system. Recently, however, the boundaries of race and culture have been realigned so as to present a stark dichotomy composed of Spanish citizens (members of the European Union and the Caucasian race), on the one hand, and racially and culturally distinct African immigrants, on the other. Furthermore, as we will see, this transformation of ethnic and cultural identity goes hand in hand with the shifting identity of Andalusian peasants as full-fledged members of the Spanish nation-state, and as citizens of the European Union.

Thranhardt and Miles (1995, 5) comment on the effects of "globalization":[2] "There will be one single organized club of rich countries," with citizens of poor countries consigned to the margins. Further, "Underlying and shaping the practice of exclusion are not only utilitarian economic considerations, but also racist conceptions of 'otherness'" (ibid., 3). Goldberg (1993, 6) underscores liberal modernity's role in the construction and perpetuation of racism at the same time that it preaches tolerance:

> So the irony of modernity, the liberal paradox comes down to this: As modernity commits itself progressively to idealized principles of liberty, equality, and fraternity, as it increasingly insists upon the moral irrelevance of race, there is a multiplication of racial identities and the sets of exclusions they prompt and rationalize, enable and sustain.

We will argue that Spanish immigration law systematically creates and re-creates illegality while preaching integration, much as the modern state nourishes racial categorizations while at the same time "insist[ing] upon the moral irrelevance of race." Further, this construction of illegality in Spanish immigration law is part and parcel of the construction of racial categories of otherness to which Thranhardt and Miles (1995) refer.

Immigrants have frequently been characterized as the quintessential other, having crossed borders to relocate in a community other than their own. Sociologist Georg Simmel (1950) long ago discussed the notion of the immigrant as "stranger"—physically present in the community but not part of it. Bourdieu (1991, 9) has described the immigrant as "'atopos', without place, displaced," a "bastard" between citizen and real outsider. And Rogers Brubaker (1992, 47) talks about "the modern figure of the foreigner—not only as a legal category but as a political epithet . . . condensing around itself pure outsiderhood."

But, in the new economic and social order of globalization, things are more complicated than these static dichotomies of immigrant/citizen or stranger/member imply. Legally, politically, and ideologically, the community has extended beyond the nation-state to include—in the case of Spain—the European Union. Thus, not all foreigners come from "outside the community," and not all foreigners are "strangers" or "others."[3] Just as important, the lines that distinguish who is an immigrant "stranger" are continually shifting, as the law and legal culture, and notions of the national community, redraw the boundaries of membership.

Young (1996) and Simon (1993) in their eloquent discussions of the "outlaw as other" describe the processes by which the boundaries that exclude outsiders simultaneously enclose and reinforce the community itself. In other words, exclusion and inclusion not only operate *in tandem*, but may be effectively the same process (although Young depicts the exclusionary process as counterproductive to true community building). In much the same way, this case study explores the role of immigration law in illegalizing third-world immigrants and setting them apart as illegal "others" to be excluded—not so much from the territory (as they continue to play an important economic role), but from the social and moral life of the community—and the simultaneous process of constructing a universalist nation-state whose citizens are not just embraced by the national community, but have now become European citizens as well. These projects of exclusion and inclusion together help to explain the radical redefinition of African immigrants in Andalusia as culturally and racially "other."

Andalusian Peasants and Transformations
in the Spanish Political Economy

Andalusia, the southernmost region of Spain, historically has been dominated by a few quasi-feudal landowners (*latifundistas*), with the mass of the population impoverished peasants who have been described as "the most wretched class in Europe" (Carr and Fusi Aizpurua 1979, 8). Beginning in the second half of the nineteenth century, peasants became an important political force in Spain, and anarchists, communists, and socialists struggled for years to achieve an agrarian reform involving redistribution of the land. Although some of these demands were recognized during the Second Republic, the establishment of the Franco dictatorship in 1939 brought the destruction of organized labor, the rolling back of agrarian reforms, and the repression of those who had sided with the republic.

Francoist nationalist discourse elaborated an "imaginary community" that was purportedly united by its imperial past and cultural uniqueness. Official ideology held Spain to be a "'state of smallholders' . . . and heralded the supposedly natural virtues of smallholding family producers" (Collier 1987, 168). In this rendition, peasants (*campesinos*) were extolled as the true Spaniards, characterized by national Catholicism as bearers of the essence of the Spanish race, as "noble and rightful," and as the "moral reserve of the nation" (Carr and Fusi Aizpurua 1979). Such cynical demagoguery has been called by Sevilla Guzman (1979) the "sovereignty of the peasantry," coexisting with an otherwise "agrarian fascism" that brutally reinforced the class-based rural structure in southern Spain.

At the same time and in interaction with the official reading, an alternative view from below was forged by those condemned to not be able "to live on their own" ("vivir de lo suyo"), who saw the world through the lens of a stratified social structure and a controlled, segmented, and hermetic social sphere. From this perspective, the main class boundary was drawn between two groups defined by their position in this rigid structure: those who could not live on their own and whose survival always depended on someone else's decisions; and the "rich," comprising a landed oligarchy, professionals, civil servants, and politicians (Gilmore 1980; Sevilla Guzman 1979; Contreras 1991).

During the Franco period, little could be done to undermine this agrarian class structure and the quasi-feudal relations on which it depended. After the dramatic repression of anarchists, communists, and socialists who struggled for agrarian reforms in the Second Republic, an imposed apoliticism prevailed among the offspring of the vanquished (Collier 1987). Class differences were maintained and reproduced through a politics of fear perpetrated by an authoritarian political system that regularly used security forces against peasants and others who were ideologically suspect. Employers were called upon to attest to a worker's "ideological purity" or "trustworthiness," thus condemning those who did not submit to employers' wishes to permanent hiding, emigration, or nomadism (Sevilla Guzman 1979, 176; Collier 1987).

Beginning in the 1950s and 1960s, Franco initiated a series of industrialization strategies that have been called the "Europeanization of Spain," and that he explained in his 1964 New Year's message as the beginning of a "new era" (Carr and Fusi Aizpurua 1979, 54). The rapid economic growth and industrialization of this era were fueled by massive internal migrations, as poorer, more rural populations from the southern regions of Andalusia and Extremadura, and Galicia in the west, poured into Madrid and Barcelona and other more prosperous areas. By 1970, 38 percent of the population of Catalonia (the region of which Barcelona is the capital) was born elsewhere, with 16 percent coming from Andalusia (Woolard 1986, 57).

Since Franco's death in 1975, the economy has continued to expand. This growth is perhaps best reflected in per capita GNP, which in 1960 stood at approximately 56 percent of the European average, but which had increased to 76 percent by 1996 (*Economist* 1996, 4). During the high-growth period of 1986–90, more than two million new jobs were created in Spain, more than in any other European country (Maxwell and Spiegel 1994, 89).

Spain's GNP per capita was still lower than the European average by the 1990s, but the structure of employment had changed dramatically, and wages and standard of living had skyrocketed. Between 1960 and 1985, the percentage of the population employed in agriculture fell more than twenty points, from 38.7 percent to 18 percent (Jimeno and Toharia 1994, 7). During the same period, average real wages more than doubled, and the official minimum wage increased by a factor of more than twenty-five (Mate Garcia 1994, 18, 27).

Despite this stunning economic growth, Spain is still plagued by the highest unemployment rate in Europe, hitting a peak of more than 24 percent in 1994 before settling at about 22 percent in 1996 (*Boletín Mensual de Estadística* 1997, 297; *El País* 1997, 434). The figures are worse for Andalusia, where it is estimated that unemployment reached 33 percent by the mid-1990s (*Economist* 1996, 6).

A relatively generous welfare state cushions the worst impacts of this unemployment. Between 1980 and 1993, Spain registered one of the highest rates of growth on social spending in the EC (Consejo Económico y Social 1995, 491). While the bulk of this goes to old-age pensions and the national health-care system, Spain ranks first in the European Union in the proportion of social spending on unemployment compensation (ibid., 493). This compensation, which applies only to those who have been previously employed and has a maximum duration of two years, is less generous than that of some of its European neighbors but is indicative of Spain's commitment to at least minimum income-maintenance policies. In part as a result of the country's economic growth and in part because of these social welfare policies, the poverty rate in Spain has fallen substantially since 1980, regardless of what indicators are used to define poverty (Ruiz-Huerta and Martínez 1994, 47–49). Paralleling this reduction in poverty and indicative of the equalizing effect of welfare state policies, internal migrations have come to a standstill, with slight net *in-migrations* registered in Andalusia as former migrants return home for their retirement (Ministerio de Asuntos Sociales, Dirección de Migraciones 1995, 197–98).[4]

Today, the valley of the town of Alfaya (Andalusia), where the research for much of this essay was conducted, is full of people who several decades ago fled from poverty or political oppression. Although the agrarian system and class divisions based largely on land ownership play an enduring role in this valley, much has changed. As one Alfaya resident put it, "There are still rich and poor people, but now things are different because we have leveled off [*nos hemos igualao*]. Before, there was that tremendous fear, one could not say a word to the *cacique* [local security forces], we had to talk to them with our head bent downward, we coped with everything because we were afraid of their power, of the possibility of reprisals."

Before turning to a discussion of the changes in conceptions of the national community that have accompanied these economic and political transformations, the next section describes the Alien Law of 1985, focusing specifically on its criminalization of third-world immigrants and their subsequent marginalization. In the remainder of the essay, we argue that it was this marginalization of third-world immigrants and the accompanying rhetoric of their unassimilable "otherness," together with the entry of Spain onto the world stage as a modern, capitalist welfare state, that altered boundaries of exclusion/inclusion in the national community, and triggered shifts of identity among Andalusia's rural poor.

Overview of Spanish Immigration

With industrialization, democratization, and the expansion of its welfare state, Spain has gone from being a country of emigration to a country of immigration (Casey 1997, 9; Cornelius, Martin, and Hollifield 1994; Izquierdo 1996, 38–39; Solé 1995, 20). Migration into Spain includes large numbers of returning Spaniards who had sought work in northern Europe and the Americas after World War II. More pertinent here, beginning in the 1980s rapidly increasing numbers of third-world immigrants entered Spain seeking work. In 1980, approximately 66 percent of foreign residents in Spain were from western Europe and North America, but by the 1990s this percentage had shrunk to a little more than 50 percent (Comisión Interministerial de Extranjería 1995, 138; Ministerio de Asuntos Sociales. Dirección General de Migraciones 1994, 1995; Casey 1997, 12–13).

A terminological curiosity reveals the disproportionate weight of third-world immigration in the public discourse. The official term for all foreign residents in Spain—regardless of how long they intend to stay—is *extranjero* (foreigner). But, in popular parlance a distinction is made between *extranjeros*, on the one hand, and *inmigrantes*, on the other, with the latter category reserved for those who come from the third world seeking work. Thus, when the "immigration problem" is discussed in government circles, in the media, among academics, or in public opinion surveys, it invariably refers to third-world immigration, leading one commentator to refer to first-world immigrants as "authentic *desaparecidos*" (Izquierdo 1996, 71).

The single largest source country of foreign residents in Spain is Morocco, with approximately seventy-five thousand legal residents. Africa as a whole provides 19 percent of Spain's legal foreign residents, the Americas 22 percent, and Asia 8 percent (Comisión Interministerial de Extranjería 1995, 24, 22). It must be remembered that these numbers and percentages refer only to those with legal status. Were legal and illegal residents considered together, the proportions would shift substantially, because the legal status of citizens of third-world countries is dependent on elusive visas, and residence and work permits. One immigration scholar estimates that approximately 40 percent of all foreign residents in Spain—legal and illegal—are from the developed world, with 60 percent coming from the third world (interview with John Casey, Universidad Autónoma de Barcelona).

The number of legally resident foreigners in Spain increased from just over 183,000 in 1980 to almost 500,000 in 1995. Estimates of the number of foreigners living in Spain without valid residence permits range from 60,000 to 600,000 (Casey 1997, 14; Colectivo Ioe 1992; Red Cross, cited in Solé 1995, 25). It is difficult to arrive at good estimates of these *irregulares*, in part because the undocumented often leave no paper trail, but also because these are not distinct populations: not only do legal residents lose their status when their work permits expire, but periodic regularization campaigns temporarily reduce the number of illegal residents, sometimes rather dramatically. Nonetheless, the more reliable independent sources estimate that the combined number of legal and illegal residents is close to one million (see, for example, Solé 1995, 25).

Prior to 1985, Spain had no explicit immigration policy, nor any comprehensive legislation regarding the treatment of foreigners within its territory. The Spanish Constitution of 1978 had specified only that "Foreigners in Spain will enjoy the rights and liberties put forth here, according to the terms set by international treaties and the law," with the qualification that foreigners did not have the same rights as Spaniards to vote and to serve as elected officials (Spanish Constitution, articles 13 and 23; reproduced in Ministerio del Interior 1996, 210, 214). This absence of legal specificity created a kind of legal limbo for immigrants, "who carried out their work and social lives without any great anxiety and without a consciousness of being illegal" (Izquierdo 1996, 142). One study of Moroccan immigrants prior to 1985 found that they were better integrated into the social fabric than later cohorts, were more likely to be self-employed, and often had their families with them (ibid.).

The Spanish parliament passed the Ley Orgánica sobre Derechos y Libertades de los Extranjeros (LOE) in the summer of 1985, the same month it joined the European Community. Evidence suggests that the law was in part the result of negotiations surrounding Spain's entrance into the EC (Casey 1997, 24). Indeed, many observers have noted that the evolution of Spain's immigration laws goes hand in hand with the process of European integration (Borrás 1995, 21; Casey 1997, 24). It is important to note that although the European Union (EU) has increasingly attempted to coordinate its border control policies, each country retains exclusive jurisdiction over immigration matters, with coordination being confined largely to statements of intent and principles.[5]

According to its Preamble, the LOE had the dual purpose of guaranteeing foreigners' rights and controlling illegal immigration (Congreso de los Diputados 1985). The law has been called "vague and imprecise" (Sagarra and Aresté 1995, 169) and "ambiguous and incoherent" (Aresté 1995, 192), in part because of its generality and absence of detail. Together with its regulations, which were finally published in May 1986, the LOE had six main foci. First, sharp distinctions were made between types of foreigners and their corresponding rights, with a dichotomy being drawn between the *Régimen Comunitario* (which applied to EC members) and the *Régimen General* (which applied to all non-EC members), and EC members being granted all the rights of free circulation, residence, and work in Spain. Second, the new policies required for the first time that most non-EC entrants have visas (article 12). Third, in addition to these entrance visas, those who intended to stay in Spain longer than ninety days were required to obtain residence and work permits (articles 13 and 15). As a result, "The great majority [of immigrants] became illegals" (Sagarra and Aresté 1995, 165). Fourth, the law provided that legal residents have certain rights of assembly, public education, and unionization, with the proviso that these rights were operative only insofar as they did not conflict with the "national interest, security, public order, health, morality, or rights and liberties of Spaniards" (articles 7-10, in *Boletín Oficial del Estado* 1985, 20825). Fifth, the law distinguished between legal and illegal aliens, and explicitly excluded the latter (which, as a result of the law, comprised the bulk of non-EC foreigners) from any of the rights already spelled out (articles 7–10). In recognition of the vast numbers thus excluded from any legal rights, a "regularization" program was established through which foreign residents could apply for legal status within a brief window of opportunity.[6] Sixth, the LOE spelled out the grounds for deportation, including lack of proper residence and/or work permits, being involved in activities that are considered dangerous to the public order, being convicted of a felony, and being without sufficient funds (article 26).[7]

A privileged status was created for foreigners from Latin America, Portugal, the Philippines, Equatorial Guinea, Sephardic Jews, Andorrans, and natives of Gibraltar, who were not required to hold entrance visas and were given preference in obtaining residence and work permits; in addition, natives of the Maghreb countries were exempt from the visa requirement—a privilege that was soon to be revoked (article 23).

The LOE, still the only comprehensive law on the books relating to immigration matters and the rights of foreigners in Spain, comprised barely five pages in the Federal Bulletin (*Boletín Oficial del Estado* 1985, 20825–29), leaving not just the details, but vast terrains of uncharted policy to be worked out through administrative regulation. Subsequent policy has been hammered out almost entirely by administrative policies and official decrees, leading one constitutional law expert (Santos 1993, 113) to call it "à la carte" immigration policy. The most substantive of these administrative actions was the "Council of Ministers Agreement on Regularizing Foreign Workers" of June 7, 1991. This regularization program specified that illegal aliens who could verify that they were already in the country by May 15, 1991, and had ongoing work contracts, were self-employed in a lucrative, legitimate enterprise, or had previously had a valid residence and work permit could apply for legalization (reproduced in Boix 1991). This legal status was valid for only one year; renewal was possible, but was contingent on these same conditions persisting. Another government decree in 1996 (*Real Decreto* 155/1996, reproduced in Ministerio del Interior 1996) launched Spain's third regularization program, stipulating this time that it applied only to those who had once had residence and work permits, but who for a variety of reasons had been unable to renew them. A government decree in May 1991 imposed visa requirements for the first time on entrants from the Maghreb countries (Morocco, Tunisia, and Algeria), Peru, and the Dominican Republic. The new controls followed reports that these countries were the source of large numbers of illegal residents, just as Spain was experiencing stepped-up pressure from the EU upon joining the Schengen Agreement in June 1991.

Mercedes Jabardo (1995, 86–87), an anthropologist studying African farmworkers in Spain, observed of the 1985 immigration law: "The new legislation [LOE] . . . generates irregularity among the vast majority of the immigrant community . . . In other words, the Law creates the legal category of immigrant and . . . generates the category of the 'illegal.'" This is true in the obvious sense that before the LOE there was no comprehensive immigration policy in Spain, and thus there were no illegal immigrants.[8] Similarly, the 1991 visa requirement for Moroccans, Peruvians, and Dominicans ipso facto produced large numbers of illegal immigrants. But, the law produces "irregularity" in a more subtle way as well, for lapses into illegality are *built into* Spanish immigration law. This construction of illegality through law is the product of a variety of overlapping factors, the most important of which is the temporary and contingent nature of legal status.

The temporary nature of legal status is underscored by the instability inherent in the programs purportedly designed to facilitate integration—the much-touted "regularization" of illegal aliens. These legalization programs are specifically and exclusively for foreign *workers* (and, under some limited conditions, their families), and are contingent on either having a legitimate work contract or having had one in the recent past. The difficulties of illegal immigrants meeting this standard, given their concentration in the underground economy, are legion. Not only are underground employers often unwilling to formalize work contracts, but some clearly *prefer* the undocumented status of their workers, and the vulnerability that status ensures. According to qualitative studies based on in-depth interviews with Latin American and African immigrants, a number of immigrants have been fired for inquiring about legalization. (Valls, Estrada, and Ferret 1995; Pumares 1996). An Equatorial Guinean who lost his job when he asked his boss to help him with legalization put it this way: "Here when they hire an immigrant they prefer that he work in conditions that are not legitimate, and preferably illegal; that way they can pay what they want and under conditions convenient to them." A Gambian immigrant explained, "If you work in the fields, and you go to your boss and ask for a contract, that's the day you lose your job" (quoted in Valls, Estrada, and Ferret 1995, 125, 127).

Those who do manage to get regularized find it difficult to retain their legal status. In fact, Spain's legalization programs *build in* a loss of legal status unless one can demonstrate, usually on an annual basis, that the original conditions persist (most important and most daunting, a formal work contract). Some immigrants do not qualify for renewal because the work contracts on which their regularization had been based have ended; in other cases, the original contract commitments were never fulfilled by employers. For example, among Moroccans it was not uncommon for "pre-contracts" to evaporate when the employer refused to pay social security or satisfy other formalities, leaving the newly legalized immigrants to work without a contract, and making it impossible for them to renew their regularization at the end of the year (Pumares 1996, 87–89; Izquierdo 1996, 73).

The work permit system operates in conjunction with, and parallel to, these regularization programs. Foreign residents who have been legalized must secure a preliminary work contract with an employer, with which they then apply for a work permit. These work permits are temporary, with the vast majority lasting one year or less. As with regularization, securing a work permit is contingent on maintaining a legitimate work contract, an insurmountable barrier for most third-world immigrants.

Given the difficulties of securing permits, it is not surprising that most third-world immigrants work without them, illegally. In 1996, with an immigrant worker (non-EU) population of approximately 300,000, fewer than 90,000 work permits were in use (Ministerio de Trabajo y Asuntos Sociales 1997, 201). Studies of third-world immigrant communities find a preponderance of "irregulars." According to Izquierdo's calculations (1996, 24), "Among Moroccan and Algerian immigrants, irregularity is the norm, not the exception." Among African farmworkers, it is estimated that four out of five workers are illegal (Jabardo 1995).

The production and reproduction of illegality through law enhances the precariousness and marginalization of those who are thereby illegalized. And this marginalization is not limited to the illegal population; it affects those who are (temporarily) legal as well. Indeed, in this sytem, there are few real distinctions between the two, because legal status is always a fragile state and almost inevitably gives way to periods of illegality. As the director of one of the largest union immigrant advocate groups in Barcelona put it, "Immigrants in Spain always have to pass through periods of illegality" (personal interview). Valls, Estrada, and Ferret (1995, 35) follow this logic through: "If [marginalization] is true for immigrants all over the world, it is especially true in Spain, where it is so easy to go from a situation of legality to illegality . . . The notion that there is a dichotomy between legal and illegal immigrants, as if they were two intrinsically distinct categories, is false."

There is widespread recognition of the economic and social marginalization of immigrants in Spain. Not only immigrant advocates and academics, but politicians and the mass media decry the creation of immigrant "ghettos," even "apartheid," within Spanish society (Cortes Generales 1990, 2112). Indeed, public policy is almost without exception rhetorically framed in terms of the need for integration and cultural tolerance. In marked contrast to this rhetoric, Spanish law systematically reproduces illegality, marginality, and precariousness. The social and economic exclusion and marginalization of Spain's immigrants is neither unpredictable nor incidental; rather, it is the most significant achievement of Spanish immigration law.

It is this criminalization and exclusion of third-world immigrants, together with welfare-state protections for Spanish citizens and the inclusionary ideology of the European Union, that have radically transformed perceptions of community and identity among the rural peasants of Andalusia.

Shifting Boundaries of Identity in Rural Andalusia

Since the 1980s, the valley of Alfaya in rural Andalusia has been caught up in the new capitalist, intensive agricultural production that characterizes the entire region. Despite the economic transformations of Alfaya, and the relative equalization in economic relations they have brought about, the seasonality of agricultural production and the risks associated with capitalist agriculture still leave many people periodically without means of subsistence. Since the 1980s, the modern Spanish welfare state has moved to cover these gaps, and this dependence of peasants on the state has had profound consequences on identity formation, related notions of citizenship, and peasants' orientation to the immigrant workers in their midst.

The rural subsidies instituted by the Socialist Party in 1984 were a modified version of the late Francoist rural employment plans. The key changes in the system were (1) a shift from families to individuals as the basis for subsidies, and (2) replacing control by local landowners and employers, based on vertical and corporatist syndicates, to administrative control that emphasizes the individual links between citizen and state at the local, regional, and national levels. Two plans in particular make up the core of the state support system for rural areas. The Agrarian Unemployment Subsidy provides each subsidized person with a modest nine-month salary to cover structural, temporary unemployment. In addition, the Rural Employment Plan allocates funds to municipalities to hire the unemployed for public works. There is extensive evidence of clientelism, fraud, and posturing to receive the subsidies and coveted work contracts associated with these programs.

Andalusian social researchers attribute peasants' depoliticization during the 1980s and 1990s to the access they gained to social and economic rights as rural citizens. These researchers argue that peasants shifted their focus from collective mobilization involving class-based struggles centered on working conditions to individualistic strategies to gain access to public funds (Moreno 1991a, 28). Furthermore, these subsidies are often supplemented by the rural population with work in the proliferating underground economy. Thus, a central concern is to be as "invisible" to the state as possible, in order to continue combining formal and informal economic strategies of survival (personal interview with immigrant worker in Andalusia).

There are obvious contradictions in the way a semiperipheral European state deals with marginal and vulnerable economic sectors and regions such as rural Andalusia. On the one hand, there is a need for public intervention to deal with such structural distortions as the high unemployment rate; on the other hand, the European Union requirements for a common currency are imposing policies of austerity in public expenditures. Compounding this contradiction, Spain has tolerated the underground economy and illegal labor conditions, especially at harvesttime, but increasingly the state is held accountable for guaranteeing the socioeconomic rights of Spaniards and legal foreign workers, and for preventing exploitation in the workplace (*Boletín Oficial del Estado* 1991).[9] In this politically delicate situation, the Spanish state has chosen to target illegal African immigration as both the fuel of the underground economy and a burden on state resources. And the focus on immigrants and their control fits well with the demands of the EU to seal off the southern border of the European fortress.

Although the symbolic and real violence of the mechanisms employed by the state against immigrants is resented at the local level, nonetheless the rural population of Alfaya has fallen prey to the depiction of African immigrants—criminalized and marginalized by the Alien Law of 1985—as a danger to the interests of European citizens. These political, economic, and legal processes of criminalization and demonization cumulatively foster an emergent identity for Andalusians that feeds upon the new legal ideology of bourgeois liberalism, in which "formal equality and freedom mask and serve to legitimate exploitative economic relations. Each legal subject stands in an individual one-to-one relation with the state without the potentially disruptive mediation of class" (Fitzpatrick 1980, 33).

Although perceptions of class divisions have, of course, not disappeared among Alfaya's largely peasant population, the class boundary has increasingly been replaced by one that marks off rightful members of the national community from illegal nonmembers. The peasants of Alfaya have thus come to see themselves as Spanish citizens—and citizens of the larger European Union—with rights and entitlements, in contrast to their African immigrant counterparts, who not only have no such rights, but are increasingly seen as culturally and morally suspect.

This transformation is perhaps best described with the words of one directly involved. Assane, an immigrant from Senegal who had been one of the pioneer African migrants to Alfaya, told about the changes in Alfaya and his perception of the treatment now accorded immigrants like himself: "Alfaya is now like the big places . . . Alfaya is already like New York City, you see? Like Paris. Like London. It is not Alfaya anymore. It is Alfaya City. And here, as in New York, I can be persecuted just because of my skin. There I would be a Harlem Negro; here I am a black Muslim from Senegal" (personal interview).

Conclusion

The exclusionary dynamics of liberal modernity are played out in a particularly visible fashion in rural Andalusia, where Spanish peasants and African immigrants toil in the fields together and have, until recently, identified with each other as members of a disempowered class of farmworkers in a rigid, quasi-feudal class system. As Spain has joined the roster of advanced capitalist democracies, immigrant workers are increasingly marginalized, racialized, and symbolically excluded from the national community. Thus, as rural peasants in Spain's poorest southern regions come to view themselves as citizens with rights, as full members of the national community—and the larger European Union as well—they increasingly disassociate themselves from the now racialized and marginalized immigrant other. Three developments are critical to this construction of third-world immigrants as racially and culturally other and the corresponding shifts in identity among Andalusian peasants.

First, as we have seen, Spain's rapid economic growth beginning in the post–World War II period and accelerating in the 1980s, and the evolution of its welfare-state democracy after Franco's death, almost overnight transformed Spain from a country of emigration to a country of immigration. By the 1990s, approximately one million legal and illegal immigrants were living in Spain. The Spanish economy has come to depend on the labor of several hundred thousand third-world immigrants, most of whom are concentrated in the underground economy, where they provide "flexibility" to what policy makers and employers describe as an overly "rigid" labor market (Director-General of Migration, quoted in *Mercado* 1992, 27; Director-General of Domestic Policy, quoted in *La Vanguardia* 1993, 10; Ministerio de Asuntos Sociales 1995, 29; see also Jabardo 1995). Indeed, as Spain's standard of living has improved and welfare-state protections have cushioned Spanish citizens from the worst effects of structural dislocations in the capitalist economy and the seasonal unemployment associated with agricultural production, Andalusians and those from other poor regions in Spain no longer can be counted on to supply the desperate and nomadic workforces on which the economy depended in the past. In this context, Spanish policy makers argue that immigrants from the third world are a critical safety valve.

Second, during this period Spain entered the European Community, thereby solidifying its status as an advanced capitalist democracy. In the course of a decade, poor peasants from southern Spain had thus been transformed from effectively disenfranchised underclasses on the margins of a peripheral country to equal citizens in a modern democratic state with all the rights and privileges of membership in the European Union.

Third—and an integral part of these developments—the Alien Law of 1985 for the first time spelled out the rights of foreigners in Spain and drew sharp distinctions between EC members and third-world immigrants. Despite the rhetoric of integration and assimilation, this law and subsequent policies systematically illegalize most third-world immi-grants by making it virtually impossible for them to retain legal status. With lapses into illegality built into the system, Spanish immigration policy not only continually reproduces an extensive illegal population, but ensures the precariousness of its (temporarily) legal immigrants as well. Responding to pressure from the EU to shore up its borders as the southern wall of Europe, but drawing vast economic benefits from this labor source, Spain has crafted immigration policies that, instead of con-trolling *immigration*, control *immigrants*, ensuring their marginalization and their continued contribution to the economy as "flexible" workers.

Race plays a part in this marginalization, but is not the definitive criterion, nor could it be because race itself is socially constructed. Just as Spanish and Italian workers in Germany, France, and Switzerland in the 1950s and 1960s were considered racially and culturally inferior, only to become "Caucasians" and members of the European Community thirty years later, so it is with the marginalized workers of the Maghreb and certain South American countries in Spain: race, exclusion, and economic function are of one piece. The law plays a central role in this alchemy. For migrants who have crossed geographic borders, the law sorts and ranks and, for some, symbolically reconstitutes those borders.

As Andalusian peasants increasingly see themselves not in terms of their membership in the rural working class, but as individual citizens in relationship to the liberal welfare state, they draw sharp boundaries between themselves as full and rightful citizens of the national commu-nity and those who have been constructed in the law and in the national discourse as outsiders. The LOE of 1985, largely precipitated by Spain's entry into the European Community, itself plays a part in the shifting boundaries of community even in this remote region on Europe's south-ern border. As Goldberg (1993, 6) has pointed out, the inclusive prin-ciples of "liberty, equality, and fraternity" essential to the conception of the modern democratic state—and symbolically linking poor peasants in rural Alfaya to affluent professionals in Madrid and Barcelona—have paradoxically given rise to new categories of otherness and new mecha-nisms of exclusion.

Notes

1. The full title of this legislation was Ley Orgánica sobre Derechos y Libertades de los Extranjeros en España (Organic Law on the Rights and Liberties of Foreigners in Spain).

2. Overbeck (1995) suggests that the widely used term *globalization* may be a misnomer. He argues that instead of increasing economic integration of the world economy, the contemporary period is undergoing a capital *"contraction"* with economic activity increasingly centered in three principal regions (North America, Western Europe, and East Asia), and the third world—especially Africa—heavily marginalized in this global restructuring.

3. Non-European Union foreigners in Spain are evocatively called *extracomunitarios*, or community outsiders.

4. Regional disparities in the standard of living persist, with real per capita income in Andalusia only 80 percent of the national average (*Informe España 2002*, 366).

5. The third major step in European unification—the Maastricht Treaty, which officially created European citizens—was signed by EC members in February 1992, to be effective in November 1993, when the European Community became the European Union (EU). Title VI of this agreement dealt with asylum, border controls, immigration, drugs, and establishing a European policing system (Europol). It also formed a committee to advise the Council of Ministers of Interior and Justice of the member countries. While Schengen and Maastricht have attempted to move toward a coordinated European policy on immigration and asylum, as one high official put it, there remain "teething problems" (quoted in Benyon 1996, 365).

6. There were only 44,000 applicants to this program, which was widely criticized for its lack of publicity and coordination, and which was launched at a time of fear and confusion among immigrants who had become illegal overnight as a conseqeunce of the new visa and permit requirements. Of these applicants, only 23,000 were able to fulfill the program requirements relating to ongoing, legitimate work contracts or other means of support in the formal economy (Colectivo Ioe 1992; Izquierdo 1992).

7. A provision that would have allowed administrative authorities to conduct deportations without judicial input was declared unconstitutional in 1987 (Tribunal Constitucional, Sentencia Num. 115/1987).

8. There were, of course, immigrants who were working illegally in the

underground economy, but they were under no threat of deportation, and were reportedly better integrated into the community than later cohorts (Izquierdo 1996).

9. Modernization is assumed to go hand in hand with the disappearance of nonregistered, and usually exploitative, social relations of production. However, social scientists have long acknowledged the structural role of the informal sector in the development of capitalism, both in peripheral countries and in the core (Sassen-Koob 1988; Fernandez-Kelly 1983; Portes 1990; Portes, Castells, and Benton 1989; Calavita 1994).

References

Anderson, Benedict. 1991. *Imagined Communities: Reflections on the Origins and Spread of Nationalism.* 2d ed. London: Verso.

Aresté, Pedro. 1995. "Los cupos de trabajadores en 1993 y 1994." In *Diez años de la Ley de Extranjería: Balance y perspectivas*, ed. Alegría Borrás. Barcelona: Itinera Libros.

Beiner, Ronald, ed. 1995. *Theorizing Citizenship.* Albany: State University of New York Press.

Benyon, John. 1996. "The Politics of Police Cooperation in the European Union." *International Journal of the Sociology of Law* 24: 353.

Boix, Vicente Font. 1991. *El trabajador extranjero y la regularización de 1991.* Barcelona: Itinera Cuadernos.

Boletín Mensual de Estadística. 1997. Vol. 64. April. Madrid: Instituto Nacional de Estadística.

Boletín Oficial del Estado. 1985. Number 158. July 3.

——. 1991. Number 257. October 26.

Borrás, Alegría. 1995. *Diez años de la Ley de Extranjería: Balance y perspectivas.* Barcelona: Itinera Libros.

Bourdieu, Pierre. 1991. "Preface." In Sayad Abdelmalek, *L'immigration: Ou les paradoxes de l'altérité.* Brussels: De Boeck-Wesmael.

Brubaker, Rogers W. 1992. *Citizenship and Nationhood in France and Germany.* Cambridge: Harvard University Press.

Calavita, Kitty. 1994. "Italy and the New Immigration." In *Controlling Immigration: A Global Perspective*, ed. Wayne Cornelius, Phillip Martin, and James Hollifield. Stanford, Calif.: Stanford University Press.

Carr, Raymon, and Juan Pablo Fusi Aizpurua. 1979. *Spain, Dictatorship to Democracy.* London: George Allen and Unwin.

Casey, John. 1997. "La admisión e integración de los inmigrantes extranjeros." In *Las polítícas públicas en España*, ed. J. Goma and R. Goma. Madrid: Ariel.

Cohn, Bernard S., and Nicholas B. Dirks. 1988. "Beyond the Fringe: The Nation-State, Colonialism and Technologies of Power." *Journal of Historical Sociology* 1: 224–29.

Colectivo Ioe. 1992. *Los trabajadores extranjeros en España: Informe para el Instituto Sindical de Estudios.* Madrid: Colectivo Ioe.

Collier, George A. 1987. *Socialists of Rural Andalusia: Unacknowledged Revolutionaries of the Second Republic.* Stanford, Calif.: Stanford University Press.

Comisión Interministerial de Extranjería. 1995. *Anuario Estadístico de Extranjería.* Madrid: Secretaría General Técnica. Ministerio de Justicia e Interior.

Congreso de los Diputados. 1985. *Boletín Oficial de las Cortes Generales.* Number 132.

Consejo Económico y Social. 1995. *Economía, trabajo y seguridad: Memorias sobre la situación socioeconómica y laboral, España.* Madrid: Consejo Económico y Social.

Contreras, J. 1991. "Estratificación social y relaciones de poder." In *Antropología de los pueblos de España*, ed. J. Prat, U. Martinez, J. Contreras, and I. Moreno. Madrid: Taurus Universitaria.

Conway, Dennis. 1994. "Are There New Complexities in Global Migration Systems of Consequence for the United States 'Nation-State'?" *Indiana Journal of Global Legal Studies* 2: 31–44.

Cornelius, Wayne A., Philip L. Martin, and James F. Hollifield, eds. 1994. *Controlling Immigration: A Global Perspective.* Stanford, Calif.: Stanford University Press.

Cortes Generales. 1990. *Diario de sesiones del Congreso de los Diputados.* Number 44. June 13.

Danielsen, Dan, and Karen Engle, eds. 1995. *After Identity: A Reader in Law and Culture.* New York: Routledge.

Delbruck, Jost. 1994. "Global Migration—Immigration—Multiethnicity: Challenges to the Concept of the Nation-State." *Indiana Journal of Global Legal Studies* 2: 45–64.

de Lucas, Javier. 1996. *Puertas que se cierran: Europa como fortaleza.* Barcelona: Icaria.

den Boer, Monica. 1995. "Moving between Bogus and Bona Fide: The Policing of Inclusion and Exclusion in Europe." In *Migration and European Integration:*

The Dynamics of Inclusion and Exclusion, ed. Robert Miles and Dietrich Thran-hardt. London: Pinter Publishers.

Economist. 1996. "A Survey of Spain." *Economist*, December 14, 3–18.

El País. 1997. *Anuario el País*. Madrid: Ediciones El País.

Falk, Richard. 2000. "The Decline of Citizenship in an Era of Globalization." *Citizenship Studies* 4: 5–17.

Fernandez-Kelly, Patricia. 1983. *For We Are Sold: Women and Industry in Mexico's Frontier*. Albany: State University of New York Press.

Fitzpatrick, Peter. 1980. *Law and State in Papua New Guinea*. New York: Academic Press.

———. 1992. *The Mythology of Modern Law*. New York: Routledge.

Gilmore, David D. 1980. *The People of the Plain: Class and Community in Lower Andalusia*. New York: Columbia University Press.

Goldberg, David Theo. 1993. *Racist Culture: Philosophy and the Politics of Meaning*. Cambridge, Mass.: Blackwell Publishers.

Hammar, Thomas. 1990. *Democracy and the Nation-State: Aliens, Denizens and Citizens in a World of International Migration*. Aldershot, England: Gower Publishing.

Hobsbawm, Eric J. 1990. *Nations and Nationalism since 1780*. Cambridge: Cambridge University Press.

Hobsbawm, Eric J., and Terence Ranger. 1983. *The Invention of Tradition*. Cambridge: Cambridge University Press.

Ignatiev, Noel. 1995. *How the Irish Became White*. New York: Routledge.

Informe España 2002. 2002. Madrid: Fundación Encuentro.

Izquierdo, Antonio. 1992. *La inmigración en España: 1980–1990*. Madrid: Ministerio de Trabajo y de la Seguridad Social.

———. 1996. *La inmigración inesperada*. Madrid: Editorial Trotta.

Jabardo, Mercedes. 1995. "Etnicidad y mercado de trabajo: Inmigración africana en la agricultura." *Perspectiva Social* 36: 81.

Jimeno, Juan, and Luis Toharia. 1994. *Unemployment and Labor Market Flexibility: Spain*. Geneva: International Labour Office.

La Vanguardia. 1993. "El Sindic de Grueges pide una actitud mas integradora hacia los inmigrantes." October 8, 10.

Marshall, T. H. 1950. *Citizenship and Social Class and Other Essays*. Cambridge: Cambridge University Press.

Maté García, Jorge J. 1994. *Demanda, oferta y ajustes salariales en el mercado de trabajo español*. Valladolid: University of Madrid Press.

Maxwell, Kenneth, and Steven Spiegel. 1994. *The New Spain: From Isolation to Influence*. New York: Council on Foreign Relations Press.

Mercado. 1992. "Miedo a lo Desconocido." February 24, 27.

Ministerio de Asuntos Sociales. 1995. *Plan para la integración social de los inmigrantes*. Madrid: Ministerio de Asuntos Sociales.

Ministerio de Asuntos Sociales. Dirección General de Migraciones. 1994. *Anuario de Migraciones*. Madrid: Ministerio de Asuntos Sociales.

———. 1995. *Anuario de Migraciones*. Madrid: Ministerio de Asuntos Sociales.

Ministerio del Interior. 1996. *Normativa Básica de Extranjería*. Madrid: Ministerio del Interior.

Ministerio de Trabajo y Asuntos Sociales. 1997. *Boletín de Estadísticas Laborales*. Number 143. April. Madrid: Ministerio de Trabajo y Asuntos Sociales.

Moreno Navarro, I. 1991. "Desarrollo del capitalismo agrario y mercado de trabajo en Andalucía." *Revista de Estudios Regionales* 31: 19–29.

Omi, Michael, and Howard Winant. 1986. *Racial Formation in the United States: From the 1960s to the 1980s*. New York: Routledge and Kegan Paul.

Overbeck, Henk. 1995. "Towards a New International Migration Regime: Globalization, Migration and the Internationalization of the State." In *Migration and European Integration: The Dynamics of Inclusion and Exclusion*, ed. Robert Miles and Dietrich Thranhardt. London: Pinter Publishers.

Portes, Alejandro. 1990. *Immigrant America*. Berkeley: University of California Press.

Portes, Alejandro, Manuel Castells, and L. Benton. 1989. *The Informal Economy: Studies in Advanced and Less Developed Countries*. Baltimore: Johns Hopkins University Press.

Pugliese, Enrico. 1995. "New International Migrations and the 'European Fortress.'" In *Europe at the Margins: New Mosaics of Inequality*, ed. Costis Hadjimichalis and David Sadler. New York: John Wiley and Sons.

Pumares, Pablo. 1996. *La integración de los inmigrantes marroquíes: Familias marroquíes en la comunidad de Madrid*. Barcelona: Fundación "La Caixa."

Ruiz-Huerta, Jesús, and Rosa Martínez. 1994. "La pobreza en España: ¿Qué nos muestran las EPF?" *Documentación Social* 96: 15–109.

Sagarra, Eduard, and Pedro Aresté. 1995. "Evolución en la administración desde 1985 en el tratamiento de la extranjería." In *Diez años de la Ley de Extranjería: Balance y perspectivas*, ed. Alegría Borrás. Barcelona: Itinera Libros.

Santos, Lidia. 1993. "Elementos jurídicos de la integración de los extranjeros."

In *Inmigración e integración en Europa*, ed. Georges Tapinos. Barcelona: Itinera Libros.

Sassen-Koob, Saskia. 1988. *The Mobility of Labor and Capital*. Cambridge: Cambridge University Press.

Schuck, Peter H. 1998. *Citizens, Strangers, and In-Betweens: Essays on Immigration and Citizenship*. Boulder, Colo.: Westview Press.

Sevilla Guzman, E. 1979. *La evolución del campesinado andaluz*. Barcelona: Península.

Simmel, Georg. 1950. *The Sociology of Georg Simmel*. Trans., ed., and with an Introduction by Kurt H. Wolff. New York: Free Press.

Simon, Jonathan. 1993. *Poor Discipline: Parole and the Social Control of the Underclass. 1890–1990*. Chicago: University of Chicago Press.

Solé, Carlota. 1995. *Discriminación racial en el mercado de trabajo*. Madrid: Consejo Económico y Social.

Tapper, Richard. 1989. "Ethnic Identities and Social Categories in Iran and Afghanistan." In *History and Ethnicity*, ed. Elizabeth Tonkin, Maryon McDonald, and Malcolm Chapman. New York: Routledge.

Thranhardt, Dietrich, and Robert Miles. 1995. "Introduction." In *Migration and European Integration: The Dynamics of Inclusion and Exclusion*, ed. Robert Miles and Dietrich Thranhardt. London: Pinter Publishers.

Tonkin, Elizabeth, Maryon McDonald, and Malcolm Chapman, eds. 1989. *History and Ethnicity*. New York: Routledge.

Torpey, John. 2000. *The Invention of the Passport: Surveillance, Citizenship, and the State*. Cambridge, England: Cambridge University Press.

Valls, Andreu Domingo, Jaume Clapés Estrada, and Maria Prats Ferret. 1995. *Condicions de vida de la població d'origen Africà i Llatinoamericà a la regió metropolitana de Barcelona: Una aproximació qualitativa*. Barcelona: Diputació de Barcelona.

Woolard, Kathryn A. 1986. "The 'Crisis in the Concept of Identity' in Contemporary Catalonia, 1976–1982." In *Conflict in Catalonia: Images of an Urban Society*, ed. G. W. McDonogh. Gainesville: University Press of Florida.

Young, Alison. 1996. *Imagining Crime: Textual Outlaws and Criminal Conversations*. London: Sage.

Yuval-Davis, Nira. 1990. "Women, the State, and Ethnic Processes." Paper presented at conference on racism and migration in Europe. Hamburg.

Zolberg, Aristide R. 1994 "Changing Sovereignty Games and International Migration." *Indiana Journal of Global Legal Studies* 2: 153–70.

CHAPTER 5

South Asian Workers in the Gulf: Jockeying for Places

Karen Leonard

Even children's books in South Asia now assume familiarity with the experience of expatriates working in the Persian Gulf. Thus *The Case of the Shady Sheikh and Other Stories* (Singh 1993) features an Indian labor contractor and a Gulf sheikh who cheats poor men, taking money from them and promising passports, visas, and work permits for jobs in the Middle East. The criminals are foiled by a band of children who become detectives and expose their shady dealings.[1] That a children's book should deal with such themes is quite appropriate, for some of the most highly publicized South Asian workers in the Gulf states are children, young boys from Bangladesh, India, and Pakistan who are used as jockeys in camel racing. Brought by agents from South Asia, the small boys are light in weight; tied or Velcroed to the backs of the camels, their screams increase the animals' speed. When they grow older they are replaced by younger boys.[2] Few of the older South Asian businessmen and professionals working in the Gulf would liken themselves to these exploited boys, tied to their jobs and racing at the pleasure of their Arab masters, but there are certain similarities, and they are increasing.

For South Asian expatriates in the Gulf, the internationalism of postwar capitalism has produced opportunities to use their skills for higher pay and in better working conditions than at home. Businessmen, professionals, service workers, and laborers have left their home countries to become part of a flexible international labor force in which "the

space of flows . . . supersede[s] the space of places" (Watts 1991, 9; citing
Henderson and Castells 1987, 7). Yet it is not the expatriate workers
but the Arab rulers who control these flows through laws that set a
"steel frame" for work and family life.[3] In the Gulf, we see a unique
example, perhaps, of transnationalism as a deliberate strategy of economic and political governance.

Transnationalism has something of a romantic aura in much of
the literature, despite its rooting in processes of global capitalist pene-
tration. Widely used definitions of transnationalism and transmigrants
put forward in 1992 by Nina Glick Schiller, Linda Basch, and Cristina
Blanc-Szanton stress the development of social fields linking the country of origin and of settlement (1992, 11). These connections are viewed
positively, described as "maintained, reinforced, and . . . vital and growing" and as creators of "fluid and multiple identities grounded both in
their society of origin and in the host societies." Even Roger Rouse,
while drawing attention to the challenges and contradictions of the
migrant experience, talks of "cultural bifocality, a capacity to see the
world alternately through quite different kinds of lenses" (1992, 41).
Rosina Wiltshire speaks of "multiple national loyalties" (1992, 175)
and Arjun Appadurai goes further, postulating that transmigrants have
"loyalty to a nonterritorial transnation first" (1996, 173, 176). He firmly
connects transnationalism to postnationality. Basch, Schiller, and Blanc
(1994), like Appadurai, discuss deterritorialized nation-states and global
cultural constructions as aspects of transnationalism.

David Harvey views the collapse of spatial and national barriers
quite differently, and far more negatively, as provoking "an increasing
sense of nationalism and localism." To him, the "small-scale and finely
graded differences between the qualities of places (their labor supply,
their infrastructures and political receptivity, their resource mixes, their
market niches, etc.) become even more important because multinational
capital is in a better position to exploit them" (Harvey 1990, 427–28;
see also Silbey 1997, 213–17). This view is echoed by Hassan Gardezi,
who states that "globalization's neo-colonial agenda" has most drastically affected "the ordinary people of post-colonial societies" (1997, 116),

and Saskia Sassen, who sees a new phase of the world economy in the 1980s that is an assault on all working-class people (1993, 61–65).

Focusing on Indians and Pakistanis in Kuwait and Dubai to delineate how notions of globalization and transnationalism actually play out in workers' lives, one can see both enabling and disruptive consequences of their work across national boundaries.[4] Although South Asian workers at all levels intended to improve their lives and those of their children in their home countries, that goal is being achieved more certainly by the lower-class and lower-middle-class workers. For middle-class migrants, the Gulf has often turned out to be a stopping place on the way to Western countries, a further and unanticipated displacement and one that can mean downward mobility.

The Political Economy in the Gulf

When South Asians talk about the Gulf, they mean the six monarchies of Saudi Arabia, Kuwait, Bahrain, Oman, Qatar, and the United Arab Emirates (UAE). These six belong to the Gulf Cooperation Council (GCC), formed in 1981 primarily for security reasons. There are only two categories of residents in the Gulf states, citizens and noncitizens, and the limitation of citizenship to "nationals" or "locals" rests more on a "genealogical" conception of nationalism than on the logic of modern capitalism.[5] The ruling families conceive of the states as theirs, their fellow tribesmen as their subjects and citizens,[6] and the large numbers of expatriate workers of all classes and national origins as perpetual outsiders.[7] There is no pretense that immigration is occurring or that migrant workers are being integrated into the Gulf states. Like the other Gulf rulers, the Arab rulers of Kuwait and the seven emirates that make up the federation of the UAE delegate few political rights even to their own citizens.[8]

The Gulf rulers launched their states into the modern world with the help of expatriates. Just at the time that external events contributed to the collapse of the pearling and fishing economies of the Gulf states in the 1930s, foreign oil companies began to arrive in search of concessions. The pearl industry, mainstay of most Gulf economies prior to

Japan's development of its cultured pearl industry, was based on indigenous technology and expertise, but the oil concessions established a reliance on expatriate expertise and manpower, which has persisted beyond
the termination of the foreign oil concessions in the late 1970s.[9] The
Gulf states are trying to develop and diversify their economies, but their
small and relatively unskilled populations still need the help of expatriate
managers and workers (Sayigah 1972, 293; Stoakes 1972, 203; Zahlan
1989, 70–72). These Gulf oil-exporting states are exceptionally wealthy,
and their citizens receive many economic benefits. Home ownership is
nearly universal for citizens, and water, power, and telephones are heavily

Map 5.1. The Gulf states.

subsidized; sanitation services are free. Free education often includes education abroad, and free, or nearly free, health care can include care abroad. The expatriate workers also benefit from state subsidies.

Workers come to the Gulf from all over the world, providing its rulers with an international and flexible workforce. Of the total population of these six GCC countries in the 1990s, estimated at twenty-three million, some ten million are foreigners, one million of them maids. Expatriates are the backbone of the urban working and professional classes. At first, such expatriate workers were drawn from Iran and from neighboring Arab countries, but the number of workers from Asia has steadily increased. Treating the six GCC countries as a unit, the general picture in 1985 (before the Gulf war) showed that 43 percent of the foreign workforce in the Gulf was from South Asia, 30 percent was from other Arab countries, and 20 percent was from Southeast Asia. Pakistanis moved into the Gulf countries in the early 1970s, followed and surpassed by Indians in the 1980s, with strong representation from Bangladesh and Sri Lanka by the 1990s. The Philippines, Thailand, and South Korea now send many workers to the Gulf, and the "better trained and disciplined" Southeast Asians have intensified the competition for jobs and contributed to the lowering of wages and salaries in recent years.[10]

This globalization of the labor market does not erase difference, but "revalidates and reconstitutes place, locality, and difference" (Watt 1991, 10). Foreign workers are ranked by place of origin, receiving differential payment and treatment. Most of the Gulf states do not release detailed statistics about the expatriate workers' origins, but they sometimes use general "nationality" categories to produce crime and other statistics. In the UAE, these categories are UAE, Gulf (GCC), Other Arab, and Asian, and GCC citizens can generally enter one another's countries without visas, whereas other Arabs and Asians need visas.[11] The categories also roughly reflect salary differences, with other Arabs ranked above Asians, and with gradations within these groups as well. Thus the other Arabs of Lebanese, Palestinian, and Syrian origin command the highest wages and salaries, Egyptians and Sudanese receive half as much, and South and Southeast Asians receive one-third as much.

Among laborers, Indians reportedly rank above Pakistanis, who rank above Bangladeshis and Chinese. There are also strong gender differences within and across citizen and noncitizen categories. What little political participation has been extended to citizens has gone only to males, and although expatriate male laborers are covered by state labor codes, domestic workers (predominantly female) are not.[12]

The centrality of the state in the economies and a dependence on multinational capital are features that the Gulf states share with other oil exporters, but there are sharp differences, most notably the combination of a homogeneous class of citizens with large numbers of heterogeneous noncitizens working within each state.[13] One can compare the Gulf states with other "growth-region" states, as in Henk Overbeek's analysis of the contemporary medium-duration "conjuncture" produced by the growth of the European Union and the collapse of the USSR (Overbeek 1995, 16–22).[14] In the Gulf, however, expatriate workers are arguably better off than in Western Europe. Their status is unambiguous, whereas Kitty Calavita (2001) shows that in Spain confusing and contradictory laws serve not to integrate but to marginalize immigrant workers.[15] Another comparison is with Japan, with its growing and heterogeneous population of noncitizen workers (Yamanaka 1993, 1997a, 1997b), but in Japan the Japanese are the majority population, and in Kuwait and Dubai noncitizens outnumber the citizens. There are similarities to Aihwa Ong's regional "growth triangle" model of differential treatment of workers via the implementation of integrated labor policies by Malaysia and its Southeast Asian neighbors, but the workers are, in her cases, all citizens, albeit sorted into geographic economic zones of "varied sovereignty."[16]

India and Pakistan are major suppliers of labor to the Gulf, which is correspondingly important to these South Asian states. The favored destinations for Indians have been Saudi Arabia, closely followed by Oman and the UAE, and then Kuwait and Bahrain (Mowli 1992, 81, 83). For Pakistanis, the figures are harder to obtain (it is estimated that as many Pakistanis go to the Gulf illegally as legally [Gardezi 1991, 192]), but there are more Pakistanis than Indians in Saudi Arabia.

Although the percentage of India's export earnings from remittances is not very significant, remittances from abroad, 75 percent of them from the Middle East, constitute the single largest source of export earnings for Pakistan.[17] Thus, the declining numbers of Indian and Pakistani workers in the Gulf in the late 1980s and especially after the Gulf war of 1990–91 have been disruptive. In 1995, Pakistan reported that its manpower exports to the Gulf had dropped by more than 50 percent since 1985 because of increased competition and a shift from unskilled to skilled workers and professionals (*Pakistan Link*, February 17, 1995, 42). India has also seen a decrease in the annual outflow of manpower.[18]

South Asians are the largest expatriate group in Kuwait and the UAE. Indians are approximately double the number of Pakistanis in each place, with slightly more Bangladeshis and Sri Lankans than Pakistanis. The population of Kuwait is about two-thirds noncitizens, and most foreign workers in Kuwait are bachelors, with a sex ratio of 225 to 100 (males to females), or 31 percent female.[19] In the UAE, 75 percent of the population is said to be expatriate, and in Dubai that proportion is higher, perhaps 80 percent. The sex ratio among expatriates in the UAE is 70 percent male and 30 percent female, almost identical to that in Kuwait.[20] Women come as maids, but also as wives, doctors, teachers, and nurses. In Kuwait, most maids are from the Philippines, whereas in the UAE most are from Sri Lanka; other maids come from Bangladesh, India, and Indonesia (*Pakistan Link*, September 16, 1994, 20).

The Gulf state boundaries are viewed, in a memorable phrase, as "sifters of labour rather than as barriers to its movement" (Ranger 1994, 287, but there are stiff requirements.[21] Those who meet them— visa, sponsor, work permit, residence permit, and medical checkup requirements—gain access to economic opportunities. Recruitment starts in the home countries and involves brokers and manpower recruiting agencies at both ends; costs are high and some are unofficial.[22] The rules are detailed and quite similar in Kuwait and Dubai. Citizen sponsors are needed even for a visitor's visa (save for GCC citizens), and residence visas are of three types: work, dependent, and servant. Expatriates, whether businessmen, professionals, or workers, over the age of

Table 5.1 The Gulf countries

Country	Square miles	Estimated population	% Expatriate	Expatriate % of 15–64-year-olds	Expatriate origins	%
Bahrain	239	603,318	37	44.39	Asians	13
					Other Arabs	10
					Iranians	8
Kuwait	6,880	1,834,269	75 (62–67)	72.07	South Asians	46
					Indians	18
					Sri Lankans	10
					Bangladeshis	10
					Pakistanis	8
					Egyptians	23
Oman	82,031	2,264,590	25	NA	Arabs	
					Baluchi	
					South Asians	
					Africans	
Qatar	4,416	670,274	77	83.49	Other Arabs	40
					Pakistanis	18
					Indians	18
					Iranians	10

					Afro-Asians	
					Egyptians	
					Pakistanis	
					Indians	
					Filipinos	
Saudia Arabia	756,981	20,087,965	26	35.87		
UAE	32,000	2,262,309	68 (75–80)	75.73	South Asians	50
					Other Arabs & Iranians	23
Abu Dhabi	26,000					
Dubai	1,500					
Sharjah	1,000					
Ras Al Khaimah	650					
Fujairah	450					
Um Al Quwain	300					
Amjan	100					

Sources: Unless otherwise indicated, and for the sake of comparability, all figures come from *The 1997 World Fact Book* put out by the U.S. Central Intelligence Agency. This can be accessed on the Web at http://www.odci.gov/cia/publications/factbook/index.html. I have converted square kilometers to square miles and computed the expatriate percentages of the populations.

The estimates of percentages of expatriates in the fourth and fifth columns are from *The World Fact Book 1994* (Washington, D.C.: U.S. Government, Central Intelligence Agency, 1995), 299. Note that the *Economist* (September 20, 1997, 52) gives different percentages for expatriates: 67 percent for Kuwait and 80 percent for the UAE, which I use in the text. The *Kuwait Pocket Guide '95* gives a still lower figure for Kuwait (62 percent). These alternative figures appear in parentheses in the table.

The *Kuwait Pocket Guide '95* (p. 116) gives detailed and very different information about the origins of expatriates, which I have used here instead of the pre–Gulf war information in *The 1997 World Fact Book*. I have also used more detailed information about Saudi Arabian expatriates from Gardezi (1991, 191), although figures are not available for Saudi Arabia and Oman.

The square-mile breakdown by emirates is from Christine Osborne, *The Gulf States and Oman* (London: Croom Helm, 1997), 34 and 61.

sixty are not permitted. A noncitizen can do private business in Kuwait in several closely regulated ways, most of them involving a local agent, sponsor, or partner (in Kuwait this must be a man, but it can be a woman in the UAE). These working relationships are typically quite nominal, with sponsors taking commissions from many foreigners annually but not participating in the businesses. The laws governing expatriates in the UAE are slightly more flexible: visitors' visas for tourists are easier to get, and, although the age limit of sixty pertains in theory, many older businessmen and major investors are allowed in (thus the transnationalism of capital is encouraged although the transnationalism of workers is limited) (*India-West*, January 16, 1996, A38; see Roberts 2001, 3).

Family life for expatriates depends on their class. Once he has secured a residence visa, a man who makes a certain amount of money monthly can sponsor his wife and children to live with him; the amount is high (very slightly less in the UAE than in Kuwait), to discourage workers from bringing their families. If both spouses are working, their salaries can be added together. Wives cannot sponsor husbands in Kuwait, but women doctors and teachers can sponsor husbands in the UAE. In both sites, adult (over eighteen) and unmarried daughters can be sponsored, but not adult sons, and no dependents can work without their own sponsors and work visas. Parents can visit for one to three months (since 1995 in Kuwait, they can stay longer for a high annual fee).[23] Foreigners (save GCC citizens) cannot own land or real estate and must rent accommodations, customarily unfurnished ones.

In both Kuwait and Dubai, expatriates can and do employ other expatriates. They may sponsor one full-time household servant (again, there is a minimum salary requirement). If a man sponsors a female servant, he must be married and have his wife living with him. Maids must be between twenty and fifty years of age, and family members cannot be brought in as servants. Maids and other domestic workers live in their employers' households, while male laborers and service workers usually live in groups of six or more in rooms or dormitories, and they commonly contract for either two or three meals a day at dining halls.[24]

South Asian expatriates benefit substantially from working in the Gulf. For unskilled and skilled workers, professionals, and businessmen, salaries are many times those at home, and one's income is tax-free.[25] Working conditions are excellent, with modern facilities and technology, and living conditions are also good, with cheap and dependable water, electricity, air conditioning, and other amenities. In Kuwait, expatriates and their dependents got free health care until 1994, when (low) fees began to be set for nonemergency procedures. Maternity care is still almost entirely free there, although marriage certificates must be shown at all hospitals and husbands cannot be in the delivery room at the state hospitals. Food in both places is government-subsidized. Because of the extremely hot summer, government workers get one month's leave and private workers get at least that every year, plenty of time to vacation in Europe, have a long visit home, or drop in on relatives elsewhere. Although residences have to be rented, leases can be arranged for five-year stretches.

An important reason professional and business people give for working in the Gulf is that they were still in an Asian context—the Gulf is also called West Asia, in South Asia.[26] Both Kuwait and Dubai compare very favorably to cities in the Western world, and yet they are culturally non-Western, an important consideration for those who view Western culture as threatening to personal safety or to family and religious values. Law and order are strictly maintained, and in Kuwait and Dubai (but not Saudi Arabia) one can freely practice one's religion. Those who work in Dubai have additional incentives. Dubai is fun, although people save less because enjoyable diversions are plentiful and it is easier to bring families (thus increasing costs).

The one certainty is that expatriates cannot stay in the Gulf permanently. At some point, they must leave, and they are psychologically prepared for this: "One becomes defensive. One has to inwardly accept the terms and be prepared to leave tomorrow, and then it's OK."[27] They retain strongly positive relationships with India or Pakistan, seeing themselves as overseas citizens of, and eventual returnees to, those states. South Asians working in the Gulf invest in consumer durables, house building and repair, family celebrations, and schooling for their children back in the home countries (see Sharieff 1994). Furthermore, middle-class expatriates have begun to hold multiple citizenships or immigration rights. Along with Indian citizenship, a person might secure a U.S. and/or Canadian green card, and Pakistanis are allowed to hold dual citizenship with the United Kingdom or Canada. The laborers typically have fewer options, but are just as prepared to return home or go elsewhere to work. In some respects, then, these South Asian workers are transmigrants, participants in transnationalism, yet their experiences in the Gulf require closer examination.

Contrasting Environments

Rivalries in the Gulf region abound, partly reflected by the changing rankings in the United Nations' "human development" rankings. In 1994, Kuwait secured the highest ranking in the Arab world in the United Nations Human Development Index, but in 1995 Bahrain and the UAE jumped ahead (to numbers 44 and 45, with Qatar 56, Kuwait 61, Saudi Arabia 76, and Oman 91). The UAE remained ahead of Kuwait in 1997 in this annual index, and it also leads in the Gulf competition for "who has the highest tower."[28] The Kuwait Communication Towers used to be the highest, then Dubai's thirty-nine-story World Trade Center, but now Abu Dhabi in the UAE has erected an even higher building and tower.

Kuwait and Dubai share certain features of physical environment and work culture. Both are on the coast, with long, hot, and dry summers and short, warm, and (sometimes) wet winters. Summer temperatures often approach 50 degrees centigrade (122 degrees Fahrenheit), a temperature at which outside physical labor is legally prohibited in both places.[29] The work is demanding, going from 7 or 8 A.M. to noon or 1 P.M., when the midday heat encourages long lunches and perhaps naps; people work again from 4 to at least 8 P.M. Most people eat dinner at 8:30 or later. Far more than government employment, private business is competitive and demanding, and the hours are long. For many businessmen, lunches are also business meetings, and sometimes international business timings mean that there is no real break at mid-day. Wives complain about how little they see of their husbands, and family recreation can occur at the end of the long, hot days when children are taken to swim in the sea after midnight!

Kuwait and Dubai offer modern, urban environments, both cities having undergone major transformations in a very short time. Low-lying landscapes with wind towers poking up to channel breezes down into the interior courtyards of old houses have given way to the high profiles of architecturally innovative new buildings. Clusters of spectacular hotels, banks, shopping malls, and apartment buildings house international commerce and industry. Luxury hotels are excellent, providing a full range of international cuisine in stylish settings; there are many fast-food restaurants. Ultramodern constructions invoke tradition: the interior of Kuwait's international airport and the roofs of the National Assembly buildings suggest tents, and the mushroom-shaped water towers that punctuate the suburban skyline are meant to evoke palm trees around an oasis. Dubai is a green city, with four golf courses (three of them green, unlike the brown ones in Kuwait). The architecturally stunning Emirates Golf Club clubhouse resembles an assembly of royal tents, and the equally venturesome Dubai Creek Golf and Yacht Club resembles a dhow, the traditional fishing boat. While Kuwait city's residential areas tend to be segregated, with Kuwaiti villas in some localities and expatriate families' homes and apartments in others, and the bachelor workers' apartments and barracks further out, low-cost housing for expatriate workers is scattered throughout Dubai city, an example of the late Sheikh Rashid's liberal policies, which made Dubai the Gulf's leading industrial, commercial, and trading center.[30]

For expatriate workers, the Gulf states offer a range of work environments. Legal, financial, and cultural conditions present various trade-offs. The prevailing cultural orientations in Saudi Arabia and Kuwait are thoroughly Arabic in both language and culture, reflecting a dominant culture heavy with Islamic resonances and meanings. The UAE reflects a more cosmopolitan hybrid culture, with its frequent use of Urdu and broadly secular South Asian resonances and meanings.

Within the UAE, Abu Dhabi, the site of the federation's capital and the home of its president, is more culturally Arabic, while its rival, Dubai, is more South Asian. Traditional gender conventions weigh less heavily on expatriate women in Dubai than in Saudi Arabia, Kuwait, or Abu Dhabi. In Kuwait, workers are paid more. However, there is more of a bureaucracy there, staffed by other Arab intermediaries, and despite that, there is less state regulation of working conditions than in Saudi Arabia and the UAE.[31]

The sociocultural environments and the experiences of South Asians in Kuwait and Dubai are quite different (see Leonard 2001), largely owing to their different relationships with South Asia and Great Britain in the past.[32] Historical ties between South Asia and some of the Gulf states, particularly Oman and the emirates of the UAE, are long-standing, and were intensified in the eighteenth century by British empire building in India, when British efforts to protect the trade route to India meant dealing with maritime Gulf powers.[33] In the nineteenth century, the small polities of the Gulf signed separate treaties or truces with the British government, a process beginning in 1820 and sealed in 1853 with the Perpetual Maritime Truce signed by the present members of the UAE. Bahrain signed a separate treaty in 1861, and Kuwait and Qatar came under British influence even later through treaties in 1899 and 1916, respectively (Zahlan 1989, 5–9).

Under British dominance, and still oriented toward India, the Gulf states evolved distinct identities.[34] Their boundaries and relations with one another had been historically fluid, but Britain conducted separate relations with each state, leading to separate flags, travel documents or passports, and ultimately national anthems.[35] British dominance also produced important commonalities. The Indian rupee was the principal currency in the Gulf, Indian stamps were used (overlaid with state names), British Indian regulations were applied by the political officers, and Urdu (Hindustani) words infiltrated the Arabic coastal dialect (ibid., 10–13).[36] In addition, Yemeni and other Gulf Arabs worked as soldiers in Indian native states, particularly Hyderabad (Khalidi 1997), and smuggling of all kinds linked western India, east Africa, and the Gulf states.

Kuwait is closer to the Middle East in terms of language, religious observances, and general lifestyle. Kuwait's constitution declares the religion of the state to be Islam and the Islamic *sharia* the main source of law. The official language is Arabic and that is the street language as well, learned to some degree by most expatriate workers. Drinking liquor is forbidden in Kuwait, to Kuwaitis and foreigners alike.[37] Non-Muslims can practice their religion and there are several Christian churches, but Hindu temples are not allowed.

Dubai, as a member of the UAE, also follows Islamic *sharia* and Arabic is its official language, but it was strongly influenced by the British and South Asian connection. Thus, in Dubai, Sharjah, and most of the UAE emirates, Urdu (Hindustani) is readily spoken and understood by many Arabs.[38] Urdu and English, rather than Arabic, are the languages one hears on the streets; expatriates do not need to learn Arabic. Not only are non-Muslim religions freely practiced, but there are two Hindu temples. In Dubai, non-Muslims can drink alcohol, by paying fees for permits and patronizing popular pubs. The city feels cosmopolitan, even South Asian, rather than Arab. A Christian couple from India felt at home in Dubai: "We feel we are staying in our own country," the husband said.[39] Popular culture from South Asia, very much part of the South Asian expatriate world in Kuwait, is even more widespread in the UAE. There have been many marriages between Arabs and young Muslim women from India's Hyderabad State, so South Asian culture is part of the home life as well as the work life of many UAE Arabs.[40] Hindi films and film songs, traveling comedians, poets, singers, and sports events attract locals as well as South Asians. Well-known smuggling and underworld connections between India (particularly Bombay) and Pakistan and the UAE even link criminal activities across state boundaries.[41]

The historical roots of South Asian business, professional, and working-class people in Dubai and the UAE are deeper than in Kuwait and the numbers have always been large.[42] South Asian businessmen and workers began coming to the UAE in the 1960s. In those early days, many came by launch, a trip of about three days from Bombay to Dubai.

Sometimes they swam ashore, to be greeted by a queue of three or four taxis waiting at a (blazingly hot) beach. Most of the early shopkeepers were from Kerala, or they were Indian Arabs, descendants of Arabs who had gone to work in India in earlier times. Many South Asian business and professional people feel that they have been partners in the development of the UAE, and particularly Dubai, if not leaders of it.

In Kuwait, South Asian businessmen and professionals also began coming in the 1960s, when Kuwaiti sponsors were often uneducated and experienced foreigners could get licenses to do business directly in Kuwait. Now, most sponsors are educated and all foreigners must work through them. Other Arabs were already well placed in government and private positions there. Palestinians (and, after the Gulf war, Lebanese) fill the crucial positions of *mandoubas* or intermediaries, the Arabic speakers who obtain the proper forms, fill them out in Arabic, and interface with Kuwaiti officialdom on behalf of expatriate businessmen.[43] Even the essential *harris*, the building watchman or concierge, was and is always an expatriate Arab. South Asian workers began coming in numbers only in the mid-1970s. Then, a longtime Indian businessman there remarked, "the ABCDs came flooding in: the *ayahs*, butlers, cooks, and drivers."[44] Thus, in Kuwait a small elite South Asian business and professional class has been swamped by workers, who are a larger part of the expatriate population in Kuwait than in the UAE. The high proportion of South Asian maids, drivers, and cooks has produced a "master–servant mentality," several men told me, so that Kuwaitis tend to see all South Asians as servants.[45]

Relationships with the "nationals," the term used in Kuwait, or the "locals," the term used in Dubai, are slightly different in the two places; even these usages convey distance and easy familiarity, respectively. People familiar with the different Gulf states characterized the Kuwaitis as the least pleasant people with whom to work, perhaps even more so after the Gulf war. In contrast, they said, the late Sheikh Rashid of Dubai (1958–86) favored Indian merchants and treated them very well, and the liking was and is mutual. Many South Asians commented that the locals in Dubai were "the nicest, the most accessible to business, the least arrogant." "We do socialize more with the locals, men only, of course; that reservation is always there. This is better than Kuwait, and the locals have been educated in Karachi or Bombay, they have been exposed to South Asians," one man told me, and others echoed him.[46]

An important difference between Kuwait and Dubai concerns the agents of authority—the officials and the police. The kinds of expatriates filling these roles and the languages they use significantly affect the lives of South Asian expatriates. Kuwaiti agents of the state, chiefly drawn from the non-Gulf Arab category, strongly intimidate the poorer South Asian workers there, who express helplessness in the face of the bureaucracy or the police. If a worker was arrested and accused of drunkenness or fighting, his fellow workers had to desert him for fear of arrest and deportation themselves. If workers were not paid or were underpaid, their legal remedies were few and slowly implemented. The emirates vary in the impact of UAE authorities on workers' lives. Abu Dhabi, the capital of the federation, is more like Kuwait, where government institutions and officials play the major roles in public life. Even more important is the constitution of the police forces. There are mainly non-Gulf Arabs on the Abu Dhabi police force, and "the police speak Arabic only (although of course they know Urdu) and are out to get you; in Dubai, they speak Urdu politely to you, will listen to your explanation, and often let you go." In Dubai, the police are given cordiality lessons, and the chief is Yemeni, while the force consists of locals, Sudanese, Barkas men (Arabs from Hyderabad, India), Iranis, and Baluchis.[47]

Although Dubai's more international lifestyle and tolerant attitudes make it particularly attractive to visitors and to businesspeople, both cities exhibit many aspects of modern transglobal culture. There are English-language newspapers and international satellite TV, the latter competing with state-run TV channels and bringing in CNN, Star TV, the BBC, and popular shows (in 1995) such as *Oprah* and *The Bold and the Beautiful*. In Dubai, there is no dress code of the sort encouraged in Kuwait and every style of clothing can be seen, including bikinis at the beaches. One author remarks that Dubai has "become a convention-center oasis, a jumbo-jet-serviced ultramodern bazaar and playground on the edge of the desert, halfway between Rome and Singapore as the 747 flies . . . Westerners lived here as if in a dream" (Dickey 1990, 168). Perhaps reflecting Dubai's commercial emphasis and its large numbers of British and Indian Christians, Christmas is lavishly celebrated with official displays of decorated trees.[48] Dubai also has a well-developed tourist industry, adding golf, water sports, sand-skiing, "wadi-bashing" (desert driving in four-wheel-drive vehicles), desert feasts, and visits to Bedouin villages to the traditional male sports of falconry, camel racing, and horse racing in the Gulf.

In both Kuwait and Dubai, expatriate workers are conspicuous on Fridays, when most have their day off. The spaces of the city come alive with workers shopping and visiting with each other. Popular restaurants overflow. Video and audiocassette shops sell Hindustani film and music favorites, and empty tapes for the men to record their messages home; for many, that is easier than writing letters. Workers congregate in Kuwait city by national origin, the Bangladeshis in one section of a huge mall and the Indian men in another, while maids from India's state of Andhra Pradesh, divided into groups by districts (Cuddapah and Karim-nagar), meet in an adjacent smaller shopping center. The Pakistanis can always be found in yet another location, and so on. Employers' cars drop workers off at set places and times and then pick them up again at the end of the day. In Dubai too, the markets and malls are crowded on Fridays, but the spaces are not so well defined as in Kuwait, and the larger numbers of families lessen the visual impact of the workers' groups. People gather at the many inexpensive Indian and Pakistani Mughlai restaurants, and there are also sweet shops, South Indian and Afghan restaurants, and *pan* shops in nearby Sharjah (*pan* is outlawed in Kuwait and Dubai, because of the red stains left as chewers spit betel nut on sidewalks and walls).

The two-tier class structure so strong among expatriate South Asians in Kuwait is more muted in the UAE, with more families present and greater mixing across class lines.[49] South Asians of lower-class origins who are upwardly mobile in the Gulf, "people with no manners," may nevertheless be part of the everyday social worlds of South Asians from "noble clans," crossing a gulf in the UAE that is harder to cross in Kuwait, with more mixing across national boundaries as well. Lower-middle-class professionals did most of their business with other expatriates. An encyclopedia salesman reported that he had to laugh at the way Filipinos, Thais, Egyptians, Palestinians, and Iranis spoke Urdu (note that Urdu is the common language).[50]

Relationships among South Asians in the Gulf strongly reflect political and social divisions from home. Indian–Pakistani interaction among workers is minimal, as occupations tend to be dominated by one or the other—or employers use one or the other—category of workers. From the remoter areas of Pakistan, Baluch and Pukhtun tribesmen migrate to the UAE to work on the roads, serve as drivers, and do construction work. Most taxi drivers in the UAE are Pakistanis, Pushtu speakers from Peshawar and its hinterland, and the construction workers in Al Ain (Abu Dhabi) come from the same background. Most South Asian maids are from India or Sri Lanka.

Even among the business and professional expatriates there is rivalry and distance between Indians and Pakistanis, though less than in the case of the service workers and laborers. This is partly because of the existence of historical and marital ties between Indian and Pakistani Muslims (classmates and relatives divided by Partition in 1947 can be reunited in the Gulf, and some marriages are arranged across those boundaries). Indian and Pakistani children may attend the same elite schools, although most attend embassy-affiliated schools, thereby confirming national boundaries.[51] Hindus have always been prominent among the big Indian businessmen in the UAE, and Indian and Pakistani Muslims report that the Hindus do as well or better than South Asian Muslims there. Sindhis dominate the business classes and Keralites dominate the service classes in the UAE, and there is a sizable community of Indian Christians.[52]

Political events in India and Pakistan have repercussions in the Gulf, demonstrating the extension of these nationalisms abroad, not their attenuation in a neutral setting. When Hindu fanatics pulled down the Babri Masjid in India in December of 1992, the incident provoked demonstrations such as had never been seen in the UAE by expatriates or locals. Ironically, it was mostly Pakistani, not Indian, Muslims who caused problems. They protested at the Indian consulate in Abu Dhabi, but the UAE police controlled the crowds without firing shots or mounting charges against the public. In Dubai, riot police in full gear with armored vehicles were required to restore order in the (Hindu-dominated) Sona Bazar or Gold Souk. In Abu Dhabi and Sharjah, Indian shops were closed, and in Al Ain (Abu Dhabi), Pukhtun laborers from Pakistan staged illegal demonstrations and consequently were deported (*India-West*, December 11, 1992, 29 and February 1, 1993, 39). Less serious eruptions of Indian and Pakistani patriotism arise whenever the Sharjah-hosted cricket competition, the Australasia Cup, pits the two nations against each other. Tensions are evident in the emirates, but also back in the homelands, because a television audience of millions watches the games there.

The Indian and Pakistani consulates actively work on behalf of their constituents in the Gulf. The South Asian consuls are called on by the UAE government to help with disputes over wages or working conditions.[53] The consulates assist maids escaping domestic abuse, which includes nonpayment, overwork, and verbal and physical abuse, including rape. The abusers are most often the Arab employers (both male and female), but they can be Indian, Pakistani, or other expatriates. The Sri Lankan, Indian, Bangladeshi, and Filipino embassies all run safe houses for maids who have left their sponsors and are requesting repatriation (see, for example, Bonner 1992 and *India-West*, March 6, 1992, and October 1, 1993).

Contracting Environments

Despite soaring local birthrates and the rising educational qualifications of their own young people, Gulf employers still prefer to hire cheaper and more exploitable expatriates.[54] However, the recruitment of labor has become more wide-ranging, bringing increased competition and less desirable salaries and working conditions. The Gulf war of 1990–91 was a turning point, particularly in Kuwait.[55] Workers at all levels of the Kuwaiti economy were expelled or evacuated. Air India's airlift from Kuwait was allegedly the largest one in history, taking out between 133,000 and 135,000 people.[56] The return of South Asian expatriates to gainful employment in Kuwait was problematic. Kuwaiti sponsors and employers exercised selectivity when bringing workers back later, with many choosing not to bring back older longtime workers but turning instead to younger, inexperienced, and cheaper ones.[57] The age limit for expatriates was enforced, and the state stopped the allowances for expatriate children (Kuwaitis continue to receive a monthly allowance per child). Most important, government and private employers kept the wage level the same as before the war, but by 1995 prices had reportedly risen by at least 10 or 15 percent, in some cases 30–40 percent.[58]

The Gulf war produced South Asian expatriate victims across class lines. Homes and businesses were looted and damaged. Workingmen who left were unable to reestablish claims of any sort on the state or private employers, forfeiting pay and unable to renew their lapsed work permits. Maids were deserted and left without resources in the embattled city. A very few businessmen of long standing in Kuwait stayed throughout the war and were lauded for their service to the state. In other cases, war service went unrewarded. Professionals, particularly doctors, who were entreated to stay and continue to work, found that payment for this seven months of service never materialized, despite repeated promises and the eventual payment of those Kuwaiti colleagues who had remained.

Deliberate government policies after the war have cut the numbers of noncitizens in Kuwait. Before 1990, Kuwaitis officially made up 27 percent of the population, and now they make up 38 percent (*KPG '95*). The expulsion of large numbers of Palestinians, Jordanians, Sudanese, and others whose governments sided with Iraq was a major factor. Among expatriate workers, Arabs from Palestine and Egypt dominated before the Gulf war, but now Asians outnumber expatriate Arabs. In post-1991 Kuwait, the taxi drivers are still from Egypt, but the bus and car drivers are from India, the workers at McDonald's from the Philippines and Korea, the cleaners from Bangladesh, and the most recently arrived construction workers from China.[59]

The Kuwaiti government has continued to stiffen the entry and working conditions for expatriates. In 1992, the income requirements for bringing dependents were raised.[60] In 1993, having already set a ceiling for expatriates as government employees, the Kuwaiti government set a ceiling of half a million expatriates for the private sector. This affects South Asians disproportionately because Indians are the largest group of non-Arab expatriates working in the private sector (63,304, or 17.8 percent), followed by Pakistanis (at 34,445) (*India-West*, March 26, 1993). In 1995, the rules for switching sponsors were tightened, requiring expatriates who had not completed two years' service with the first sponsor to return to their countries to secure new residence and work permits with a subsequent sponsor (*Kuwait Times*, August 6, 1995).

Like Kuwait, Saudi Arabia and the UAE are tightening requirements and recruiting more widely.[61] In the UAE, banks were told in 1994 to ensure that UAE citizens were at least 10 percent of their staffs. Fees for visas and medical examinations were raised in 1994, to five or more than ten times as much as before, and salary requirements for bringing spouses and children were raised to 5,000 dirham a month ($1,362).[62] A crackdown on those switching jobs illegally or arriving on visitors' visas and then working illegally led to many arrests and deportations (the UAE jail for deportees in Abu Dhabi is said to be always full) (*India Today*, October 15, 1994, 116). The changes and tough policies subject expatriate workers to traumatic uncertainties.

Expatriates in the UAE faced two crises in 1995, as the government moved to cut down on Asian labor in favor of Arab labor. The first concerned expatriate schools, and the second concerned flights back to the Gulf after the summer vacations in India. Expatriate schools, good but expensive, are maintained by fee-paying students and are licensed and closely regulated by the Gulf states. School license renewal fees also increased in 1994, and these increased fees had a domino effect on schools in both the UAE and India. The expatriate schools had to raise their own fees, so steeply that many Indian and Pakistani students decided to transfer back to South Asia at the June summer break (*India-West*, June 30, 1995, A47). Transfer certificates issued by the UAE Education Ministry numbered around three hundred per day that June. Some 30 percent of the South Asian children leaving schools in the UAE were estimated to be from the lower classes, and, because their school fees had not been cleared, they could not secure official transfer certificates. The loss of pupils and the uncollected fees caused expatriate schools to raise their fees again, pressing expatriate families in the UAE even harder. In India, families bringing their children back from the Gulf tried to get the domicile criterion waived for students seeking college admissions—those without domicile status (NRIs, or nonresident Indians) had to pay huge sums for admission to many colleges, and often admission quotas limited their enrollment (ibid.).

The second crisis in 1995 concerned flights from India back to the Gulf. Gulf Air (the UAE airline) had mounted extra flights in June and July for the summer exodus of South Asian workers from the Gulf, but the presold tickets back to the UAE relied on extra return flights as well. At the end of August, as Gulf workers tried to return to their jobs, India delayed granting Gulf Air permission for extra flights from India to the Gulf. This endangered people's work permits (which had to be renewed within a certain time period) and the attendance of their children at Gulf schools (which opened September 1). India finally gave permission for the extra flights after UAE employers spoke out about the need for the return of the Indian labor force, citing major construction projects involving housing, roads, and hospitals (*Khaleej Times*, August 19, 1995, 3 and August 26, 1995, 3). This incident highlighted the crucial role of the expatriates in the UAE economy, but also their vulnerability.

The fall of 1996 brought another crisis, a new UAE crackdown on illegal workers. This brought a flood of emergency exit permit applications to Indian and Pakistani diplomatic offices from workers without proper travel documents (some workers in the Gulf destroy their passports when their residence visas expire and stay on illegally). Undocumented workers had to leave before a UAE amnesty expired on

September 30 and around 10 percent of the five hundred thousand Indian workers in the UAE were there illegally, an Indian official estimated. India's national airlines had to schedule extra flights and the government flew many people back home free, because most of those departing were housemaids or laborers who could not pay the airfare. Tens of thousands of workers were unable to leave in time because airlines and shipping companies could not cope with the mass exodus, so the UAE had to extend the amnesty. By the end of September, some one hundred thousand exit permits had been issued and another hundred thousand were anticipated (*Pakistan Link*, September 27, 1996, A36).

The tough new laws against illegal workers in the Gulf had severe consequences in South Asia. According to Indian officials, some thirty thousand Malayalees needed to be resettled in Kerala and the 2.5 million people belonging to their families would be severely affected by the loss of remittances. Land and real-estate prices in Kerala were expected to fall drastically. The same laws would affect some 150,000 Bangladeshis, most of them men who had gone on short-term visas through recruitment agencies, then had destroyed their passports (when the visas expired), taken new identities, and stayed on (*India-West*, October 4, 1996, A10; *Pakistan Link*, September 27, 1996, A37). UAE construction firms again found themselves without enough workers and major projects were delayed or suspended. Faced with a labor shortage, the UAE made it easier for workers to transfer sponsorships.[63] The competition from elsewhere in Asia, the former USSR, and eastern Europe has diminished the prospects of Indian and Pakistani entrepreneurs, professionals, and laborers, leading to changes in their long-term strategies. Although the first entrepreneurs from South Asia in the UAE had learned that "to make it you have to mix with the nationals," the historical closeness between the locals and South Asians is declining. Locals used to go to Pakistan and India for education and medical treatment but now tend to go to the United Kingdom (whereas South Asian expatriate businessmen and professionals used to go to the United Kingdom for education and medical treatment but now go to the United States). The emphasis once placed on personal ties has faded in the face of international competition for market niches. To compete in the UAE now, these expatriates are sending their children to graduate schools in the West to get degrees and they are investing in malls and department stores, not small general stores (*India-West*, September 15, 1995, C7).

Expatriate workers of all classes recognize that the Gulf no longer represents assured social mobility back in the homelands. All are experiencing some ambivalence and uncertainty; perhaps the most vulnerable are the Indian and Sri Lankan women who come on their own as domestic servants, constrained by work and residency laws but unprotected by the labor laws.[64] For laborers and service workers such as air-conditioner repairmen, bus drivers, encyclopedia and other salesmen, the Gulf is still a place where one can earn money, improve the family home or build a new one, and accumulate money for one's sisters' dowries.[65] Even the Sri Lankan women returning from domestic work in the Gulf have gained materially, although their dependence on Gulf employment has become firmly established (Eelens, Shampers, and Spechmann 1992, 232–35).[66] Most workers cannot bring their families to the Gulf, and those who do save less money and expose themselves to state policies such as those concerning schools. Instead, they spend the money on their children's education at home. The owner of one of Hyderabad city's most exclusive schools, for example, reports that Gulf-returned workers, men and women who cannot speak English, are bringing their children to her English-medium school, even donating money for its expansion so that their children can be accommodated.[67]

The middle-class families living in the Gulf have faced different implications for their own and their children's mobility. The plan was to return to the homelands, to new homes and to systems of higher education that would prepare their children for professional careers. The families lived well, enjoying the modern technology and material abundance of the Gulf states while thinking that they were not exposing themselves or their children to the disruptive effects of Western culture. But "a consumerist orientation toward global citizenship" and "full exposure to western socioeconomic modes of life" have occurred for parents and children alike.[68] Despite the temporary nature of South Asian children's residence in the Gulf states, people found that the children's daily experiences were unsettling their knowledge of and commitment to their parents' home nations.[69] Residence in the Gulf sites has had an irreversible impact on the children.

The consequences of the Gulf war brought these realities home abruptly. Families and family strategies based in Kuwait were most dramatically affected, but throughout the Gulf the war disrupted the flow of workers, commodities, and money across national borders and unsettled the long-term family strategies of expatriate business and professional people. The national and generational displacement of South Asian men, women, and children returning from the Gulf became clear during their months of prolonged residence in the South Asian homelands. Living "at home" without material comforts and with exposure to political and communal conflicts of all kinds forced the parents to think again about eventual resettlement in their homelands.[70] Many middle-class expatriates, having made "only a short-term move," found themselves reluctantly forced to make decisions along unanticipated (and previously resisted) lines. They reconsidered their own long-term futures, looking hard at Canada, Australia, or the United States, and prepared to sacrifice their own careers to relocate in places more advantageous for their children.

Almost every year brings stronger feelings of disillusionment and imminent displacement for South Asian expatriate workers in the Gulf. The citizens are rising through the educational system and beginning to fill jobs once held by expatriates, and the increasing internationalization of labor means that the Gulf workforces are becoming more diverse and competitive at every level. Workers from China come for very low wages, and Polish engineers are now available at half the cost of Indian ones. Engineering consultants, once primarily Lebanese, Egyptians, and Jordanians, have become a very diverse group, and even local engineers are becoming partners in government firms, and, more slowly, in private firms. Some people still want to stay. An Anglo Indian woman who supervises construction workers in the UAE said, "They keep on changing the rules here, they want to keep us insecure . . . yet I've been here thirteen to fifteen years, I owe this country a lot; from nothing I've become something, I can afford it all here. I've seen other parts of the world, and my dad had a personal audience with the pope! I can shout at the Pathans, they give me respect here." Others are more ambivalent. One man said, "Previously the Gulf was good, but now more locals are involved in the work and their own mentality comes into it." A slang term for the locals, "IBM," shows that mentality, or rather an expatriate stereotype of it: Inshallah (Allah willing), Bukaram (tomorrow), and Malosh (possibly, or never). Others said, "It is still a place to earn, compared to home, but fees are doubling, conditions are not so good now"; "The expatriates have built the UAE, running the banks and everything . . . [now they should not] make life miserable for those who built it up"; and "Everything is done to discourage expatriates from settling down; they don't want us to put down our roots here. Therefore all the rules and policies are tailored to push us out." The last speaker felt that the constant threats to one's status had an effect on personality.[71]

Finally, the world situation has changed significantly. As one person in Dubai put it, "With the dirham tied to the dollar, and the liberalization in India, and inflation in the UAE—why are we here, why not go back or go west?"[72] The modernity and sophistication of the Gulf environments have changed expectations, and the heavy impact of Western culture and material goods on the Gulf societies means that the non-Western "home away from home" is vanishing before the middle-class expatriates' eyes. Their identities as short-term economic migrants intending to return home have been challenged by unforeseen economic-political determinations that they cannot control, both in the Gulf and at home. Many parents now consider relocating to another overseas destination rather than simply going "home" as their children grow up. To return to the image of the boy jockeys, it is time to take the reins and seize control, change horses, perhaps even racecourses. Jockeying for places in the global marketplace is risky at best, and for some expatriates, downward mobility has been a consequence.

Changing Places: Transnationalism?

Narratives of transnationalism rest on and often overlap with those of globalization; it is sometimes hard to separate the two. Moving between South Asia and the Gulf states, the South Asian expatriates, like their places of origin and migration, escape easy categorization in the globalization and transnationalism literature. Clearly, their economic opportunities in the Gulf have been shaped increasingly by developments beyond both their places of origin and the sites in which they work. Market forces rather than individual agency are driving the expatriate workers in the Gulf. While the experiences of working in the various Gulf states continue to be strikingly different (that is, historic relationships continue to shape specific work environments), global capitalism now produces working conditions and workforces increasingly unrelated to the past hegemonic actions of global powers in the region.[73] Yet working-class migrants from South Asia have persistently seen themselves as benefiting from employment there and it can be argued that mobility is now less problematic for them than for higher-class expatriates. Just as clearly, the fundamental orientation of expatriates in the Gulf was not a transnational or transmigrant one, for, although "their public identities are configured in relationship to more than one nation-state," the relationship to the Gulf states was basically a negative one, one of nonbelonging save through work.[74] This nonbelonging in the Gulf had important, if unintended, consequences for their belonging in their homelands. They did not set out to be transmigrants, yet many of the middle-class families among them have been compelled to become so. They were loyal to their South Asian homelands while in the Gulf, and those who are reluctantly moving elsewhere now for the sake of their children may be choosing new homelands rather than stretching loyalties across nation-states as transnational migrants.

Most narratives of globalization, those that idealize and those that demonize, are firmly anchored in Western culture and implicitly assume the ascendance of the liberal nation-state. Susan Silbey (1997) outlines some of those narratives, while William Maurer (in this volume) calls for alternative constructions, other narratives of globalization and transnationalism. Maurer reminds us that offshore financial centers and Islamic banking challenge the dominant definitions of finance and economics. Aihwa Ong (in this volume) finds some Southeast Asian nations mandating inequality, exclusion, and difference within and across boundaries to maximize their participation in the new global economy. These essays, and mine, suggest that positioning oneself outside the dominant theoretical constructions, viewing globalization and transnationalism from less familiar standpoints, enables us to see more diverse and complex ways for individuals and populations to manage and be managed within and across the boundaries of nation-states. Certainly the South Asian expatriates in the Gulf experience the forces of globalization and transnationalism, forces that powerfully constrain and redirect their participation in nationhood, citizenship, and civil society.

Notes

1. The "Gulfan" (Gulf-returned man) is a new social category in the South Indian state of Kerala and elsewhere.

2. Camel jockeys are supposed to be ten years old, but Bangladeshi boys as young as two to four have been rescued by police in India from adults taking them to the Gulf. Previously tied onto the backs of the camels, they are now attached with Velcro to the saddle. Despite protests from journalists (Dickey 1990, 199–200) and others, the practice goes on (*India-West*, March 6, 1998).

3. Sara Suleri (1992, 766) argues that lived experience for women can best be approached through the narratives provided by the law; this is also true for expatriate men in the Gulf.

4. Funding for the research on Indians and Pakistanis originally from Hyderabad, India, was provided by the Committee on American Overseas Research Centers (CAORC): Kuwait city, July 31–August 12, 1995; UAE, August 12–26, 1995, and February 9–12, 1996. I especially thank Mirza Shamsher Ali Beg and Parveen and Shahid Ali Mirza in Kuwait and Anees and Maqsood Ali and Sharafat and Sultana Walajahi in Dubai for greatly facilitating my work, and Junaid Adil, Dubai, for his careful reading of an early draft; I am, of course, responsible for any errors.

5. See Andrew Shyrock's work on Bedouins in Jordan, *Nationalism and the Genealogical Imagination* (1997).

6. Bedouins historically moved back and forth across the Iraq–Kuwait frontier, but after the Gulf war, Kuwait declared those Bedouins who had not fulfilled the complex citizenship registration requirements non-Kuwaitis, although they were one-third of the indigenous population (Goodwin 1995, 175–76).

7. There are some exceptions to this, particularly in Dubai in earlier decades when some Iranians and Indians were given passports.

8. Since the eighteenth century, the Emir of Kuwait has been from the Al-Sabah family. The UAE was formed in 1971 from the seven emirates of Dubai, Abu Dhabi, Sharjah, Um Al Quwain, Ras Al Khaimah, Ajman, and Fujairah. The president of the federation is the Sheikh of Abu Dhabi, Sheikh Zayed, and the vice president is the Sheikh of Dubai, Sheikh Maktum.

The powerful royal families of the Gulf states present obstacles to electoral democracy (Owen 1993, 33–40). Kuwait was a relatively free and open society in the 1960s and 1970s, but royal control was tightened in the 1980s, and the National Assembly was dissolved in 1986. After the Gulf war of 1990–91, the Kuwait Assembly was reconvened. Elections were held in 1992 and again in 1996. Kuwaiti voters are men over twenty-one years of age of proven Kuwaiti ancestry, that is, from families in the country since 1920; this meant that some 100,000 of the 750,000 citizens in a population of just over two million elected Assembly members in 1996 (*Economist*, October 12, 1996, 50). The UAE was set up in 1971, but it is still run under an interim constitution, which is extended every five years by the rulers. In 1993, the president revived the Federal National Council, a move toward democracy (*Dawn*, August 30, 1993).

9. The dependency of Gulf states on pearls ranged from 20 to 48 percent (Zahlan 1989, 22, 70).

10. *India-West*, 1995, 40; *Pakistan Link*, September 16, 1994, 20; Gardezi 1991, 190–91. Seventy percent of Sri Lankan workers in the Gulf are female domestics (Eelens, Shampers, and Spechmann 1992, 3).

11. Those holding residence visas of any GCC state, except menial laborers, are given visas on entry to the UAE, Oman, and Qatar. British citizens can get short-term visas upon arrival in the UAE, and Americans can be similarly favored in Kuwait, thanks to historical ties between Britain and the emirates and the U.S. role in the Gulf war, respectively.

12. Much of the literature on the Gulf states reads as though expatriates were not there, and when they are included they are talked about as men. Gardezi (1991, 192), in an otherwise informative article, remarks only that female

domestics from the Philippines and prostitutes from Pakistan are often smuggled in illegally. See Leonard 2001.

13. See Ong, in this volume, about Southeast Asian states; Coronil, 1997, 6–7, about Venezuela. This mix of citizens and noncitizens confounds Overbeek's matrix of state forms, which proposes a simple two-by-two table of homogeneous and heterogeneous populations versus hegemonic control (civil society, with power founded on consent) and Hobbesian control (minimal civil society, state domination) (Overbeek 1995, 25–27). Eelens, Shampers, and Spechmann have tables comparing the Gulf states and Europe with respect to migrants in the 1980s (1992, 70).

14. Consideration of the Gulf states shows the inadequacy of Overbeek's North/South, East/West, third-world labels (Lewis and Wigen 1997 discuss such inadequacies).

15. Workers in the Gulf are in a better position than many workers in the United States, where it is not entrance that is curtailed, but legal and social status that would allow undocumented workers entitlements.

16. See Ong and Coutin, in this volume. Coutin's treatment of the space of nonexistence in the United States is relevant, although it is far harder to escape the laws in the Gulf states.

17. Gardezi (1991, 191), quoting the government of Pakistan *Economic Survey*, 1987–88 (Islamabad, 1989, 159) and the World Bank *World Development Report*, 1989 (New York: Oxford University Press, 1989), respectively.

18. Consequences for the state of Kerala were particularly heavy, because it furnished almost 50 percent of India's Gulf labor force (Mowli 1992, 54, 81, 61).

19. A breakdown of the expatriate population in Kuwait in 1994 compiled from residency permits recorded from liberation in February 1991 to January 1, 1994, puts Egyptians at 23 percent, Indians at 18 percent, Bangladeshis and Sri Lankans at 10 percent each, and Pakistanis at 8 percent of the total of 889,347 (*Kuwait Pocket Guide '95* [hereafter, *KPG '95*], 116). The total is below that given for the citizen—noncitizen tabulation in the text, where the expatriates number 1,099,868, or 62 percent of the total population (*KPG '95*, 20). The sex-ratio figure is from *KPG '95* (21).

20. *Economist* (September 20, 1997, 52) gives a population figure for the UAE of 2,210,000 and asserts that more than 80 percent are expatriates.

21. Ranger was referring to colonial powers drawing the borders within Africa.

22. *India Today* (February 15, 1997, 39–40) gives a smuggling fee of 1.5 to 2

lakh rupees (150,000 to 200,000 rupees, or $4,280 to $5,700), paid to brokers and agencies in India for sea passage to the Gulf countries. I found women agents recruiting men in both India and Pakistan in the 1990s (in Islamabad, Pakistan, and Hyderabad, India). For Sri Lanka, see Eelens, Shampers, and Spechmann (1992, 48–59).

23. The fee for parents is two hundred Kuwaiti dinar ($690) a year; the dinar has been a very stable currency, and one KD equals $3.30 (*KPG '95*, 38).

24. In Dubai, one must draw 7,000 dirham (about $1,900) per month to sponsor a maid, higher than for a dependent, and the government collects an annual tax equal to her salary, which should be not less than 400 dirham ($108) per month. Thus one pays about 800 dirham a month or 9,600 dirham ($2,400) a year for a maid (*Pakistan Link*, September 16, 1994, 20). The dirham has been 3.67 to the dollar since 1980.

25. Men who are bus drivers or air-conditioner repairmen in Kuwait earn from 90 to 120 KD ($297–$396) per month, and they typically spend about 45 KD ($148.50) for accommodations and food. Meals at a contract dining hall range from 18 KD ($59.40) per month for three meals a day to 20 KD ($66) a month for two (better-quality) meals a day. Laborers can earn as little as 20 KD ($66) a month, the wage allegedly paid to workers from China (Mirza Shamsher Ali Beg, interview, August 2, 1995, Kuwait). In the UAE, laborers' wages range between $250 and $500 per month (with $115 at the low end), with food costs about $100–$110 per month (*Pakistan Link*, September 27, 1996). For living conditions of Sri Lankans, see Eelens, Shampers, and Spechmann (1992, 92–95), particularly on enclave-type camps. Interviews with Indians and Pakistanis brought estimates of five to ten times as much, and Eelens, Shampers, and Spechmann (on Sri Lankans in the 1980s) estimate five to fifteen times as much (1992, 90).

26. Lewis and Wigen (1997) insightfully discuss varying labels for this part of the world.

27. Arsalan Mirza, interview, August 21, 1995, Dubai.

28. In 1994, Kuwait was number 53 out of 173 countries, highest in the Arab world and second highest among Muslim countries (*KPG '95*, 33). For the 1995 rankings (for 1992, actually), see *Khaleej Times*, August 18, 1995 (omitting Bahrain's ranking). See also *Human Development Report* (1995, 20; 1997 [for 1994, where Bahrain is 43, the UAE 44, Kuwait 53, Qatar 55, Saudi Arabia 73, and Oman 88], 45).

29. It was 120 degrees F (almost 50 degrees Centigrade) when I was in Kuwait, and people told me that when it is 50 degrees C, official temperatures are not reported, lest a day's work be lost.

30. In Kuwait, Western expatriates cluster by the sea in Salmiya, South Asians and other expatriates reside in Salmiya and Salwa, businessmen prefer Shark, and bachelor workers from Kerala and elsewhere live in Farwaniyah, Abasiya, and the outlying Hawasi district. In Dubai, housing is still inadequate, and makeshift shantytowns such as Jarnia Fur house many South Asian, Egyptian, and Sudanese workers (Ahmed 1984, 270).

31. Another disadvantage of Kuwait is that Kuwaiti employers seldom include a free air ticket home (Mr. Mohammed Yousufuddin, interview, August 3, 1995).

32. The range of contextualized experiences for women (and men) in the Gulf has Saudi Arabia at one end, with the fewest opportunities and the most constraints for both men and women. Kuwait falls somewhere in the middle, and the UAE emirate of Dubai falls at the other end. A widow, I was unable to go to Saudi Arabia because a woman visitor must be accompanied by her husband or a male blood relative (I did not ask my son to accompany me).

33. The maritime empires of the Omani sultanate and the Qawasim tribal confederacy, the latter based in Sharjah and Ras Al Khaimah, traded and fought aggressively in the Gulf and beyond. Nineteenth-century battles of the Qawasim confederacy with British forces led to the trucial system.

34. British relationships with the Gulf polities were first directed by the provincial government of Bombay, then, after 1873, by the colonial government of India, and after 1947 (the independence of India and Pakistan) by the British Foreign Office.

35. A British Political Resident (stationed in southern Iran to 1946 and thereafter in Bahrain) had subordinate Political Agents posted in several Gulf locations who conducted all foreign relations for the Gulf states (Zahlan 1989, 16).

36. Oman too was affected by this system, as even in the late 1920s its mail for the west was routed through Bombay. The Omani sultanate ruled part of the Pakistani (Makran) coast until 1958 (Peyton 1983, 24, 54), although it lost its Zanzibari outpost through British arbitration in 1861 (Zahlan 1989, 108). Other links to India developed through the pearl-diving industry, which sent pearls to Hyderabad, India, for stringing and setting into jewelry.

37. The famous 1994 incident of two American men "getting lost" and missing the border to Iraq was really a liquor run; they were deliberately evading the

border guards to bring liquor back into Kuwait. This Kuwaiti gossip explains the low-key treatment of the incident by the United States.

38. Hindustani is Urdu if written in the Arabic script and Hindi if written in the Sanskrit script; the former draws on Arabic and Persian and the latter on Sanskrit vocabulary.

39. Anthony David, interview, August 9, 1995, Dubai.

40. Among older Arabs, some 10 to 20 percent had wives from India, Muslim women descended from Arabs settled in Hyderabad, Deccan (thus even South Asian domestic culture was familiar to many Gulf Arabs). In some areas the percentages of Indian wives were far higher.

41. Among those executed for murder in Sharjah and Dubai in 1997 were three Indians from the Bombay underworld found guilty of 1995 rival gang killings (*India-West* August 1, 1997, A20).

42. Current figures are hard to find. Dubai's Chamber of Commerce gives no breakdown by nationalities, although detailed figures reportedly exist but are not released. The categories used are only those of citizens and noncitizens, and then Asian, Other Arab, Gulf, and UAE.

43. The Palestinians in Kuwait made major contributions to the state's development, and felt close to it much as South Asians did in the UAE. They and their families back home lost heavily after the Gulf war (Abdo 1993, 119–20).

44. Mr. Syed Bilgrami, interview, August 1, 1995, Kuwait. Kuwait's ties with India were minimal until recently. Back in 1961, one old-timer told me, there were only 150 Indians in Kuwait, whereas in 1995 there were between 180,000 and 200,000 (Mr. and Mrs. Azimuddin, interview, August 2, 1995, Kuwait; Mr. D. P. Jain, second secretary of the Indian embassy, interview, August 3, 1995, Kuwait). Mr. Jain told me (telephone, August 6) that the Indian embassy has not tried to keep registers of its citizens working in Kuwait, and "certainly not by religion; India is a secular country."

45. Further damaging the image of the elite class is the fact that many new Indian and Pakistani business and professional people are upwardly mobile, from working-class backgrounds rather than from well-established families in South Asia. This bipolar class distribution contrasts with the more balanced range of backgrounds represented in the UAE; several different informants pointed this out explicitly in Kuwait.

46. Hasan Bozai, interview, August 20, 1995, Dubai.

47. Ali Ishrati, Junaid Adil, and Anees Ali, interview, August 31, 1995, Dubai.

Other symbols of (male) authority are motor vehicles. "In Abu Dhabi, no expatriate can own a four-wheel-drive vehicle—only locals can own them, or your company can own one for you. But in Dubai you can own one yourself," I was told.

48. According to an Indian Muslim friend in Dubai, there was an emphasis on Islamic life-cycle observances in Abu Dhabi (the UAE emirate closest in atmosphere to Kuwait), whereas there was an emphasis on birthday parties in Dubai.

49. The relatively liberal attitudes of Dubai encourage more South Asian expatriate families there than elsewhere. In Dubai, vital statistics show noncitizens (80 percent of the population) with double the number of births as citizens; they also have double the number of deaths, but only about half the numbers of marriages and 55 percent of the divorces per year (*Dubai Facts and Figures* 1994, 2).

50. He said that Filipinos bought the most encyclopedias—they knew about them, wanted them for their children's education, and wanted the English-language versions, which were cheaper in the UAE than in the Philippines. The encyclopedia salesman worked only on commission (no salary), lived in a group accommodation, and had a meal plan arrangement with a Tiffin carrier (Arun De Souza [aka Mr. Ganesh], interview, Dubai, August 16, 1995).

51. This means that Indian children are taught Hindi and Pakistani ones Urdu, so Muslim children from India cannot take advantage of Urdu schooling despite its prevalence in the Gulf.

52. In the UAE I was told many jokes about Keralites, such as the following: What do you call a successful Keralite? Pheno Menon. What do you call a dangerous Keralite? Dober Menon.

53. In a Sharjah case involving some one hundred Indian workers, it took almost a year to resolve disputes over outstanding wages and termination dues (*Khaleej Times*, August 21, 1995).

54. See the *Economist* (April 12, 1997) on rising birth and unemployment rates for GCC citizens.

55. Although the recovery from the Gulf war in Kuwait was remarkably rapid, Kuwaitization is moving slowly: 93 percent of all employed Kuwaitis work for the government (the constitution guarantees jobs to every citizen), yet Kuwaitis, about one-third of the country's population, are just one-sixth of the workforce (*Economist*, October 12, 1996, 50).

56. But the majority of the Indian community had returned to Kuwait by 1993, according to India's external affairs minister (*India-West*, February 19, 1993, 16).

57. Mr. Mohammed Hoshdar Khan and Mir Ibrahim Ali Khan, interview, August 7, 1995, Kuwait.

58. Mr. and Mrs. Hamad Nazmuddin, interview, August 3, 1995, Kuwait; members of the Hyderabad Muslim Welfare Association, interview, August 9, 1995, Kuwait.

59. Asians have become dominant in Kuwait, as they have been in the UAE and other Gulf states for some time (*Economist*, November 30, 1991, 41).

60. The monthly salary for a government employee had to be 450 KD or $1,500 and for a private employee 650 KD or $2,200 (*Dawn*, September 10, 1992). These were still the levels in 1995.

61. Saudi Arabia is enacting the most aggressive policies. From a fourth to a half of the population of Saudi Arabia are foreign workers, but more than half the indigenous population is under twenty years of age and some Saudi university graduates are unemployed. Needing jobs for the Saudi young people (*Economist*, September 20, 1997, 52), the government is decreasing the number of expatriate workers. In 1995, it de-recognized Indian and Pakistani pharmacy degrees, leading to cancellation of licenses of those practicing in the country (*Kuwait Times*, August 10, 1995), and in 1996 it banned non-Muslims and non-Christians, leading to a decline in workers from India (the ban was being lifted at the end of 1997 [*India-West*, November 7, 1997, A11]). In 1997, the Saudi government launched a drive to deport illegals, many of them Indians and Pakistanis who overstayed after pilgrimages and hoped to get work (*Pakistan Link*, November 7, 1997). It also discourages expatriates from bringing their families by closing schools. Following temporary closures of South Asian and other foreign embassy–run schools in 1995 for alleged failures to comply with various laws and traditions (such as segregation of the sexes), a closing that reportedly affected some ten thousand Indian children, the Saudi government closed all private schools being run by the foreign communities in 1997, leaving only the respective embassy schools in Jidda for the children of foreigners (*Pakistan Link*, May 26, 1995, 19 and June 27, 1997, 8).

62. Three-year visa fees were raised from 50 or 60 dirham to 300, and medical checkup fees from 15 dirham to 200. If free housing is part of an expatriate's payment, he must earn 4000 dirhams ($1,089) to bring his family (*Pakistan Link*, September 16, 1994, 20; *India-West*, September 9, 1994).

63. If a no-objection certificate could be obtained from the previous sponsor, the process was shortened to only four to seven days (*Pakistan Link*, September 27, 1996).

64. There is talk of including domestic servants under the labor codes in the Gulf, but their situation is worsening. In earlier decades, educated maids from Sri Lanka or the Philippines might accompany their mistresses to school and do their homework for them, but young mothers in Kuwait and Dubai are now educated themselves. One avenue of upward mobility has been marriages with local Arab men, but in these two Gulf societies, the domestic realms are now less secure (Leonard 2001).

65. For Indians, see Sharieff (1994), Kurien (1993); for Sri Lankan women, see Eelens, Shampers, and Spechmann (1992, 35, 222–23).

66. Eelens, Shampers, and Spechmann (1992) had to broaden their definition of investment in order to find material gains, and they qualify their conclusions in other ways as well.

67. This means transporting the children out of the old city, escaping the residential segregation that has limited Muslim opportunities there despite the skills and aspirations the fathers have acquired in the Gulf (Anees Khan, Nasr School, interview, February 1996, Hyderabad, India).

68. The first quote is from Falk (1993, 50); the second, from Seikaly (1993, 8), is about Bahrain but is applicable to all the Gulf states. Falk speaks of the world as a homogenizing supermarket for those with means, a perspective distinct from that of a global civil society or global citizenship.

69. Some children are confused about their nationality, self-identifying as Kuwaitis or Dubaites on occasion. The better children's schools in the Gulf enroll students from all over the world, blurring national identities and enhancing consciousness of the immediate location.

70. When sent home for seven to nine months during the Gulf war, some South Asian children asked to be sent back to the war zone. They complained of unsanitary urban conditions, crowded and equipment-deficient schools, and the unavailability or unreliability of such things as electricity, water, air conditioning, and telephones. They missed the kinds of fast food they had gotten in the Gulf and the many luxurious malls and stores. Not only did the relatives in the homelands, in constant contact with the evacuees, hear these complaints, but other relatives in the transnational kinship networks now common for this class and South Asians throughout the Gulf heard them. The families also

experienced Indian and Pakistani political and communal conflicts (primarily Hindu–Muslim, in India, and Punjabi–Pathan–Sindhi–Muhajir in Pakistan). In Hyderabad, India, Hindu–Muslim riots in the fall of 1990 terrified refugees from the Gulf, some of whom took shelter with relatives during citywide curfews, standing guard all night with guns at the ready.

71. Arsalan Mirza, Junaid Adil, and Ali Ishrati, interview, August 21, 1995, Dubai; Maqsood Ali, interview, August 24, 1995, Dubai; Elizabeth Ellis, interview, August 26, 1995, Dubai.

72. Vipin Singh, interview, August 23, 1995, Dubai.

73. This is contrary to Alejandro Portes's observations about international migration patterns (1995, 20).

74. See Schiller, Basch, and Blanc-Szanton (1995) for an attempt to establish this new and somewhat ideal type, the transmigrant.

References

Abdo, Nabla. 1993. "New World Order: Old Arab World Problems." In *Global Visions: Beyond the New World Order*, ed. Jeremy Brecher, John Brown Childs, and Jill Cutler. Boston: South End Press. 113–26.

Ahmed, Akbar S. 1984. "Dubai Chalo," *Asian Affairs* 15: 161–76.

Appadurai, Arjun. 1996. *Modernity at Large: Cultural Dimensions of Globalization*. Minneapolis: University of Minnesota Press.

Basch, Linda, Nina Glick Schiller, and Cristina Szanton Blanc. 1994. *Nations Unbound: Transnational Projects, Postcolonial Predicaments, and Deterritorialized Nation-States*. Amsterdam: Overseas Publishers Association.

Bonner, Raymond. 1992. "A Woman's Place." *New Yorker* (November 16): 56–66.

Coronil, Fernando. 1997. *The Magical State: Nature, Money, and Modernity in Venezuela*. Chicago: University of Chicago Press.

Dawn. 1992–93. Karachi, Pakistan.

Dickey, Christopher. 1990. *Expats: Travels in Arabia, from Tripoli to Teheran*. New York: Atlantic Monthly.

Dubai Facts and Figures. 1994. Dubai: Dubai Chamber of Commerce and Industry.

Economist. 1991–98. London.

Eelens, F., T. Shampers, and J. D. Spechmann. 1992. *Labor Migration to the Middle East: From Sri Lanka to the Gulf*. New York: Kegan Paul.

Falk, Richard. 1993. "The Making of Global Citizenship." In *Global Visions: Beyond the New World Order*, ed. Jeremy Brecher, John Brown Childs, and Jill Cutler. Boston: South End Press. 39–50.

Gardezi, Hassan N. 1991. "Asian Workers in the Gulf States of the Middle East." *Journal of Contemporary Asia* 21(2): 179–94.

———. 1997. "Making of the Neo-Colonial State in South Asia: The Pakistan Experience." *Comparative Studies of South Asia, Africa, and the Middle East* 17(2): 108–17.

Goodwin, Jan. 1995. *Price of Honor: Muslim Women Lift the Veil of Silence on the Islamic World*. New York: Penguin.

Harvey, David. 1990. "Between Space and Time: Reflections on the Geographical Imagination." *Annals of the Association of American Geographers* 80(3): 418–34.

Henderson, Jeffrey, and Manuel Castells. 1987. "Introduction". In *Global Restructuring and Territorial Development*. London: Sage. 1–17.

Human Development Report. 1995. New York: United Nations, Oxford University Press.

———. 1997. New York: United Nations, Oxford University Press.

India Today. 1991–98. Delhi, India.

India-West. 1991–98. Fremont, California.

Khajeej Times. 1995. Dubai, UAE.

Khalidi, Omar. 1997. "The Hadhrami Role in the Politics and Society of Colonial India, 1750s–1950s." In *Hadrami Traders, Scholars and Statesmen in the Indian Ocean, 1750s to 1960*, ed. Ulrike Freitag and William Clarence-Smith. Leiden: E. J. Brill. 67–81.

Kurien, Prema Ann. 1993. "Ethnicity, Migration and Social Change: A Study of Three Emigrant Communities in Kerala, India." Ph.D. dissertation, sociology, Brown University.

Kuwait Pocket Guide '95. 1995. Kuwait: Multimedia Publishing and Distribution.

Kuwait Times. 1995. Kuwait.

Leonard, Karen. 2001. "South Asian Women in the Gulf: Families and Futures Reconfigured." In *Marking Times and Territories: Genders in the Globalization of South and Southeast Asia*, ed. Esha De and Sonita Sarker. Durham, N.C.: Duke University Press. 213–31.

Lewis, Martin W., and Karen E. Wigen. 1997. *The Myth of Continents: A Critique of Metageography*. Berkeley: University of California Press.

Mowli, V. Chandra. 1992. *Bridging the "Gulf": India's Manpower Migrations to West Asia*. New Delhi: Sterling Publishers.

The 1997 World Fact Book. 1997. Washington, D.C.: U.S. Government, Central Intelligence Agency (http://www.odci.gov/cia/publications/factbook/index.html).

Osborne, Christine. 1977. *The Gulf States and Oman*. London: Croom Helm.

Overbeek, Henk. 1995. "Towards a New International Migration Regime: Globalization, Migration and the Internationalization of the State." In *Migration and European Integration: the Dynamics of Inclusion and Exclusion*, ed. Robert Miles and Dietrich Thranhardt. London: Fairleigh Dickinson University Press. 15–36.

Owen, Roger. 1993. "The Practice of Electoral Democracy in the Arab East and North Africa: Some Lessons from Nearly a Century's Experience." In *Rules and Rights in the Middle East: Democracy and Society*, ed. Ellis Goldberg, Resat Kasaba, and Joel Migdal. Seattle: University of Washington Press. 17–40.

Pakistan Link. 1991–98. Los Angeles, California.

Peyton, W. D. 1983. *Old Oman*. London: Stacey International.

Portes, Alejandro, ed. 1995. *The Economic Sociology of Immigration: Essays on Networks, Ethnicity, and Entrepreneurship*. New York: Russell Sage Foundation.

Ranger, Terence. 1994. "Studying Repatriation as Part of African Social History." In *When Refugees Go Home*, ed. Tim Allen and Hubert Morsink. Trenton, N.J.: Africa World Press. 279–95.

Rouse, Roger. 1992. "Making Sense of Settlement: Class Transformation, Cultural Struggle, and Transnationalism among Mexican Migrants in the United States." In *Towards a Transnational Perspective on Migration: Race, Class, Ethnicity, and Nationalism Reconsidered*, ed. Nina Glick Schiller, Linda Basch, and Cristina Blanc-Szanton. New York: Annals of the New York Academy of Sciences, vol. 645. 25–52.

Sassen, Saskia. 1993. "Economic Globalization: A New Geography, Composition, and Institutional Framework." In *Global Visions: Beyond the New World Order*, ed. Jeremy Brecher, John Brown Childs, and Jill Cutler. Boston: South End Press. 61–66.

Sayigah, Yusif A. 1972. "Problems and Prospects of Development in the Arabian Peninsula." In *The Arabian Peninsula: Society and Politics*, ed. Derek Hopwood, Totowa, N.J.: Rowman and Littlefield. 286–309.

Schiller, Nina Glick, Linda Basch, and Cristina Blanc-Szanton. 1992. *Towards a Transnational Perspective on Migration: Race, Class, Ethnicity, and Nationalism*

Reconsidered. New York: Annals of the New York Academy of Sciences, vol. 645.

———. 1995. "From Immigrant to Transmigrant. Theorizing Transnational Migration." *Anthropological Quarterly* 68(1): 48–63.

Seikaly, May. 1993. "Women and Social Change in Bahrain: A Historical Perspective." Working paper no. 21, G. E. von Grunebaum Center for Near Eastern Studies, UCLA.

Sharieff, Afzal. 1994. "Socio-Economic Transformation of the Kuwaiti Repatriates—a Case Study of Hyderabad." Ph.D. dissertation, geography, Osmania University, Hyderabad.

Shryock, Andrew. 1997. *Nationalism and the Genealogical Imagination.* Berkeley: University of California Press.

Silbey, Susan. 1997. "Let Them Eat Cake: Globalization, Postmodern Colonialism, and the Possibilities of Justice." *Law and Society Review* 31: 207–35.

Singh, Jacquelin. 1993. *The Case of the Shady Sheikh and Other Stories.* New Delhi: Penguin.

Stoakes, Frank. 1972. "Social and Political Change in the Third World: Some Peculiarities of Oil-Producing Principalities of the Persian Gulf." In *The Arabian Peninsula: Society and Politics*, ed. Derek Hopwood. Totowa, N.J.: Rowman and Littlefield. 189–215.

Suleri, Sara. 1992. "Woman Skin Deep: Feminism and the Postcolonial Condition." *Critical Inquiry* 18 (summer): 756–69.

Watts, Michael J. 1991. "Mapping Meaning, Denoting Difference, Imagining Identity: Dialectical Images and Postmodern Geographies." *Geografiska Annaler* 73 B: 7–16.

Wiltshire, Rosina. 1992. "Implications of Transnational Migration for Nationalism: The Caribbean Example." In *Towards a Transnational Perspective on Migration: Race, Class, Ethnicity, and Nationalism Reconsidered*, ed. Nina Glick Schiller, Linda Basch, and Cristina Blanc-Szanton. New York: Annals of the New York Academy of Sciences, vol. 645. 175–88.

The World Fact Book 1994. 1995. Washington, D.C.: U.S. Government, Central Intelligence Agency.

Yamanaka, Keiko. 1993. "New Immigration Policy and Unskilled Foreign Workers in Japan." *Pacific Affairs* 66(1): 72–90.

———. 1997a. "Return Migration of Japanese Brazilian Women: Household Strategies and Search for the 'Homeland.'" In *Beyond Boundaries: Selected Papers* on *Refugees and Immigrants*, vol. 5, ed. Ruth Krulfeld and Diane Baxter. Arlington, Va.: American Anthropological Association. 11–34.

———. 1997b. Review of Michael Weiner, *Race and Migration in Imperial Japan*. *Asian and Pacific Migration Journal* 6: 260–61.

Zahlan, Rosemarie Said. 1989. *The Making of the Modern Gulf States: Kuwait, Bahrain, Qatar, the United Arab Emirates, and Oman*. London: Unwin Hyman.

CHAPTER 6

Illegality, Borderlands, and the Space of Nonexistence

Susan Bibler Coutin

At a time when national boundaries seem increasingly insignificant and the rationales for ethnic, gender, and other divisions have come under attack, scholars have begun to examine "borderlands" as sites that transcend boundaries and that may generate new cultural forms. Borderlands have been celebrated for their bricolage, innovation, and interstitiality. Gupta and Ferguson (1997, 48) note that borderlands are not "a fixed topographical site between two other fixed locales (nations, societies, cultures) but an interstitial zone of deterritorialization and hybridization." Borderlands are spaces that defy categories and paradigms, that "don't fit," and that therefore reveal the criteria that determine fittedness, spaces whose very existence is simultaneously denied and demanded by the socially powerful. Borderlands are targets of repression and zones of militarization, as can be seen by the recent deployment of weaponry and guardsmen along the U.S.–Mexico border. Borderlands are marginalized yet strategic, inviolate yet continually violated, forgotten yet significant. Sometimes economically "backward" and "peripheral," borderlands are nonetheless defended by military might when infringed upon. Because they defy categorization, borderlands have been seen as sites of resistance, as sources of alternatives to the status quo, as places where a modus vivendi that redefines the social order can be devised (Rosaldo 1989). Borderlands are therefore productive, in multiple senses. Sites of key industries (such as *maquiladoras*), and of syncretic cultural forms, borderlands

also demarcate that which is peripheral. The productivity of borderlands is clear in Gloria Anzaldúa's (1987, 22) description of *mestizaje*:

> What I want is accounting with all three [of my] cultures—white, Mexi-
> can, Indian. I want the freedom to carve and chisel my own face, to staunch
> the bleeding with ashes, to fashion my own gods out of my entrails. And
> if going home is denied me then I will have to stand and claim my space,
> making a new culture—*una cultura mestiza*—with my own lumber, my
> own bricks and mortar and my own feminist architecture.

In contrast to Anzaldúa's expression of proud determination, this
essay will examine a borderland that I cannot celebrate: the space of
nonexistence. Unauthorized immigrants from El Salvador have told me
of this space. An activist involved in Salvadoran immigrants' struggle for
legal status in the United States said: "We need to be here legally or
it's like we're not here." Another activist who had worked clandestinely
with a Salvadoran political organization recalled his days as an undocumented immigrant: "Everything we did was illegal! We had no recognition from the United States government, we had no recognition from
the Salvadoran government! We didn't exist!" A Salvadoran community
college student said that getting a work permit brought her out of an
underground to the surface. She explained: "[Without a work permit],
you don't exist. Well, they know you are there, but they ignore you.
They don't see you as like you exist. And this is the people who raise
children, and you know, whenever they come, 'Well, they're illegals.'" I
characterize this space of nonexistence as a borderland because it divides
the legal and the illegal, the legitimate and the illegitimate, the overt and
the clandestine. Legality is spatialized in that those who do not exist
legally are imagined to be "outside," in an "underground," or "not there"
(cf. Coombe 1997). Like other borderlands, the space of nonexistence
defies categorization in that its boundaries and membership are continually being negotiated (Coutin 2000). This space excludes people, limits
rights, restricts services, and erases personhood. The space of nonexistence is largely a space of subjugation.

This essay presents an ethnography of the space of nonexistence. This space is both imagined and real. Like its residents, it both is and is not "there." This space is imagined in that, like other social spaces, it is culturally constructed and demarcated (Anderson 1991; Caldeira 1996; Clifford 1997; Gupta and Ferguson 1997; Malkki 1992; Shapiro 1988; Sorkin 1992). Moreover, as the undocumented *do* exist, at least in a physical sense, references to nonexistence are merely descriptive. At the same time, this space is real in that the practices that make people not exist have material effects. The undocumented are denied legal rights, social services, and full personhood, and can be detained and deported if apprehended by immigration authorities. The space of illegality is nevertheless a necessary space, in that defining that which is illegal simultaneously indicates what is legal, determining who is to be excluded also reveals the criteria for inclusion, and borders could not exist unless there was something to divide (Coutin 2000; Fitzpatrick 1992, 1993; Holston 1991). But perhaps it is too binary to speak only of existence and nonexistence. In fact, there are multiple nonexistences and there are gradations of existence. Individuals do not only enter a space of nonexistence when they become undocumented; they also cease to exist when they are involved in clandestine activities, when they are abducted and secretly assassinated by death squads, and when they hide in order to prevent being captured and tortured. It would not be inaccurate to view refugees' entire sojourn in the United States as an attempt to escape persecution by making themselves not exist in their homelands. And yet, clearly, regardless of their legal status, migrants *do* exist in that they live, work, go to school, play, have parties, ride buses, and so forth. It might be most accurate to say that, like characters who experience a temporal rift in a *Star Trek* episode, they come in and out of existence, and exist simultaneously in multiple ways, depending on the frame of reality being used.

I begin my ethnography of nonexistence by describing the dimensions and characteristics of the space occupied by undocumented immigrants in the United States. I next discuss the multiplicity of nonexistences by detailing the forms of clandestinity created in response to death-squad activity and U.S. immigration practices. Following this discussion, I examine the *partiality* of nonexistence—the various senses in which the undocumented *do* exist and in which legal status is irrelevant. I conclude by noting some of the ways that immigrants can turn nonexistence to their advantage and thus subvert the power of immigration law. This ethnography is about more than immigration. It is also about human rights, subjugation, and the violence of law.

The Space of Nonexistence

August 20, 1997. I am sitting in the office of a paralegal who is interviewing a client to assess her legalization possibilities. The paralegal marks an 800 number and enters the woman's Alien Number. Over the speakerphone we hear a recording confirm the woman's name. The paralegal pushes more buttons, and the recording summarizes the history of the woman's case: "May 19, 1987. Voluntary departure. April 30, 1990. Board of Immigration Appeals finished considering the case. There are no current appointments to appear in Immigration court. There is no clock running." No clock running. No clock running . . .

The space of nonexistence occupied by the undocumented has its own characteristics, temporalities, and dimensions. Individuals enter this space when they come to the United States without authorization from the U.S. government, or when they remain in the United States after their authorization has expired. Although they are physically present within U.S. territory, such individuals are neither temporarily nor permanently party to the social contract embodied in U.S. law and are therefore officially outside of the social body. Lacking a juridical existence, even the physical presence of the undocumented becomes suspect (Coutin 1993). The undocumented have been referred to as "'shadow' people who slip in and out of sight" (Hull 1985, 14) and who live in an "underground" (Harwood 1986) or a "netherworld" (Hull 1985, 14). Official U.S. policy is to detain and eventually deport these troubling, ambiguous, shadowy people (see Chavez 1991, 1992), and thus to remove even the trace of their physical presence. Even if they are not deported, the undocumented are set apart from the juridically authorized by laws that dispense rights and services on the basis of legal identity. The un-documented therefore exist in a nondomain, a space of illegality (cf. Sanchez 1997). Often conflated with criminals (Malkki 1992), the undoc-umented are "outside the law" (Hull 1985; Fuchs 1985)—even though it is law itself that denies their existence by distinguishing between citizens and aliens. To identify the physical and social qualities of this space of nonexistence, I propose to enter this space, assuming for the moment that people can be confined to its reality.

In the space of nonexistence, physical presence is unregistered. It is impossible to "reside" in any kind of documented way. Recent arrivals often live with relatives, friends, or coworkers, with as many as ten or more individuals in a one-bedroom apartment. Their names do not appear on utility accounts, leases, or rent receipts. Women who work as live-in domestics reside in homes that are not their own (Maher 1997). These women's employers—many of whom are violating tax and labor codes (Hondagneu-Sotelo 2001)—are not eager to officially acknowledge their employees' presence (Hagan 1994). Because even the unauthorized are not fully confined to the space of nonexistence, some record of their presence is often generated. Nonetheless, to the degree that their residence is unregistered, the undocumented are not officially "here." If they later attempt to prove that they have been continuously present in the United States since a certain date, which is a prerequisite for qualifying for the 1986 amnesty program, suspension of deporta-tion, or cancellation of removal, they find that unregistered presences are deemed absences. The residence of the undocumented is unofficial; it does not count, carries no weight, and cannot be demonstrated. Un-registered, undocumented, unrecorded, those who lack legal status are nowhere. They do not exist.[1]

Despite the fact that their presence is unregistered, the nonexis-tence of the undocumented is measured temporally. There are multiple temporalities in the space of nonexistence. Because accumulating years of continuous residence can help to qualify the undocumented for legal-ization, attorneys and immigration officials speak as though an invisible immigration timepiece is measuring the temporal presence of illegal aliens. For example, seven years of continuous presence are required to qualify for suspension of deportation. As a result, an undocumented immigrant who has only been in the United States for five years must manage to remain in this country for another two years so that the clock will strike seven. And yet, the space of nonexistence is also characterized by timelessness. As already noted, presences that are completely unregistered cannot count toward completing required periods of continuous residence for legalization purposes. Moreover, temporal presences that fall short of the requirements do not confer any equity on the undocumented. Additionally, the "clock" can be "stopped" on the accumulation of time, propelling the undocumented into a temporal void. According to the 1996 Illegal Immigration Reform and Immigrant Responsibility Act (IIRIRA), the issuance of a notice to appear in court stops the immigration timepiece, such that, for example, an immigrant who has only been in the United States for five years when summoned to court can never accumulate more time, no matter how long the person remains in the United States. IIRIRA also created a new temporality: "illegal time." Individuals who are in the United States without authorization after April 1, 1997, accumulate illegal time. If these individuals accumulate 180 days of illegal time and then leave the United States, they are barred from reentering for a period of three years. A full year of illegal time activates a ten-year bar on reentry.[2] Like a financial account, a surfeit of illegal time must be balanced by a period of nonresidency.

Work cannot occur in the space of nonexistence. The right to work—a key marker of presence, personhood, and citizenship (Coutin 2000; Engel and Munger 1996; Thomas 1985)—is denied to the undocumented.[3] Without work authorization, the undocumented cannot officially work. Some try to define their labor as something other than work. For example, the undocumented can provide gardening and other services as independent contracters, or can be self-employed street vendors, participating in the informal economy. Domestic workers are often paid in cash, leaving no record of their supposed employment. When asked to recount their work history for the past five years, as is required on many immigration forms, such unofficial workers hesitate, saying,

"I was only paid in cash." As it is unreported, unregistered, and untaxed, prohibited work may not actually have occurred. Other immigrants work under false pretenses, with fake IDs and invented Social Security numbers. To work, immigrants have to pretend to exist.

Social ties are not recognized in the space of nonexistence. The unauthorized have no "right" to be with their families. Lacking legal status themselves, the undocumented cannot petition for the legalization of their parents or other relatives. Nor do they have the right to leave and reenter the United States so that they can visit relatives abroad. Their family ties are severed. The undocumented can be arbitrarily separated from their relatives. For example, suppose that a man who is a legal permanent resident marries a woman who is undocumented, and they have two children, who are U.S. citizens by birth. The man can petition for legal status for his wife, but until a visa is available, she remains undocumented and can be deported from her spouse and children. The controversy over section 245(i) of immigration law exposes the legal aconsanguinity of the undocumented. Section 245(i) permitted undocumented immigrants to adjust their status in the United States instead of having to return to their countries of origin. When IIRIRA created "illegal time," with its consequent bars on reentry, 245(i) assumed new significance. Without the extension of this program, which was scheduled to expire in September 1997, those who accumulated illegal time by remaining in the United States while waiting for family visa petitions to become current would be unable to reenter the United States after leaving to claim their visas. Families had to choose between splitting up so that they could preserve rights to green cards, or foregoing the possibility of legalization. The unauthorized discovered that they could not reverse the laws of descent such that having U.S. citizen children conferred legal rights on undocumented parents. In the space of nonexistence, they could not be full social persons.

The space of nonexistence is a space of illegality. Surviving requires engaging in illicit practices. To pretend to exist, the undocumented purchase false ID cards. Those whose income is not reported do not pay their income taxes. The undocumented perform unauthorized work. They labor in sweatshops, fields, homes, and elsewhere, often in conditions that violate federal and state labor codes. Denied a driver's license (in California, at least), they drive without authorization. Without a driver's license, they cannot obtain car insurance as required by law. Lacking travel documents, their entries and exits are clandestine. Instead of petitioning for relatives, in some cases they smuggle them into the country. When they occur "outside the law" in the space of nonexistence, such commonplace actions as working, traveling, and driving become illicit.

Mobility is restricted in the space of nonexistence. Subjected to detention and deportation if apprehended, the undocumented limit their travel, staying home, avoiding areas where immigration officials conduct raids, staying away from checkpoints, and only moving about as necessary. One Guatemalan migrant characterized this situation as "democracy with a stick." He explained: "You are free to move about to whatever place within the United States as long as you have the required papers. A visa or green card is required to leave the Los Angeles area.[4] If you are illegal, you don't have freedom of movement. You go from your workplace to your house and as much as possible you avoid contact with the authorities." A Salvadoran immigrant expressed a similar sense of confinement, noting that he and his wife could not take their daughter to Sea World until his wife received a new work permit. Without the work permit, the family would not be able to pass through the San Clemente checkpoint on their way between their home in Los Angeles and Sea World in San Diego. Ironically, or perhaps logically, it is the unauthorized movement of the undocumented that renders them immobile. Sometimes defined by their mobility as "boat people," "feet people," or a "flood" (see Coutin 1993), when they enter the space of nonexistence, the undocumented are confined to social and territorial nonlocations. Immobility, which is also a sign of death, prevents full social personhood. Because they are denied public assistance, financial aid, college admission, and work authorization, the undocumented find that their social mobility is as limited as their physical mobility (Jenkins 1978; Portes 1978).

Paradoxically, the space of nonexistence is a hidden dimension of the space of existence, sometimes making it difficult to determine the location of particular individuals. The space of nonexistence is often referred to as "another place," "elsewhere," distant from the reality inhabited by those who are legal. For example, a *Los Angeles Times* article about the legalization quest of a Salvadoran man who had lived in the United States for years was titled "Hunting a Way In" (McDonnell 1997). Where are those who, like animals, "hunt" a way "in"? Where is the space of nonexistence? Terms such as *underground* and *netherworld* suggest that this is a place frequented by shady characters, perhaps the sort of place that mobsters hung out in during the 1930s, or where drug dealers do business. Where is this forbidden place? Consider for a moment the actual places where the undocumented can be found. The mall. Apartment buildings. Restaurants. Buses. Factories. Businesses. Grocery stores. Homes. These places only become "an underground" when the undocumented are present, and they are only forbidden to the undocumented. In short, the forbidden space occupied by the undocumented is the United States itself. The physical dimensions of the space of nonexistence coincide with the territorial boundaries of the United States. Because their bases for social membership are negated—blood ties, labor, movement, humanity—the undocumented are forbidden to be in the United States. They are therefore situated "outside" of U.S. territory, in a realm of nonexistence.

There are multiple senses in which migrants can be said to not exist. In the case of Salvadorans, among whom I have been doing research since the mid-1980s, becoming an unauthorized immigrant is often a continuation rather than an initiation of nonexistence.

Disappearing

September 1996. A former client of the Central American Resource Center in Los Angeles has given me permission to look through her case file. Browsing through a bulging and frayed folder, I discover a transcript of her deportation hearing. According to the transcript, she fled El Salvador after ten girls from her school were disappeared. During the hearing, the judge asked her to define "disappeared." She answered that this meant being captured, kidnapped, and killed. Incredibly, the judge then suggested that the missing girls may simply have dropped out of school. Multiple realities, multiple truths. And multiple nonexistences.

Central Americans' narratives about civil war, political persecution, and immigration to the United States reveal multiple sorts of nonexistence. To these immigrants, the legal nonexistence conferred by entering the United States without authorization is merely the latest in a series of violent erasures of personhood. Death-squad activity in El Salvador and Guatemala not only killed people, it annihilated them, ripping them from their homes, tearing them limb from limb, destroying houses and property, massacring communities, and discarding limbs and bodies in trash dumps or in the street. Those who feared that they would be subjected to such violence sought to prevent it by disappearing before authorities could destroy them. Potential death-squad targets cut off their social ties, avoided family and friends, stopped working, gave up their studies, abandoned their homes, moved from place to place, slept in the fields instead of houses, went into hiding, and sometimes left the country. Emigrating to the United States can therefore be understood as an attempt to make oneself *not* exist in one's country of origin. I encountered people who had had these experiences during the 1980s when I did research about congregations that had declared themselves "sanctuaries" for Salvadoran and Guatemalan refugees, and in the 1990s, when I conducted a study of Salvadoran immigrants' efforts to negotiate their legal status in the United States. Both of these projects entailed interviewing Salvadoran and Guatemalan immigrants, participating in the preparation of asylum and other immigration cases, and observing deportation hearings during which Central Americans recounted their experiences of persecution. During interviews—less so during formal immigration proceedings—Central Americans compared the INS to death squads, deportation to exile, and U.S. immigration policy to political repression. My analysis of the multiplicity of nonexistence draws on their analysis.

Central Americans who were not yet affected by civil conflict and who had not yet emigrated existed legally, socially, and physically in their countries of origin. María Bonilla, a Salvadoran woman who had been targeted by the military because of a nephew's involvement with the guerrillas, recalled her life in El Salvador: "Why did I have to leave my mother and my father and everything that I had and come to this country? There we had a business. And we had a house. We were building onto the house. And we were poor, but we had beds for all of us." Note that her description of her earlier life mentions family, a home, a business, plans for the future, and residential belonging—the "beds" for every family member.[5] These are precisely the elements of existence that are denied to migrants who are in the space of nonexistence. Similarly, a former Salvadoran political prisoner told me of the indignation he felt when an asylum official suggested that he had come to the United States for economic reasons. He said that he told the official, "Do you know what I was doing in El Salvador? I was going to school. I worked. I had my own office. I had three secretaries. I dressed in a suit. And my wife, she was a doctor, she was very respected." As a professional, this man may have been better off than many migrants, but his description of the completeness of his life—family, friends, studies, a home, a profession, respect—is typical. In retrospect, the normalcy of their former lives seems a sharp contrast to their current illicitness. Ángela Reyes, who was detained in Texas shortly after entering the United States, described her reaction to being imprisoned: "This was so different from my earlier experience. In El Salvador, I'd been studying, I'd been going to school, I was living with my family. It was terrible." Before civil war jeopardized their futures, migrants were forming families, pursuing careers, participating in social networks. They existed.

The outbreak of armed conflict in El Salvador at the end of the 1970s created new forms of nonexistence. Repression was nothing new to El Salvador, where some twenty-five thousand people were killed in 1932 following a peasant uprising (Byrne 1996). Prolonged civil war, however, created a polarization that left no room for neutrality. As a former political prisoner explained, "For the [Salvadoran] government, political struggle is stronger [than armed struggle] . . . And this is the reason for the huge repression and the huge massacres, because they [the authorities] abducted people. Upon suspecting someone, they captured him and killed his family." The Salvadoran civil war lasted until 1992 and produced eighty thousand dead and seven thousand disappeared (Montgomery 1995; Stephen 1995). Although I do not have access to death-squad members' descriptions of these assassinations, I have heard hundreds of accounts of their practices from victims and observers. Typically, suspects were abducted in their homes, workplaces, or the street by numerous heavily armed men wearing civilian clothing and driving vehicles that witnesses identified as being of government issue. Homes were ransacked in search of arms, women were raped, and residents were lined up and massacred. Victims who were abducted were often interrogated under torture, killed, dismembered, and discarded. A survivor described her experience:

> They abducted my father and me . . . [and] four other men, including my cousin, other cousins, and an uncle of mine . . . They wanted to take us to an isolated place, where there was nothing . . . And they took us, but little by little they were letting people go, and I spoke to them, "My uncle is in the civil patrols." But they didn't listen. But thus we walked and walked. By then it was about midnight, maybe, when they released my two cousins, they released my uncle, and they only had my cousin, my father, and me. They took us because to them I was the leader of the guerrillas. About which they were very mistaken. But I begged to God and said, "My God! It isn't possible, they are going to kill us unjustly! But I'm going to die together with my father."

> [After walking about three kilometers, the commander] said, "We are going to let you go, but you're going to run!" But my cousin wasn't released. They only released my father and me . . . And yes, they got into a group and told us, "Go! Run! Go away! Run!" And I put my father in front, I covered my father with my back. "Papá!" I said to him, "Papaíto, run, Papaíto! Run, Papá! Run!" I could feel the bullets! I could feel the

bullets! But I wanted to cover myself. If they fell on me, let them fall, but not on my father. But no, they didn't shoot at us, and we arrived home.

But my cousin—there, when they released us in the middle of the night, there, in that place where they released us, there they just took my cousin to a coffee field and my cousin, they killed my cousin there, that same night. They broke his arms behind him, alive. Because there was a family who heard the cries. The family lived on that ranch, and . . . they heard my cousin cry like a child. Crying, calling for my uncle, my aunt, like a child! They broke his arms behind him, they put out his eyes, they broke his fingers, finger by finger. Because when they found him, that's how they found him. They skinned his head . . . The last thing that they did was slit his throat. That was the end. Afterwards they cut out his tongue. They tortured him completely.

From such accounts it is possible to reconstruct the mentality of the torturers. To the authorities, the "subversive" or "guerrilla" was someone who had betrayed the social order, someone who was dirty, dangerous, an animal—someone who deserved to be tortured, stamped out of existence, the body discarded as an example to others, someone who had no rights. Death-squad members seemingly did not differentiate between guerrillas, guerrilla supporters, and the uninvolved. Instead, the entire population was suspect (Green 1994; Stephen 1995). Torturers twisted, pulled, stamped, kicked, and cut suspected guerrillas, exposing their interiors. Like trash, victims were then thrown away. But as they were destroyed, alleged subversives were interrogated, a process that simultaneously defined and erased victims. Victims were defined in that they were named as subversives, guerrillas, the unwanted, illegals (cf. Coutin and Hirsch 1998). They were erased in that they were defaced, killed, or forced into exile. As they were defined and erased, pulled in and out of existence, victims were torn apart. The space of nonexistence is a space of violence.

Central Americans who feared that persecution was imminent placed themselves in a space of nonexistence, saving authorities the trouble. Signs of having been targeted by death squads included anonymous threatening phone calls, warning letters left under one's door, unidentified individuals asking one's whereabouts, knocks on the door in the middle of the night, shots fired into one's house, threatening visits by armed men, and the abduction of relatives or colleagues. Confronted with such signs, potential victims often went into hiding, ceasing to work, abandoning their studies, moving from place to place, distancing themselves from family and friends. They hid their existence, trying to be "not there." Sonya Hernández, a Salvadoran woman whose family had experienced political difficulties when the government business where she worked became unionized, recalled fleeing her hometown when she was nineteen: "We had to leave and move to the city. We can't go back to our *canton*, to where we're from, because there, they know us, so we're afraid. In the city, we weren't so afraid, because no one knew who we were. But, we had to leave without anything. We left behind our money, our clothes, our land, everything." Fearing that they would fall victim to death squads, Sonya and her family became socially nonexistent. When two of Sonya's brothers were killed, the family dispersed even further, with her parents moving to the Guatemalan border and the rest of the family coming to the United States. The places where they were "known" became *forever* forbidden, as Sonya explained: "There, we have houses and we have lands, but it isn't safe for us. There, in the town that we're from, we're known, and the people who killed my brothers are still there and their hatred is deep. There's a lot of desire for vengeance. We can't go back there."

When Central Americans' experiences of persecution are taken into account, their stay in the United States can be understood as an effort to not exist in their homelands. The space of legal nonexistence occupied by unauthorized immigrants is therefore another dimension of a previously entered space of social nonexistence. Like the undocumented, individuals who go into hiding within their countries of origin cannot work, be with their families, have residences, move about freely, or fulfill their plans for the future. Like legal nonexistence, social nonexistence is a spatial and temporal void. It is an asocial space, the *monte* or the "wild" where people sleep in order to avoid being captured by death squads (see Anker 1992). Like undocumented immigrants, the socially nonexistent engage in clandestine, illicit practices. They assume false identities, hire smugglers, pay bribes, travel through mountains and deserts, and enter a land where they continue to not exist. Clandestinity, not migration, marks many Central Americans' entry into nonexistence.

Many Central Americans draw connections between being victims of political persecution and being unauthorized immigrants. For example, Rodolfo Nuñez, a Salvadoran student activist who narrowly escaped assassination, commented that in the United States,

> It seems like we are living through the same anxiety that we lived through there in El Salvador, right? That is, sometimes when they say, "Here comes Immigration." Exactly like when they said there, "Here comes the [National] Guard," see. Everyone looks for a way of surviving at that moment, at that instant. There, to save one's life, here to save one's life too, to not have to return to one's country.

Like Rodolfo Nuñez, Roberto and Alicia Méndez, Guatemalan migrants who had fled to the United States after Roberto was detained and tortured, saw connections between their need to exist legally in the United States and their fear of ceasing to exist physically in Guatemala. After a judge denied their asylum petition, Alicia told me, "The judge was making our tomb." Jorge Lima, a Salvadoran who had been active in opposition groups in both the United States and El Salvador, attributed such judicial decisions to the United States' lack of responsibility regarding the consequences of U.S. policies that destroyed lives in El Salvador. Jorge told me that the situation of Central American immigrants "is like when a woman has been raped and is pregnant, see? Then there's a reality! Understand? She has conceived, and however you try to exterminate that fact, it's a reality! You can't keep it a secret. You may not register it in your structures, as though it never existed. But yes, it did exist!" In this graphic image, El Salvador is a raped woman, the United States is the rapist, Central American immigrants are the illegitimate child, and U.S. immigration law is a means of denying the child's existence. Yet, though its existence is denied, unregistered, even exterminated, the child continues to reassert itself. Nonexistence cannot be sustained.

The Quotidian

November 5, 1997. I am in front of the Los Angeles Federal Building, where Central American activists have organized a weeklong fast and vigil in support of residency for Central American immigrants. Walking in a circle, the two hundred fasters and supporters chant, "Aquí estamos! Y no nos vamos" (Here we are! And we're not leaving). Suddenly, I am reminded of the Dr. Seuss story "Horton Hears a Who." In order to prevent the destruction of their world by those who doubted its existence, all of the Whos in Whoville had to shout "We are here! We are here!" The assertion "Aquí estamos" begins to seem more important than the defiant "Y no nos vamos." What does it mean to be here? How do you "rise to the surface," as the community college student put it? Why do people who are here have to prove that they're here in order to prevent the destruction of their worlds? And where are the nonexistent?

The undocumented are not, of course, confined to the space of nonexistence. Like the illegitimate child referred to by Jorge Lima, they are a reality. Although they are not legally present, the undocumented get jobs, rent apartments, buy property, go to school, get married, have children, join churches, found organizations, and develop friendships. On a day-to-day basis, their illegality may be irrelevant to most of their activities, only becoming an issue in certain contexts, such as when changing jobs, applying for college, or encountering an immigration official. The undocumented thus move in and out of existence. Much of the time they are undifferentiated from those around them, but suddenly, when legal reality is superimposed on daily life, they are once more in a space of nonexistence. The borders between existence and nonexistence nonetheless remain fuzzy and permeable.

Legal nonexistence does not prevent physical presence and social

participation because illegal immigration has long been officially prohibited but unofficially tolerated (Calavita 1992; Chavez 1992; Delgado
1993; Harwood 1985). Kitty Calavita (1994) attributes this contradiction to three underlying tensions within U.S. policy: (1) employers want
cheap, immigrant labor but native workers want immigration controls in
order to prevent wages from declining; (2) policies that are in the interests of the native labor force and that could prevent illegal immigration,
such as enforcing U.S. labor laws, are politically unpalatable; and (3) liberal democratic ideals conflict with the policing that would be required
to bar illegal immigration. As a result, the legal sanctions that do exist
can be easily flouted. Those who are deported can reenter the country,
false identity documents are readily available to those who need them,
employer sanctions are not fully enforced (Bean, Edmonston, and Passel
1990; Calavita 1990), and most INS enforcement efforts are directed
toward the U.S.–Mexico border, creating a de facto tolerance for those
who make it to the interior (Chavez 1992; Delgado 1993). Although they
are barred from working, obtaining a valid driver's license, or receiving
certain social services, the undocumented are not legally prohibited from
engaging in other sorts of transactions, such as renting or purchasing
homes. As a result, many who are officially illegal manage to live in the
United States for years. Immigration law does affect the undocumented
in profound, even life-threatening ways, but there are also many contexts
in which it is simply irrelevant.

Because the legally nonexistent do exist socially and physically,
records of their presences are generated. Attending classes produces
school records, seeking medical assistance produces medical records,
working can produce check stubs, and renting or purchasing a home
produces deeds, leases, rent receipts, and utility bills. As the undocumented foray out of the space of nonexistence, their presence becomes
"documented."

If it is powerful enough, the social existence of the undocumented
can confer legal status and thus pull them completely out of the space
of legal nonexistence. Some scholars have argued that there is an implicit contract between migrant workers and the states in which their

labor is employed (Bosniak 1991; Hammar 1994; Holston and Appadurai 1996). According to this implicit contract, when migrants contribute to a society through their labor, the society incurs certain obligations to them, such as the obligation to recognize them as full social and legal persons. Through various forms of social participation (going to school, having a family, obtaining an address, working), migrants "imitate citizens" and thus *act on* the rights that this implied contract promises. According to the notion of reliance interest in contract law as well as legal decisions regarding palimony (Singer 1988), even unwritten contracts are binding if they endure long enough. The principle that social citizenship and territorial presence confer legality has been recognized to some degree in U.S. immigration law as well. The rationale for creating an "amnesty" for immigrants who had been continuously and illegally present in the United States since January 1, 1982 (Hing 1986), was that individuals who were already de facto members of society ought to be allowed to regularize their stay. Suspension of deportation and cancellation of removal—two defenses available to aliens who are in deportation proceedings—also base residency on developing extensive social ties in the United States and on long periods of physical presence.[6] Those who manage to make legal nonexistence irrelevant for long periods of time can eventually make it permanently irrelevant.

For Central Americans who came to the United States fearing that they would cease to exist physically in their countries of origin, extensive social existence and lengthy physical presence have become the strongest rationale for legalization. In the early 1980s, Salvadorans and Guatamalans who were trying to hide their existence in their countries of origin were under little pressure to try to legalize their stays in the United States. Before the passage of the 1986 Immigration Reform and Control Act (IRCA), U.S. immigration law imposed fewer hardships on the undocumented, many viewed their stay in the United States as temporary, and political asylum, the only means of legalization for which most were eligible, was rarely granted to Salvadorans and Guatemalans.[7] Most Central Americans applied for asylum only as a last resort, to prevent deportation if they were apprehended by INS officials.[8] As their stay in the United States lengthened and civil war in El Salvador became prolonged, these immigrants' desire to remain in the United States grew. At the same time, Central American activists realized that if the United States granted refugee status to Salvadorans and Guatemalans, it would in essence be recognizing the horrific human-rights record of the Salvadoran and Guatemalan governments, which would make it difficult for the United States to sustain its Cold War policy of aiding these governments in their fight against supposed "communist insurgents." Accordingly, Central American activists launched a solidarity movement that in 1990 resulted in legislation granting Temporary Protected Status (TPS) to Salvadorans and a court settlement that allowed Salvadorans and Guatemalans to reapply for political asylum (see Coutin 2000; 1998).[9] By the mid-1990s, Salvadorans' Temporary Protected Status had expired, and peace accords in both El Salvador and Guatemala made asylum grants unlikely for most migrants. A new campaign for legalization again resulted in legislative relief. In November 1997, the U.S. Congress passed the Nicaraguan Adjustment and Central American Relief Act (NACARA), permitting Salvadorans and Guatemalans to apply for residency on the basis of their lengthy stay in the United States, their good moral character, and the extreme hardship that they would suffer if deported.[10] Physical presence and extensive social ties in the United States have proven stronger rationales for legalization than was the need to escape physical destruction.

Although the space of nonexistence is largely a space of subjugation that most would like to leave, there are sometimes advantages to not existing, as those who do not exist have discovered.

The Art of Not Existing

January 1996. I am sitting among approximately fifty Central Americans who have gathered at the offices of a community organization in Los Angeles to hear a staff member explain U.S. immigration law. A man sitting behind me asks whether the fact that he left the United States to visit relatives and thus interrupted his continuous presence disqualifies him for the benefits of a legal settlement for Salvadoran and Guatemalan asylum seekers. The staff member asks how he traveled. "Pues, mojado," the man answers, illegally. The people around me chuckle, and a woman calls out, "At least he's honest." Choosing his words carefully, the staff member explains, "You don't qualify. You don't qualify because you went to El Salvador without permission. But you are the only one who knows you went." Multiple truths, multiple realities.

Because they are placed "outside" the law, those who do not exist legally are, in a sense, "free." Theirs may be the nebulous and oppressive "freedom" experienced by the homeless and the unemployed, but it is nonetheless worthwhile to consider for a moment the "subversiveness" of the space that the undocumented occupy. If they are not party to the social contract, the undocumented are not subject to legal obligations. Although they can, in fact, be tried for crimes and thus held legally accountable for their actions, their illicit presence is, in and of itself, a challenge to the legal order, as advocates of immigration reform have noted (Fuchs 1985; Hull 1985). Theoretically, illegal aliens' movements cannot be regulated or documented, their income can be untaxed, and their actions are clandestine.[11] The space of nonexistence intrinsically defies a discipline that, according to Foucault (1977, 143), seeks to

> eliminate the effects of imprecise distributions, the uncontrolled disappearance of individuals, their diffuse circulation, their unusable and dangerous coagulation; it [discipline] was a tactic of anti-desertion, anti-vagabondage, anti-concentration. Its aim was to establish presences and absences, to know where and how to locate individuals, to set up useful communications, to interrupt others, to be able at each moment to supervise the conduct of each individual, to assess it, to judge it, to calculate its qualities or merits.

Unknowable, unquantifiable, and illicit, the legally nonexistent seem potentially subversive to authorities.[12] It is not a coincidence that the 1996 Anti-terrorism and Effective Death Penalty Act (AEDPA) addressed immigration issues.[13]

The potential utility of nonexistence was not lost on Salvadoran activists who perfected the art of clandestinity. Just as targets of death-squad activity hid their social existence in El Salvador, hoping to avoid being assassinated, political activists who deliberately engaged in politically risky activities sometimes cut off their social ties, assumed false identities, and distanced themselves from homes and relatives. These measures were taken to protect themselves, their relatives, and their organizations. A former member of one of the organizations that made up the Farabundo Martí National Liberation Front (FMLN) explained that joining the political struggle meant that "you have to sacrifice many things—your family, your studies, your children, what you love—so that you can dedicate yourself to [the struggle]." Activists who emigrated to the United States both to save their lives and as emissaries for their political movements also experienced such denial of self, as one participant related: "We were denying ourselves everything. There were lots of divorces among my *compañeros*. Your life was at risk all the time! Physically, emotionally, mentally." The clandestinity of their political work securing funding, supplies, legitimacy, even arms for their organizations in El Salvador was matched by their legal clandestinity as undocumented immigrants. A man who was involved in such work in Los Angeles in the 1980s recalled: "For us, being illegal was like a form of civil disobedience. It was part of the radicalism that we were practicing."

Even if they are politically inactive, the undocumented occasionally exploit their nonexistence. Unlike those who are temporarily "legal" in that they have a pending immigration case, those who are thoroughly undocumented can enter and leave the United States, as long as they are not detected.[14] Undocumented, clandestine absences do not officially interrupt one's continuous presence in the United States. The undocumented can be paid under the table, and, depending on their relationship with their employers, can sometimes choose whether to disclose their income to the government. The undocumented thus have some flexibility regarding what to make official and what to keep unofficial and therefore nonexistent. The undocumented also have some ability to create realities, by, for example, using false documents to create a presence that was really an absence. Such fabrications were apparently quite common during the 1986 amnesty program. According to Hagan (1994, 98), the INS's willingness to accept affidavits as proof of presence transformed the problem of not having been present in the United States since January 1, 1982—the cutoff date to be eligible for legalization—into "a short-term technical consideration, one that could be overcome (for at least some groups in the [undocumented Mayan] community." Finally, clandestinity may be comforting to those who are trying to escape human-rights abuses in their countries of origin.

Like other borderlands, the space of illegality is productive. Underground economies and illicit labor are profitable. Far from being a "natural resource" of a given nation (see Chock 1995), migrants participate in multiple and globalized economies (Sassen 1989; Schiller, Basch, and Blanc 1995). In the case of El Salvador, remittances from Salvadoran migrants are a major source of national income (Darling 1996; *La Opinión* 1996). In the United States, unauthorized Central American immigrants have also fueled local economies, through the development of courier services and ethnic businesses (Lopez, Popkin, and Telles 1996; Hagan 1994; Mahler 1995). In contrast to the notion that one can only belong to one place (Malkki 1992; Gupta and Ferguson 1992), undocumented migrants, who live on the legal if not geographic boundary of nations, devise new notions of citizenship and belonging (Basch, Schiller, and Szanton Blanc 1994; Hammar 1990). With families that span borders (Hondagneu-Sotelo 1994), transnational community relations (Hagan 1994; Kearney 1995), and claims on multiple states, unauthorized immigrants can become constituencies in more than one locality. During a visit in 1997 to Salvadorans in Los Angeles, the mayor of San Salvador told his audience that he and the mayor of Los Angeles "are the only two people in this world who are mayors of a city that has more than 250,000 Salvadorans." The same activists who greeted the mayor of San Salvador as "our mayor" have been campaigning for residency for Salvadorans in the United States. Multiple nonexistences give rise to multiple existences as an underestimated consequence of that which is politically, economically, and legally clandestine.

Conclusion

I cannot celebrate the space of nonexistence. Even if this space is in some ways subversive, even if its boundaries are permeable, and even if it is sometimes irrelevant to individuals' everyday lives, nonexistence can be deadly. Legal nonexistence can mean being detained and deported, perhaps to life-threatening conditions. It can mean working for low wages in a sweatshop, or being unemployed. It can mean the denial of medical care, food, social services, education, and public housing. And it can mean an erasure of rights and personhood such that violence becomes not only legitimate but even required. Legal, social, and physical non-existences coalesce and separate. The violence that destroys lives also demands an erasure of legal personhood (cf. Sanchez 1997). Placing "subversives" or "guerrillas" outside of the legal order in a "lawless" realm justifies extreme actions and exempts authorities from their legal obligations to their citizenries. Likewise, the rights of those who do not exist legally in the United States are ambiguous (Hull 1985; Neuman 1996). Legal notions of agency, causation, and individual culpability (Shapiro 1988; Wagner-Pacifici 1994) make it difficult to ascertain responsibility for illegal immigrants who drown in the Rio Grande, perish in the mountains when the INS militarizes easier routes, or are injured in confrontations with border patrol officers who, after all, are only enforcing the law. Do not such victims "choose" their deaths when they "choose" to migrate (cf. Kearney 1995; Sanchez 1997)? Moreover, social nonexistence is connected to physical and legal nonexistence in that hiding one's social existence is a means of preventing physical execution, and those who do not exist legally are made to not exist socially as well. Nonetheless, physical, legal, and social nonexistences are not the same thing, as demonstrated by the physical and social presence of the legally nonexistent. Identifying the relationships between, yet incommensurability of, multiple nonexistences is critical to understanding the power relations intrinsic to U.S. immigration law.

As borderlands, the spaces of nonexistence shed light on the nature and limitations of dichotomies between globalization and localism, transnationalism and the nation-state, and law and the illicit. Legal nonexistence is defined in relation to the nation-state as the arbiter of citizenship. Individuals only become "illegal aliens" in relation to a state that delimits the boundaries and accessibility of legal personhood. Immigration laws thus reproduce the nation-state model, even as the necessity for immigration laws is a product of that model's inability to characterize social reality. At the same time, the physical and social presence of illegal aliens may be more important than their legal nonexistence given that illicit travelers create transnational communities and develop underground economies and exchanges, such as the remittances that migrants send "home" to their families. Policies designed to render the legally nonexistent socially and physically absent produce the phenomenon that they counter. In other words, there would be no "illegal immigration" if nations did not make governmental authorization a prerequisite for entering their borders. Geographically, the space of nonexistence is *outside* of national territory, a sort of void where the "stateless" are sent.[15] Yet this space coincides with national boundaries in that the space that is forbidden to the undocumented is the territory in which they lack legal rights. Defining that which does not belong also clarifies the nature of belonging, just as demarcating criminality defines the boundaries of legality. I therefore would not say that spaces of nonexistence are an intermediate zone between the global and the local. Rather, such spaces demonstrate that the global and the local, transnationalism and the nation, and law and illegality are mutually constitutive yet sometimes indistinguishable. Like the undocumented, who do and do not exist simultaneously, illegal immigration reproduces, yet defies, the nation-state, and violates, yet is created through, law. Although I do not celebrate nonexistence, I acknowledge that this space is not likely to disappear anytime soon.

Epilogue

When I was working with the Mothers of the Disappeared in Argentina in 1985, I used to try to imagine the dimension occupied by the disappeared. I *saw* the disappeared. I saw their photographs in the Mothers' office, I saw their names embroidered on the scarves that the Mothers wore, I saw their silhouettes when the Mothers and their supporters painted them on the sidewalks and walls of Buenos Aires. I pictured them together, whole, laughing, walking, watching. Watching us. What would it take to bring them back? And what would it take to prevent others from being compelled into this space of nonexistence?

Notes

1. Consider the following hypothetical example. Suppose that a woman enters the United States in 1987 and works as a live-in domestic for two years. In 1989, she moves into her own apartment, obtains a California ID card, and gets a job in the garment industry, where she is officially on the payroll. In 1996, she applies for asylum, thinking that this is a means of obtaining a work permit. She loses her asylum case, never receives a work permit, and is placed in deportation proceedings. At her court hearing, she attempts to apply for cancellation of removal, on the grounds that she has been in the United States for ten years, has a U.S. citizen son who would suffer if she were deported, and has demonstrated good moral character. She has no documentation of her first two years in the United States, however, as all residential records were in her employer's name, her employer will not sign an affidavit certifying that she was here, and she has no medical records, school records, or other records of her presence during this period. A judge will most likely deny her application, on the grounds that she can only prove continuous residence for eight years. So, where was she during the first two years? She was not in her country of origin, but she was not here either. She was in a space of nonexistence.

2. The creation of illegal time has aroused a controversy over a section of immigration law known as 245(i). This section allowed undocumented immigrants to adjust their statuses in the United States rather than returning to their countries of origin. When 245(i) was scheduled to expire in September of 1997, undocumented immigrants who were in the United States waiting for family petitions to become current faced the possibility that, by the time their visas became available, they would have accrued enough illegal time to trigger one of the bars if they left the country to claim their visas and then tried to reenter. Section 245(i) has been temporarily extended several times.

3. Work, presence, time, and legalization are interconnected. For example, in suspension of deportation cases, check stubs count as proof of residence, evidence of continuous employment indicates that aliens' time in the United States

has been well spent, and proof of employment also helps to demonstrate that aliens are not a public charge.

4. Although technically no travel documents are required to leave the Los Angeles area, this migrant correctly observes that when they leave Los Angeles, migrants encounter Immigration and Naturalization Service (INS) officials at checkpoints, bus stops, train stations, and so forth. As these officials may, in fact, request proof of legal presence, the speaker's comment is accurate.

5. At the time of the interview María, her husband, and their two daughters were sharing a one-bedroom apartment in Los Angeles, a step up from their initial residence, which was shared with fifteen other migrants and therefore lacked privacy.

6. To qualify for suspension of deportation, aliens must demonstrate seven years of continuous physical presence in the United States, good moral character, and that their deportation would pose an extreme hardship to themselves or their U.S. citizen or legal permanent resident relatives. Qualifying for cancellation of removal, which was created through the 1996 Illegal Immigration Reform and Immigrant Responsibility Act (IIRIRA), requires ten years of continuous residence, good moral character, and demonstrating that being deported would cause an extreme and exceptional hardship to an alien's U.S. citizen or legal permanent resident spouse, parent, or child. Suspension of deportation was eliminated by IIRIRA; hence, the only suspension cases pending are those that began before IIRIRA took effect. NACARA permitted Salvadorans to apply for "special rule cancellation" of removal, which is the equivalent of suspension.

7. Other means of legalization, such as suspension of deportation, family petitions, and labor certification, require lengthy periods of residency, close relatives with legal status in the United States, and employers who are willing to sponsor their employees. During the early 1980s, when large influx of Central American immigration to the United States began, few Salvadorans and Guatemalans met these requirements. The approval rate for Central American asylum applicants during this period was only 2 percent (USCR 1986). As a result, legalization was largely beyond the grasp of most Central American migrants.

8. But note that those who did not know that they had the right to apply for asylum did not do so, and that the INS sometimes coerced Salvadoran detainees into departing the country. See *Orantes-Hernandez v. Meese*, F.Supp. 1488 (C.D.Cal. 1988).

9. The 1990 Immigration Act created a new form of legal status known as "Temporary Protected Status," and designated Salvadorans as the first recipients. In 1991, a legal settlement known as *American Baptist Churches v. Thornburgh* granted certain Salvadorans and Guatemalans the right to apply or reapply for asylum under special rules designed to ensure a fair hearing of their claims. See Blum (1991), Frelick and Kohnen (1994), *Interpreter Releases* (1990), and Wasem n.d. for further details.

10. In essence, Salvadorans and Guatemalans who either were ABC class members (see note 9), or who applied for asylum before 1990, were allowed to apply for suspension of deportation under pre-IIRIRA immigration law. NACARA applicants have been granted a presumption of hardship, and asylum officials have been authorized to hear NACARA claims.

11. Note, however, that in fact the undocumented may pay more in taxes than they receive in benefits. This imbalance occurs because aliens who work under false Social Security numbers sometimes have taxes removed from their paychecks but do not file tax returns or claim refunds; see Simon (1989) for further discussion. Also, some have argued that immigration law is itself a means of "disciplining" the labor force (see Jenkins 1978; Portes 1978).

12. A newspaper article about the 1986 amnesty program begins, "A state agency trying to count the uncountable has concluded that there are 1.7 million illegal immigrants in California who qualify" (McLeod 1987, 8).

13. The Anti-terrorism and Effective Death Penalty Act placed aliens who had entered the United States without inspection in exclusion proceedings rather than in deportation proceedings. Individuals who are in exclusion proceedings are ineligible to apply for suspension of deportation as they are deemed to be "outside" of the United States seeking entry, and therefore cannot accrue years of continuous residence within the United States (*Interpreter Releases* 1996). IIRIRA eliminated the distinction between exclusion and deportation and created a single process, known as "removal."

14. Individuals who have pending applications for political asylum or for suspension of deportation and who leave the United States without advanced parole are deemed to have abandoned their cases. International travel is therefore difficult for such temporarily legalized immigrants. ABC class members are in such a temporarily legal state, and during interviews, many complained to me that they were unable to visit relatives in El Salvador and Guatemala for years.

15. I do not mean that the undocumented are *actually* stateless in the sense of

the individuals left stateless when war redefines national boundaries (see Marrus 1985). Rather, these individuals are "stateless" in that they do not "belong" in their countries of residence. The fact that they have citizenship elsewhere is largely irrelevant to their current condition of illegality.

References

Anderson, Benedict. 1991. *Imagined Communities: Reflections on the Origin and Spread of Nationalism*. 2d ed. London: Verso.

Anker, Deborah E. 1992. "Determining Asylum Claims in the United States: A Case Study on the Implementation of Legal Norms in an Unstructured Adjudicatory Environment." *New York University Review of Law and Social Change* 19(3): 433–528.

Anzaldúa, Gloria. 1987. *Borderlands/La Frontera: The New Mestiza*. San Francisco: Spinsters/Aunt Lute.

Basch, Linda, Nina Glick Schiller, and Cristina Szanton Blanc. 1994. *Nations Unbound: Transnational Projects, Postcolonial Predicaments, and Deterritorialized Nation-states*. Langhorne, Pa.: Gordon and Breach.

Bean, Frank D., Barry Edmonston, and Jeffrey S. Passel, eds. 1990. *Undocumented Migration to the United States: IRCA and the Experience of the 1980s*. Washington, D.C.: Urban Institute Press.

Blum, Carolyn Patty. 1991. "The Settlement of American Baptist Churches v. Thornburg: Landmark Victory for Central American Asylum-Seekers." *International Journal of Refugee Law* 3(2): 347–56.

Bosniak, Linda S. 1991. "Human Rights, State Sovereignty and the Protection of Undocumented Migrants under the International Migrant Workers Convention." *International Migration Review* 25(4): 737–70.

Byrne, Hugh. 1996. *El Salvador's Civil War: A Study of Revolution*. Boulder, Colo.: Lynne Rienner.

Calavita, Kitty. 1990. "Employer Sanctions Violations: Toward a Dialectical Model of White-Collar Crime." *Law and Society Review* 24(4): 1041–69.

———. 1992. *Inside the State: The Bracero Program, Immigration, and the I.N.S.* New York: Routledge.

———. 1994. "U.S. Immigration and Policy Responses: The Limits of Legislation." In *Controlling Immigration: A Global Perspective*, ed. Wayne A. Cornelius, Philip L. Martin, and James F. Hollifield. Stanford, Calif.: Stanford University Press. 55–82.

Caldeira, Teresa P. R. 1996. "Fortified Enclaves: The New Urban Segregation." *Public Culture* 8: 303–28.

Chavez, Leo. 1991. "Outside the Imagined Community: Undocumented Settlers and Experiences of Incorporation." *American Ethnologist* 18(2): 257–78.

————. 1992. *Shadowed Lives: Undocumented Immigrants in American Society.* Fort Worth: Harcourt Brace Jovanovich.

Chock, Phyllis. 1995. "Ambiguity in Policy Discourse: Congressional Talk about Immigration." *Policy Sciences* 28: 165–84.

Clifford, James. 1997. *Routes: Travel and Translation in the Late Twentieth Century.* Cambridge: Harvard University Press.

Coombe, Rosemary J. 1997. "The Demonic Place of the 'Not There': Trademark Rumors in the Postindustrial Imaginary." In *Culture, Power, Place: Explorations in Critical Anthropology,* ed. Akhil Gupta and James Ferguson. Durham, N.C.: Duke University Press. 249–76.

Coutin, Susan Bibler. 1993. *The Culture of Protest: Religious Activism and the U.S. Sanctuary Movement.* Boulder, Colo.: Westview Press.

————. 1998. "From Refugees to Immigrants: The Legalization Strategies of Salvadoran Immigrants and Activists." *International Migration Review* 32(4): 901–25.

————. 2000. *Legalizing Moves: Salvadoran Immigrants' Struggle for U.S. Residency.* Ann Arbor: University of Michigan Press.

————. 2001. "The Oppressed, the Suspect, and the Citizen: Subjectivity in Competing Accounts of Political Violence." *Law and Social Inquiry* 26(1): 63–94.

Coutin, Susan Bibler, and Susan F. Hirsch. 1998. "Naming Resistance: Dissidents, States and Ethnographers." *Anthropological Quarterly* 71(1): 1–17.

Darling, Juanita. 1996. "U.S. Dollars Sent South Now Fuel Salvador Economy." *Los Angeles Times,* January 28, A1, A6.

Delgado, Hector. 1993. *New Immigrants, Old Unions: Organizing Undocumented Workers in Los Angeles.* Philadelphia: Temple University Press.

Engel, David M., and Frank W. Munger. 1996. "Rights, Remembrance, and the Reconciliation of Difference." *Law and Society Review* 30(1): 7–53.

Fitzpatrick, Peter. 1992. *The Mythology of Modern Law.* London: Routledge.

————. 1993. "The Impossibility of Popular Justice." In *The Possibility of Popular Justice: A Case Study of Community Mediation in the United States,* ed. Sally

Engle Merry and Neal Milner. Ann Arbor: University of Michigan Press. 453–74.

Foucault, Michel. 1977. *Discipline and Punish: The Birth of the Prison.* Trans. Alan Sheridan. New York: Pantheon Books.

Frelick, Bill, and Barbara Kohnen. 1994. "Filling the Gap: Temporary Protected Status." Washington, D.C.: U.S. Committee for Refugees.

Fuchs, Lawrence H. 1985. "The Search for a Sound Immigration Policy: A Personal View." In *Clamor at the Gates: The New American Immigration*, ed. Nathan Glazer. San Francisco: Institute for Contemporary Studies. 17–48.

Green, Linda. 1994. "Fear as a Way of Life." *Cultural Anthropology* 9(2): 227–56.

Gupta, Akhil, and James Ferguson. 1997. "Beyond 'Culture': Space, Identity, and the Politics of Difference." In *Culture, Power, Place: Explorations in Critical Anthropology*, ed. Akhil Gupta and James Ferguson. Durham, N.C.: Duke University Press. 33–51.

Hagan, Jacqueline Maria. 1994. *Deciding to Be Legal: A Maya Community in Houston.* Philadelphia: Temple University Press.

Hammar, Tomas. 1990. *Democracy and the Nation State: Aliens, Denizens and Citizens in a World of International Migration.* Aldershot, England: Avebury.

———. 1994. "Legal Time of Residence and the Status of Immigrants." In *From Aliens to Citizens: Redefining the Status of Immigrants in Europe*, ed. Rainer Baubock. Aldershot, England: Avebury. 187–97.

Harwood, Edwin. 1985. "How Should We Enforce Immigration Law?" In *Clamor at the Gates: The New American Immigration*, ed. Nathan Glazer. San Francisco: Institute for Contemporary Studies. 73–91.

———. 1986. *In Liberty's Shadow: Illegal Aliens and Immigration Law Enforcement.* Stanford, Calif.: Stanford University Press.

Hing, Bill Ong. 1986. *The Immigration Reform and Control Act of 1986: Its Provisions, Applications, and Effect on Immigration Practice.* San Francisco: Immigrant Legal Resource Center.

Holston, James. 1991. "The Misrule of Law: Land and Usurpation in Brazil." *Comparative Studies in Society and History* 33(4): 695–725.

Holston, James, and Arjun Appadurai. 1996. "Cities and Citizenship." *Public Culture* 8: 187–204.

Hondagneu-Sotelo, Pierrette. 1994. *Gendered Transitions: Mexican Experiences of Immigration.* Berkeley: University of California Press.

———. 2001. *Doméstica: Immigrant Workers Cleaning and Caring in the Shadows of Affluence.* Berkeley: University of California Press.

Hull, Elizabeth. 1985. *Without Justice for All: The Constitutional Rights of Aliens.* Westport, Conn.: Greenwood Press.

Interpreter Releases. 1990. "Section-by-Section Summary of the 'Immigration Act of 1990.'" 67: 1277–92.

———. 1996. "Final Anti-Terrorism Bill Contains Major Immigration Changes." 73: 521–30.

Jenkins, J. Craig. 1978. "The Demand for Immigrant Workers: Labor Scarcity or Social Control?" *International Migration Review* 12(4): 514–35.

Kearney, Michael. 1986. "From the Invisible Hand to Visible Feet: Anthropological Studies of Migration and Development." *Annual Review of Anthropology* 15: 331–61.

———. 1995. "The Effects of Transnational Culture, Economy, and Migration on Mixtec Identity in Oaxacalifornia." In *The Bubbling Cauldron: Race, Ethnicity, and the Urban Crisis,* ed. Michael Peter Smith and Joe R. Feagin. Minneapolis: University of Minnesota Press. 226–43.

Lopez, David E., Eric Popkin, and Edward Telles. 1996. "Central Americans: At the Bottom, Struggling to Get Ahead." In *Ethnic Los Angeles,* ed. Roger Waldinger and Mehdi Bozorgmehr. New York: Russell Sage Foundation.

Maher, Kristen Hill. 1997. "Space, Race, Class, and Immigrant Labor: Latino Workers in Fortressed Middle-Class Neighborhoods." Paper presented at the Annual Meeting of the American Political Science Association, Washington, D.C., August 28–31.

Mahler, Sarah J. 1995. *American Dreaming: Immigrant Life on the Margins.* Princeton, N.J.: Princeton University Press.

Malkki, Liisa. 1992. "National Geographic: The Rooting of Peoples and the Territorialization of National Identity among Scholars and Refugees." *Cultural Anthropology* 7(1): 24–44.

Marrus, Michael R. 1985. *The Unwanted: European Refugees in the Twentieth Century.* New York: Oxford University Press.

McDonnell, Patrick J. 1997. "Hunting a Way In: Illegal Immigrants Grapple with Law That Will Speed Deportation." *Los Angeles Times,* March 9, A3.

McLeod, Ramon G. 1987. "1.7 Million Aliens in State May Be Eligible for Amnesty." *San Francisco Chronicle,* July 7, 8.

Montgomery, Tommie Sue. 1995. *Revolution in El Salvador: From Civil Strife to Civil Peace.* 2d ed. Boulder, Colo.: Westview Press.

Neuman, Gerald L. 1996. *Strangers to the Constitution: Immigrants, Borders, and Fundamental Law.* Princeton, N.J.: Princeton University Press.

La Opinión. 1996. "Reformas en EU afectaran a El Salvador: Ponen en peligro el envío de remesas familiares." Los Angeles. 3A, 5A.

Portes, Alejandro. 1978. "Toward a Structural Analysis of Illegal (Undocumented) Immigration." *International Migration Review* 12(4): 469–84.

Rosaldo, Renato. 1989. *Culture and Truth: The Remaking of Social Analysis.* Boston: Beacon Press.

Sanchez, Lisa. 1997. "Boundaries of Legitimacy: Sex, Violence, Citizenship and Community in a Local Sexual Economy." *Law and Social Inquiry* 22: 543–80.

Sassen, Saskia. 1989. "America's Immigration 'Problem': The Real Causes." *World Policy Journal* 6(4): 811–31.

Schiller, Nina Glick, Linda Basch, and Cristina Szanton Blanc. 1995. "From Immigrant to Transmigrant: Theorizing Transnational Migration." *Anthropological Quarterly* 68(1): 48–63.

Shapiro, Michael J. 1988. "The Constitution of the Central American Other: The Case of 'Guatemala.'" In *The Politics of Representation: Writing Practices in Biography, Photography, and Policy Analysis.* Madison: University of Wisconsin Press. 89–123.

Simon, Julian Lincoln. 1989. *The Economic Consequences of Immigration.* Oxford: Basil Blackwell.

Singer, Joseph William. 1988. "The Reliance Interest in Property." *Stanford Law Review* 40(3): 611–751.

Sorkin, Michael, ed. 1992. *Variations on a Theme Park: The New American City and the End of Public Space.* New York: Hill and Wang.

Stephen, Lynn. 1995. "Women's Rights Are Human Rights: The Merging of Feminine and Feminist Interests among El Salvador's Mothers of the Disappeared (CO-MADRES)." *American Ethnologist* 22(4): 807–27.

Thomas, Robert J. 1985. *Citizenship, Gender, and Work: Social Organization of Industrial Agriculture.* Berkeley: University of California Press.

USCR (United States Committee on Refugees). 1986. *Despite a Generous Spirit.* Washington, D.C.: American Council for Nationalities Service.

Wagner-Pacifici, Robin. 1994. *Discourse and Destruction: The City of Philadelphia versus MOVE.* Chicago: University of Chicago Press.

Wasem, Ruth Ellen. N.d. *Temporary Protections under U.S. Immigration Law.* Washington, D.C.: Congressional Research Service, Library of Congress.

CHAPTER 7

Christian Conversion and "Racial" Labor Capacities: Constructing Racialized Identities in Hawai'i

Sally Engle Merry

Forming Racialized Identities on a Terrain of Social Ambiguity

Racialized identities depend on etching sharp lines through the continuities and ambiguities of social personhood. Essentialized centers are centrifugally spun from national, cultural, class, and physical variation. Endless struggle is required to create the marks of difference and to hold them firm as populations themselves blend and change. Although it is clear that racial identities are social constructs developed over time, this essay describes how they are created and regulated in one social setting. It examines the institutional factors that gave shape and meaning to identities in Hawai'i during the Americanization of the sovereign kingdom in the nineteenth century and its period of U.S. colonial control in the early twentieth.

There are several aspects to this process: (1) the legal definition of identity through citizenship, immigration regulation, jobs, and rates of pay; (2) declarations of identity through processes of counting, marking, classifying, and labeling populations in the course of governance; (3) the policing of social and spatial boundaries through regulations of marriage, sociability, residence, and schooling. Through these forms of regulation, fixed identities are forged from variable social markers; lines and edges are shaped in social fields characterized by ambiguities; and boundaries to social interaction and spatial intermingling are sharpened and enforced.

This is clearly a local process, but it is also a profoundly global one. Even in the nineteenth century, ideas and practices about racial identities and their regulation were circulated transnationally. The idea of racialized labor capacities was widespread in late-nineteenth- and early-twentieth-century plantation economies, for example. The contrast between "coolie labor" and "citizen labor"—between workers thought undesirable as permanent residents versus those thought suitable for citizenship—emerged in Fiji, Australia, the United States, and many other parts of the world. These identities were rooted in the local sugar plantation economy and its labor relations, but they were also shaped by the global transfer of meanings and practices concerning labor and the racial basis of citizenship in Euro-American societies. Similarly, the imagining of Chinese workers as dangerous and threatening in late-nineteenth-century Hawai'i built on ideas imported from California. Chinese were virtually prohibited from immigrating to the United States in 1882 and from Hawai'i only a few years later. Global cultural understandings shaped Hawaiian responses to Chinese immigrants despite the different economic and social conditions in the islands and California.

Racial identities are always created in oppositional forms, so that the construction of one identity stands in contrast to one or more others. Here I explore the creation of an oppositional set of racial identities in nineteenth- and early-twentieth-century Hawai'i. I examine the legal and social factors that constructed these identities and the extent to which each set of identities incorporated transnational conceptions of personhood and virtue, focusing on the small harbor town of Hilo, Hawai'i.

By the late twentieth century, the town of Hilo, along with other urban areas of Hawai'i, was a field of interconnected and complex identities. Despite the crosshatching of ancestry of this community, its members are imagined and counted as a series of distinct and bounded populations. According to the 1990 census, the racial breakdown of the district of South Hilo was 34 percent Japanese, 26 percent white, 19 percent Hawaiian, 12 percent Filipino, 3 percent Chinese, 1 percent Korean, 1 percent other Asian or Pacific Islander, 0.5 percent black, and

0.5 percent Native American. These figures, based on self-report on the census form, imply that the categories of ethnic identity are unambiguous. In practice, most of the population is extensively intermarried, so that ethnicity is a matter of some choice among possible alternatives and is heavily influenced by lifestyle, social class, and self-perception. The Japanese American community is predominant in government and educational activities and largely middle-class. The white population consists of two groups, those descended from Portuguese sugar workers, who consider themselves Portuguese rather than *haole*, the local term for white, and whites from the mainland or other origins who are called *haole*.

Crosscutting these ethnic divisions is the important distinction of local or outsider, marked largely by accent. Locals speak pidgin, an inflected version of English that immediately marks its speaker as someone who belongs on the island and separates him or her from newcomers. At the same time, speaking "standard" English is essential to upward social mobility and professional status. Those who speak only pidgin face obstacles in job advancement, particularly in the tourist industry. Older plantation workers were taught that this was a second-rate language and are often very apologetic about their "bad" English. Many professionals who grew up in Hawai'i are able to speak both pidgin and standard English and can switch easily between them.

An examination of historical processes of identity formation in Hilo, as elsewhere in Hawai'i, provides some insight into how these identities have been distilled out of the tumultuous changes of nineteenth- and early-twentieth-century Hilo. The major influences were the Christian mission of the early nineteenth century, the burgeoning sugar plantation economy of the late nineteenth century, and the land trusts and other benefits established to compensate Native Hawaiians for U.S. takings of their lands in the early twentieth century. This analysis indicates that the local situation was formative, but that it was given shape and meaning by global discourses about plantation labor, Chinese threats, and approaches to handling indigenous peoples in expanding Euro-American settler states.

The Historical Context

Early-nineteenth-century Hawai'i was dominated by trading relation-ships between the chiefly elite of Hawaiian society, the *ali'i*, and a band of adventurers and merchants, largely from New England, who settled in the port towns of Honolulu, Lahaina, and Hilo to engage in provi-sioning the ships of the China trade and, from the 1820s until the 1860s, servicing the ships of the burgeoning Pacific whale fishery. Congre-gational and other Calvinist missionaries arrived from New England in 1820, seeking to convert the "heathen" native peoples and antagoniz-ing the merchant community in the process. Disputes erupted between these two foreign communities about whether commerce or Christian-ity was the more effective route to civilization; none doubted the final objective of the process. By 1850, however, the Native Hawaiian popu-lation was plummeting from introduced diseases and economic displace-ment as well as some out-migration, while changes in the legal structure of the Kingdom of Hawai'i allowed aliens to purchase land for the first time. By 1876, the sugar plantation economy was booming, demanding a larger labor supply than the dwindling Hawaiian community could provide. Decades of labor importation from Asia and Europe produced an extraordinarily heterogeneous community by the turn of the century, when U.S. imperialism swept up the islands in an 1898 takeover and 1900 annexation. By the end of the century, plantation areas consisted of a largely Chinese, Japanese, and Portuguese labor force under the management of predominantly American and British supervisors and plantation managers. A racialized labor system was well entrenched.

Yet the Native Hawaiians did not become incorporated into this system. Instead, their identities were forged by their earlier encounter with missionaries, in which the key opposition was between the heathen and the saved. With Christian conversion, the heathen identity can be replaced, although the possibilities of slippage are great and the number of backsliders considerable. The missionaries sought to incorporate those Hawaiians who partook of a Christian life as church members and con-verts, although those who failed to abide by their principles of sexual containment within marriage, for example, were suspended as members or excommunicated. Unlike many other parts of the colonial world, in nineteenth-century Hawai'i incorporation and assimilation dominated relations between foreign and indigenous populations. After persuading the *ali'i* to adopt a predominant Christian and Anglo-American legal system, the missionaries brought all Hawaiian people under its authority. In marked contrast to the dual legal systems prevalent in much of British colonial Africa and other colonial states, the assumption in Hawai'i (under the influence of politically powerful missionaries) was that Native Hawaiians who changed their cultural practices and loyalties could be accepted into at least the legal and political systems of white society.

The lot of the Asian laborers was vastly different. As the need for labor in the expanding sugar plantations became acute, planters imported a succession of foreign laborers from China, Japan, Portugal, Puerto Rico, Korea, the Philippines, and, more recently, the Pacific Islands and Mexico. The population of white Americans and non-Portuguese Europeans, who tended to occupy top managerial positions, remained small and socially separated from the largely Asian labor force.

Plantations, with their distinctive forms of discipline and order, increasingly dominated Hilo, while the labor they imported changed its social composition dramatically. The low pay, grim working and living conditions, brutal treatment by overseers (*lunas*), and quasi-slave contract labor system drove each group of immigrants out of the plantations as soon as possible. Planters constantly sought new sources of labor. During the 1860s, Hawaiians did much of the arduous work of hoeing, cutting, and hauling cane, but by the 1870s, the practice of importing foreign laborers under three-year contracts, after which they were expected to return home, was widespread (Beechert 1985). Despite complaints in the U.S. press that this was a quasi-slave system, it was not abolished until formal annexation to the United States in 1900 made it illegal. Chinese labor was imported beginning in 1852 and continued slowly until 1875, accelerating until public protest against Chinese immigrants induced the government to restrict this flow in 1886 (Sullivan 1923, 511). A law banning Chinese immigration, the Chinese Exclusion Act, had been passed only four years earlier in the United States. In 1893, Chinese immigrants were excluded unless they were willing to work as contract laborers and leave as soon as they finished their contracts (George 1948, 27).

The Chinese had a distressing (to the planters) tendency to leave the plantations after their contracts expired for more remunerative work in independent rice farming or in retail or service trades in the urban centers (Takaki 1989, 147). In 1882, the Chinese were 49 percent of the plantation workforce, but only 5,037 (37 percent) of the 13,500 Chinese living in the Hawaiian kingdom worked on sugar plantations. By 1890, they were down to 25 percent of the workforce and by 1892, 12 percent (Okihiro 1991, 23). Planters, anxious for a white population whom they imagined would make better citizens than the Chinese, imported workers and their families from Portugal between 1877 and 1913, mostly from Madeira and the Azores (Lydon 1975, 52). The major labor supply, however, was imported from Japan between 1885 and 1907.

By 1896, the population of the Hawaiian Islands was 109,020, of which 28 percent were Native Hawaiians, 22 percent Japanese, 20 percent Chinese, 14 percent Portuguese, 8 percent part Hawaiian, 3 percent American, and 2 percent British (Thurston n.d.).[1] In 1900, laborers were brought from Puerto Rico and Korea (George 1948, 28–29; Okihiro 1991, 24). From 1906 until 1934, large numbers came from the new U.S. colony of the Philippines (Sullivan 1923, 511; Daws 1968; Beechert 1985, 232). The proportion of Native Hawaiians to imported sugar workers continued to fall in the early twentieth century as labor immigration continued. By the 1920 census, out of a total population of 255,912, there were 9 percent Native Hawaiians, 43 percent Japanese, 11 percent Portuguese, 9 percent Chinese, 8 percent Filipino, 8 percent other Caucasians, 7 percent part Hawaiians, 2 percent Puerto Rican, 2 percent Korean, and 1 percent Spanish (Sullivan 1923, 513). By the late 1930s, however, large-scale importation of foreign labor had virtually ended. By this time, a small number of white Americans and Europeans controlled a largely Hawaiian, Portuguese, and Asian labor force.

Because the planters believed that whites were incapable of doing grueling fieldwork under the tropical sun for such low pay, they never envisioned the area as one for white settlement. Nor was there a substantial white working class to compete for jobs with the immigrants. The pervasive racialized hierarchy of the plantation allocated members of each nationality to clearly defined statuses, with the whites virtually always at the top. However, continuing patterns of intermarriage introduced complexities into this system of ethnicity that these statistics—which imply unambiguous, essentialized categories of identity—fail to represent. Instead, these statistics construct a certainty of identity produced by an array of social mechanisms. The racial hierarchy of the plantation system was a major one.

Although the earliest plantations in the 1850s and 1860s in Hilo were often run by Chinese managers employing Native Hawaiian workers, by the 1880s this pattern had changed. Instead, the management was largely American and British and the workers Portuguese, Chinese, and Japanese. A list of plantations in the Hilo region in 1887 mentions eighteen plantations employing predominantly Portuguese, Chinese, and Japanese laborers and a few Hawaiian workers. Native Hawaiians were often hired as camp police. A list of plantation officers on the island of Hawai'i from 1889 suggests that, with the exception of one plantation with a Chinese manager, all plantations were managed by Americans or Britons. The 1884 census reported 25,000 people living on the island of Hawai'i, with a 2:1 ratio of males to females. Of this number, there were 12,000 Hawaiians, 800 "half-castes" (presumably part Hawaiians), almost 5,000 Chinese, of which only 170 were women, 5,000 Portuguese, evenly divided between males and females, and 400 Americans, of which only 100 were women, and about 600 Caucasians of other nationalities. Six thousand, or one in four, were contract laborers.

By the early twentieth century, there were some thirteen plantations along the Hamakua Coast, virtually all under Scottish managers (Leithead 1973, 53). Ownership of land and buildings was heavily concentrated in the hands of Anglo-Saxons, despite their numerical minority (George 1948, 41). Because landing cargo and loading sugar cane was always difficult along this coast, some plantations adopted a system of long cables to raise goods and people up the cliffs from the decks of ships anchored offshore. Hilo, with its harbor, remained the commercial and administrative center for this plantation economy, as it had been for the early mercantile economy based on the whaling ships.

Creating Racialized Identities

Early contact and labor immigration in Hilo produced two distinct patterns of racial and class subordination, and consequently two rather different sets of identities. First, the relationship between Euro-Americans and Native Hawaiians was a classic colonial relationship. The Europeans arrived in an overseas location seeking to transform the society of the indigenous people and then wrest political control from them. Hawai'i was an American colony (Territory) from 1900 to 1959. Although in the early Territory years Native Hawaiians were relatively well off with opportunities in government and police work, plantation supervision, and ranching, as well as having considerable electoral power (Handy and Pukui 1958; Trask 1993), they began to lose political power and economic position by mid-century. This group now ranks at the bottom of the social hierarchy in income, educational attainment, health, and longevity and has become a largely poor, urban population (Blaisdell and Mokuau 1994). Since the 1980s, a powerful movement to reclaim Hawaiian language and culture and assert sovereignty has swept Hawaiian urban and rural communities, paralleling similar movements among colonized indigenous peoples in New Zealand, Canada, Australia, and the mainland United States (Trask 1993; Hasager and Friedman 1994; Merry 1997).

Second, the immigrant sugar workers had a typical immigrant relationship to the *haole*/Hawaiian leadership of the Hawaiian Kingdom and later Territory of Hawai'i. Like other instances of immigrant labor in capitalist agriculture, after a long period of initial subordination in the workplace and community under strict paternalistic control, there was some long-term upward mobility, although less than in urban areas. The sugar workers who stayed and raised families in Hawai'i managed to move out of the plantation in the next generation, by and large.

Although people of Asian ancestry were denied naturalized citizenship in Hawai'i as in the United States, their U.S.- born children were able to vote and claim full citizenship as Americans.

Incorporation and Assimilation: The Native Hawaiians

One of the intriguing features of these two relationships is the very different images the *haole* elites developed about the groups. The Native Hawaiians were regarded as "our" natives by the whites and treated as childlike but benign, lazy, irresponsible with money, and friendly, although too sensuous. When the missionaries arrived in the 1820s, the dominant discourse was one of savagery and heathenism and the need to minister to souls on these dark shores. As the Hawaiians proved resistant to the enormous cultural and moral changes envisioned by the mission, the missionaries began to search for "natural" flaws in their character or intellect to account for this failure, such as an inability to think abstractly (Andrews 1836). By the middle of the nineteenth century, as *haoles* attempted to make Native Hawaiians into a plantation labor force, this discourse was replaced by one of childlike indolence and laziness. The frustrating efforts to transform marriage and sexual practices added a recurring complaint about licentiousness, heard loudly in missionary reports from the field in 1846 (Kingdom of Hawai'i 1846). Looking back in the 1880s, Titus Coan, a missionary who lived in Hilo for almost fifty years, described the Hawaiians as a primitive race, claiming that "our native converts were as children, and up to this day many of them need milk rather than strong meat" (1882, 249).

Coan argues that the "natives" are not yet ready to be in charge of the churches because they are slack in church discipline and remiss in keeping track of wandering church members. Their church statistics are past remedy. He bemoans the tendency of Hawaiians to wander away from one church, to fail to take letters of dismissal and present them to the new church, and to change their names as they please (ibid., 255). The frequency with which missionary reports are peppered with statistics about members, readers, writers, dismissed members, deceased members, suspended members, and so on, indicates that enumerating and fixing the population was a critical part of the mission project. This was a process of rendering the Hawaiian mass known and accountable. Yet frequent movement and name changes conformed to Hawaiian kinship practices and were governed by a social geography of relatives and friends. The logic of movement seemed incoherent to those who thought in terms of fixed domiciles and permanent identity and citizenship.

The Hawaiians are "naturally indolent" and although they are hard workers when necessary, they "lack economy," in Coan's view. "We teach them industry, economy, frugality, and generosity, but their progress in these virtues is slow. They are like children needing wise parents or guardians" (ibid., 254–55). The character of this "infant race" is amorous and subject to bad influences from foreigners and by some laws that encourage licentiousness and others that, while wholesome, are unenforced (ibid., 256). They are also followers rather than leaders. They are inclined to be untruthful, speaking lies as soon as they are born, but this trait also is rooted in their racialized nature: "This is a severe charge, but it is a trait probably in all savage races" (ibid.). Coan concludes that their piety is imperfect: "Their easy and susceptible natures, their impulsive and fickle traits, need great care and faithful watching" (ibid., 257).

Thus, elite whites produced a Hawaiian identity that allowed them to define themselves as adults, even fathers, in relation to feminized children, while the agentic capacity of the Hawaiians themselves was progressively diminished. Writing in a missionary newspaper in 1844, Robert Wyllie praised Hawaiian seamen as both docile and competent: "I have never heard any captain of a vessel who did not speak highly of the native seamen whom he had employed. They are eminently subordinate, docile, good natured and trustworthy; and with proper training they become good efficient seamen" (Wyllie 1844). In an 1864 article, along with discussions about the possibility that all Native Hawaiians would soon die out, one author describes them as "children of the Pacific; they have an aesthetic love of the beautiful beyond what is found in the most highly-cultivated circles" (Anon 1864,

255). But, the author continues, although these people are brave, kind, and beautiful, they are disappearing because, he thinks, of infanticide. "The mothers are idle, they dislike the trouble of bringing up families, and they desire above all things to preserve their charms, which the nursing of children diminishes. They are very far from cruel." He adds, "They are very licentious" (ibid.). A missionary writer in the 1880s, retrospectively describing Hilo in 1837, evokes the childlike image as he describes the area: "15,000 natives scattered up and down the sea-belt, grouped in villages of from 100 to 300 persons, a sensual, shameless, yet kindly and tractable people, slaves to the chiefs, and herding together almost like animals—to this parish, occupying the eastern third of the island of Hawaii, a strange mingling of crags and valleys, of beauty and barrenness, and to this interesting people, was called the young missionary Titus Coan" (Humphrey n.d., 2). The same images contained in this passage—the animal-like nature of the Hawaiian people, their tractability, their sexuality, and their indolence—appear over and over in nineteenth- and twentieth-century texts, while references to their capacities and courage diminish over time.

By 1888, these traits had taken on a less benign hue, and one writer, mocking David Kalakaua, the Hawaiian king of the period, remarked, "The natives have the virtue of hospitality, good nature, and honesty; but they are incorrigibly indolent and have no more care for the morrow than the American Indian . . . Given an abundant supply of *poi*, a species of flour made from the root of the taro plant, and the Hawaiian is content" (Fitch 1888, 126). An 1891 account furthers the infantilization and link with nature and animals, describing how "Their frank open countenances, soft and flashing eyes, simple manners, and child-like deportment win the hearts of all beholders. Their simplicity, easy good humor, and implicit trust in nature to provide for them are characteristics found only in the people of the tropics" (Ingram 1891, 755)—or, more often, in conquered peoples who have been forced to abandon their militaristic past. These images helped to legitimate the *haole*-led overthrow of Queen Liliu'okalani in 1893 and the formation of the Republic of Hawai'i. Rev. Sereno E. Bishop, a missionary descendant, echoed Republic President Sanford Dole's opinion of Hawaiians when he wrote: "The common people were not intrusted with rule, because in their childishness and general incapacity, they were totally unfit for such rule." Hawai'i's government, he continued, should be in the hands of the few for the benefit of the masses, who were "babes in character and intellect" (quoted in Okihiro 1991, 12).

The routine denigration of Hawaiians as child-like, indolent, and sensual was so well entrenched by the turn of the century that a minister in 1908 objects to the phrase "just like a Hawaiian," which is commonly used as a term of disparagement (Oleson 1908). "It is just as much like an Anglo-Saxon as it is like a Hawaiian to do some things that are foolish, that are disappointing, that are even at times disreputable. On the other hand, it is just as much like a Hawaiian as it is like an Anglo-Saxon to do things that are commendable, that evince strength of character, that reveal genuine response to high ideals" (ibid.). By this time the *haole* had constituted himself as the adult to the Hawaiian child, the energetic to the lazy, the strong and wise to the simple and trusting in virtually hegemonic form.

The infantilization of Hawaiian people and their naturalization persisted well into the twentieth century. Even as Hawaiians were denigrated as inferior, sensual, and lazy, their music, dance, crafts, and foods were admired and appropriated for tourism. *Haole* elites from the mid-nineteenth century through the 1950s felt a paternalistic concern for Native Hawaiians as the group disappeared through death and assimilation, at the same time as the tourist industry increasingly relied on displays of Hawaiian cultural practices and fantasies of Hawaiian sexuality to attract business. This infantilized and sexualized image of Hawaiians is still central to the tourist industry and its portrayal of Hawai'i as a libidinous paradise distant from the disciplinary regimes of the clock and the workplace, as an oppositional world constructed to provide relief from the everyday in which the Hawaiian becomes the sign of difference (see Trask 1993). When the Hawaiian sovereignty movement staged a massive demonstration to protest the overthrow of Queen Liliu'okalani at its centennial in 1993 and draped the Iolani Palace in downtown

Honolulu in black, tourists were encouraged by the Hawaiian Visitor's Bureau to stay away.

Exclusion and Alienation: The Asians

Asian immigrant groups, on the other hand, were viewed by *haoles* as threatening Orientals, unable to assimilate and prone to socially dangerous habits such as opium smoking or cockfighting. As the Hawaiians were romanticized and economically marginalized, the immigrant groups from Asia were viewed as a threat by *haole* elites, undesirable as citizens and characterized by morally repugnant habits such as gambling, thievery, and opium smoking attached to essentialized biological identities. These practices were seen as threatening to the fragile moral capacity of the Native Hawaiians. As the planters demanded more and more labor, they confronted local resistance to bringing in each immigrant group. During the 1860s and 1870s, the Chinese were particularly subject to public attack (Lydon 1975). There had been Chinese inhabitants of the kingdom since at least the 1820s working as sugar masters, merchants, and rice farmers, but these individuals did not evoke any

Table 7.1 Chinese population in Hawai'i

Year	Number of Chinese	Population of Kingdom	Percentage Chinese
1850	200 (estimated)	84,165	0.2
1853	500 (estimated)	73,134	0.6
1860	816	66,984	1.2
1866	1,206	62,959	1.9
1872	1,938	56,987	3.5
1878	5,916	57,985	10.3
1884	18,254	80,578	22.2
1890	16,752	89,990	18.8

Sources: Polynesian, August 28, 1858; *Advertiser*, April 6, 1867, July 10, 1869, March 15, 1873, February 22, 1879, February 16, 1885; Kuykendall, 1938, 387; 1953, 177; Lind, 1955, 27. Table in Lydon 1975, 18.

comparable resistance. Between 1852 and 1875, Chinese immigration involved fewer than two thousand people, but between 1875 and 1887, 25,497 entered and 10,196 left, with a net gain of 15,000 Chinese residents. By 1884, the kingdom was 22.2 percent Chinese. Because of the steep decline in the Native Hawaiian population, by that time there were only twice as many Native Hawaiians (44,000) as Chinese residents (18,254) living in the kingdom, and almost all of the Chinese were men (ibid., 18). By 1890, the Chinese population had dropped to 16,752, or 18.8 percent, as the number of Japanese workers soared.

As early as the 1850s, debates began about the Chinese workers. Planters claimed that they were good laborers, while long-term residents, including many Native Hawaiians, complained that they were troublesome and prone to quarrels, thefts, suicides, and other misdemeanors (Lydon 1975, 23–24). The anti-Chinese movement was fed by Native Hawaiian fears that their shrinking numbers would be engulfed by newcomers. The burgeoning anti-Chinese movement in California, increasingly the most important area for Hawai'i's contact and trade with the United States in the post–Gold Rush era, was also significant. The missionary element worried that the Chinese were a bad moral influence on the Native Hawaiian population.

Alleged Chinese criminality was at the heart of the anti-Chinese movement. Opium was a major area of contention. The Honolulu press worried that it had a bad influence on Hawaiians and caused suicides and serious riots (ibid., 27). Allegations of violence were also foci of concern. Reports in the press of violent assaults on *lunas* in the cane fields exacerbated the public perception that the Chinese, now envisioned as a unitary race with a fixed character, were prone to violent crimes and resistant to planter control (ibid., 29). When a Chinese employee murdered his employer, the anti-Chinese press emphasized the danger.[2]

Drawing on an allegedly global discourse, an editorial in the Honolulu newspaper *Advertiser* after an incident in 1881 observed that Europeans the world over had learned "to distrust him [the Chinese] as treacherous, and ready to shed human blood and take human life in revenge for the slightest provocation" (quoted in ibid., 50). Henry M.

Whitney, editor of the *Advertiser*, carried on an extensive anti-Chinese editorial campaign in the late 1860s and 1870s, complaining that the Chinese (in the essentialized singular) was a pagan and had no regard for life so that all who dealt with the coolie had a feeling of insecurity. He thundered from his newspaper pages that Chinese brought disease, smoked opium, and had a demoralizing effect on "the Hawaiian" (ibid., 31). R. G. Davies (a part-Hawaiian lawyer in Honolulu), in an influential statement, articulated the opposition between the interests of the Native Hawaiians and the Asian immigrant workers, redeploying the language of civilization and race:

> Our own people, the Hawaiians are dying off. Shall we import another element of destruction to hasten their extinction? The planters say that they must have more labor, and the coolies are the cheapest and best. Well, suppose they send for a thousand or two of these uncivilizable coolies. They will go on making sugar for the next ten years, and then retire with their fortunes made to travel in Europe or to enjoy their sugar-made wealth in a villa beneath the lovely skies of Italy on the banks of the lake of Como, leaving their agents to manage their plantations here, and we the people to manage the discharged coolies as best we may. We have as many coolies here as the courts can take care of. In order to resuscitate this nation, and bring prosperity to all, let us have a new infusion of good blood. (Quoted in ibid., 37; published in *Pacific Commercial Advertiser* 1869)

The imagining of the Chinese as a site of disease, gambling, opium, theft, and violence, characteristics embedded in the body and marking their undesirability, was thus substantiated by the apparently objective, scientific evidence of crime statistics.

The absence of Chinese women exacerbated the criminal image of the immigrants. In the period from 1853 to 1890, the Chinese population was only about 5–10 percent female. A petition from 1876, signed by the prime minister, Walter Murray Gibson, who used the anti-Chinese movement to increase his popularity among Native Hawaiians, says that Chinese males, "utterly unchaste in character, must aggravate still more the sterility of Hawaiian women, and so tend to increase the rate of deterioration of your Majesty's Hawaiian Subjects" (quoted in ibid., 43, from *Advertiser* 1876). When, in 1874, an elderly Chinese man raped a ten-year-old Hawaiian girl and was tried and sentenced to eighteen months' hard labor, the author of the article in the *Advertiser* concluded, "These beastly low-class Chinese are doing a fearful work among the female native children" (ibid.). Indeed, Chinese competition for Hawaiian women may have fueled Hawaiian resistance to more Chinese immigration. An 1880 bill passed by the legislature but not signed by King Kalakaua (probably in response to planter pressure) restricted the immigration of male "Asiatics" by specifying that for each five male immigrants there should be three females (ibid., 62).

By 1877, there was considerable pressure to stop Chinese immigration altogether based on the perceived threats to public health and safety and encouraged by the growing anti-Chinese movement in California. For example, one Hawaiian who had been to California said that the California Chinese were regarded as "thieves and assassins and were looked upon as the lowest of the low" (ibid., 47). In 1886, Chinese immigration was virtually ended, but Walter Murray Gibson, the prime minister, was able to engineer this cessation only by offering the planters a new source of labor: Japan. Between 1886 and 1894, 29,000 Japanese came and about 8,000 left, but this number is dwarfed by the next four years, in which private Japanese contractors brought in 64,000 more workers (Beechert 1985, 88–89). At the same time, a new law passed in 1890 allowed Chinese workers to come to Hawai'i as long as they did only agricultural labor and stayed no more than five years. Declared unconstitutional in 1892, the law was passed as a constitutional amendment in 1892 (ibid., 92–93). Between 1879 and 1898, some 49,000 Chinese workers arrived, half in the final four years to beat the ban on Chinese immigration that would follow annexation to the United States (ibid., 91). Yet, many left the plantations. Of 14,000 laborers imported to work under contract between 1876 and 1882, only about 5,000 were still working on the plantations in 1882 (ibid.).

But by the 1880s, an anti-Japanese movement was under way,

again fueled by the American movement (Takaki 1989; Okihiro 1991). In 1896, the population was 22 percent Japanese and the planters succeeded in resuming large-scale Chinese immigration for contract laborers who were required to return home (Lydon 1975, 78). The large population of Chinese and Japanese free laborers was characterized as shiftless and lazy, requiring regulation to direct their work into useful ends (Okihiro 1991, 36).

After annexation, the planters attempted to institute a passbook system for workers and to use an old vagrancy statute to compel workers to work on public works as prisoners (ibid.). Because annexation increased the possibilities of Japanese migration to the mainland, the anti-Japanese movement in the United States resulted in a 1907 executive order keeping Japanese, among others, from the mainland and produced the 1908 Gentlemen's Agreement, by which Japan agreed to restrict emigration.[3] As a result, the flow of labor from Japan was cut off, except for parents, wives, and children of Japanese residents. By 1909, new immigration from Japan had virtually stopped. However, an increase in picture brides produced a shift in gender ratios: in 1890, only 19 percent of the population were women, in 1900, 22 percent, and in 1920, 43 percent (ibid., 38, 58). By 1902, Japanese immigrants were 73.5 percent of the plantation workforce (ibid., 59). When the Japanese workers engineered a strike in 1909, they were seen as an alien threat, even as they began to make claims in American terms to equal pay for equal work (Okihiro 1991). By this time, perhaps 70 percent of the Japanese workers were literate and many read one of the eleven Japanese newspapers on the islands (Beechert 1985, 169). But the notion that essentialized racial identities were linked to particular patterns of disorder and criminality was virtually unquestioned among the white settlers and planter elite.

Thus, whites constructed Asians as far more threatening and different from them than Native Hawaiians. This vision of the social order emerges in an intriguing document produced by Lorrin Thurston, a leading businessman and central figure in the overthrow and a third-generation missionary descendant. The date is probably 1897. This *Handbook on the Annexation of Hawaii* tries to sell an increasingly racially nativist and balky American public fearful of the multihued population of the islands on the benefits of annexation. Thurston describes the Native Hawaiians, "only 33,000 in number," as "a conservative, peaceful and generous people" (Thurston n.d., 27). He reminds readers that the Hawaiians are not Africans but Polynesians, brown rather than black. There is, he says, no color line between whites and native Hawaiians in marriage or in political, social, or religious affairs. He describes the Portuguese as constructive members of society, emphasizing that they commit a smaller proportion of criminal offenses than any other nationality in the country and are "a hard-working industrious, home-creating and home-loving people who would be of advantage to any developing country. They constitute the best laboring element in Hawaii" (ibid., 28). They are, of course, the only significant element of the workforce that is white.[4]

Asians are portrayed very differently. The Chinese and Japanese are "an undesirable population from a political standpoint, because they do not understand American principles of government" (ibid.). In flagrant disregard of actual population movements, he asserts that these groups neither want to stay permanently in Hawai'i nor to migrate to the United States:

> The Asiatic population of Hawaii consists, however, of laborers who are temporarily in the country for what they can make out of it. As soon as they accumulate a few hundred dollars they return home. Shut off the source of supply, and in ten years there will not be Asiatics enough left in Hawaii to have any appreciable effect. (ibid.)

Another assertion reveals how closely the racial policies of the United States shaped those of Hawai'i:

> Individually, the Chinese and Japanese in Hawaii are industrious, peaceable citizens, and as long as they do not take part in the political control of the country, what danger can the comparatively small number there be to this country? They are not citizens, and by the Constitution of Hawaii,

they are not eligible to become citizens; they are aliens in America and aliens in Hawaii; annexation will give them no rights which they do not now possess, either in Hawaii or in the United States. (Ibid.)

The remaining inhabitants, Thurston continues, are Americans, English, and Germans, "strong, virile men who have impressed their form of government upon the much larger population living there, and have acquired the ownership of more than three-fourths of all the property in the country. If they were able to do this against the hostility and in the face of an unfavorable monarchy, why is there any reason to believe that they will be any less strong under the fostering influence of the republican Government of the United States?" (ibid., 29). Instead of noting the fatal combination of gunboats, greed, and capitalism that prevailed against determined Hawaiian resistance in the nineteenth century, Thurston celebrates these changes as the victory of masculinized white racial supremacy. He draws on the developing transnational consciousness of white racial supremacy, always male, linked to the high colonialism of Europe as well as the United States.

For Thurston, as for Cecil Rhodes, Rudyard Kipling, and other imperialist thinkers, the image of Hawai'i governed by a class of about four thousand Americans and other Anglo-Saxon peoples ruling over 145,000 others of different racial/ethnic heritage seemed perfectly reasonable, legitimated by racialized and gendered conceptions of identity. Citizenship laws underscored and reinforced these conceptions, enacting them in the realm of legal definitions of identity (see Maurer 1997). Because American laws denied naturalization to Asian immigrants, nearly 60 percent of Hawai'i's population at the time of annexation was disenfranchised (Okihiro 1991, 13). Antagonism to Chinese and Japanese had taken on the essentialized understandings of race characteristic of the United States at this time, an era of increasing nativism and exclusionism marked by the passage of laws in California in 1913 that prohibited aliens from owning land, thus denying land ownership to all nonwhite groups excluded from naturalization (Takaki 1989, 203). The early twentieth century saw the growth of a racial exclusion movement, racially based nativist movements such as the Ku Klux Klan, and the passage of a racially based immigration law in 1924 targeting Japanese as well as many European groups (see ibid., 209; Higham 1955).

The Gendering and Racialization of Power: The Whites

The whites defined themselves in opposition to both Hawaiian and Asian groups, again only in the masculine. In an article written in 1922 about Hilo in 1873, a *haole* writer says: "Naturally by virtue of education, culture, refinement, and moral dignity, the missionaries were looked upon as the leading people in all matters of social and intellectual activities. These missionaries were: Rev. Titus Coan, Rev. D. B. Lyman and Dr. C. H. Wetmore, to which may be added the Hitchcock brothers, who were missionary descendants of the first generation, and who ranked with the missionaries themselves." The names Lyman and Hitchcock appear as judges and attorneys in the Hilo district and circuit courts. Sullivan comments in 1923 that "there are practically no Anglo-Saxon laborers in Hawaii, or at least no field-laborers. The Anglo-Saxon element is of exceptional quality. The men who control the industries are largely of 'Old American,' British, German, and Scandinavian stock" (1923, 533).

Indeed, from annexation until 1946, a small, interrelated group of *haole* businessmen exerted enormous political and economic power over a numerous and heterogenous nonpropertied class (Okihiro 1991, 13). Island politics revolved around the delegate to Congress, the governor appointed by the U.S. president, and the territorial legislature. During the 1930s, the so-called Big Five companies controlled thirty-six of the Territory's thirty-eight sugar plantations, as well as banking, insurance, transportation, utilities, and wholesale and retail merchandising. Interlocking directorates, intermarriages, and social associations bound this financial oligarchy closely together. By 1940, a dozen or so men managed the economy. During the Territory period, almost half the land was owned by fewer than eighty individuals, and the government owned most of the rest, producing a concentration of wealth and power more extreme than elsewhere in the United States (ibid., 14–15).

White power was described as paternal, both male and mature, and physically marked by stature. Writing a retrospective newspaper article in 1940 about his arrival in Hilo in 1898, Carl Carlsmith, one of the leading attorneys in Hilo, expresses the ideology of racialism and planter paternalism as he describes his steamer trip with frequent stops at plantation landings:

> At that time the plantation ordered oriental laborers as it did any other merchandise and if 40 men were to go to John Watt at Honokaa the ship hove to and that many human beings were hoisted in a crate to the upper cliff. (*Hilo Tribune Herald*, December 30, 1940, 37)

Carlsmith's account of the importance of the plantation managers to Hilo society in the 1890s indicates that the judiciary was part of this planter paternalism:[5]

> To be a plantation manager in the 1890s was to possess not only wealth but social and political position and a right to guide the destinies and affairs of people in the district. Judges, sheriffs and all other officers were appointed by the government residing at Honolulu. A new appointment was not usually made till approved by the managers. New enterprises were not likely to succeed unless they met with the managerial sanction. At Waiakea was C. C. Kennedy and at Wainaku was John A. Scott. Both had grown old in the sugar industry and both were charitable and kindly even if strict in the conduct of all local affairs.
>
> Beyond Waiakea there was Goodale at Onomea, Deakon at Pepeekeo, Moir at Honomu, George Ross at Hakalau, McLellan at Laupahoehoe, Walker at Ookala, Albert Horner at Kukalau, Lidgate at Paauallo, Moore at Paahau, John Watt at Honokaa and Forbes at Kukuihaele. *These were all men of great dignity, tall of stature and important because of the responsibilities given into their keeping.* (Ibid.; emphasis added)

Their height is more symbolic than physical, since at least one, John Scott, was quite short, according to one of Carlsmith's descendants who knew him. Carlsmith also comments on the power that this social class exercised over the trial courts, again reminiscing about the 1890s:

> Every three months the circuit court had a term session. The attorney general came from Honolulu and with him Chinese, Japanese, and Portuguese interpreters, lawyers, clerks, and sometimes witnesses or litigants in important cases increased the crowd. The trial jury always had plantation managers, merchants, and the first men of the circuit and rarely did anyone ask to be excused. Crimes and civil differences were adjudicated by the men of substance and standing. (Ibid.)

Carlsmith came to Hilo to be the law partner of D. H. Hitchcock, building the firm that in 1940 was Carlsmith and Carlsmith, where Carl practiced with his two sons. Here he translates power and authority into tallness and masculinity as well as whiteness, just as in the earlier descriptions of Native Hawaiians subordination and powerlessness were translated into soft eyes and feminine acquiescence.

Practices of Demarcation
Space and Work in the Racialized Labor Hierarchy of the Plantation
As the plantations expanded in the late nineteenth century, a distinctive cultural order emerged linking social class, gender, and essentialized and homogenized conceptions of nationality. As the discourse of race flourished in the United States and in Hawai'i, difference was increasingly imagined as biological. The term *paternalistic racism* describes the position in which the dominant whites imagined themselves during the plantation era. There were, as we have seen, two different versions of paternalistic racism, one for Native Hawaiians, which envisioned them as childlike, benign, and foolish but not threatening, and one for the laborers on the plantation, who needed authority to hold them in check because they lacked the self-restraint and self-control found among other races, such as the whites. Laborers who were Christians, as a few were, seem to have been regarded more sympathetically, as were those who were racially white. The image of the Native Hawaiians reflects the missionary past and their conversion to Christianity.

I use the term *paternalism* along with *racism* because this is an image of power that is gendered as well as raced. As we have seen, white privilege is always located in a male body, often a tall or virile male body. The dominant whites did not imagine themselves engaged in maternal caretaking but in paternal disciplining, exerting a benevolent but stern form of authority. The masculinized authority drew added strength from the reformist element of Hawai'i missionary society because it was thought to improve the character of its subjects. The image of paternal power enabled violence to be thought of as discipline, justifying the considerable use of flogging and whips on the plantations. There were, of course, forms of violence that were thought to be excessive, just as paternal authority in the home required violence—but not excessive violence—to establish and maintain discipline. Together, paternalism and racism provided a language for thinking about the violence of plantation life, tying together masculinity and whiteness. The whip was part of the necessary discipline of subordinate races, who deserved—indeed, even chose—this violence when they failed to go along with the rules, just as women who fail to abide by their husbands' commands choose violence. Women choose violence by talking back to their husbands, as did workers who resisted the orders of the *lunas*, their supervisors. As with male discipline over women, the violence was envisioned as improving the subordinates.

Although the discourses are similar, the practices of exclusion in Hawai'i differed from those of the mainland, particularly California. Because Hawai'i was not envisioned as a place for white settlement, immigrant workers did not compete with working-class whites as they did in California. There, the competition raised intense and violent ethnic antagonism. But in Hawai'i, the immigrants had ways of weaving themselves and their cultures into Hawai'i in a way not possible on the continent (Takaki 1989, 176). The white planters were opposed largely by Native Hawaiians rather than by a white working class.

Planters did have a racial preference for European workers, who were imagined to make better citizens than "coolie" labor. But these Europeans were unwilling to stay on the plantations and work for such low wages under such degrading discipline. They typically complained bitterly and left. Efforts to import Germans and Norwegians failed, and even the Portuguese, who came in far greater numbers, left the plantations as soon as they could. A set of Hilo newspaper articles from the late nineteenth century describes the Portuguese as good people—industrious and helpful—but unfortunately leaving for better opportunities in California.[6]

The system of discipline created by the plantations depended on the creation of a hierarchy of racial and gendered identities grounded in alleged labor capacities and marked by spatial segregation. When the plantations imported laborers for the cane fields, they constructed ethnically segregated housing for them, which was generally labeled as the "Japanese camp," the "Puerto Rican camp," the "Filipino camp" (Sharma 1980, 97). Supervisors, called *lunas*, who were generally *haole* (white), Native Hawaiian, Portuguese, or, by mid-century, Japanese, lived in special parts of the plantation housing divided from those of other backgrounds by roads and by rules not to play with the children across the street.

Linked to this economic hierarchy was an ideology of planter paternalism in which planters justified their extensive systems of regulation, surveillance, and control in terms of the need for a strong hand of authority against workers envisioned as "coolies." Okihiro quotes an editorial from the July 26, 1904, *Pacific Commercial Advertiser* on the psychology of the "plantation coolie":

> Yield to his demands and he thinks he is the master and makes new demands; use the strong hand and he recognizes the power to which, from immemorial times, he has abjectly bowed. There is one word which holds the lower classes of every nation in check and that is Authority. (Okihiro 1991, 35)

This authority was exercised through the system of contract labor and its penal sanctions for violation of the contract, local police and plantation police, a system of rules and fines, physical abuse, and fear generated by lynchings such as the 1889 murder of Goto, a well-known advocate of Japanese workers on the Hamakua Coast north of Hilo by five whites employed as foremen on nearby plantations (ibid.). The whites were found guilty of manslaughter but were released on bail pending an appeal and promptly left the islands (Beechert 1985, 115).

Planter paternalism incorporated missionary ideas of Christian charity and benevolence into the old rhetoric of civilization: "A plantation is a means of civilization," says the 1886 *Planter's Monthly*. "It has come in very many instances like a mission of progress into a barbarous region and stamped its character on the neighborhood for miles around" (Okihiro 1991, 40). As Okihiro notes, plantations upheld Christianity and civilization in the wilderness and the plantation master, through discipline and parental affection, cultivated cane and morality among his impressionable charges. An essay in the *Planter's Monthly*, "A Manager's Influence," talks about the master's burden: "Every manager has a grave responsibility in keeping up discipline and order on his plantation as well as a healthy moral tone." The plantation order was a moral order in which the manager controlled virtually all aspects of workers' lives (ibid.).

Planters' paternalistic discourse toward workers was couched in the language of an essentialized racial/national identity definitive of labor capacities. For example, in 1870, E. G. Hitchcock, a judge, sugar planter, and brother of D. H. Hitchcock, also a prominent local attorney, in responding to a questionnaire from the Department of Finance with reference to his plantation of 65.5 acres, remarked: "Native laborers are much superior to any other laborers, if kept out of debt, well fed, and kindly but strictly treated."[7] Plantation documents described workers in categories that merged tasks with racial and gender identities. The manager's report from the Olaa Sugar Company, for example, lists its workers in 1901 and 1902, the first few years of its operation, as shown in Table 7.2.

This curious list of employees, similar to that provided in other plantation managers' reports, blends occupation, nationality, and gender as if they all refer to the same thing. In other words, work is so deeply understood in categories of race and gender that these identities stand in for occupational identities, just as the first three categories of occupation similarly encode a racial and gender designation of *haole* male, although this identity is simply implicit. Race and gender provided the categories by which *haole* elites talked about work and the job to which a person was assigned, to a large extent: there were clearly female jobs and male jobs, while top management was reserved for *haoles* and middle management (*lunas*) largely for *haoles* or Portuguese. In the language of H. P. Baldwin, a prominent *haole* planter, writing in 1894:

Table 7.2 Labor statement, Olaa Sugar Company

	1901	1902
Management and Office	11	13
Lunas	34	14
Mechanics	42	18
Chinese Cane Cultivation Contractors	21	46
Japanese Cane Cultivation Contractors	399	577
Japanese day laborers	805	424
Japanese day women	38	6
Chinese	206	2
Portuguese	100	91
Hawaiians	20	9
Porto Ricans	220	85
Porto Rican Women	17	2
Other Nationalities	19	7
Sundry Clearing Contracts	550	...
Harvesting Contracts		
Japanese		496
Chinese		89
Porto Ricans		45
	2485	1924

Source: Manager's report, Olaa Sugar Company, 1902, 23 (reproduced exactly as in original report), from Hawaiian Collection of the University of Hawai'i/Hilo.

The field or ordinary labor on our plantations is done by Hawaiian, Portuguese, Chinese and Japanese. All these classes make good all-round plantation laborers. The Portuguese, who come from Madeira and the Azores, are the best for heavy work; the Hawaiians make good teamsters, and the Chinese and Japanese excel for factory work. The Japanese are good workers, but are not so easily managed as Chinese, and where there is a large number of them on a plantation they are apt to combine and make trouble in various ways. (Baldwin 1894, 668)

The various groups are identified as "classes" and their essentialized identities defined by alleged shared labor capacities.

The widespread practice of paying different wage rates to workers of different nationalities for the same work powerfully underscored the meanings of these essentialized identities. For example, on one plantation in Honokaa, north of Hilo, Portuguese workers were paid fifteen to sixteen dollars a month in 1885, while newly arrived Japanese were paid nine dollars (Okihiro 1991, 60). Between 1915 and 1933, Filipino males were typically paid eighteen to twenty dollars a month, while Filipino women were paid twelve to fourteen dollars (Sharma 1980, 98). Such wage differentials, which were common, fueled discontent and were important grievances in the early labor movements in the twentieth century (Okihiro 1991; Takaki 1989). They impeded the formation of cross-national labor unions during the early years of the twentieth century, but as plantation workers joined across these lines, their union efforts were more successful (Beechert 1985).

Gender, race, and occupation also determined housing. The Hawaiian Sugar Planter's Association developed blueprints for plantation camps in 1920 that showed how these differences in identity were reflected in the design of houses. The overall plan for the camp suggests the orderly grid of control and surveillance that Michel Foucault sees as central to the disciplinary society. Camps were segregated by ethnicity as well as by occupational rank. As the sugar industry has declined, some of these barriers to housing have slowly and grudgingly given way. For example, the great house of the Olaa Sugar Company, a massive structure overlooking fields and the ocean, was home to its first non-*haole* when a Japanese American was hired as manager to oversee the last years of the plantation's operation in the late 1970s.

Thus, the variegated identities of immigrant and settled populations were homogenized and essentialized in the social order of nineteenth- and early-twentieth-century Hilo: Japanese became a single identity, regardless of prefecture of origin, as did Filipino, despite the significant regional variations in the Philippines. The multiplicity of regions of China were subsumed into a single identity marker in the context of Hilo identity formation. Hawaiian also became singular, despite significant differences in rank.

People are marked in court records in terms of these essentialized identities just as they are classified into such groups for purposes of disciplining and ordering a plantation labor force and reinforcing the hierarchy and the planter paternalism on which it depends. Not only subordinates become homogenized, of course, but also the *haole* elites, who themselves took on a uniformity of identity, extending even to the body, as they all came to be "strong and virile," or "tall of stature." This identity, when it was one of authority, was also masculine.

Naming Identities and Strategies of Governance

The discourse of nationality, as identities were named in the plantations, was fundamental to official communications and planter journals as well as court records at least until the 1940s. As the structure of governmentality, based on measuring and administering populations developed, these populations were always seen as raced and gendered units. The 1884 census counted people by gender and ethnicity as well as by place of residence. Police arrest statistics until the 1940s listed arrests by nationality. Court records are quite explicit about ethnicity, particularly in the nineteenth century, typically identifying defendants by an unambiguous ethnic label. Of a total set of 5,628 district and circuit court cases from Hilo beginning in 1853 until 1985, half (51 percent) mentioned the ethnic identity of the defendants. During the 1860s, 1870s, and 1880s, ethnicity was mentioned in about half the cases. The percentage was highest in the 1890s and 1900s, when ethnic identity was mentioned in more than three-fourths of all cases, then fell to under 20 percent in the twentieth century. In 2,510 Hilo circuit court cases from 1852 to 1892, 62 percent mentioned the defendant's nationality, and in the district court of the same period, 54 percent identified nationality, reaching a high of 89 percent in 1893. These variations reflect the fact that Puerto Ricans and Japanese were almost always identified by nationality, while Hawaiians were rarely identified (20 percent of the cases) and *haoles* (whites) even less often (12 percent). Nineteenth-century district court case records frequently refer to witnesses and defendants as "the Chinaman" or "Jap" rather than by name, but *haoles* are generally identified by name. Hawaiians are identified by name and gender (because names do not specify gender), but not nationality. Asian defendants are identified by name and nationality but not gender, probably because the vast majority were male. In the late nineteenth century, they are also often identified by a number, presumably the "bango" number assigned by the plantation. *Haole* defendants are the only ones identified by name and title (such as Mr. or Mrs.). During the latter part of the nineteenth century, *haoles* are sometimes identified in the court record by "F," which presumably means foreign.

The practice of stating the defendant's nationality in the docket book diminished in the twentieth century, as only 9 percent of the 805 Hilo circuit court cases I examined between 1905 and 1985 stated the nationality of the defendant, but practices of identifying defendants by nationality occur throughout the detailed case records, probation reports, psychological examinations, and other information considered in case processing well into the 1940s. Intermarriage and cultural blending increasingly rendered these identities far more malleable and ambiguous than they were imagined to be, but official documents such as court records, police reports, and census forms resolutely refuse to incorporate this ambiguity. These identities represented the crystallization of complex local and regional identities in the locations from which they came into essentialized national identities within the Hawaiian context.

Assimilation, Incorporation, and the Blood Quantum

In 1920, the U.S. Congress allocated a large stretch of land to the Native Hawaiian people to serve as a homeland. The Hawaiian Homelands were to be awarded to any Native Hawaiian of a blood quantum of 50 percent or higher who applied. Plots were allocated as homesteads and as ranches. Despite the promise of this scheme, large numbers of Native Hawaiians lingered for years on waiting lists and substantial portions of Homelands property were leased to plantations and government and commercial uses such as airports and shopping malls. Moreover, the divisive effects of the blood quantum system are a major concern for contemporary Hawaiian sovereignty activists (see Trask 1993; Hasager and Friedman 1994). As the proportion of the population of Native Hawaiians with the requisite blood quantum falls, the number eligible for this benefit also drops. Moreover, the allocation of a benefit on the basis of blood rather than self-identification violates contemporary understandings of Hawaiian identity, creating a line different from that of everyday social practice. Other benefits to Native Hawaiians, such as attendance at the Kamehameha School (a private school designed for Native Hawaiians only) or participation in a plebiscite on the future of Native Hawaiian sovereignty held in 1996, depend on self-identification as Native Hawaiian and the possession of some Native Hawaiian ancestry rather than percentage Native Hawaiian ancestry. These conflicting and crosscutting definitions of identity attached to entitlements fracture the Hawaiian community and draw lines at variance from those of social practice.

The concept of blood quantum was imported to colonial Hawai'i from the policies toward Native Americans. The notion of blood quantum was fundamental to the approach to Native Americans, because it envisioned the ultimate assimilation of the Native Americans into the cultural and biological mainstream of American society (Hoxie 1989). The notion of defining identity by blood quantum, rather than according to the "one-drop" rule sometimes adopted toward African American populations, focuses on incorporation and the ultimate disappearance of the group rather than its permanent marking and exclusion.

It is no coincidence that this approach to defining identity was adopted toward those two groups that possessed extensive land claims that stood in the way of American economic and political expansion. Moreover, both groups were heavily subjected to Christian missionization. The missionary endeavor was fundamentally incorporative and assimilative: its goal was to save and transform, and then to retain, the convert in the fold of new forms of belief and conduct rather than to mark and exclude. Boundaries were drawn on the basis of behavior, with those who failed to conform excluded from churches and excommunicated from membership in the Christian community. Thus, the logic was fundamentally different from that applied to the Asians and more similar to that used with Native Americans. Here again, there is a global context within which these approaches were developed and applied and a global transfer of mechanisms of defining and dividing identities.

Conclusions

Several processes were critically important in forging discrete identities out of the multiplicity of persons and ancestries in Hilo. One was the dynamics of the initial encounter and the cultural categories that determined them. The Christian missionary encounter with the Hawaiian people well predated any attempt to convert the Hawaiian commoners into a plantation labor force. Instead, Hawaiians were understood as potential converts subject to transformation and incorporation, although the failure of this project propelled the missionaries to attribute inherent flaws of character and intellect to the Hawaiian population. In contrast, the encounter between the planters and the Asian laborers was structured by labor demands and the exigencies of producing sugar. This encounter was also shaped by ideas of racial labor capacities and the need for authoritarian control of nonwhite workers by plantation managers.

A second process was the introduction of legal regulations of citizenship, immigration, and labor. The notion that whites and Native Hawaiians were citizens or potential citizens if they were willing to swear an oath of allegiance to the kingdom differed significantly from the assumption that Asians could never become naturalized citizens. This was the essence of the "coolie" labor designation. Although there was no effort to restrict miscegenation in Hawai'i as there was in California, there was concern by Native Hawaiians about the number of Chinese men arriving without wives and an effort to change the gender ratio of these immigrants. The differential preference for various groups of laborers led to different patterns of immigration as well. Portuguese workers were allowed to come as families; Chinese and Filipino workers were brought as single men. Although Japanese workers usually came as single men, they were allowed to import wives from Japan. The consequences of these differences in immigration policies were enormous to a community's ability to create its own institutions and produce an assimilated second generation.

Differential treatment of laborers on the plantations also contributed significantly to the creation of essentialized and bounded identities. The strict allocation of jobs and housing on the basis of "nationality" reinforced social boundaries, while differential pay rates exacerbated hostilities. In the early twentieth century, all social life was conceived through these categories, including baseball teams and schools. Early union movements followed these lines as well, although by the 1920s cross-national unions gradually emerged and became more effective.

Finally, a third social process concerns practices of governmentality: forms of counting, measuring, and knowledge production about the population. Categories of the census changed over time but race remained a distinct and fundamental concept. Court records similarly encoded identities, reflecting an assumption that these identities represented knowledge essential for the judgment of criminal cases. In the post–World War II period, efforts to count and measure continue, although the difficulty of sorting and labeling has become more obvious. The shift to a self-report strategy in the census as well as in police and court records retains the notion of a fixed identity but transfers the locus of announcement to the individual himself or herself. The use of multiple identity categories in the 2000 census is a further recognition of these problems.

In describing these processes, it is clear that they are deeply rooted in local situations. Yet they are also formed by the transfer of global categories of identity. The Christian mission was a transnational phenomenon, deeply shaped by the experiences of other missionary endeavors in its approaches and forms of understanding. Missionaries frequently moved from one field to another and communicated with each other through missionary publications such as the *Missionary Herald*. Similarly, the sugar plantation is a transnational institution whose forms of labor management and social ordering were developed through shared discourses across national and colonial boundaries (Curtin 1990). The contract labor system and its underlying legislation was a global institution, circulated along with ideas about distinctive racialized labor capacities. Finally, conceptions of indigenous peoples were transplanted from mainland North America to Hawai'i to shape evolving policies toward Native Hawaiians. In sum, the emergence of a new world order is not simply a recent phenomenon, but was also fundamental to nineteenth- and early-twentieth-century imperialism.

Notes

The research in this essay was generously funded by grants from the National Science Foundation, both the Law and Social Sciences Program and the Cultural Anthropology Program, the National Endowment for the Humanities, and the Canadian Institute for Advanced Research. The Bunting Institute at Radcliffe College provided an ideal working environment. I have also received support from Wellesley College in conjunction with my chair, the Class of 1949 Chair in Ethics.

1. *Planter's Monthly* 6 (1887): 499. In Hawai'i as a whole, the plantation labor force in 1887 was 12 percent Hawaiian, 26 percent Portuguese, 14 percent Japanese, 39 percent Chinese, 3 percent South Sea Islanders, and 5 percent other nationalities (ibid.).

2. In 1866, the French consul in Hawai'i was murdered by his Chinese cook, Asee, fanning the flames of fear, even though Chinese merchants in Honolulu contributed to offering a reward for Asee's capture. In 1879, a group of Chinese workers attacked their *luna* with cane knives and in 1881 a Chinese employee murdered his employer (Lydon 1975, 59).

3. Thousands of Japanese workers left for the mainland and higher wages after their contracts were filled. By early 1907, forty thousand Japanese had left Hawai'i for the West Coast. The 1907 order prohibiting Japanese from Hawai'i from going to the mainland trapped many eager emigrants in Hawai'i (Takaki 1989, 148).

4. This same bifurcation of notions of race and virtue was replicated in Fiji, but the indigenous Fijians were viewed by the British colonial government as childlike, whereas the laborers imported from India to work the cane received the same disdain as the Chinese, Japanese, and Portuguese in Hawai'i (Kelly 1994).

5. Takaki (1989) also uses the term *planter paternalism*, but without explicit attention to its gendered meaning.

6. Luther Severance, a prominent member of Hilo society, kept a scrapbook of newspaper clippings about Hilo covering the end of the nineteenth century. Many of the clippings are undated, presumably cut from Honolulu papers. This scrapbook is an invaluable resource on Hilo history. It is in the Lyman House Memorial Museum in Hilo, Hawai'i (cited hereafter as Severance Scrapbook).

7. Hawaiian Kingdom, Finance Office, March 10, 1870, Hawaii State Archives; quoted in Kelly, Nakamura, and Barrere (1981, 87).

References

Andrews, Lorrin. 1836. "Letter from Lahainaluna." *Missionary Herald* (October): 390–91.

Anon. 1864. *From Chamber's Journal.* "A Doomed People." *Eclectic Magazine* 64 (February): 250–56.

Baldwin, H. P. 1894. "The Sugar Industry in Hawaii." *Overland Monthly* 25: 663–68.

Beechert, Edward D. 1985. *Working in Hawaii: A Labor History.* Honolulu: University of Hawaii Press.

———. 1993. "Patterns of Resistance and the Social Relations of Production in Hawaii." In *Plantation Workers: Resistance and Accomodation*, ed. Brij V. Lal, Doug Munro, and Edward Beechert. Honolulu: University of Hawaii Press. 45–69.

Blaisdell, Kekuni, and Noreen Mokuau. 1994. *"Kanaka Maoli*: Indigenous Hawaiians." In *Hawai'i: Return to Nationhood*, ed. Ulla Hasager and Jonathan Friedman. Copenhagen: International Work Group for Indigenous Affairs, Document no. 75. 49–68.

Coan, Titus. 1882. *Life in Hawaii: An Autobiographic Sketch of Mission Life and Labors (1835–1881)*. New York: Anson D. F. Randolph & Company.

Curtin, Philip. 1990. *The Rise and Fall of the Plantation Complex: Essays in Atlantic History*. Cambridge: Cambridge University Press.

Daws, Gavan. 1968. *Shoal of Time: A History of the Hawaiian Islands*. Honolulu: University of Hawaii Press.

Fitch, George H. 1888. "The Pygmy Kingdom of a Debauchee." *The Cosmopolitan* 4: 123–33.

George, Milton C. 1948. *The Development of Hilo, Hawaii, TH or; a Slice through Time at a Place Called Hilo*. Ann Arbor, Mich.: Edwards Letter Shop.

Godkin, E. L. 1893. "Hawaii." *Nation* 56 (1441): 96.

Handy, E. S. Craighill, and Mary Kawena Pukui. [1958] 1972. *The Polynesian Family System in Ka-'u, Hawai'i*. Rutland, Vt.: Charles E. Tuttle.

Hasager, Ulla, and Jonathan Friedman, eds. 1994. *Hawai'i: Return to Nationhood*. Copenhagen: International Work Group for Indigenous Affairs, Document no. 75.

Higham, John. 1955. *Strangers in the Land: Patterns of American Nativism, 1860–1925*. Reprint. New York: Atheneum, 1970.

Hoxie, Frederick E. 1989. *A Final Promise: The Campaign to Assimilate the Indians, 1880–1920*. Cambridge: Cambridge University Press.

Humphrey, Rev., S.J. N.d. *Titus Coan: Missionary and Explorer, 1801–1882*. From "American Heroes on Mission Fields," by permission of the American Tract Society. Worcester, Mass.: Archives of American Antiquarian Society.

Kelly, John D. 1994. *The Politics of Virtue*. Princeton, N.J.: Princeton University Press.

Kelly, Marion, Barry Nakamura, and Dorothy B. Barrere. 1981. "Hilo Bay: A Chronological History." Prepared for U.S. Army Engineer District, Honolulu. Typescript.

Kingdom of Hawai'i. 1846. *Answers to Questions: Proposed by His Excellency R. C. Wyllie, His Hawaiian Majesty's Minister of Foreign Relations, and addressed to all the Missionaries in the Hawaiian Islands, May 1846*. Honolulu: Kingdom of Hawaii.

Kuykendall, Ralph S. 1938. *The Hawaiian Kingdom*, vol. 1, *1778–1854*. Honolulu: University of Hawaii Press.

———. 1953. *The Hawaiian Kingdom*, vol. 2, *1854–1874, Twenty Critical Years*. Honolulu: University of Hawaii Press.

————. 1967. *The Hawaiian Kingdom*, vol. 3, *1874–1893, The Kakakaua Dynasty*. Honolulu: University of Hawaii Press.

Leithead, A. Scott. 1974. "Hilo, Hawaii: Its Origins and the Pattern of Its Growth, 1778–1900." Unpublished B.A. honor's thesis, University of Hawaii, Department of History.

Lind, A. W. 1955. *Hawaii's People*. Honolulu: University of Hawai'i Press.

Lydon, Edward C. 1975. *The Anti-Chinese Movement in the Hawaiian Kingdom, 1852–1886*. San Francisco: R and E Research Associates.

Maurer, Bill. 1997. *Recharting the Caribbean: Land, Law, and Citizenship in the British Virgin Islands*. Ann Arbor: University of Michigan Press.

Merry, Sally Engle. 1997. "Legal Vernacularization and Transnational Culture: The Ka Ho'okolokolonui Kanaka Maoli, Hawai'i 1993." In *Human Rights, Culture and Context: Anthropological Perspectives*, ed. Richard Wilson. London: Pluto Press. 28–49.

Okihiro, Gary. 1991. *Cane Fires*. Philadelphia: Temple University Press.

Oleson, Rev. William Brewster. 1908. "Just like a Hawaiian." *The Friend* (October): 80.

Sharma, Miriam. 1980. "Pinoy in Paradise: Environment and Adaptation of Philipinos in Hawaii, 1906–1946." *Amerasia Journal* 7: 91–117.

Sullivan, Louis R. 1923. "The Labor Crisis in Hawaii." *Asia Magazine* 23: 511–34.

Takaki, Ronald. 1989. *Strangers from a Different Shore: A History of Asian Americans*. Boston: Little, Brown.

Thurston, Lorrin A. N.d. (circa 1897). *A Handbook on the Annexation of Hawaii*. Pamphlet. N.p.

Trask, Haunani-Kay. 1993. *From a Native Daughter: Colonialism and Sovereignty in Hawai'i*. Monroe, Maine: Common Courage Press.

Wyllie, Robert. 1844. "Native Seamen." *The Friend*, 79.

CHAPTER 8

Sex and Space in the Global City

Lisa Sanchez

In 1989, the first "all-nude" strip club opened its doors in the city of
Portland, Oregon.[1] The conversion of ten area topless bars to all-nude
strip clubs following a Supreme Court ruling that legalized full nudity
in business establishments took place so quietly as to seem mundane,
unremarkable. Three years later, the number of all-nude dance clubs in
Portland had grown to fifty, neighborhood taverns had converted to
strip clubs, pornography stores were advertising "live nude models," and
escort services were on the rise. In addition, new forms of adult entertainment, such as "lingerie clubs" and "gentleman's tanning salons,"
surfaced on the Eastside, creating a plethora of images and spaces for
sexual commerce in Portland. Given the rapid expansion of these commercial sex markets, many Portlanders thought that the commercial sex
industry had reached a peak by 1992. However, between 1992 and 1997,
the number of legal adult businesses continued to rise—in 1994 there
were nearly eighty strip clubs, and by 1995, the number of strip clubs
and other adult entertainment businesses continued to increase. In the
summer of 1997, the city witnessed its first visible sign that the market
for sexual labor and consumption might finally have reached a satura-
tion point. The most vivid indication of this possibility appeared on a
billboard located just south of the city limits along the main highway
leading into east Portland. Advertising casino gambling at one of five
Indian reservations, most of the space of the billboard for the casino

was consumed with a larger-than-life portrait of an older white woman wearing a sequined bikini and feathered headdress. Adorned in garish clothing, the woman on the billboard appeared wrinkled and haggard, mascara running down her face and dark circles under her eyes. The sign, which read "Welcome to Ghost Ranch Casino, *No* Girls, Girls, Girls," played upon the local knowledge that in Portland entertainment venues, the absence of dancers was the exception rather than the rule.

Studies of commercial sex practices, as well as the legal and regulatory regimes that govern them, focus overwhelmingly on prostitution and on normative questions regarding the sexual conduct and motivations of individual sex workers. Such studies are characteristically dislocated from the broader political economy of capital, labor, and consumption. This narrow focus has reproduced a monolithic and historically immutable picture of commercial sex, overshadowing the diversity of sexual practices that constitute commercial sex markets and the historical and cultural specificity of the political economies in which they emerge.

This essay focuses on the relationship between global economic restructuring and the formation of local labor and consumption markets specializing in commercial sex services and performances. Framing sexual commerce against the backdrop of globalization, with its transnational labor flows and markets, it draws upon field research in licit and illicit commercial sex markets in Portland and regional data on labor and consumption. The essay argues that the emergence of a flourishing economy of commercial sex in Portland should be understood in relation to cultural images and practices that are circulated in the national and global economy within the context of late-modern global capitalism. Second, it traces the emergence of the "prostitution-free zone ordinance," which utilizes trespass law to exclude women involved in street-level prostitution from public spaces and city streets. This new regulatory strategy has developed in response to local conflicts over the commercial sex industry. As an emergent strategy of "spatial governmentality," the prostitution-free zone ordinance is one outgrowth of global economic change. It is situated at the crossroads of cultural and economic development and of the unique political and spatial economy of the city.

Global Cities, Regional Nodes, and Informal Economies

Contemporary scholarship on globalization has focused on global finance, law, and labor (Sassen 1988, 1991, 1994; Maurer 1997; Darian-Smith 1997), migration and immigration (Cesarini and Fulbrook 1996; Calavita 1998), feminized labor and service work (Ong 1987; Sassen 1988; Enloe 1990), and the cultural dimensions of globalization (Harvey 1989; Hannerz 1990; Featherstone 1990; Appadurai 1996). In *The Global City*, Saskia Sassen (1991) suggests that global economic restructuring produces an economy of centrality and marginality within the dominant centers of finance and technology (e.g., New York, Tokyo, and London), increasing wealth disparities and urban segregation, and enabling new forms of labor exploitation in the global cities. This economy of centrality and marginality has usually been viewed in terms of the duality of highly developed and less developed countries (Sassen 1991, 1994). As Calavita suggests, the so-called global economy has "crystallized around a few decision-making capitals in the first world, some low-wage manufacturing in third-world countries, and the majority of the world's population marginalized from this 'global' process" (1998, 315). But although scholars have often drawn attention to the way in which global relations of capital have produced marginalized labor forces in developing countries, economic polarization and disinvestment in local human capital are also evident in economically advanced countries and across neighborhood enclaves within cities. Alongside global economic restructuring, deindustrialization has accelerated economic polarization domestically, shifting the weight of economic activity from production places to centers of finance and service and leaving the industrial centers of manufacturing and heavy industry in flux (Bluestone and Harrison 1982; Harvey 1989; Sassen 1991).

According to the global cities model, the "regional node" occupies a third kind of spatial and economic position in relation to the global economy. Regional nodes include cities and rural regions that are peripherally linked to the global economy, providing goods and services to the dominant centers of finance and capital (Sassen 1994). There is some evidence to suggest that regional nodes are arising in cities that were formerly major industrial centers. Thus, some of those regions that were hit hardest by deindustrialization may have adapted to the sharp decline in domestic production by taking a secondary role in the global economy. Unlike the global cities, Portland does not have the status or infrastructure to support global financial markets, and it has not developed a broad-scale service economy to support such markets. Rather, Portland's economic planners focused on attracting business enterprises that are necessary to the development of global finance and capital centered in distant global cities. Occupying the position of a regional node, which services the dominant centers of finance and capital, Portland has taken neither a central nor a wholly marginal role in the new world economy.

Portland's position in the global economy has resulted in a number of local economic and social transitions. Most notably it has resulted in a shift in the primary economic base from a resource extraction model centered on logging and shipping to high-tech electronics, software development, and nonpolluting light industry. Two major global economic factors have contributed to this transformation of Portland's political economy. First, the primary economies of timber extraction, processing, and shipping have taken a downturn in recent years because of increased competition from developing countries and environmental restrictions on air pollution and clear-cutting. Portland's home state is one of the largest producers of lumber and paper products in the world, with processing industries located in the outskirts of the city and in the suburbs. But in recent years, attempts to limit clear-cutting and preserve animal species indigenous to the region in the face of competition from rapidly deforesting nations that cannot afford to limit their primary economic base have decreased the city's potential to use timber to generate revenues.

Second, in an effort to jockey for some position in a changing world economy, Portland encoded a series of new tax laws intended to draw nonpolluting light industry and technological enterprises to the region. Two major incentives for industrial investment include the Enterprise Zone Program and the Strategic Investment Program. The Enterprise Zone Program allows local jurisdictions to vote to waive property taxes on new buildings and equipment for technology and light industry for three years, or up to five years for companies creating "especially high-paying jobs" (Report of the Economic Development Department, 1997). The strategic investment law allows local governments to approve property tax abatements for up to fifteen years for key industrial companies investing more than $100 million of assessed value in property and equipment. According to the Economic Development Department, the purpose of the tax incentive is to bring employment to the region by "encouraging extremely capital-intensive investments, especially investments in high technology" (ibid.). Part of the motivation to enact the law was to encourage Intel to retain its world-leading microprocessor development group in the region. Intel designed the Pentium chip in Portland, prompting the Economic Development Department to contribute $12 million to assist in the development of technology that will resolve the "millennium problem" (ibid.). Not surprisingly, the five companies that have taken advantage of the Strategic Investment Program include Intel, IDT, Sumitomo, Fujitso, and LSI Logic. These companies are located in the middle-class and upper-income neighborhoods of Portland's Westside and in the outlying regions of the city.

The past two decades of business-friendly tax laws have attracted some new corporations and jobs to the region. However, these jobs have been available primarily to highly skilled workers and professionals trained in technology and business marketing and management, and the labor force in these new enterprises consists of a large proportion of migrants who were recruited from out of town. The Economic Development Department's report on net personal income by industry provides one means of comparing the growth in traditional manufacturing and resource extraction industries with high-tech industries. Between 1986 and 1995, figures on the comparative growth of select industries show electronics to have increased by 290 percent, and technological machinery and equipment to have increased by 120 percent. By comparison, forestry increased by only 31 percent, lumber and wood products by 18 percent, and fishing decreased by 25 percent during the same period.

It has been widely acknowledged that one of the key features of the contemporary global economy is the broad expansion of service sectors in a number of regions across the globe (Daniels 1985; Sassen 1991, 1994; Lash and Urry 1994). Although service industries existed to support production and enhance the quality of life in centers of production long before deindustrialization, services have become more diversified and specialized in the postindustrial era (Daniels 1985). This shift from manufacturing to service and light industry has taken shape as a gendered reorganization of labor, with traditionally male-dominated industrial economies being displaced by a growing service sector consisting largely of women and immigrant workers. Although these changes may appear as a more egalitarian distribution of labor represented by less gender-based structures of work, they may instead reveal "yet another step in the formation of a supply of cheap and powerless workers" (Sassen 1991, 286).

There is a growing body of literature on the relationship between globalization and informal and illicit economies (Portes, Castells, and Benton 1989; Sassen 1991). Underground economies, informal economies, and tax evasion are three forms of economic activity that are distinct from the formal economy in that they are not recorded in official economic statistics, and the commodities and services produced are sold and assembled outside the regulatory apparatus that governs zoning, tax, and labor law (Sassen 1991). Street vending, software and video piracy, piecework, casual labor, and illicit drug manufacturing and sales are each examples of unrecorded informal and illicit economic activity that fluctuate in relation to the economic polarization and urban ghettoization of a globally restructured economy. Whether licit or illicit, commercial sex in Portland is most closely constituted as informal or illicit economic activity because it is officially unacknowledged and either legally prohibited or performed under conditions that fail to meet the minimum requirements of formal labor markets.[2] Participation in these sexualized forms of illicit and informal labor partially mimic and partially diverge from participation in other forms of feminized labor and service work.

The Sociospatial Economy of Commercial Sex in Portland: Local Effects of Global Processes

The restructuring of Portland's economy can be described as a series of geographic and economic dislocations and relocations. Increased social and economic disparities are expressed in the city as a visible difference in the quality of life or "neighborhood livability" of the spendy Westside neighborhoods and the economically deteriorated Eastside. To understand these disparities, it is instructive to consider the history of land use and planning, and the local sentiments toward property ownership in Portland. Located along the western frontier, Portland's home state places a high value on property ownership and "wise land-use practices." Property is a key cultural symbol in Portland, giving character and meaning to the lived experience of city dwellers and rural residents alike. What one does with one's "own" property is respected in the culture and usually met with little interference from the state; even those who do not own their home or the land beneath it are likely to subscribe to these values. Advocating wise land-use and development practices, the city has managed urban growth and preserved its natural environment in a way that is unmatched in most cities in the United States (Kunstler 1993). Portland's particular blend of economic and cultural values has produced a city politics that celebrates a deregulated market and a planning politics that enhances business liberties but holds a tight rein on developers. Within this kind of sociopolitical climate, Portland has attempted to preserve an older way of life and development has been tightly controlled in the built environments of the city.

But, not unlike other urban areas, Portland has its share of economic deterioration and urban decay. The decline of manufacturing and resource extraction economies in Portland, coupled with a growing disinvestment in local human capital, has accelerated economic and geographic polarization within the boundaries of the city. While funds for regentrification projects have flowed from both public and private sources into the business districts of the Westside and the downtown area, the city has focused little energy on rebuilding the economically depressed communities of the Eastside, particularly southeast Portland. For more than 20 years, the federal Model Cities program has provided funds for capital construction projects, but these funds were not distributed to all regions of the city. Southeast Portland was the only sector of the metropolitan area that was left out of the Model Cities program, which provided federal funding for urban renewal projects across the country (Report of the Office of Neighborhood Associations, November 1975). The exclusion of the city's most transitional and socioeconomically disenfranchised community from the Model Cities program makes it possible to present a public image of high-quality living against the backdrop of clear blue skies and Portland trees for all Portland residents.

In the 1980s and early 1990s, the most deteriorated areas in the city included the predominantly African American business districts and residential enclaves of north and inner northeast Portland (Sanchez 1997a, 1997b, 1998). But the shape and texture of the local landscape has changed in recent years. Between 1995 and 1997, residents of inner northeast Portland have successfully appealed to the preventionist factions of local and state government. Using a variation of the "broken windows" argument focused on deterring gang activities, prostitution, and drug sales from their area (Wilson and Kelling 1982), the residents of inner northeast Portland have secured city, state, and private funds for major regentrification efforts, and street prostitution has all but disappeared from the area. Although the African American residents of inner northeast Portland are no less marginalized than their Anglo-American neighbors in southeast Portland, they have a critical mass of grassroots activists focused on social and economic inclusion. In contrast, the predominantly white neighborhood enclaves of southeast Portland lack a focused political subjectivity, and remain a community of quietly disenfranchised poor. As one city commissioner explained, capital construction is needed to produce jobs in Southeast Portland: "We're painting storefronts in Southeast and funding major capital construction projects in Northeast" (*Oregonian*, January 7, 1997). The problem is not just that many of the poor and working-class residents of the Eastside have been left without jobs. More important, they are lacking a stable economic base, as well as the public and private funding to rebuild their economy.

Beginning in the late 1980s, however, a wide variety of adult entertainment venues opened in the city, providing a new source of revenue for east Portland and boosting alcohol sales in the clubs and taverns that hosted these venues. Although the rapid growth in Portland's commercial sex industry may seem to defy the conservative planning politics of the city, the trend is paradoxically predictable. There are a couple of reasons that the development of the adult entertainment industry has taken this path. First, the state's libertarian-influenced high courts have ruled consistently in favor of the expansion and minimal regulation of legal adult businesses. In 1989, a Ninth Circuit Court judge ruled that full nudity could no longer be prohibited by city ordinance because it discriminated against business establishments selling alcohol (*Oregonian*, May 1990). By contrast, public nudity was allowed in art classes, in the making of pornography, and at some river beaches and county fairs (one particular county fair is known for its open toleration of nudity and marijuana use). Under the new ruling, nude dancing was defined as a form of symbolic speech, and was therefore protected by a "right to free expression" standard broader than the federal free-speech guidelines (*Oregonian*, April 1993). Similarly, proposed zoning regulations that would keep legal sex-related businesses at least one thousand feet from residences and schools have been consistently struck down on constitutional grounds, as has a proposed ordinance that would require nude dancers and their customers to maintain a distance of two feet between them at all times (the failed "two-foot law"). With the backing of the courts, a relatively powerful coalition of adult business entrepreneurs has successfully argued that such proposed regulations would send them down the slippery slope toward repression, threatening everyone's right to free expression.

Seizing upon the opportunities opened by the libertarian-influenced state supreme court, entrepreneurs and business-minded locals have taken advantage of the ever-expanding and diversifying East-side market niches in adult entertainment. As a result of the legal and regulatory decisions of the late 1980s, "all-nude" strip clubs and other adult businesses increased from ten in 1989 to nearly a hundred in 1995. Although a few of the larger strip clubs were built for the express purpose of operating an exotic dance business, most clubs emerged in existing taverns and pool halls that added a dance stage and converted to strip bars to compete for business with the larger strip clubs. Accompanying the growth in strip bars, pornography stores, "live-nude" modeling businesses, and "tanning salons for gentlemen" have flourished, and escort services totaled more than a hundred in 1997, according to local police (police interview, August 1997).[3] Thus, in spite of protests from residents and neighborhood association leaders, as long as one does not significantly alter the built environment, legal adult sex businesses are rarely prevented from getting a liquor license and any other necessary credentials to open shop.

Along with the ten-year expansion in legal adult businesses, there has been a rapid upswing in legal gambling within city limits. Owing its robust economy largely to the institution of video poker in 1994, there has been an economic boom in the state-run gaming industry. After the State Lottery Commission voted to legalize video gambling, many taverns, strip bars, convenience stores, and restaurants introduced video poker machines in an effort to capture a share of the gambling market held by casinos located on Indian reservations. Because Oregon does not collect sales tax, the lottery commission justified its decision by appealing to the funding needs of public education and social programs. Marketed in the form of widely available pamphlets listing and describing the educational and social programs that gambling revenues fund, video poker was an "easy sell" to the Portland public. With the addition of strip bars and video poker machines, the city's traditional markets for alcohol consumption (taverns, pool halls, and nightclubs) have expanded and diversified.

Although the commercial sex industry provides ample, if exploitative, economic opportunities for many young women in Portland, not every woman can work in legal adult businesses. The selection of women for legal sexual labor depends, in part, on age, embodiment, race and ethnicity, and geographic mobility. Given the primary construction of sexual value in race and class-stratified society, legal sex businesses such as strip bars and nude modeling businesses select young, white women who appeal to the local and global desire for youthful "all-American" faces and bodies that exude a desirous, yet approachable feminine sexuality. Within this cultural framework, there is some room to push the boundaries of feminine sexual performance and embodiment, but women who challenge the tastes of this particular consumer culture too harshly cannot obtain work in legal adult businesses. Alongside legally sanctioned sex markets, there is a market for women whose lifestyle or appearance does not conform to the dictates of such consumption niches. Although legal adult businesses do not explicitly qualify sex workers based on body type and physical attributes, this task is effectively accomplished through the cultural messages of marketing and advertisement. In addition, women are channeled into a specific position in the sex trade by a third party, such as a sex-club manager, an agent, or a pimp, or through a self-selection process based on their own interpretation of the cultural messages of sex industry advertising. As one woman who worked in prostitution explained, "I couldn't work for the strip bars. You know I wasn't a size five and I wasn't a beauty queen. So I just found it curious."

Along with the gendered and racialized logic that positions women into particular niches of the sex industry, women's drug use, social and geographic mobility, and housing needs play a role in how they are positioned in the local sexual economy. Although legal sex businesses, and strip bars in particular, are known to attract drug dealers and both dancers and strip-club managers frequently report using drugs inside and outside the clubs (Sanchez 1997a, 1998), access to legal sex markets is limited by drug-use patterns. Women who inject drugs are usually precluded from legal work because their drug use leaves marks on their bodies and structures their time according to physical cycles of addiction. Because chemical substances drive the daily routines of heroin, crack cocaine, and methamphetamine users, in particular, such women are usually unable to comply with externally imposed time schedules and requirements on the physical maintenance of their bodies. Similarly, poor and homeless women, and many women with children, may not be in a position to maintain externally imposed schedules or to go through the extensive bodily preparations needed to maintain that freshly desirous look so valued by customers and employers.

As carefully cultivated enclaves of habit and taste, the geography of gambling and sex consumption markets can be traced according to the local spatial politics and regulatory culture in Portland. Although the zoning and regulatory policies of the State Lottery Commission, which regulates the gaming industry, and those of the Liquor Control Commission, which governs the strip bars, apply to all regions of the city, some locals have greater influence over the enforcement of gambling and sex industry regulations. The wealthier Westside residents have publicly opposed the introduction of adult sex businesses and video poker machines into their neighborhoods. They have staged protests, launched media campaigns, and lobbied the police bureau to recommend against granting liquor licenses to adult businesses and to nightclubs and taverns applying for a permit to locate video poker machines on the premises. Taking the path of least resistance, businesspeople interested in using commercial spaces for nude dancing and video poker have settled primarily in southeast and northeast Portland, where some residents welcome these businesses for the jobs and the entertainment they bring, and others silently acquiesce. As evidence of the effects of these cultural practices, southeast Portland is home to more than half of the adult businesses in town, as compared to the 10 percent that occupy the wealthier district of southwest Portland. On the same side of the river, northeast Portland has the second-highest concentration of adult businesses at 25 percent.

Given the spatial politics of the city, it is no coincidence that the consumer market for street-level prostitution is also concentrated in southeast Portland. Traditionally, there have been four major street markets for prostitution in Portland. In the 1980s, the most active area was the "Hollywood District" of inner northeast Portland, with a highly active, but geographically dispersed, street market in southeast Portland, and two smaller, more concentrated locations downtown and in north Portland. Since the early 1990s, however, regentrification projects in the Hollywood District, downtown, and north Portland have significantly curtailed street prostitution activities in those areas. Although the street market for prostitution in the Hollywood District is currently almost undetectable, arrest statistics show that a small market for street prostitution still exists in that area. Regentrification efforts in Hollywood, a historic theater district, have been highly successful, and Hollywood has become one of the most heavily patrolled areas for street prostitution. Not surprisingly, the largest and most active street market for prostitution is located in southeast Portland, with the number of arrests in 1996 totaling more than three hundred. Thus, the geography of adult entertainment and commercial sex in Portland mirrors the global cities model, with private business and state and municipal funds concentrated in the dominant economic centers and wealthier residential enclaves, and urban decay and informal/illicit economic activity centered in those communities that are already the most disenfranchised.

Culture and Consumption in the Erotic Economy

The consumer market for sexual commerce reveals another dimension of social and economic transformation in the city of Portland. A substantial base of local consumers gravitates toward the strip clubs and street prostitution markets. Portland strip clubs have become a familiar element of local culture, providing a social space for men to meet friends or gather for special occasions, such as birthdays and bachelor parties. Most strip clubs are housed in visible locations on the main boulevards, and minimal regulations on storefront advertising permit strip clubs to draw customers with lighted signs, graphic designs of nude female bodies, and photographs of partially clad dancers displayed in the window boxes in front of these clubs. Two local adult entertainment magazines advertising strip clubs and adult sex shops are widely available in strip clubs, stores, and on street-corner newsstands. These magazines keep a running tally on the number of strip clubs and sex businesses in the greater metropolitan area, providing the names and locations of these businesses, and dramatizing the opening of each new club with a kind of boastful pride in Portland's high threshold for sexual entertainment. Escort services, which cater to business travelers, tourists, and some locals, also advertise in these adult entertainment magazines, as well as in the mainstream newspapers.

Nationally, Portland has gained a reputation as a key site for sexual commerce. Portland sex businesses advertise nationally in magazines, on-line zines, and mail-order catalogs specializing in adult entertainment products and services, as well as on the Internet. In 1994, one adult entertainment magazine reported that Portland had more nude dancing bars per capita than any other U.S. city; that report was reproduced in one of Portland's mainstream newspapers (*Oregonian*, August 15, 1994). And a 1995 article in an adult entertainment rag graphically detailed Portland's first ever public "sex train," in which one woman had sexual intercourse with numerous men consecutively. That event made national news in the form of tabloid television, bolstering Portland's reputation as a domestic haven for adult entertainment. In addition to direct advertising, ethnographic research in Portland reveals that some consumers learn about the Portland sex trade from sex workers who travel across the country in what is known as a circuit (Sanchez 1998). The circuit follows market flows in sexual commerce, and for women involved in prostitution, travel helps them avoid police detection. Pimps, adult sex service agencies, and managers of adult business enterprises often coerce or facilitate circuit travel. For example, during a ride along with a Portland vice sergeant, one woman stated that she had traveled to twenty-three cities in six months with her "boyfriend," engaging in street prostitution in each of those cities (field interview, August 1997). And in another case, two dancers I spoke with answered an advertisement soliciting for dancers in a local newspaper. Upon answering the ad, they were sent to New Mexico for "training," then sent to Connecticut to work in a strip bar (field interview, September 1995). When they arrived, they made fifteen dollars a day and they were expected to live off their tips, but to earn tips, club management encouraged them to leave the premises and engage in prostitution with customers who propositioned them. Once the two young women had arrived on the East Coast, the agency provided no return ticket to Portland. As one of them explained, "Jody and I were both underage, and we had gotten there on Jody's last paycheck . . . we'd spent all that so we had no choices. I mean, we had no way of getting back home."

There is some evidence to suggest that sex consumption is cultivated through images and products that are circulated globally. The Internet provides one source of transmitting this information globally. Because a steady flow of business travelers and tourists are exposed to the diverse array of consumer sex markets annually, word of mouth is undoubtedly another means of transmitting information about Portland's sex industry to potential customers from out of town. To the extent that Portland participates in global technological enterprises, its key location in relation to the Pacific Rim has brought a number of elite businessmen and investors from Japan and other East Asian countries to the region. Although it is difficult to measure the extent to which East Asian men or any other international business traveler, tourist, or migrant worker uses commercial sex services, field interviews with escort owners and the women who work for them suggest that a significant proportion of their customers are from overseas (field interviews, September 1995, August 1997).

The circulation of cultural images has attracted local, national, and international sex consumers to adult sex markets in Portland. As a regional node that attracts business travelers, set in a city that is nestled against snowcapped mountaintops, clear blue skies, and lush forests, Portland can be compared to other cities that have played upon the promise of leisurely pleasure to attract domestic and international dollars to the region. Historically, a number of cities across the globe have developed entertainment economies and commercial sex markets to attract revenues from nearby centers of economic activity, such as international markets and seasonal industries, and centers of conflict, such as war zones and occupied regions. As feminist scholars have observed, the transterritorial influx of businessmen, travelers, immigrant laborers, and military personnel—that is, single men and married men whose "*own*" women are temporarily absent—into any city or rural region is often accompanied by a rise in licit and illicit commercial sex in those regions (Enloe 1990; Truong 1986; Gilfoyle 1992). For example, the prevalence of prostitution increased in Thailand as Bangkok was transformed into a destination of rest and recreation for American military men during the Vietnam War (Truong 1986; Enloe 1990). After the war, Thailand's sex markets were transformed into major markets of international sex tourism, catering to men from North America, Western Europe, Japan, and the Middle East (Truong 1986). In other regions, international networks of sex tourism have facilitated travel to third-world countries. For example, Ferdinand Marcos's political regime used the "reputed beauty and generosity of Filipino women as a 'natural resource' to compete in the international tourism market" (Enloe 1990, 38). Such countries have rather explicitly relied on sex workers to attract tourist dollars for speedy economic development. As Cynthia Enloe suggests, it has taken calculated policies to sustain the relationship between sexual commerce and transnational military and economic activity. These policies "shape men's sexuality, ensure battle readiness, determine the location of businesses, structure women's economic opportunities, and affect wives, entertainment and public health" (Enloe 1990, 81).

Global and domestic economic processes have both enhanced the consumer market for commercial sex and complicated the Eastside economy, making these neighborhoods ripe for the development of sexual commerce. The introduction of legal adult businesses has played a key role in salvaging the depressed economies of Portland's Eastside, but these businesses occupy a contradictory position in the fabric of social and economic life. To some extent, they stimulate the depleted Eastside economies, but they have also engendered new forms of labor exploitation and new consumption costs for some locals. In the early 1990s, immediately following the Supreme Court's decision to legalize full nudity, strippers usually performed individually, on one stage, collecting tips and then exiting the stage for the next dancer to appear. As the industry expanded, dancers began performing two and three at a time, competing for tips on a single stage, while some clubs built additional stages and others began to specialize in novelty performances, such as table dances, shower dances, beanbag dances, and booth dances. Probably the most popular variation of the "one-on-one" performance is lap dancing, a form of dance involving contact between dancers and customers. By 1995, most Portland strip clubs offered lap dancing, and many required dancers to solicit lap dances from customers at fifteen to twenty dollars per dance, and to pay a percentage of their earnings to the club as a condition of their employment. This kind of diversification of niche markets in exotic dancing and other adult businesses was undoubtedly set in motion by the competition for a share of Portland's flourishing commercial sex markets. The simplest interpretation of this trend is that niche markets were created to fill an existing demand for erotic entertainment. Perhaps more plausibly, however, the diversification of markets in erotic entertainment has generated repetitious consumption habits and produced increased demands for diversity of performance and service.

As sex markets have expanded and diversified, employment practices in the sex industry have become increasingly exploitative. For example, in the late 1980s and early 1990s, legal sex workers usually earned a small wage plus tips, but in the mid-1990s, they were almost universally hired as private contractors, liable to pay income taxes individually, but ineligible for basic benefits such as health insurance and worker's compensation. As the decade wore on, not only were women in the strip industry and other on-site venues working for tips alone, they were required to pay a percentage of their tips to the host club, and some clubs even required a stage fee. In effect, most sex workers have been reduced to paying for the "privilege" to work in Portland's commercial sex markets. Further contributing to the devaluation of labor in the strip clubs, most strip clubs hold a weekly "amateur night" in which any woman can enter the club and perform for free. Such a ploy is commonly used to attract business, but it also decreases job security for the dancers who are already on schedule by bringing in "new blood" (young, inexperienced dancers who are willing to work for free). Thus, in theory, the growth and diversification of adult entertainment economies might be viewed as opening new possibilities for sex workers to make money and engage in a wider variety of services and performances, but in practice, it limits their choices by requiring them to engage in a style of performance that they might not otherwise have chosen and it reduces their capacity to make money by normalizing the market, thereby increasing competition. Under these employment practices, Portland sex workers have become "a dime a dozen," as their labor becomes increasingly devalued and their work conditions increasingly exploitative.

Women perform most of the work in the sex industry, but the industry also offers secondary jobs for men who drive dancers and escorts from location to location, or work as security guards, bartenders, disk jockeys, and sex-club managers. Additionally, drug dealers commonly frequent strip clubs and other adult sex businesses. Operating behind the closed doors of loosely regulated, dimly lit clubs, drug dealers use the clubs as a social gathering place and a place to conduct business. Many of these dealers are partnered with women who work in legal sex clubs, escort services, or street prostitution markets. Purchasing their drugs directly or having customers purchase for them, sex workers constitute a substantial consumer market in illicit drugs. This synergism between illicit drug economies and sexual economies creates consumption costs for some sex workers and their customers, and filters some of the money made in the adult sex industry into the illicit drug economy.

Employment patterns and consumption pressures among those involved in Portland's commercial sex industry have effectively reorganized socioeconomic relations among many of the families and heterosexual couples involved. Sex workers' earnings in tips usually support them only at the subsistence level, and their clothing and body maintenance products and services produce additional costs that they must bear. Additional money made by sex workers is often spent on entertainment for themselves and their partners. Because they routinely navigate entertainment spaces, they constitute an important part of the consumer market for alcohol, drugs, and video poker, and are themselves targeted consumers. Underlining this point, one dancer I interviewed deposited her tips in a video poker machine located on the premises during each break. After she had spent all of the money she earned in tips, she borrowed an additional twenty dollars from one of her customers. Romantic partnerships between Portland sex workers and men who are unemployed or who perform child care and/or household duties are not only common, but strikingly conspicuous. In my experience as a researcher, it was precisely the frequency with which I observed this kind of reversal of traditional social and economic arrangements among working-class couples that inspired me to ask broader questions about the relationship between gender, labor, and economy in Portland. Thus, although sex workers in Portland appear to have achieved some measure of economic independence, the coupling of their social and economic position with the increased disenfranchisement of working-class men has produced conflict as gender and power relations shift among romantic couples in the area.

At a broader economic level, the Eastside economies and neighborhood enclaves have little to show for the money that flows through adult businesses and entertainment economies. Sex-industry dollars are certainly not regenerated into capital construction projects or business enterprises that would help rebuild the Eastside economy. Because much of the money made in the sex industry is channeled upward into the hands of a few wealthy entrepreneurs, that money also tends to flow outward to the rural and suburban residential enclaves where these entrepreneurs live and to distant cities and countries where they leisure and consume. This pattern accelerates the process of socioeconomic polarization in the city; it marks the Eastside as a socially marginalized location and keeps it economically stagnant.

Portland's Prostitution-Free Zone and
the New Spatial Governmentality

Although legal adult businesses have been permitted to operate almost without legal sanction since 1989, the recent growth and transformation of commercial sex in Portland has not come without cost or conflict. Public protests in front of strip bars and other adult businesses have become commonplace. Although such conflicts have underlying moral currents, they have surfaced primarily as concerns about property values and struggles over land-use decisions. Although the libertarian factions of the Portland business and legal community have prevailed in their development efforts and antiregulatory stance, many residents associate the adult sex industry with a decline in Portland's "quality of life." With the onset of community policing and the growing strength of Portland neighborhood associations in the mid-1990s, these residents were better situated to influence the decisions of the city council and the Police Bureau. Nevertheless, their influence had little bearing on the ongoing growth and deregulation of legal adult businesses.

Given the community-policing emphasis on crime prevention and the failure of some activists to persuade city government to tighten the regulatory reins on legal adult businesses, community activists eventually turned their attention to illicit commercial sex. In 1995, these activists instigated a crackdown on street prostitution, helping to write and enact a new law called the "prostitution-free zone ordinance" (city ordinance 137816). Reversing the zoning logic that historically confined legal adult businesses *inside* a set spatial boundary, the prostitution-free zone maps out "high-vice" areas and *excludes* those caught soliciting for prostitution from those areas. According to the ordinance, people arrested for prostitution or prostitution procurement within five hundred feet of the zone are excluded from that area for ninety days. If convicted, they are excluded for an additional year; if the police find them in the area during that time, they can be arrested for trespassing.

Enforcement of the zoning ordinance, commonly referred to as the "exclusion law," is a spatial form of governance, one that seeks to draw a boundary between the life spaces of privileged, propertied residents and the visibly sexual/sexualized body of the prostitute. The prostitution-free zone law has been celebrated by some as the most important tool for the police to "protect the public" and an opportunity for the community to "take back their neighborhoods and business districts plagued by drug dealing and prostitution" (*Oregonian*, March 27, 1997). Supporters of the prostitution-free zone ordinance claim that the law focuses on citizen concerns rather than punishment. As one deputy district attorney put it:

> The ordinances do not focus on the person, but on a *geographic area* . . .
> Their purpose is not retribution or deterrence, which are the typical goals
> of punishment. Instead, the ordinances try to fix neighborhood crime
> problems. (Ibid.; emphasis added)

In the more common sentiments of a local resident: "If [people] are doing drugs or prostitution, they shouldn't be allowed there. I understand it's their constitutional right to be around, but it's making life totally unbearable for people who live there" (*Oregonian*, April 25, 1997). Reflecting local assumptions that those who are involved in prostitution or drug use are alienated strangers who cannot possibly live in the area or have family and friends nearby, such locals express their concerns as an issue of "neighborhood livability"—a problem of geography rather than punishment. Using a language of exclusivity that masquerades as a kind of liberal pluralism—prostitutes and drug users can do what they choose, just "not in my backyard"—supporters of the prostitution-free zone ordinance diffuse the potential for charges of moral reformism.

Although the exclusion law has been in effect since 1995, it has come under fire from a small group of lawyers, judges, and community members. One defense attorney claimed that the ordinance is "the rough equivalent of banishment" (*Oregonian*, April 25, 1997). But the ordinance also raises constitutional questions regarding double jeopardy and freedom of travel, and it contradicts federal criminal procedure statutes, requiring criminal prosecutions to focus on a person's conduct rather than her status. The ordinance bans people from public city spaces regardless of the reason for occupying them, and it does so upon arrest, that is, prior to their being convicted of a crime. In framing prostitution as a problem of *geography* rather than one of *status* or even *conduct*, legal practitioners have attempted to circumvent entanglement in the thorny legal questions raised by a law that effectively amounts to a status offense.

In April of 1997, a circuit court judge ruled that the exclusions violated the Fifth Amendment ban on double jeopardy because the ordinance excludes a person from a part of the city and then prosecutes the person for the same crime. Since the ruling, two hundred to three hundred cases have been dismissed, but the constitutionality of the ordinance has yet to be challenged in the state supreme court. In the meantime, the city council, the prosecutor's office, and the police bureau have devised patchwork remedies in response to criticisms. As a temporary measure, the assistant police chief ordered officers to stop issuing exclusions and arrests simultaneously, and those who live or work in the spaces from which they were excluded can now obtain passes allowing them access to those locations by a specific route (*Oregonian*, August 1997). However, the fact that a new pass must be requested for each condition of travel within the zone makes the modification unrealistic by any standard. As a long-term solution to the double-jeopardy problem, the district attorney drafted an amendment in 1998 that would require conviction before exclusion. Offenders would still be excluded from the zone after conviction and would be subject to trespass charges if they are found in the area within a year of their conviction, whether or not they are engaged in prostitution or prostitution procurement when they are questioned.

Ultimately, the legal questions raised by the prostitution-free zone ordinance will have to be resolved by the state supreme court. In the meantime, police officers continue to enforce the law and prosecutors are busy directing law enforcement to "get the numbers needed to justify the law" (deputy district attorney, at city council meeting, August 1997). In the summer of 1997, the city council voted to establish a new prostitution-free zone on West Riverside Boulevard after local residents and business owners complained that the Hollywood Street prostitution-free zone had diverted prostitution activities westward into their neighborhood. At the meeting, city council members, prosecutors, and police officers discussed how to shield the ordinance from attack. A deputy district attorney, strategizing the best spatial location for conducting prostitution missions, which supply the so-called magic numbers needed to justify the law, stated:

> There is no magic number . . . We need to make our ordinance more defensible relative to attack. We need to focus on prostitute numbers not John numbers. Johns are not an accurate predictor of the amount of prostitution occurring in an area. Johns will go wherever the prostitutes go. (At City Council meeting, August 1997)

Revealing the reluctance with which local officials have come to approach any efforts to regulate legal adult businesses, a city council member added, "We can't attack adult businesses because we'll be challenged."

The emotionally charged meeting, heavily publicized by the local television stations and newspapers, featured impassioned testimonials by community members concerned about the effects of prostitution on property values, routine business dealings, and criminal activities. By displacing disempowered individuals from the public spaces that privileged residents have claimed as their own, these officials and activists send a symbolic message that they are working with *the* community to "clean up *their* neighborhoods" and "keep criminals out."

In Portland, police officers take pride in enforcing the prostitution-free zone ordinance. The fervor with which officers enforce the exclusion law was perhaps best expressed by one prostitution detail officer who referred to the law as "a great tool" and to himself as "the big hammer":

> I'm the big hammer; I get them off the street. They feel it's *their* street so they can do what they want. I'm not hands on—I don't talk to them. Even if they didn't do anything, I just get them off *my* street. (Field interview, August 1997)

Resisting reference to the Freudian connotations of this officer's statements, his language reflects the territorial logic of community policing. Representing himself as a "tool" of the state, the officer's claim to ownership of public city streets constructs the geographic battle lines of this conflict as a struggle over real and imagined entitlements to community property and land-use decisions.

In Portland, conflicts over public space are rooted in antiquated, if unwitting, attempts to redefine citizenship rights vis-à-vis property ownership.[4] The moral content of these conflicts, and the proprietary quality of the regulatory strategies established to address them, are encoded in a discourse of "neighborhood livability." Elsewhere, I have considered these regulatory discourses and strategies as an example of "spatial governmentality" (Sanchez 1997a, 1998, 2001; Perry and Sanchez 1998).[5] Spatial governmentality describes strategies of governmentality that manipulate the spatial order of a region or community. Techniques of spatial governmentality effect social order by *managing populations in place.* They rely on the managerial logic of the governmental state (see, e.g., Foucault 1991) to order and regulate public and private spaces and to manage the flow of bodies into and out of these spaces. They include civil ordinances and zoning codes that govern public and commercial land uses, and criminal codes that establish and police boundaries between public and private space (e.g., trespass, vagrancy). They also include urban planning and architectural strategies, as well as the new "communitarian" strategies, such as the currently popular "quality-of-life" discourses. Regimes of spatial governmentality thus join modern technological advances, population management systems, and discourses of citizenship, community, and property with techniques of sociospatial control, producing enclosed spaces and zones of exclusion.

Portland's regulatory strategies and contemporary zoning laws, such as the prostitution-free zone ordinance, allow the state to manage identities, bodies, and populations by prohibiting specific forms of visible conduct in some spaces, and by "directing the flow of population into certain regions [and] activities" (Foucault 1991, 100). The placement and displacement of people inside or outside the normative and sociospatial boundaries of community, and the organization of people in space as legitimately including some and excluding others, highlight the coercive effects of spatial governmentality on American lives.

Conclusion

This essay has pursued questions suggested by the scholarly literature on globalization as a first step of inquiry into the connections and disjunctures between global economic processes and informal labor and consumption markets, specializing in commercial sex services and performances. Following the pattern illustrated in the global cities model, Portland's urban economy has become economically and spatially polarized, with wealth concentrated in select industries and among the higher-income residential enclaves, and poverty and informal economic activity centered in the economically depressed area of east Portland. The spatial economy of sex, gambling, and drug markets can thus be mapped onto a more general geography of centrality and marginality within the boundaries of Portland City. For both the women and men who participated in the study, the sociospatial production of sex markets and consumption niches carefully crafted around the manipulation of taste and the patient nurturing of habit contribute to social stratification and economic polarization in the city. The particular forms of sexual labor and consumption that have developed in the lower-income residential enclaves of east Portland serve as class markers of identity and geographic space. They distract Eastside residents from the larger social and economic problems facing them by cultivating repetitious labor and consumption habits that serve to manage their time, their bodies, and the spaces through which they travel. From this perspective, sexual performances and forms of consumption that exploit pleasure and amusement can be viewed as a disciplinary technique that "kills the time" and "keeps the place" of Eastside residents, metaphorically and geographically speaking.

As part of the contemporary picture of global culture and economy, the trend of Portland sex markets replicates a long history of North American and Western European colonization. In the case of international sex tourism in Thailand and the Philippines, men of first-world countries colonized a geographic corner of the developing nation while simultaneously colonizing the bodies of the feminine "exotic other." But transnational markets of commercial sex are not the exclusive domain of developing countries, and the consumers of commercial sex services do not consist solely of businessmen and wealthy travelers from the first world. The development of commercial sex markets in Portland, a relatively stable regional economy in a country that is a leading economic power, illustrates how the lives of American women can also be subordinated to the international relations of global capital, as young women provide sexual services to domestic and international businessmen, immigrants, and local men of all socioeconomic classes.

At one level, the flow of capital and consumers stimulated directly and indirectly by licit and illicit commercial sex markets can be viewed as a contribution to the depleted working-class economies of Portland's Eastside, one that subordinates the interests of working-class women to the economic interests of the region. Such practices parallel the use of sex tourism in Southeast Asia to spark the flow of international capital into the region. Portland's commercial sex economies draw upon the reputed beauty and sensuality of local women to cement social and economic bonds with other nations in the name of capitalism. In the gift-like exchange of women between socioeconomically linked entities, these women serve as offerings or items of exchange between transacting men or countries (Mauss 1924; Rubin 1975)—the flow of value is transmitted from one man or country to another through the body of woman. Thus, one significant effect of the feminized sexual labor being performed in Portland is the symbolic elision of woman and nation in the transnational markets of sexual commerce.

The growth in legal adult sex businesses has created new pressures to find creative regulatory strategies to manage the conflicts born of the fruits of development. The prostitution-free zone ordinance serves to appease local residents opposed to the adult sex industry with minimal interference in the business interests of legal commercial sex enterprises. Applying the logic of exclusion and enclosure directly to the population rather than to land, property, or architectural structure, the ordinance zones *people out of place*, using a rhetoric of community that appears rational and impersonal even as it is deeply exclusionary and moralistic (recall the deputy district attorney's claim that the ordinance does not focus "on the person, but on a geographic area"). Enforcement of the prostitution-free zone ordinance relies, in important ways, on a legitimating discourse of community that fits with the new objectives of community policing and the currently popular discourse of "neighborhood livability." Although the effort to enhance the quality of life in the residential enclaves of Portland is an admirable goal in the abstract, in practice, such efforts foreground property ownership as the primary means of verifying citizenship and the primary criterion for making rights claims. But the effects of the new techniques of spatial governmentality remain largely unintelligible because they involve the populace in the systematic governance of self and other, and in the policing of boundaries between the inside and outside of community. Both "totalizing" and "individualizing," the logic of spatial governmentality gives "legitimate" citizens a stake in managing their own affairs and monitoring their communities.

While women in prostitution are subject to a form of regulatory violence by their direct exclusion from public places, women working in legal markets are subject to violence in the form of sex and labor exploitation. The exclusionary violence of the prostitution-free zone is surely a step in the wrong direction, but the libertarian ideal of state withdrawal may not be the answer to the far too closely governed and exploited lives of Portland's sexual laborers. Just as commercial sex practices are never not negotiated and never not contextually embedded, they are also never not regulated. Deregulation is itself a form of regulation, one that transfers the regulation of sex markets and their participants from the legal regime to the market and to informal measures of social control, and one in which the logic of capital is sure to do its most destructive work on those whose lives are already most marginalized.

Although it is currently fashionable for scholars to interpret a diverse array of commercial sex services and performances as part of the larger "postidentity" project of gender transgression, the metamorphosis of commercial sex on the contemporary global scene remains volatile and unpredictable. In sexual commerce, the boundaries between erotic/affective activity and economic activity are blurred as the performance of sexual personae and the sensate experiences of the body are marketed and sold through specific systems of valuation and economic exchange. Thus, what the state tries to regulate, in all its inadequacies, misappropriations, and injustices, is not simply sexual expression or identity, but rather, the contradictions of bodily commodification under the specific cultural and economic relations of capital. What regulators must manage, then, are the dialectical contradictions between the logic of capital and the cultural anxiety about the commodification of bodies on the capitalist marketplace.

Social theorists interested in understanding the experiences of commercial sex participants have focused disproportionately on the labor side of the commercial sex equation, and on the questions of agency and identity that the provision of commercial sex services suggests. These scholars have yet to question how market directives have changed the face of commercial sex today, and they have yet to understand the effects of increasingly deregulated markets on commercial sex participants. As with other informal and illicit economies, deregulated consumer markets tend to produce consumers who are readily habituated to their own consumption, and unregulated labor markets produce highly volatile work conditions and highly docile, exploited workers. The current global economy has stimulated the cultural production of sex as an assortment of images and sensations that can be packaged and sold on the marketplace in a seemingly endless stream of novel products and services. Under these same cultural and economic conditions, the interests and capacities of state and local jurisdictions to appropriately regulate the markets produced by these new cultural practices appear to be waning. As these processes accelerate under the logic of late-modern global capitalism, the bodies of the young women who labor in the markets of commercial sex become ever more compelled into the treadmill of a global culture of commodified sex.

Notes

1. All proper names of businesses and participants have been changed to protect the identities of those who participated in this study. In previous work, I used the pseudonym "Evergreen" to describe Portland, Oregon, the northwestern United States city where I conducted field research for this study (see Sanchez 1997a, 1997b); however, this is no longer necessary. The specificity of the city is given here to retain the integrity of the urban and economic analysis in this essay.

2. Although illicit commercial sex activities are not recorded in the official data on labor and economy for obvious reasons, even legal sex businesses do not appear in the official statistics of the State Labor Department or the Economic Development Department. Working with a director of Portland's Economic Development Department, I tried to untangle labor, employment, and industry statistics from available data, but there is no specific category for adult sex businesses, making economic activity in those enterprises virtually indistinguishable from entertainment and alcohol and food-service income and revenues. Even though many of the taverns and clubs draw primary revenues from sex work and would not stay in business without such entertainment or service, the state and local statistics reflect the fact that sexual labor is still marginal enough that it is not considered relevant or official economic activity. The papering over of sex work under other entertainment economies probably also reflects some effort, however informal, on the part of state and local officials, to downplay the role of sex businesses in the Eastside economy. If sex businesses remain officially unacknowleged and geographically segregated off from the popular tourist locations, the city can retain that wholesome public image necessary to attract tourists and federal funds for urban projects and social programs. As unrecorded economic activity, adult sex businesses are less accountable to local, state, and national regulatory agencies, leaving business owners free to manage and promote business as they see fit, with little concern for regulatory limits on employment practices or work conditions.

3. One official in the Portland police bureau provided the figure of 220 escort services. His estimate is based on investigations and case files in process, and marketing analysis. It is difficult to estimate with any certainty the exact number of escort services operating at one time, and even more difficult to estimate the number of women working in these businesses or to gauge the number of

businesses operating illegally as fronts for prostitution, because some escort agencies advertise in multiple places under more than one name to increase business, and some services change their name continuously over time to avoid police detection. "Private dance" businesses often operate as escort services in terms of the kinds of services performed and the organization of business operations, and women who work as escorts and private dancers often work for multiple agencies. In addition, some advertisements for escorts are placed by individual women who are primarily involved in local and street markets of prostitution or by pimps who are running prostitutes. Although the figure of 220 quoted by the officer interviewed may seem high, given the volume of advertising in adult magazines and mainstream newspapers and the number of cases processed or under current investigation in the police department, it is probably accurate to say that the number of businesses operating at any given time is in the hundreds. The number of escorts working in these businesses is probably about double the number of escort businesses, given that escorts often work concurrently or consecutively for more than one business. By any estimation, escort businesses in Portland are abundant, occupying multiple market niches and serving a variety of local, national, and international consumers.

4. See the discussion in Yuval-Davis (1997) regarding the historically and culturally varied criteria for defining citizenship. Yuval-Davis defines citizenship broadly, as full membership in a community, focusing on the rights and exclusions of specific citizens and noncitizens, rather than on the legal definition of inclusion or exclusion from membership in the nation.

5. Following Michel Foucault's work, governmentality is defined as a logic of governance that emphasizes not moral ideals or transcendental rules, but the proper functioning of government itself (Foucault 1991). According to Foucault, the legitimacy of such a system of managerial governance lies in the rational administration of the knowledge and science of *populations*. Governmental regimes aim not only to govern *over* the population efficiently, but to govern *through* the population, that is, to elicit the desired form of self-governance from its citizenry. In contrast to older regimes of sovereignty, government has had as its purpose the "welfare of the population, the improvement of its condition, the increase of its wealth, longevity, health, etc." (Foucault 1991, 100). Scholars following Foucault have focused on the management and manipulation of populations and the statistical representation of risk (see, e.g., Reichman 1986; Simon 1987, 1988, 1993; O'Malley 1992; Deflem 1997; Sanchez 2001; Merry 1998;

Perry and Sanchez 1998; Valverde 1998). Contemporary governmental regimes are characterized by an array of technologies for monitoring and managing populations, including regional, national, and global health, social security and criminal records, police surveillance technologies, and geographic profiling systems. Other strategies of governmentality that make use of architecture, planning, zoning, and other creative techniques of spatial organization and control may be more properly considered "spatial governmentality." Thus, as I am using it here, spatial governmentality draws upon the theory of governmentality to describe spatially organized forms of governance. This notion of spatial governmentality has developed in dialogue with scholars in a collective research project undertaken at the University of California, Irvine, under a research initiative titled "Law as Regimes of Culture," organized by Richard Perry. See, for example, Sanchez 1997a, 1998, 2001; Perry and Sanchez 1998.

References

Appadurai, Arjun. 1996. *Modernity at Large: Cultural Dimensions of Globalization.* Minneapolis: University of Minnesota Press.

Bluestone, Barry, and Bennett Harrison. 1982. *The Deindustrialization of America.* New York: Basic Books.

Burchell, Graham, Colin Gordon, and Peter Miller, eds. 1991. *The Foucault Effect: Studies in Governmentality.* Chicago: University of Chicago Press.

Calavita, Kitty. 1998. "Immigration, Law, and Marginalization in a Global Economy: Notes from Spain." *Law and Society Review* 32(3): 529–66.

Cesarini, David, and Mary Fulbrook, eds. 1996. *Citizenship, Nationality and Migration in Europe.* London: Routledge.

Daniels, P. W. 1985. *Service Industries: A Geographical Analysis.* London: Methuen.

Darian-Smith, Eve. 1997. "Globalizing the Legal Self?: Rethinking Intellectual Property Law in Postcolonial Hong Kong." Paper presented at the Global Peace and Conflict Studies colloquium, University of California, Irvine.

Deflem, Mathieu. 1997. "Surveillance and Criminal Statistics: Historical Foundations of Governmentality." *Studies in Law, Politics and Society* 17: 149–84.

Enloe, Cynthia. 1990. *Bananas, Beaches and Bases: Making Feminist Sense of International Politics.* Berkeley: University of California Press.

Featherstone, Mike. 1990. *Global Culture and Postmodernism.* London: Sage.

Foucault, Michel. 1991. "Governmentality." In *The Foucault Effect: Studies in*

Governmentality, ed. Graham Burchell, Colin Gordon, and Peter Miller. Chicago: University of Chicago Press. 87–105.

Gilfoyle, Timothy J. 1992. *City of Eros: New York City, Prostitution and the Commercialization of Sex, 1820–1920*. New York: W. W. Norton.

Hannerz, Ulf. 1990. "Cosmopolitans and Locals in World Culture." *Theory, Culture and Society* 7: 237–51.

Harvey, David. 1989. *The Condition of Postmodernity*. Baltimore: Johns Hopkins University Press.

Kunstler, James. 1993. *The Geography of Nowhere: The Rise and Decline of the American Manmade Landscape*. New York: Simon and Schuster.

Lash, Scott, and John Urry. 1994. *Economies of Signs and Spaces*. London: Sage.

Maurer, Bill. 1997. *Recharting the Caribbean: Land, Law, and Citizenship in the British Virgin Islands*. Ann Arbor: University of Michigan Press.

Mauss, Marcel. 1924. *The Gift: Forms and Functions of Exchange in Archaic Society*. Trans. Ian Cunnison. Glencoe, Ill.: Free Press.

Merry, Sally Engle. 1998. "The Kapu on Women Going Out to Ships: Spatial Governmentality on the Fringes of Empire." Paper presented at the annual meeting of the Law and Society Association, Aspen, Colorado.

O'Malley, Pat. 1992. "Risk, Power and Crime Prevention." *Economy and Society* 21: 252–75.

Ong, Aihwa. 1987. *Spirits of Resistance and Capitalist Discipline: Factory Women in Malaysia*. Albany: State University of New York Press.

Perry, Richard, and Lisa Sanchez. 1998. "Transactions in the Flesh: Toward an Ethnography of Embodied Sexual Reason." *Studies in Law, Politics and Society* 18: 29–76.

Portes, Alejandro, Manuel Castells, and Lauren Benton, eds. 1989. *The Informal Economy: Studies in Advanced and Less Developed Countries*. Baltimore: Johns Hopkins University Press.

Reichman, Nancy. 1986. "Managing Crime Risks: Toward an Insurance Based Model of Social Control." *Research in Law, Deviance and Social Control* 8: 151–72.

Rubin, Gayle. 1975. "The Traffic in Women: Notes of the 'Political Economy' of Sex." In *Toward an Anthropology of Women*, ed. Rayna Reiter. New York: Monthly Review Press.

Sanchez, Lisa E. 1997a. "Boundaries of Legitimacy: Sex, Violence, Citizenship and Community." *Law and Social Inquiry* 22(3): 543–80.

———. 1997b. "Spatial Practices and Bodily Maneuvers: Negotiating at the Margins of a Local Sexual Economy." *PoLAR: Political and Legal Anthropology Review* 21(2): 47–62.

———. 1998. "Sex, Violence, Citizenship and Community: An Ethnography and Legal Geography of Commercial Sex in One American City." Dissertation, University of California, Irvine.

———. 2001. "Enclosure Acts and Exclusionary Practices: Neighborhood Associations, Community Police, and the Expulsion of the Sexual Outlaw." In *Between Law and Culture: Relocating Legal Studies*, ed. David Goldberg, Michael Musheno, and Lisa Bower. Minneapolis: University of Minnesota Press. 122–40.

Sassen, Saskia. 1988. *The Mobility of Labor and Capital: A Study in International Investment and Labor Flow*. New York: Cambridge University Press.

———. 1991. *The Global City: New York, London, Tokyo*. Princeton, N.J.: Princeton University Press.

———. 1994. *Cities in a World Economy*. Thousand Oaks, Calif.: Pine Forge Press.

Simon, Jonathan. 1987. "The Emergence of a Risk Society: Insurance, Law, and the State." *Socialist Review* 95: 61–89

———. 1988. "The Ideological Effects of Actuarial Practices." *Law and Society Review* 22: 771–800.

———. 1993. "For the Government of Its Servants: Law and Disciplinary Power in the Work Place, 1870–1906." *Studies in Law, Politics and Society* 13: 105–36.

Truong, Thanh-Dam. 1986. *Virtue, Order, Health and Money: Towards a Comprehensive Perspective on Female Prostitution in Asia*. Bangkok: United Nations Economic and Social Commission for Asia and the Pacific.

Valverde, Mariana. 1998. "Governing out of Habit." *Studies in Law, Politics and Society* 18: 217–42.

Wilson, James Q., and George L. Kelling. 1982. "Broken Windows: Police and Neighborhood Safety." *Atlantic Monthly* 249 (March): 29–38.

Yuval-Davis, Nira. 1997. *Gender and Nation*. London: Sage Publications.

CHAPTER 9

Works in Progress: Traditional Knowledge, Biological Diversity, and Intellectual Property in a Neoliberal Era

Rosemary J. Coombe

When giving this paper orally, I always began with a proverbial apologia, that uniquely superior form of special pleading that characterizes the disclaimer that one's presentation is "a work in progress." What does it mean, I asked, to represent one's efforts as a "work" that can be situated in some temporal process designated as "progress"? What forms of authority do we appeal to and what mediums of legitimation do we evoke when we so casually adopt such phases? In contemporary fields of power and knowledge, it appears, particular values are indeed bestowed upon individual and collective labors to the extent that they can be represented as "works" and thus positioned as singular, signed contributions to a particular linear trajectory represented as "progress." In any case, it would be more accurate to represent this essay as an effort in regress—a contribution toward an unworking of some particular anthropological prejudices about "culture" and "tradition" and their political potential in international legal arenas.[1]

As an anthropologist who has only recently begun to do research and fieldwork in international legal arenas, I quickly found myself in a position of some ambivalence. Although anthropologists have been quite hostile to the concept of culture in the past two decades, in other disciplinary fields it has been embraced enthusiastically. In international law, in particular, the concept is very much alive and appears to be performing an ever-greater amount of complex ideological work. As an anthropologist, I was disturbed by rhetorical deployments of culture as a noun—something that can be recognized, enjoyed, possessed, maintained, disseminated, and preserved, according to the major human-rights covenants—but nonetheless found myself intrigued by the political possibilities afforded by affirmations of culture in global struggles for social justice. This optimism did not come easily. Among critical legal scholars, as well, emphasis on "culture" is nearly always seen to represent conservative, if not authoritarian, tendencies that serve to demonize others, justify local forms of domination and subordination, obscure racism, and mask more fundamental forms of social inequality.

Nonetheless, in this period of accelerating globalization and the emergence of a so-called new world order based on the growing hegemony of information capital, we are witnessing renewed attention to "cultural rights" based on possessive relations to traditions in a number of international forums. "Information capital," it must be said, is something of an oxymoron. Information only becomes capital when it ceases to be information, and becomes commodified—aggregated in some way as an identifiable work of human labor and protected against unauthorized forms of dissemination. This is accomplished legally, through intellectual property protections, which, until quite recently, were understood as cultural rights—to benefit from the fruits of one's creative labors, to claim works as one's own, and to contribute to and share in the accumulated heritage of humankind—loosely associated with rights of cultural identity and cultural integrity. The association between these various cultural rights is rarely articulated; but contemporary economic, political, and legal developments are making this task increasingly imperative as neoliberal trade regimes assume ever-greater hegemony.

Intellectual property is a doctrinal field that relies on modern European understandings of progress, science, and civilization and the significance of cultural works in developing both national canons and "human heritage." These understandings pose challenges and possibilities for non-Western others (including the West's own internal others—nomads, artisans, and peasants, as well as internally colonized nations) who seek to protect alternative forms of creative world making from appropriations and exploitations in Western commodity markets. In a more utopian and normative moment, I have visited the issue of protecting "traditional" or "indigenous" knowledge as a form of intellectual property through the prism of the major international human-rights covenants and their commitment to preserving and maintaining human culture (Coombe 1998b). In this essay, I will shift position, simultaneously voicing and interrogating my anthropological ambivalence toward this normative aspiration. I will do so by critically exploring the tropes that so vigorously thrive and proliferate in the rhetorical fields in which claims to indigenous knowledge are made. First, however, some delineation of the international legal contexts in which these rhetorics flourish is appropriate.

The Convention on Biological Diversity (CBD) specifically acknowledges the importance of traditional knowledge in biodiversity preservation and sustainable development. The CBD is a legally binding international framework that requires that those states that are party to it (187 of them) to "respect, preserve, and maintain knowledge, innovations, and practices of indigenous and local communities embodying traditional lifestyles" (relevant to the preservation of biological diversity). I will use the acronym TK—traditional knowledge—to refer to this nexus of practices, innovations, techniques, and knowledges. The CBD insists that states "promote the wider application of TK with the approval and involvement of the holders of such knowledge," while encouraging the equitable sharing of benefits from its use. Finding appropriate means of implementing this requirement is an ongoing endeavor. As Arturo Escobar (1998) has suggested, "an ethnography of the CBD and related network activities remains to be done," and he points to the need to attend to national, regional, and international meetings leading up to Convention of the Parties meetings, the practice of national delegations, the emergence of new knowledge and policy areas, the proliferation of issues, and the growing role of nongovernmental organizations (NGOs) and social movements in this process. I doubt that any singular ethnography of such a global process is possible; nonetheless, my own work is a contribution to this larger project.[2]

The Convention mandates its state parties to use their intellectual property systems to further Convention objectives. Since May of 1998, the World Intellectual Property Organization (WIPO) has been working in cooperation with the Convention parties to make international intellectual property agreements supportive of CBD objectives. A special Open-Ended Ad Hoc Inter-Sessional Working Group has been created to further the implementation of article 8(j)—the provision dealing with traditional knowledge—and this Group, with a partially funded indigenous caucus, has been meeting biannually with delegates from all state parties. This is the first instance in which indigenous peoples have been given supported standing in any United Nations forum other than those specifically addressing an autonomous set of indigenous human rights. Thus it provides an important global political forum to put indigenous issues in front of a much wider group of decision makers.

These negotiations bring together hundreds of indigenous NGOs from around the world (Maori and Aboriginal peoples, as well as First Nations and tribal peoples, but also peoples from the Mongolian steppes, the Solomon Islands, descendants of escaped slaves in the Americas—the very meaning of the "indigenous" is being politically negotiated here), together with traditional healers' associations (from Africa, Asia, and former socialist countries), third-world feminist activists, environmental NGOs, representatives from global financial and development institutions, civil servants, government lawyers, and scientists. In these negotiations we witness the emergence of incipient forms of governance and governmentality—as networks of citizens, NGOs, governments, and fourth-world political representatives pressure first-world governments and UN institutions to insist on justice, equity, and accountability in the expropriation of genetic resources, in the use of TK of likely economic and social value, and in the international formulation and exercise of intellectual property rights, while simultaneously creating new regimes of access and use at local, regional, and national levels. Lawmaking in this arena is emergent, iterative, and performative—it reproduces like a virus as model legislation, contracting practices, database models, protocols, and declarations are spread across the Internet and adapted, adopted, and proclaimed in local communities, regional networks, national government agencies, and legislatures.[3] This is a global arena of intense multisectoral legal pluralism as international conventions and global declarations are put into dialogue and articulation with national legislation, regional positionings, local protocols, and customary laws—both indigenous and international. Like most attempts to fundamentally shift and transform relationships of power, it is fueled by rhetorical forms and empowering fictions—in this case, narratives of tragedy, loss, salvation, and potential redemption.

Abstract, amorphous, and ambiguous as it often appears in international political discourse, TK is nonetheless embraced as essential to the preservation of biological diversity, to the livelihoods of the poor, and to prospects for sustainable development, while integrally related to fundamental cultural differences and endangered identities (Posey 1999). It is accepted that the world's greatest concentrations of biological diversity are areas occupied by peoples who have distinctive cultures that are themselves endangered.[4] Cultures are represented here as more or less synonymous with distinctive languages, and such languages are acknowledged, with alarm, to be vanishing. An estimated four to five thousand of the six thousand languages in the world are spoken by indigenous peoples (although the states in which these peoples reside may not recognize them as such). Those countries that contain peoples speaking the largest numbers of languages are also those that house the greatest biological diversity in terms of species and interspecies variations (Australia 1998).[5] These are also states in which the greatest numbers of indigenous and peoples with "traditional," or near-subsistence, livelihoods reside. The numbers of people who live in direct dependence on their knowledge of and use of local ecosystem resources is substantial. These biologically rich resources are also disappearing at an alarming rate

> through activities such as logging, land clearance and mining, large-scale "development" projects threatening . . . indigenous peoples whose livelihoods depend on these environments. There is in this sense a direct relationship between biological diversity and cultural diversity; maintenance

of the former can help preserve the latter. The reverse is also true; since indigenous peoples are often the custodians and stewards of biological diversity and do so through their culturally specific knowledges of local environments, the maintenance of cultural diversity is an important factor in the conservation of biological diversity. (Crucible II Group, 2000, 9–10)

Local and indigenous peoples who speak ancestral languages are often threatened by a loss of control over land, resources, and cultural traditions. As they become increasingly marginalized, these peoples lose innovative capacities and local wisdom about species and ecosystem management. Influential linguists and ethnobotanists assert that "any reduction of language diversity diminishes the adaptational strength of our species because it lowers the pool of knowledge from which we can draw" (Maffi 1998). As one prominent multisectoral report on the issue explained, "the loss of traditional farm communities, languages, and indigenous cultures all represent the erosion of human intellectual capital on a massive scale" (Crucible II Group 2000, 9). Because threats to traditional ways of life and threats to biodiversity are twin perils, *in situ* rather than *ex situ* forms of conservation are encouraged, to maintain the ongoing cultural production of biological diversity—local ecosystems are to be maintained, in other words, as works in progress.

A critical contemporary linguistics might well look askance at the UNESCO assertion that half of the world's languages will disappear within the next century. The discourse of vanishing languages and its presuppositions adopts, and strategically deploys, the tenets of an older form of anthropology in which the mapping of species, cultures, and languages was a museological or taxonomically inspired enterprise. Either it betrays an ignorance of contemporary understandings that the stabilities of languages are ideological constructs emergent from political and economic histories, or it is simply "evidence of the way such nineteenth-century concepts provide resources for twentieth-century international social projects" (Silverstein 2000, 5). As Michael Silverstein suggests, "the image of 'disappearing' or—to use the green metaphor—'endangered' languages and cultures is really a duplex one, produced as much by the change in the way we go about doing linguistic and sociocultural anthropology as by any forces of globalizing homogenization" (ibid.). Silverstein reasonably suggests that languages are always already in a dialectics of formation and dissolution, permeable to one another, and only ever relatively stable. Nonetheless, he does acknowledge that there are increasingly powerful social, political, and economic "forces that ever more efficiently and directly interfere with the modes of autonomous 'localization' of language and culture in relatively small-scale groups," which may be recognized as "loss" to the extent that "these nodes of our taxonomic trees of difference do indeed become extinct as autonomous localized language/cultures" (ibid.). The language of loss, however, fails to acknowledge "microvariation within politicoeconomically larger-scale units—a new and emergent fact of descriptive life somewhat jolting to the taxonomic and museological views" (ibid.).

Speciations of languages, like speciations of cultures, are clearly not natural facts, but sociocultural facts relative to which groupness is constituted and transformed and a group's differential identity relative to others is asserted. Still, it is hard to understand how "microvariation" within larger scale-units can substitute for the specificities of knowledge of habitat that uniquely distinguishes autonomous and localized languages. For the environmentalist, ecosystems and their properties are of inestimable and unknown value to humankind in terms of the resources they may hold for future human development and the security they provide against the risks posed by excessive reliance on narrow numbers of crops, animals, and agricultural techniques. Those ecosystems that are most at risk are those that harbor the greatest biological diversity, and those peoples who know the most about these habitats and the relationships between and distinctions within their species hold this knowledge in linguistically specific ways.

Because language plays a crucial role in the acquisition, accumulation, maintenance, and transmission of human knowledge concerning the natural environment and ways of interacting with it, the problem of localized language endangerment raises critical issues about the survival of knowledge that may be of use in the conservation of the world's ecosystems. The knowledge contained in indigenous languages has much to contribute to scientific theories through the uncovering of potentially valuable perspectives on a variety of problems such as land management, marine technology, plant cultivation, and animal husbandry (Nettle and Romaine 2000, 27 and 51).

The enormous intensity of interest in TK in international policy-making circles and the amount of energy expended on the discussion of how to preserve it over the last decade may well have more to do with identifying and tapping into reservoirs of insight, technique, and systemic knowledge that hold promise for future developments in science and technology than it does with the maintenance of local people's livelihoods, the alleviation of their poverty, or the promotion of their political autonomy. Nonetheless, I will suggest that to the extent that the discourse provides grounds for the recognition and valorization of cultural differences, it also thereby provides a means of making potential linkages to other human rights associated with cultural distinction and thus a covert ground for pressing more political claims. It does so, however, in rhetorically specific ways.

Global efforts to respect, preserve, and value TK deploy a peculiar discourse of power and persuasion, one that braves the perils of primitivism and depoliticizes positions of impoverishment by throwing the more acceptable mantel of "culture" over conditions of degradation and local exploitation. Inviting a global "we" to embrace narratives of portending linguistic and biological loss as our own "loss of human capital," the discourse asks "us" to embrace impoverished others as human subjects on whom "we" are or might at some future point be dependent—or so it now seems—this political project is itself, however, very much a work in progress. The ideological work of "culture," I will argue, is erected here as a bulwark to transformations in capital accumulation that create greater and greater pressures to harness "information" so that it can be aggregated and transformed into privately held works of intellectual property that are deemed to further technological progress.

Globalization refers not only to an integration of markets, but to the minimizing of the time it takes for information to flow and to be acted upon—for information to become capital as well as to be capitalized upon. The production and dissemination of "informational goods" is accelerated with the increase in global networks of electronic communications. Goods that are informational are valuable primarily because of their symbolic components rather than their physical substrate or medium of delivery. Such goods, like music, brands, computer software, choreography, perfume blends, screenplays, pharmaceutical formulas, manufacturing techniques, or integrated circuit designs, are, in economists' terms, "public goods." Until they are artificially commodified— protected against unauthorized reproduction by the imposition and exercise of legal rights of exclusivity—their value cannot be possessed and exploited once they have been publicly circulated. The process of commodifying cultural forms is a long historical process of extending, expanding, and proliferating intellectual property rights. As technologies provide ever-greater means for ever more extensive communication and reproduction of cultural forms and greater opportunities for unauthorized exploitation, greater and greater monopoly rights over these intellectual properties have been created.

The culmination of this process occured with the passage, largely at the behest of multinational corporate actors, of the TRIPs Agreement (Trade Related Aspects of Intellectual Property Rights, including trade in counterfeit goods) at the conclusion of the Uruguay Round of the GATT trade deliberations in 1993. As a consquence of this agreement—passed with next to no public deliberation or participation by any elected officials—states across the planet have obligated themselves (as a precondition of engaging in trade under favorable terms and under threat of severe trade retaliation measures) to implement the most expansive set of intellectual property protections ever proposed in world history. This legally binding instrument was promoted almost entirely by industry capture of government regulatory agencies and by industries with the most to gain from greater protection for informational goods (the pharmaceutical, entertainment, electronics, publishing, and agropetrochemical industries chief among them).[6] During the last decade, we have also witnessed an unprecedented increase in legally recognized patentable subject matter, as well as the extension of intellectual property protection to mere aggregations of data in some jurisdictions. For the purposes of considering the relationship between biological diversity and TK, it is important to recognize that technological advances in DNA extraction, identification, and sequencing have turned all elements of nature into "informational goods" subject to commodification:

> [W]hat had once been understood as simply a material *resource*—plants, animals, some bark or seeds—had become also, with biotechnology's capacity to access the genetic or biochemical components within it, what could be referred to as *an informational resource*. It is now possible to extract genetic or biochemical information from living organisms, to *process* it by replicating, modifying, or transforming it, and to *produce from it* minor modifications of this information that are themselves able to be utilized as raw materials, commodified as resources. The genetic information embodied within material resources has become, in effect, the *instrument of production, not only for that resource, but also for a range of other potential resources that could be produced by recombining the information in an almost limitless number of ways.* (Perry 2000, 383; emphasis in original)

The biotechnology industries, like other industrial forces with large investments in informational goods, realized that the best way to maintain "competitive advantage" (or an anticompetitive privilege, as some might deem it) was to control the networks through which information could be traded and the means by which it could be reproduced. The capacity to restrict the circulation of such information was most effectively secured by global recognition of patents in the materials they had extracted, identified, sequenced, or modified—ensuring their holders exclusive rights to market these materials and a share of the profits from any products derived from these informational resources.

The so-called level playing field for international trade ensures that some goods (genetic resources, materials, design, timber, textiles, techniques, know-how, practices, and knowledges that are extracted from the "less developed countries") flow freely, whereas others (genetically modified or industrially developed seeds, fertilizers, pesticides, software, and medicines) do not flow freely in trade but are received as monopolies that command lengthy requirements of rent payments (royalties) for each and every usage of their informational content. The field is, therefore, not a level one at all. Those peoples who merely provide resources or information (as well as resources whose "information" can be extracted through the technologies of others and claimed as exclusive properties) are at a profound disadvantage because they are unable to protect these as works of intellectual property while they become obligated to pay an ever-greater number of royalties to others.

Opposition to the TRIPs Agreement emerged only after the ink was dry. At first glance the Convention on Biological Diversity (CBD) appears to partake of the same neoliberal logic; it is part of a series of international environmental initiatives in which "nature" is seen to be a "public good" best managed through market mechanisms. Biological resources are represented as goods that are most appropriately dealt with in an open system of flows that need to be efficiently mapped, monitored, and transferred so that information about genetic resources can be globally cumulated, communicated, and, most important, capitalized upon. The so-called common heritage of biological diversity is replaced by the principle of national sovereignty to ensure its better management, its availability for national development projects, and, it would seem, to invite nation-states to create the juridical conditions enabling the security of possession necessary for contractual relations involving its exploitation. The potential profits to be derived from "biotechnology and especially recombinant DNA technology are creating new incentives to inventorize and screen the whole range of known and unknown organisms" (Flitner 1998, 144). The biotechnology industry requires certainty for commercial transactions and regulatory regimes that facilitate access to genetic resources, local knowledge, and ecosystem expertise so as to both price these undervalued resources and create market-based incentives for their trade. The CBD, arguably, is first and foremost a legal regime designed to meet these economic needs.

The CBD attempts to establish a reciprocity of both access to and benefits from the use of genetic resources by linking a Northern right to access to resources and knowledge (with the prior informed consent and compensation of Southern states and/or communities) to a Southern right (yet to be realized) to enhanced access to useful technologies for achieving sustainable development purposes. According to Michael Flitner, "the very functioning of the CBD depends on the restriction of both access to 'raw biodiversity' (and local knowledge thereof) and access to technologies and organisms derived therefrom" (ibid). To the extent that resources and knowledge thereof, however, flow in global markets simply as raw materials and raw data, the benefits to be derived from restricting access to them and/or pricing them as raw goods are limited compared to the benefits to be reaped from restricting access to and pricing derivative technologies that may command monopoly rents through their protection as intellectual properties.

Biodiversity is, as anthropologist Corinne Hayden remarks in a discussion of the practice of "biodiversity prospecting," a distinctive kind of natural resource:

> Unlike prospecting for material commodities such as minerals and timber, biodiversity prospecting is not dependent on large-scale harvests of raw material. Rather, its key objects of value are biochemical compounds extracted from plants, microbes, or insects, which biochemists and pharmacologists attempt to synthesize in laboratories for product development. The value of biodiversity thus ultimately lies in its ability to be radically scaled-up: a few milligrams of extract might be all it takes to provide the lead to a useful compound. And if biochemists succeed in synthesizing the compound in question, or in producing a modification thereof (by no means an inevitable outcome), they no longer need access to the raw material in order to mass-produce a drug. It is this potential for turning plants into "information," and information into a product, that allows proponents to label bio-prospecting a form of sustainable—or ecologically friendly—economic development. (Hayden 2002, 62)

Compounds derived from isolated and modified biological resources are being protected in many jurisdictions as patentable innovations. This creates an exclusive right to collect royalties from most
other uses of that compound, even if it is independently created from
other sources. It also creates a right to prevent others from using the
so-called innovation. (It is beyond the scope of this essay to make the
argument, but it is arguable that such activities and products do not, in
fact, pass the necessary threshold tests for patentability and that patents
granted on such products are and should be considered invalid [Amari
and Coombe n.d.].) There are now several "bioprospecting contracts" in
place that provide limited compensation for the states in whose jurisdiction the resources were located, and some others that are structured
to provide benefit sharing with local communities whose knowledge of
such resources provides guidance to where potentially valuable medicinal or agricultural properties of plant, animal, or microbial properties
might lie. Nonetheless, "indigenous" and "local communities embodying traditional lifestyles" are clearly at the low end of a complicated
hierarchy of actors with ascending levels of legal sophistication. As
Hayden points out, even those arrangements that do contain "benefit-
sharing provisions" with local peoples do so by calibrating the degree
of "innovation" that goes on at each level:

> [E]ven as prospecting helps make visible and produce ever-widening
> claims over biological resources, the construction of biodiversity as a
> potential form of intellectual property also is being used as a mechanism
> to propose and fight for new forms of market-oriented "participation"
> and rights for disenfranchised communities. That is, the definition of
> biodiversity's value as informational also opens the way for redistribut-
> ing particular kinds of claims to rights over resources, by asking, at what
> part in chains of "innovation" is value added, and by whom? (Ibid.)

The drive to represent local peoples' knowledge and practices
as innovative works—forms of intangible or intellectual property—and

integrally related to an indigenous identity or a "traditional lifestyle" emerges from within this political economy. It is in this context that we must situate efforts to "indigenize" knowledge so that it might cease to be mere information and pass, instead, in the more valuable form of culture. Only then may claims to possess, control, preserve, and maintain it be recognized and only then will peoples be respected—if only, at first, for what they "know" and its potential value to a global "we" and "our" need for new conceptual resources to further the objective of "sustainable development." Over the course of its interpretation during the last five years, the CBD has become the focus of many third-world governments, indigenous peoples, and NGO energies because it appears to represent the only major international legally binding treaty that has some potential to counter the neoliberal imperatives of the TRIPs Agreement. As indigenous peoples have become more active and sophisticated participants in this policy-making sphere and brought to it expertise honed in other United Nations venues, they have put issues of cultural integrity, democratic decision making, accountability, and self-determination squarely on the bargaining table. Their capacities to do so are greatly assisted by the rhetorical leverage provided by international human-rights norms and the central, if ambiguous, place of culture within these.

Many indigenous peoples (and many of those who may be deemed to have "traditional lifestyles") are resident in or enclosed and contained by the jurisdiction of states with which they have long historical relationships of distrust, betrayal, and violence. Rather than trust state delegates to the CBD to represent their interests, they have used the CBD agenda, forums, funding, and publicity opportunities to further press global indigenous human-rights struggles for self-determination. Those who are recognized as indigenous (and those who aspire to be), as well as supportive NGOs, have used the CBD process to further establish legitimacy and support for the Draft Declaration on the Rights of Indigenous Peoples that was negotiated almost simultaneously with debates about the implementation of the CBD. Whether or not the Draft Declaration is adopted by the UN member states in the next few years (and that appears unlikely), it has created a distinctive vocabulary of representations and claims that have been reiterated in so many contexts that they may eventually be considered a form of international customary law.

According to international legal principles, all peoples may claim self-determination, and all peoples have cultures. Indigenous peoples' rights to their lands, territories, and resources are recognized as deriving from their cultures and spiritual traditions. Peoples are entitled to pursue their cultural development and to revitalize and protect their cultural traditions. Indigenous peoples have rights to control their intellectual and cultural properties, and these include rights to special measures to control, develop, and protect their sciences, technologies, and cultural manifestations (including knowledge of local genetic resources). Draft principles for the protection of indigenous heritage define it to include knowledge transmitted intergenerationally and pertaining to a particular people or its territory. All of these nascent indigenous human rights shape the rhetoric of indigenous peoples in CBD negotiations. Emphasis is put on the dynamic and innovative nature of traditional knowledge and practices and the importance of TK in the preservation of biological diversity—culture, in other words, as a work in progress.

Meanwhile, the entire TRIPs Agreement is pending review by the Trips Council, and many third-world governments are insisting that the review consider the rights of states to make intellectual property policy to further their environmental commitments under the CBD. This may entail an expansion of those technologies that may be excluded from patent protection, including all biological materials and technologies whose "innovation" is based solely on the isolation and synthesis of active properties already known to local peoples (and thus should be considered part of the relevant prior art [Coombe 2001]). Most of the states deemed by TRIPs to be "developed" (and those that contain the largest commercial biotechnology sectors) are opposed to any amendments that would reduce the scope of patentable subject matter. Developing countries, however, seek to use CBD obligations to preserve genetic resources and protect TK as a lever to open the next round of

World Trade Organization discussions to environmental considerations, to thereby limit the power of Northern intellectual property holders, and to insist on more equitable distribution of resources and forms of technology transfer that meet development needs. In short, the movement to protect TK is one of a series of global initiatives designed to limit the proprietary powers that multinational corporate interests (backed by the coercive powers of the state) gained through the expansion of trade regimes to protect intellectual properties.

Intellectual property provides the legal and cultural means by which global flows of information are commodified, capitalized upon, managed, and policed, but it has also provided resources for movements of social resistance to the violence of "informationalism."[7] In *The Cultural Life of Intellectual Properties* (Coombe 1998a), I argued that intellectual properties are politically generative—they have productive as well as prohibitive potential—providing cultural resources (rhetorical forms, signifying vehicles, and authoritative texts) for the construction of contemporary authorities, identities, moral economies, and proprietary ethics. The expansion of intellectual property rights and an understanding of the distributional impact that the allocation of such rights will effect have motivated scholars, activists, NGOs, political ecologists, environmentalists, ecofeminists, and ecosystem peoples' movements to recognize that representations of culture, knowledge, and information have worldly consequences that threaten to effect major shifts in power and resources.[8] To understand these movements, however, it is necessary to delineate key aspects of the conceptual scaffolding that supports global regimes of intellectual property and, significantly, provides rhetorical opportunities for inverting the entitlements it affords. To the extent that industries consolidate around the management and control of information, it becomes crucial to critically scrutinize the rhetorical tropes—such as invention, discovery, originality, novelty, obviousness, and creation, culture, and progess—that legitimate the commodification and privatization of cultural forms (including local ecological knowledges) and their alienation from particular relationships within social communities of human belonging.

Such an inquiry is by necessity an inquiry into the "workings" of capital. Legal anthropologists have been instrumental in exploring the globalization of capital as a historical cultural and material process—insisting that traditional approaches to political economy and cultural perspectives on capitalism will remain both abstract and unconnected until we address the constitutive role of law in creating the cultural fictions through which capital enunciates the form and ensures the force of its entitlements (see Maurer, in this volume; see also Maurer 1995, 1999, 2002; Riles 2000). These fictions, moreover, serve to incite and to animate other rhetorical tactics that redeploy these fictions to other ends and agendas. However, it is important to recognize that "the other" never stands outside of, or beyond, the law, but is always already standing "before the law"—phrasing injustice in a productive and diacritical relationship with juridical regimes and the objects and identities they countenance.[9]

This phrasing of injustice is evident in transnational struggles to redefine "the raw and the cooked" on global terrain—the struggles of indigenous peoples, subsistence farmers, forest dwellers, and other marginalized groups to prevent local knowledge and local resources being reduced to mere data freely available to the "information-intensive industries" of a postindustrial economy. The cultural logic of intellectual property law entrenches a European colonial worldview in which individuals (including corporations) lay claim to intellectual properties by means of deploying genius and innovation to transform resources, information, and ideas into "expressions," "inventions," or the currently ubiquitous "innovations," which can be protected as "works" of intellectual property. Nature is transformed into "culture" by such processes of human creativity and such "works" are encouraged as contributions to "progress" in the arts and sciences (indeed, the U.S. Constitution explicitly grants copyright and patent powers for this purpose). In international patent practice, for instance, the idea/expression dichotomy traditionally assumed the form of a global cartography—Northern, Western individuals required unfettered access to the uncultivated resources of the South—glossed as the "common heritage of mankind."[10]

Whether represented as nature or as ideas, the resources and knowledges of non-Western others were regarded as merely the means with which Western authors could produce expressive works and technological innovations. Whether the works produced were pharmaceuticals, fertilizers, or textiles, these works contributed to "human" progress. Products of Nature become products of human Culture through Western authorship. As an incentive to promote such creative initiative, the Western innovator was given a limited monopoly on the invention to reward him for contributing it to the canon of works that compose human civilization.

This edifice is maintained by dozens of other modern misrecognitions and legal fictions (about the practices of science, for example, corporate research and development, the character of traditional agriculture, plant-breeding practices, the conditions under which scientific knowledge is generated and transmitted, the promiscuity of nature and its natural generativity, etc.). Discounting these fictions is necessary and important work, but that is not my purpose here. In any case, others have done so and doing so has assumed ever-greater importance given the increasing size and power of biotechnology industries whose profits have been enabled by the access to Southern resources this discourse legitimates. I am more concerned here with the structure of particular responses to the sudden awareness on the part of global political players that these resources are disappearing. Over the last decade, this sense of global urgency has provided a major political opportunity for repositioning the South in international legal arenas through the use of a new rhetorical politics.

I could nominate this narrative "The Knowledge Rich and the Biologically Poor," but I prefer a formulation suggested by Pat Ray Mooney (1996)—"Whether the People Who Love Panda Bears Can Respect the Genius of the Poor." Let me make it clear at the outset that my political sympathies do correspond with the redistributional aspirations that lie behind this political poetics. I am well aware that my characterization of the discourse deployed in the service of this agenda may run the risk of appearing to ridicule it. Nonetheless, it is a risk I am temporarily prepared to assume, if it helps us to better understand how this field of international legal politics is rhetorically animated. My focus on the rhetorical dimensions of these assertions should not be interpreted as any necessary skepticism about their credibility; I lack the scientific background and ethnographic experience to make such judgments. Rather, I am suggesting that economic and political claims tend to obtain credibility when they are made using discursive forms that have achieved newly hegemonic status. The sense of global urgency posed by species loss has created a symbolic opportunity strategically seized by indigenous peoples, Asian and African farmers' rights groups, and rain-forest inhabitants (and the academics, environmentalists, and NGOs that support them) to contest the colonial categorical framework that legitimates the international intellectual property system. Indeed, in international policy circles, United Nations documents, indigenous peoples' declarations, NGO statements, and academic articles during the past decade, this discourse has been turned on its head. Inverting its terms and reversing its valences, "the South" has potentially effected a rhetorical sea change in global legal discourse.

The increased use of the term *biopiracy* (Shiva 1997) following upon the Third World Network's characterization of GATT as a form of "recolonization" (Raghaven 1990a, 1990b), and the emergence of the concept of "biocolonialism" (Whitt 1998), are indicative of this inversion. Rhetorically, this inversion has been accomplished through a number of means, but arguably the most significant of these is the insistence that indigenous ecosystems are inscribed environments, the qualities of which have been put there by the deliberate development and creative cultivation activities of their inhabitants. Habitats are now represented as social texts, created by the authorial activities of peoples or communities—the result of which is a cultural work of biodiversity.

Local communities are recognized as employing creative agency in practices that nurture and improve natural resources.[11] Jungle habitats are characterized as experimental laboratories in which genetic properties are routinely discovered, synthesized, and honed by tribal peoples. Resources exist in their current form thanks to the applied knowledge of indigenous and traditional communities that monitor and improve them for specific purposes. Landraces (wild plants or partner species) are the outcome of a continuous and dynamic human development process. They are not stable products, but reflect adaptation to local agro-ecological production conditions and to the specific production preferences of different socioeconomic, gender, and ethnic groupings within farming communities—whose experimental moxy should be both safeguarded and encouraged. Peasant ecological practices comprise active processes of in situ research and innovation and by shaping genetic flows of biodiversity peasants become "small in situ biotechnologists" (Gari 1999). Even noncultivated plants found in the environs of traditional farm and indigenous communities are represented as having been nurtured or developed, or as an integrated part of forest/farming systems or community innovation systems (depending on the audience appealed to). Local recognition of the value of wild plants is seen to be evident in the preservation and improvement of the local ecosystems of which they are a part. Such preservation and improvement, it is implied, should be seen as the intentional and innovative activity of unrecognized authors who seek to produce complementarities and synergies between themselves, the flora, and the fauna. I shall quote, at length, one typical representation titled "The Indigenous Regime of Biodiversity" involving peoples in Amazonia:

> The indigenous peoples of Pastaza embody traditional ecological practices that shape the conservation, use and transformation of biodiversity in diverse Amazonian ecosystems. They have developed a complex land-use system . . . Biodiversity is essential for their agroecological practices, their food security, their primary health care, the local ecosystem resilience, and many cultural values alike. They have developed a whole indigenous agroecology, which is conveyed by both ecological practices and cultural meanings, and whose crucial component is biodiversity. They cultivate more than 50 different plant species . . . They also manage a wide genetic agrobiodiversity for many of the cultivated plants . . . fed by their cultural values as demonstrated by a culture-biodiversity curve when

comparing genetic agrobiodiversity and cultural values of the cultivated plants . . . Their planting of many fruit trees and shrubs gives rise to anthropogenic forests. From this human ecology context, the mainstream perception of Amazonia as a *wild* ecosystem and as a pool of *pristine* biodiversity resources is shown to be incorrect as other ethnoecological research also suggests. The indigenous biodiversity regime also comprises a collective system of managing and sharing plant genetic resources, which feeds an open flow of knowledge and innovations on biodiversity . . . they broadly disseminate innovations and discoveries. Their cultivated fields, and also the forests, are in-situ and in-vivo germoplasm banks, where large amounts of biodiversity are conserved, managed, shared, and cultivated . . . In fact there is a cultural codification of deep ecological insights, so that indigenous ecological knowledge is inextricable from the cultural practices. (Ibid., 6–7)

The utility of genetic resources, it is asserted, has been developed by local peoples whose knowledge is represented as perhaps more sophisticated than that of Western scientists, who appear to engage in engineering or altering rather than in any real creation, producing a dull uniformity rather than valuable diversity. Indeed, the innovations of Western scientists for which patents are granted are described as modest alterations or (better yet) minor tinkering. Patents granted for processes of treating plants and for the insecticides developed from them are sniffed at as mere derivatives—slightly modified versions of the original (Kadidal 1993). Each and every seed, it would seem, is an "original" to which we can affix a cultural, if not an individual, signature.

In this transnational discourse, the South has for too long been subsidizing the North and peoples have had to pay for the results of their own genius. The genetic resources found in ecologically diverse environments are valuable, Northern scientists assert, because of their intangible genetic information. Advocates for the South, however, argue that it is impossible to say that the collection of germ plasm does not result in deprivation to the source culture because only a few seeds are taken. The value of the work lies in its genetic structure, which is present even in the most minimal amounts of material. Just like Northern authors who cry deprivation when the hearts of their works—which embody their individual personalities—are reproduced without compensation, Southern cultures are deprived when the distinctive inscriptions of a community's traditional knowledge are reproduced in the genetic engineering of others. In short, to avoid having genetic resources essential to local livelihoods reduced to mere "information," these have been reconfigured as cultural works in progress. This rhetoric is deployed both by those who support the idea of protecting TK as a distinct form of intellectual property and by those who oppose any further extension of intellectual properties and advocate instead for an expanded public domain.

If my point here were simply to emphasize that people speak to power in the language that power understands and/or that the excesses of this rhetoric match those of the discourses it seeks to counter, I would be making a true but trite observation. I began this essay, however, by evoking my ambivalence as an anthropologist with respect to the particular position of culture in this subaltern discourse, and in the international legal arenas in which it is voiced. My own ambivalence appears to reflect in microcosm the varied and conflicted responses to the development of the category of indigenous or traditional knowledge that have emerged within the discipline of anthropology. These responses, I would suggest, illustrate and give voice to pervasive disciplinary anxieties about the concept of culture, its colonial provenance, and its contemporary deployment.

For the past two decades, critical anthropologists have been renouncing "culture"—recognizing the origins of the concept in forms of colonial governance, its complicity with Orientalism—and showing how many, if not most, constructions of tradition and cultural identity were reifications that served the interests of settler and colonial elites. Given this history, some anthropologists have taken great pains to distance themselves from the concept of culture; exhortations to go beyond culture, forget culture, transcend culture, and write against culture were ubiquitous in the late 1980s and early 1990s.[12] More recently, some critical anthropologists have suggested instead that we "site" culture, recognizing "that while anthropologists are preoccupied with de-essentializing the concept of cultural wholes, many of the very people we study are deeply involved in constructing cultural contexts which bear many resemblances to such cultural entities" (Hastrup and Olwig 1997, 3).[13]

> At the same moment that the anthropological profession experiences a loss of faith in this concept of culture, it has become embraced by a wide range of culture builders worldwide. The paradoxical result is that anthropological works are increasingly being consulted by people desiring to construct cultural identities of a totalizing sort which the anthropologist finds deeply problematic. Even though anthropologists may fear that the desired cultural identity derives from an earlier anthropological discourse that has become naturalized in various local contexts, this identity cannot be discarded as irrelevant. (Ibid.)

The discipline's new orthodoxy of "writing against culture," current practitioners' aversion to scholarly "essentialism," and the accompanying distrust of others' activities of "self-essentialism," our disapproval of practices that represent culture in any systemic form, and our anxieties about expressing any relatively autonomous forms of cultural difference (given the likelihood of being professionally wounded with accusations of "Orientalism")—not to mention our current certainties about the invention of tradition—may, however, serve to blind us to the ways in which, at the international level, cultural anthropology's traditional tropes are becoming potent tools in global struggles for social justice. From "a position of critical reflexivity," the "siting" of culture in contemporary global circumstances as a "dynamic process of self-understanding" (ibid.) requires that we contextualize actors, networks, institutions, and discourses in an economic, political, and legal framework that identifies the forces, pressures, institutional imperatives, and ideologies that are shaping emerging hegemonies and the uncanny forms of their resistance. International law provides one of the most important of these institutions of power—and the discourse of environmental preservation coupled with the discourse of international human rights are perhaps the only legitimate rhetorics of sufficiently broad normative appeal to counter the vocabulary of neoliberalism and the imperatives of capital's insistence on the magical benefits of free trade.

Not all anthropologists are adopting such positions of critical reflexivity by any means. Indeed, many anthropologists and ethnobotanists have seized the opportunity afforded by this new discourse of environmental crisis, biological loss, and indigenous wisdom to reassert precisely those images of culturally distinctive systems of knowledge and belief that were modern anthropology's academic trademark—in order to assert the anthropologist's preeminence. Within the narrative of the knowledge-rich and the biologically poor, some anthropologists are anxious to locate the new relevance and importance of their own disciplinary expertise. The "transition from capital-intensive to information-intensive development technologies" has opened the door for a new appreciation of indigenous knowledge and, concomitantly, new opportunities for anthropologists (Bentley 1998, 235). Anthropologists are to be congratulated for having been the first to recognize that "other people have their own effective science," which militates in favor of assuming an appropriate hegemony in the "development world" (Sillitoe 1998, 223). As the only experts who appreciate the significance of "sociocultural context" in understanding indigenous knowledge and consequentially the appropriate guardians against its being "treated as mere technical information," anthropologists are called upon to revive their disciplinary calling and return to what they do best—"the translation of another culture" as "the demands of development require" (ibid., 229).

The systemic view of culture that cultural anthropologists thought long discredited has thus returned with a vengeance to be embraced by applied anthropologists eager to demonstrate their usefulness in policy-making arenas. Reiterating tropes from the cultural ecology models that were abandoned by most anthropologists throughout the 1970s, these applied anthropologists represent local cultural practices as situated within "an overarching regulatory structure derived from the cybernetic and self-correcting properties of closed living systems" (Peet and Watts 1996, 5). Such images, like those sketched by the cultural ecologists that came before them, tend to conveniently obscure the fact that the social collectivities and knowledges they purport to represent are actually parts of large, complex, and open political economies, integrally imbricated with regional and global markets, state regulatory authorities, and international pressures.

Within cultural anthropology, which has long been influenced by poststructuralist currents of critique, and in which the ideological legitimations of the development industry have been largely discredited, a critique of the indigenous knowledge industry and the anthropologist's role within it comes easily.[14] Critics quickly point out that in this discourse, indigenous knowledges are presupposed to be bounded and inextricably connected to some isolable "cultural context" until disaggregated by the interpretive activities of ethnographers. This involves both misrepresentation and disciplinary hubris. Centuries of intercultural contact and cross-cultural sharing and working of agricultural and medicinal processes are being conveniently ignored here. Indigenous knowledge is represented as the knowledge of vague but similar others, defined in opposition to an authoritative "we," experts in hard systems, who have possession of scientific knowledge. This polarizes the scientific and the indigenous (Agrawal 1995)—and locates them in discrete and independent spaces (Ferradas 1998)—spaces that can exist only in Occidentalist and Orientalist fantasies.[15] Applied anthropology's enthusiasm for the indigenous knowledge industry betrays an innocence or ignorance of the political context of the discourse's emergence and the necessary shaping of its rhetorical strategies by international legal instruments (Posey 1998) in which the indigenous is a contingent, contested, and materially significant category.

For critical anthropologists, the outlines of a new global bargain or transnational contract reveal themselves. A "Northern we" will now value "Southern others" for maintaining cultural diversity because "their" cultural difference ensures "our" biodiversity. But how other must they be for us to appreciate them as having culture and when will those differences have international weight? As anthropologists Beth Conklin and Laura Graham (1995) show, Amazonian rain-forest peoples are appreciated by global environmental groups when they appear in recognizably tribal garb, claim their integral relationships to Mother Earth, engage in subsistence activities, and otherwise play the part of noble savages.[16] They are less attractive to ecopoliticians and may even be denounced as inauthentic when they show interest and acumen in the economic exploitation of local environmental resources and the capacity to engage as active participants in international decision-making processes.

Indeed, Elizabeth Povenelli's exploration of the Australian national desire to locate and respect "traditional indigenous law" suggests that such desires impose a profound violence upon Aboriginal peoples by making national recognition, public sympathy, and state resources contingent on an external scrutiny, inspection, and examination that always constitutes contemporary Aboriginal persons as failures. Aboriginal persons are scarred by, and by virtue of, their distance from and lack of sufficient identity with those ancient customs that define the authenticity of their cultural difference for a nation that is thus enabled to ignore or deny the violence of the settlement history that makes such isomorphic identifications impossible chimeras (Povinelli 1999).[17] Under international law, however, indigenous peoples are recognized as self-identifying and as the primary interpreters of their own cultures, which are recognized as evolving and changing; their own customs are recognized as the primary determinants of how heritage may be controlled. To the extent that indigenous tradition, culture, and spiritual heritage provide the legitimating basis for indigenous self-determination in international law, "tradition" and "culture" are too significant as political resources to be abandoned, despite their potential to be abused by state legislatures and judiciaries. The discourse around the CBD illustrates that some indigenous peoples have been successful in having their knowledges recognized as simultaneously traditional and innovative, customary and dynamic, integral to their own specific histories and identities, while valuable to international sustainable development efforts. Not all peoples have been equally successful on this playing field, however.

Anthropologist Marilyn Strathern once remarked that the nice thing about culture was that everyone had it. Unfortunately, however, not everyone is equally placed to convince others of the fact! Renato Rosaldo's retrospective framing of a disciplinary subconscious that distinguished between peoples with and without culture (Rosaldo 1989) now seems quaint in anthropological circles, but it is a distinction that appears to have a powerful claim on the international legal imagination. In international legal regimes, all peoples have a right to cultural identity, but all people do not. Certainly, some people who inhabit biologically rich regions have been more successful in establishing themselves as peoples than others. As Kathleen Lawrey's ethnographic work demonstrates (Lawrey 2001), these discursive strategies of representing nature as culture and tradition as innovative work in the service of the progress of humankind are not equally available to all marginalized peoples. Although Guarani Indians in the Izozog region of Bolivia are showered with NGO funding to represent their practices as integral to their cultures and encouraged to develop products based on their traditional knowledge, their mestizo neighbors find international organizations deaf to their cries that the harvesting of coca leaves is itself a traditional Inca practice that sustains biodiversity.

Designation as "a people with culture" is an important stake and site of contestation in ongoing struggles for recognition and income redistribution. Those who can make the strongest claims to possessing culture are more internationally empowered to protest local injustices. Hence, we see the emergence of strategic rhetorical moves to "indigenize" culture and "culturalize" knowledge in local resistances to and reworkings of sustainable development across the globe because indigenous peoples are those most fully recognized as in possession of cultures worthy of preservation. Rather than preening about their newfound relevance, applied anthropologists should consider when or whether it is politically or ethically appropriate to intervene in processes of cultural authentication that are not invited or instigated by these others, as well as in those that are, and in what circumstances.

Intellectual property regimes were inevitably one of the first means suggested to promote the protection and use of traditional environmental knowledge, and through it, biological diversity. Conservation, it was suggested, was not being implemented in developing countries because of the lack of any incentive structure for preserving rather than destroying biological resources. Means had to be found to value them before measures could be found to protect them. Neoliberal economists and their followers in the development industries suggested that intellectual property rights will compensate indigenous peoples for the "opportunity costs" of investing in the ongoing production of biodiversity. Treating TK as intellectual property would create opportunities for local profit making, joint ventures with government and corporate actors, the negotiation of compensation, and a market mechanism to revitalize interest in local cultures and traditional practices of resource management. There is now a vast literature (and a lively conference circuit) devoted to the possibilities for expanding intellectual property rights to recognize works of collective, intergenerational innovation, and works that involve "community innovation systems" or "traditional technologies."

Readers may be impatient by this point for some form of prescription. Should TK be protected as a form of intellectual property? Can it be? Isn't intellectual property simply a Western form of valuation that imposes a new colonial hegemony on peoples who have already suffered too many forms of European domination? Won't intellectual property protection simply strip TK of its cultural meaning, decontextualize it from social relations and ritual practices, alienating and reifying it as a simple commodity? Don't these initiatives partake of modernity's metaphysics of flows that assumes that all knowledges can be decoupled from cosmologies and appropriated instrumentally? Perhaps. Given the creativity of indigenous peoples, however, and their capacities to occupy legal categories across the grain, and to creatively hybridize legal regimes, I would hesitate to provide a definitive answer to these questions at this time. In any case, no singular position on the question seems viable given the very different political, economic, and social circumstances in which indigenous peoples and local communities of peoples preserving and developing genetic resources find themselves.

Nonetheless, it is extremely doubtful that the intellectual property regime in its existing or proposed forms is a politically or functionally viable means to accomplish the various tasks now assigned to it.[18] Indeed, as charges of biopiracy increase, patents hastily granted to corporations on technologies developed by peasant peoples are challenged, the anti-competitive and research-inhibiting implications of broad patent rights become evident, breeders' rights and patents granted on plants held sacred in indigenous communities are more publicized, and commitments made to third-world governments under the TRIPs Agreement are not met, the global intellectual property system is losing credibility. Nonetheless, the rhetorical value of debates about the viability of intellectual properties to meet the needs of the world's most vulnerable peoples—in putting impoverished peoples' grievances on the international table and drawing policy makers' attention to global inequities in distribution and compensation for resources and knowledge—has been inestimable.

Globally, it appears that attitudes toward the viability of intellectual property to deal with environmental degradation seem to divide along an axis, with those who "have culture" and thus a more secure basis to make claims to territories and resources less amenable to having their livelihoods reduced to exchange relationships among property holders. For those whom international legal regimes recognize as "indigenous," possession of cultural identity creates particular leverage. These indigenous peoples and the NGOs that represent them are far more opposed to the privatization and commodification of knowledge and living resources through intellectual property laws and they are actively involved in "no patenting of life" movements. The right not to share knowledge, to locally govern the terms and conditions of research, to restrict the commercial exploitation of any resources or information obtained to build local political capacities, and to control uses of knowledge such that local cosmologies and senses of intergenerational obligation are met are seen as much more significant rights among First Nations peoples, Maori, Australian Aboriginals, and Torres Strait Islanders, for instance. Assertions of indigenous intellectual and cultural property have indeed been made, but they have been made secondary to and inherent components of aboriginal title and self-determination, which recognizes the primacy of indigenous territoriality (Posey and Dutfield 1996).

In areas where territorial rights based on a historical connection to ancestral lands are less likely to be legally recognized, local peoples (often encouraged by NGOs and state governments) are actively involved in reflecting upon their own knowledge, shaping it for legal purposes, and reconstructing it in ways that promise to provide recognition and income. This is particularly the case in Southeast Asia, where grassroots networks of indigenous communities formally engage in knowledge sharing and crafting appropriate transfer payments between communities in seventy-five countries (Gupta 1998b). The NGOs that represent such peoples on the global plane (at international meetings, local communities embodying traditional lifestyles tend to be represented by proxy by healers' associations, farmers' associations, or university-based researchers who have established village networks for documenting TK, or are simply assumed to be represented by the delegates from the states in which they are resident) put emphasis on the conservation and valuation of local innovations in medicine, agriculture, and resource management, and the contributions such peoples' works could and should make to global progress in the arts and sciences if properly acknowledged. They are more likely to stress the role of particular individuals and families, the need to honor, reward, and compensate particular farmers and healers for their maintenance of specialized knowledges, and to downplay the collective and cosmological dimensions of such skills and their transmission. Nonetheless, to the extent that their own governments, and the governments of those Convention parties that provide them with foreign aid are obligated to help preserve the TK of those "local communities embodying traditional lifestyles," there is an impetus to continually elaborate the "traditional" basis of such "works" while developing their significance as contributions to "progress"—now glossed as sustainable development.

Claims to indigenous intellectual property rights (as well as claims to ownership of cultural forms under the more inclusive norm of self-determination) have been subjected to critical evaluation within anthropology. These responses range from the liberal alarm bells sounded by Michael Brown, who voices Enlightenment fears that "the copyrighting of culture" is likely to result in the end of science, human progress, freedom of expression, and democracy as we know it (Brown 1998), through the apocalyptic nostalgia of Michael Dove, who, with sad resignation, insists that biodiversity is the result of marginalization—once peripheries are tied into centers through such mechanisms as intellectual property, both biological and cultural diversity will vanish (Dove 1996); the social world is losing cultures at the same rate as the natural world is losing species, and the two are both inevitable and inextricably linked. More critical perspectives convey cynicism about the capacity of market mechanisms to stem market forces and caution against the new "greenwashing" politics of bypassing politics and the emergence of "Green Orientalisms" (Koptiuch 1996).

A more pragmatic approach recommends itself. If, as Kristin Koptiuch (1996) nicely put it, culture is the colonial trope by which the third world is incorporated in the first, it may also appear to be the trope with which at least some of the marginalized may take claim to the—always contested—human in human rights. The human-rights framework remains the only viable international political arena and discourse that commands sufficient legitimacy and respect to counter new liberal ideologies (and the hegemony of free trade as the basis for the governance of cultural flows or communications). If the rhetoric of informationalization increasingly insists that social life is determined by genetic codes (discovered by the genius of Western science), the response that genetic resources are themselves culturally defined by peoples' evolving knowledge is a critical intervention that displaces the debate and disrupts the integrity of the site of its emergence. It shifts the discourse from one of trade and property to one of culture and impoverishment, and in so doing reminds us that intellectual property is a *human* right.

If the new world order has established itself through new information technologies and the capitalization of its benefits through strategic deployment of intellectual property laws, we should not be surprised that the resistances it generates engage similar tactics and point them in alternative directions. Rather than approach these "factishes" (Latour 1993) as tragic capitulations to the totalizing logic of capital, I suggest we see them as calculated interventions in a large dialogue about social justice.

To the extent that indigenous peoples have put intellectual property rights "back" into the human-rights framework, they also challenge the international policy-making community to reconcile intellectual property rights with other fundamental social, economic, and political rights. They have done so, moreover, precisely through the leverage provided by the ambiguities of the rights to culture contained in the major human-rights covenants—culture as the accumulated heritage of humankind, to which we all have rights, culture as the right of self-expression, the right to engage in creative activity, the right to be compensated for the fruits of those labors, the right to benefit from scientific progress and to have access to human works as a right of cultural development, culture as a collective right to maintain and strengthen group identity through recognized attachments to objects, landscapes, resources, stories, songs, and, yes, local knowledges. The relationships between these diverse forms of culture are not straightforward—they may even come into conflict—but the resolution of their contradictions is the site of tense, but productive negotiation.

Rights to culture enshrined in international human-rights conventions exhort states to recognize peoples and rights to "enjoy their culture," manifest their culture, and develop it. The insistence that culture be recognized, protected, maintained, promoted, disseminated—the imploring demand that we "enjoy our culture" and promote the other's enjoyment of it—should no longer produce in anthropologists any particular pride, nor frustration and anxiety. Such frustrations and anxieties about culture might instead be considered symptoms of the discipline's failure to address issues of ambivalence and desire when considering issues of meaning, history, and politics. Continuing to dismiss the idea of culture as false, ideological, socially constructed, a colonial imposition, essentialist, Orientalist, the ruse of strategic essentialism, or a sop to appease anachronistic forms of legislation is to fail to do justice to its power and to discount its power to express injustice. If justice is always a deferred absence (Pavlich 1998), popular phrasings of injustice may well assume the spaces, the forms, and the tropes bestowed by colonial memory.

The identity of culture is not a positivity but a site animated by the force of ambivalence and wounded attachment—and this relationship to the historical trauma of cultural identification is also an important space of yearning and aspiration. To quote Judith Butler, "any mobilization against subjection will take subjection as its resource and that attachment to an injurious interpellation will . . . become the condition under which re-signifying that interpellation becomes possible" (Butler 1997, 104). From this perspective, it becomes less important to monitor and render judgment on progressive and reactionary deployments of colonial tropes than to consider the possibility that progressive deployments necessarily require reactionary fixations in order to effect subversive reterritorializations.

Identities are formed in constitutive relationship to juridical regimes that presume that assertion of rights and entitlements can only be made from the space of singular and injured identities—social totalizations of the particularities of historical trauma. If justice is always a deferred absence, popular phrasing of injustice assumes the spaces bestowed by colonial memory; the ultimate value of culture, then, is its ever-elastic capacity to serve as a work in progress—to give new meaning and new voice to injustice.

Notes

1. The concept of "unworking" is borrowed from Jean-Luc Nancy and is developed in the final chapter of Coombe (1998a).

2. I have attended the World Intellectual Property Organization Conference on Intellectual Property and Traditional Knowledge in November 1999 and the World Intellectual Property Intergovernmental Meetings on Genetic Resources, Traditional Knowledge and Folklore in December 2001 and December 2002, the Ad Hoc Open-ended Inter-Sessional Working Groups on Article 8(j) and Related Provisions of the Convention on Biological Diversity first meeting in Seville, Spain, in March 2000 and the second in Montreal in February 2002, the Ad Hoc Open-ended Working Group on Access and Benefit Sharing in Bonn, October 2001, the Indigenous Caucus meetings at those meetings, the CBD Convention of the Parties meetings in Nairobi in May 2000, the Canadian Open-Ended Working Group on Article 8(j) and Related Provisions of the Convention on Biological Diversity Meetings in Ottawa, November 2000, the BC Union of First Nations' Chiefs Conference on traditional knowledge in February 2000, the State of the Art Conference on Ethnobioprospecting and the International Conference on Ethnobotany, in Athens, Georgia, October 2000, and have research assistants and informants working in several interested civil society organizations and United Nations agencies.

3. For interdisciplinary discussions of the various issues thereby posed, see Brush and Stabinsky (1996); also see Guruswamy and McNeely (1998).

4. A recent estimate by Daniel Nettle and Suzanne Romaine (2000, ix), suggests "a striking correlation between areas of highest linguistic diversity, allowing us to talk about a common repository of what we will call 'biolinguistic diversity': the rich spectrum of life encompassing all the earth's species of plants and animals along with human cultures and their languages. The greatest biolinguistic diversity is found in areas inhabited by indigenous peoples, who represent around 4 percent of the world's population, but speak at least 60 percent of the world's languages."

5. For further discussion of the relationship between language, culture, and biodiversity, see Muhlhausler (1995); Maffi and Skutnabb-Kangas (1999). Nettle and Romaine (2000) is the most recent and thoroughly researched statement of this position. They estimate the number of the world's languages at between five thousand and 6,700.

6. For an excellent discussion of this process, see Sell (2001). For an abbreviated discussion, see Sell (2002).

7. The concept of "informationalism" is borrowed from Castells (1998, 18–22).

8. Varieties of environmentalism, various forms of ecological distributional conflicts, and the resistance movements that they have spawned are listed in Martinez-Alier (1997).

9. For an excellent discussion of Lyotard's concept of "phrasing injustice," see Pavlich (1998).

10. For a longer discussion of this process, see Roht-Arriaza (1997) and Whitt (1998).

11. I am providing a composite summary of some of the main features of a rhetoric drawn from hundreds of published sources. Representative examples include Alcorn (1995); Roht-Arriaza (1997); Crucible Group (1994); Haverkort and Millar (1994); Mooney (1996); Shiva (1993); issues of the on-line journal *RAFI Communiqué* (RAFI 1990–99), many articles in the *Indigenous Knowledge and Development Monitor* (Centre for International Research and Advisory Networks 1990–99), and numerous volumes published by the London publisher Intermediate Technology Publications.

12. A longer discussion can be found in Coombe (1998a, 11–18, 24).

13. See also Ferguson and Gupta (1997).

14. Three significant and influential texts addressing development within the field were Escobar (1995), Ferguson (1990), and Gupta (1998a). See also Ferguson (1997).

15. Gupta also shows the interrelation and interdependence of "modern" and "traditional" agricultural knowledges in *Postcolonial Developments* (1998a).

16. There is now a large literature disputing the propositions that indigenous peoples are always natural conservationists. See, for example, Parker (1993). On the other hand, extensive surveys of the available published evidence suggest that indigenous knowledge and skills are of immense value in preservation and ongoing production of biological diversity. See Bailey, Headland, and Sponsel (1996).

17. See also Povinelli (1998).

18. For an overview of the role of indigenous peoples in revitalizing interest in the human-rights dimensions of intellectual property, see Coombe (2001).

References

Agrawal, Arun. 1995. "Dismantling the Divide between Indigenous and Scientific Knowledge." *Development and Change* 26: 413–39.

Alcorn, Janis B. 1995. "Ethnobotanical Knowledge Systems: A Resource for Meeting Rural Development Needs." *The Cultural Dimension of Development:*

Indigenous Knowledge Systems, ed. D. Michael Warren, L. Jan Slikkerveer, and David Brokensha. London: Intermediate Technology Publications.

Amari, Bita, and Rosemary J. Coombe. N.d. "The Human Genome Diversity Project: Issues at the Intersection of Patents, Race, Culture, and Ethics." Unpublished manuscript.

Australia. 1998. *Biological Diversity and Indigenous Knowledge*, Research Paper 17 (1997–98) by Michael Davis. Department of the Parliamentary Library. Available at http://www.aph.gov.au/library/pubs/rp/1997-98/98rp17.htm.

Bailey, Robert C., Thomas N. Headland, and Leslie E. Sponsel, eds. 1996. *Tropical Deforestation: The Human Dimension*. New York: Columbia University Press.

Bentley, Jeffrey W. 1998. Untitled Commentary on Paul Sillitoe, "The Development of Indigenous Knowledge: A New Applied Anthropology." *Current Anthropology* 39: 235–36.

Boyles, James. 1996. *Shamans, Software, and Spleens: Law and the Construction of the Information Society*. Cambridge: Harvard University Press.

Brown, Michael F. 1998. "Can Culture Be Copyrighted?" *Current Anthropology* 39: 193–222.

Brush, Stephen, and Doreen Stabinsky, eds. 1996. *Valuing Local Knowledge: Indigenous People and Intellectual Property Rights*. Washington, D.C.: Island Press.

Butler, Judith. 1997. *The Psychic Life of Power Theories in Subjection*. Stanford, Calif.: Stanford University Press.

Castells, Manuel. 1998. *The Information Age: Economy, Society and Culture*, vol. 1, *The Rise of the Network Society*. Malden, Mass.: Blackwell Publishers.

Centre for International Research and Advisory Networks (CIRAN). 1990–99. *Indigenous Knowledge and Development Monitor*. Available at http://www.nuffic.nl/ciran/ikdm/index.html.

Conklin, Beth, and Laura Graham. 1995. "The Shifting Middle Ground: Amazonian Indians and Eco-Politics." *American Anthropologists* 97(4): 695–710.

Coombe, Rosemary J. 1998a. *The Cultural Life of Intellectual Properties: Authorship, Appropriation and the Law*. Durham, N.C.: Duke University Press.

———. 1998b. "Intellectual Property, Human Rights and Sovereignty: New Dilemmas in International Law Posed by the Recognition of Indigenous Knowledge and the Conservation of Biodiversity." *Indiana Journal of Global Legal Studies* 6: 59–115.

————. 2001. "The Recognition of Indigenous Peoples' and Community Traditional Knowledge in International Law." *St. Thomas Law Review* 14: 275–85.

Crucible Group. 1994. *People, Plants, and Patents; The Impact of Intellectual Property on Trade, Plant Biodiversity, and Rural Society.* Ottawa: International Development Research Centre.

Crucible II Group. 2000. *Seeding Solutions: Policy Options for Genetic Resources: Peoples, Plants and Patents Revisited.* Vol. 1. Ottawa: International Development Research Centre.

Dove, Michael. 1996. "Centre, Periphery and Biodiversity: A Paradox of Governance and a Developmental Challenge." In *Valuing Local Knowledge: Indigenous People and Intellectual Property Rights*, ed. Stephen Brush and Doreen Stabinsky. Washington, D.C.: Island Press.

Escobar, Arturo. 1995. *Encountering Development: The Making and Unmaking of the Third World.* Princeton, N.J.: Princeton University Press.

————. 1998. "Whose Knowledge, Whose Nature? Biodiversity Conservation and the Political Ecology of Social Movements." *Journal of Political Ecology* 5: 53–79.

Ferguson, James. 1990. *The Anti-Politics Machine: "Development," Depoliticization, and Bureaucratic Power in Lesotho.* Cambridge: Cambridge University Press.

————. 1997. "Anthropology and Its Evil Twin: 'Development' in the Constitution of a Discipline." In *International Development and the Social Sciences: Essays on the History and Politics of Knowledge*, ed. Frederick Cooper and Randall Packard. Berkeley: University of California Press.

Ferguson, James, and Akhil Gupta, eds. 1997. *Culture, Power, Place: Explorations in Critical Anthropology.* Durham, N.C.: Duke University Press.

Ferradas, Carmen. 1998. Untitled Commentary on Paul Sillitoe, "The Development of Indigenous Knowledge: A New Applied Anthropology." *Current Anthropology* 39: 239–40.

Flitner, Michael. 1998. "Biodiversity: Of Local Commons and Global Commodities." In *Privatizing Nature: Political Struggle for the Global Commons*, ed. Michael Goldman. New Brunswick, N.J.: Rutgers University Press.

Gari, Josep-Antoni. 1999. *Biodiversity Conservation and Use: Local and Global Considerations.* Science, Technology, and Development Discussion Paper No. 7. Cambridge: Center for International Development and Belfer Center for Science and International Affairs, Harvard University.

Gupta, Akhil. 1998a. *Postcolonial Developments: Agriculture in the Making of Modern India*. Durham, N.C.: Duke University Press.

————. 1998b. "Rewarding Local Communities for Conserving Biodiversity: The Case of the Honey Bee." In *Protection of Global Biodiversity: Converging Strategies*, ed. Lakshman D. Guruswamy and Jeffrey A. McNeely. Durham, N.C.: Duke University Press.

Guruswamy, Lakshman D., and Jeffrey A. McNeely, eds. 1998. *Protection of Global Biodiversity: Converging Strategies*. Durham, N.C.: Duke University Press.

Hastrup, Kirsten, and Karen Fog Olwig. 1997. "Introduction." In *Siting Culture: The Shifting Anthropological Object*, ed. Kirsten Hastrup and Karen Fog Olwig. New York: Routledge.

Haverkort, Bertus, and David Millar. 1994. "Constructing Biodiversity: The Active Role of Rural People in Maintaining and Enhancing Biodiversity." *Etnoecologica* 2(3): 51–63.

Hayden, Corinne P. 2003. *When Nature Goes Public: The Making and Unmaking of Bio-Prospecting in Mexico*. Princeton, N.J.: Princeton University Press.

Kadidal, Shayana. 1993. "Plants, Poverty, and Pharmaceutical Patents." *Yale Law Journal* 103: 223–58.

Koptiuch, Kristin. 1996. "Cultural Defense and Criminological Displacements." In *Displacement, Diaspora, and Geographies of Identity*, ed. Smadar Lavie and Ted Swedenburg. Durham, N.C.: Duke University Press.

Latour, Bruno. 1993. *We Have Never Been Modern*. Trans. Catherine Porter. Cambridge: Harvard University Press.

Lawrey, Kathleen B. 2001. "Indigenous Knowledge, Indigenous Networks, Indigenous Monopolies: An Alternative Perspective on Contemporary Cultural and Intellectual Property Rights Debates." Paper presented at the Society for Cultural Anthropology Biennial Conference, Montreal, Quebec, Canada, May 3–6, 2001.

Maffi, Luisa. 1998. "Linguistic and Biological Diversity: The Inextricable Link." Paper presented at the international conference "Diversity as a Resource: Relations between Cultural Diversity and Environment-Oriented Society." Rome, March 2–6.

Maffi, Luisa, and Tove Skutnabb-Kangas. 1999. "Linguistic Diversity and the 'Curse of Babel.'" In *Cultural and Spiritual Values of Biodiversity*, ed. Darrell A. Posey/United Nations Environment Programme (UNEP). London: Intermediate Technology Publications.

Martinez-Alier, Juan. 1997. "Environmental Justice (Local and Global)." *Capitalism, Nature, Socialism: A Journal of Socialist Ecology* 8(1): 91–108.

Maurer, Bill. 1995. "Complex Subjects: Offshore Finance, Complexity Theory, and the Dispersion of the Modern." *Socialist Review* 25: 113–45.

———. 1997. *Recharting the Caribbean: Land, Law and Citizenship in the British Virgin Islands.* Ann Arbor: University of Michigan Press.

———. 1999. "Forget Locke? From Proprietor to Risk-bearer in New Logics of Finance." *Public Culture* 11: 47–67.

———. 2001. "Islands in the Net: Rewiring Technological and Financial Circuits in the 'Offshore Caribbean.'" *Comparative Studies in Society and History* 43: 467–501.

———. 2002. "Repressed Futures: Financial Derivatives' Theological Unconscious." *Economy and Society* 31(1): 15–36.

Mooney, Pat Ray. 1996. "The Parts of Life: Agricultural Biodiversity, Indigenous Knowledge, and the Role of the Third System." *Development Dialogue* 1–2, special issue: 1–181.

Muhlhausler, Patrick. 1995. "The Interdependence of Linguistic and Biological Diversity." In *The Politics of Multiculturalism in Asia/Pacific*, ed. David A. Myers. Darwin, Australia: Northern Territory University Press.

Nettle, Daniel, and Suzanne Romaine. 2000. *Vanishing Voices: The Extinction of the World's Languages.* Oxford: Oxford University Press.

Parker, Eugene. 1993. "Fact and Fiction in Amazonia: The Case of the Apete." *American Anthropologist* 95: 715–23.

Pavlich, George. 1998. "Phrasing Injustice: Critique in an Uncertain Ethos." *Studies in Law, Politics and Society* 18: 45–69.

Peet, Richard, and Michael Watts. 1996. "Introduction." In *Liberation Ecologies: Environment, Development, Social Movements*, ed. Richard Peet and Michael Watts. New York: Routledge.

Parry, Bronwyn. 2000. "The Fate of the Collections: Social Justice and the Annexation of Plant Genetic Resources." In *People, Plants, and Justice: The Politics of Nature Conservation*, ed. Charles Zerner. New York: Columbia University Press.

Posey, Darrell A. 1998. Untitled Commentary on Paul Sillitoe, "The Development of Indigenous Knowledge: A New Applied Anthropology." *Current Anthropology* 39: 241–42.

———. 1999. "Introduction: Culture and Nature—The Inextricable Link." In

Cultural and Spiritual Values of Biodiversity, ed. Darrell A. Posey/United Nations Environment Programme (UNEP). London: Intermediate Technology Publications.

Posey, Darrell A., and Graham Dutfield, eds. 1996. *Beyond Intellectual Property: Towards Traditional Resource Rights for Indigenous Peoples and Local Communities.* Ottawa: International Development Resources Centre.

Povinelli, Elizabeth. 1998. "The State of Shame: Australian Multiculturalism and the Crisis of Indigenous Citizenship." *Critical Inquiry* 24: 575–610.

———. 1999. "Settler Modernity and the Quest for an Indigenous Tradition." *Public Culture* 11(1): 19–48.

RAFI (Rural Advancement Foundation International), now the ETC Group: Action Group on Erosion, Technology and Concentration. 1990–99. *RAFI Communique.* Available at http://www.etcgroup.org.

Raghaven, Chakravarthi. 1990a. "Recolonization: GATT in Its Historical Context." *Ecologist* 20(6): 205.

———. 1990b. *Recolonization: GATT, the Uruguay Round and the Third World.* London and New Jersey: Zed Books.

Riles, Annelise. 2000. *The Network Inside Out.* Ann Arbor: University of Michigan Press.

Roht-Arriaza, Naomi. 1997. "Of Seeds and Shamans: The Appropriation of the Scientific and Technical Knowledge of Indigenous and Local Communities." In *Borrowed Power: Essays on Cultural Appropriation*, ed. Bruce Ziff and Pratima Rao. New Brunswick, N.J.: Rutgers University Press.

Rosaldo, Renato. 1989. *Culture and Truth: The Remaking of Social Analysis.* Boston: Beacon Press.

Sell, Susan K. 2002. "Post-TRIPS Developments; The Tension between Commercial and Social Agendas in the Context of Intellectual Property." *Florida Journal of International Law* 14: 193–215.

———. 2003. *Private Power, Public Law: The Globalization of Intellectual Property Rights.* Cambridge: Cambridge University Press.

Shiva, Vandana. 1997. *Biopiracy: The Plunder of Nature and Knowledge.* Boston: South End Press.

———. 1993. *Monocultures of the Mind: Perspectives on Biodiversity and Biotechnology.* London: Zed Books.

Sillitoe, Paul. 1998. "The Development of Indigenous Knowledge: A New Applied Anthropology." *Current Anthropology* 39: 223–52.

Silverstein, Michael. 2000. "Languages? Cultures Are Dead! Long Live the Linguistic-Cultural!" Paper presented at the American Anthropological Association Annual Meeting in San Francisco, November.

Whitt, Laurie Ann. 1998. "Indigenous Peoples, Intellectual Property and the New Imperial Science." *Oklahoma City University Law Review* 23: 211.

CHAPTER 10

Rebooting the World Picture: Flying Windows of Globalization in the End Times

Richard Warren Perry

Shift-Control-Alt-Delete: A Prefatory Note

This essay was first written more than two years before September 11, 2001. Given the time lag, this essay's skeptical, and playfully ironic, perspective on the interwoven themes of apocalypse and redemption in globalization theorizing current at that moment should not be taken to reflect a disregard for the events of 9/11, nor a disrespect for the thousands who died then and the thousands more who continue to die in the "global war on terror" that has followed that date. Indeed, after 9/11, it is even more the case that anxieties of apocalypse, as well as various visions of redemption through self-sacrificial martyrdom, continue to be widely expressed, especially in the public cultures of South Asia and North America, over CNN, Al-Jazeera, and other global media, and this essay cannot pretend to represent these sensibilities.

Still, this essay's critique of the metaphysics of globalization theorizing is no less accurate than it was before events so dramatically outpaced both global theorizing and its critique. This is equally true in regard to the essay's focus on the religious-cosmological dimension of globalism and to the misrecognitions of histories and transnational cultures that continue to pervade globalist theorizing.

In the immediate aftermath of 9/11, a text by two analysts for the RAND Corporation's National Security Research Division exemplified this point:

Theory has struck home with a vengeance. The United States must now cope with an archetypal terrorist war of the worst kind. The same technology that aids social activists and those desiring the good of all is also available to those with the darkest intentions, bent on destruction and driven by a rage reminiscent of the Middle Ages. ("Afterword [September 2001]: The Sharpening Fight for the Future," in Arquilla and Ronfeldt 2001, 363)

Global Millenarianism: A Theory for the End of History

At the beginning of the third millennium, the future outlines of a new global order are the constant object of speculation—economic, political, metaphysical (see Cohn 1961). Popular as well as scholarly narratives of this emerging global-millennial epoch foretell it alternately as human redemption or as humankind's apocalypse. Since 1989, the world has been told that, after the meltdown of the Soviet bloc's second world and a half century in the shadow of Cold War nuclear apocalypse, all of humanity now lives, in Francis Fukuyama's epochal phrase, at the "End of History" (Fukuyama 1992).

The remarkable celebrity that immediately attached to Fukuyama's thesis (which Anthony Giddens says "deservedly projected [its] author to global fame" [1995, 30]) is itself evidence of a global-millenarian sensibility. Fukuyama argued that history—in G. W. F. Hegel's sense of a grand evolutionary dialectic between alternate and opposing visions of the human social order—has now concluded in the triumph of one of these visions. Fukuyama proposed that humankind has arrived at "a remarkable convergence" of opinions and institutions. More than a decade after he first published his thesis in 1989, Fukuyama still asserts that "[n]othing has happened in world politics or the global economy . . . that challenges the conclusion that liberal democracy and a market-oriented economic order are the only viable options for modern societies" (1999c, 16).

In Fukuyama's view, the "directionality and progressive character of human history [are] driven by the unfolding of modern natural

science" (ibid.). It is this "logic of modern science" and its closest ana-
logue in the social world, the logic of market capitalism, that "guaran-
tee," he says, an "increasing homogenization of all human societies,
regardless of their historical origins or cultural inheritances" (1992,
xiv). Fukuyama's End of History thus marks the culmination of "a universal evolution in the direction of Capitalism" (ibid., xv; the capitalization is Fukuyama's).

The glossy coffee-table monthly *National Geographic*, in an end-
of-the-century special-issue essay on "global culture" titled "A World
Together" (August 1999), declared that "[t]oday we are in the throes
of a worldwide reformation of cultures, a tectonic shift in habits and
dreams called, in the curious argot of social scientists, 'globalization'"
(Zwingle 1999: 12).[1] The cover story then continued with this quote
from a nineteenth-century text:

> Modern industry has established the world market . . . All old-established
> national industries . . . are dislodged by new industries whose . . . products
> are consumed, not only at home, but in every quarter of the globe. In
> place of the old wants . . . we find new wants, requiring for their satisfac-
> tion the products of distant lands and climes.

National Geographic matter-of-factly concludes: "Karl Marx and Friedrich
Engels wrote this statement 150 years ago in *The Communist Manifesto*.
Their statement now describes an ordinary fact of life" (ibid., 15).[2]

Just as striking as the fact that *The Communist Manifesto* is quoted
as prophetic scripture by *National Geographic* is the fact that its invo-
cation of Karl Marx as the Moses of contemporary globalization is not
the least bit anomalous in contemporary globalization discourse. In fact,
a decade after History is said to have ended with the fall of Soviet-bloc
socialism, the middlebrow public media of the first world are so generally convinced of the triumphal "inevitability of globalization" that
something very like the most reductionist version of classical Marxian
economic historical determinism now routinely passes as simple, self-
evident common sense among the investing classes.[3]

A recent review of the five most widely cited books on globalization (by Francis Fukuyama, Samuel Huntington, Benjamin Barber,
Robert Kaplan, and Kenichi Ohmae—in effect the "globalization theory canon" in political science) observes that all of the authors "echo"
Marx as they embrace "economic determinism" and all of them "agree
that the global spread of capitalism is eroding the power and autonomy
of the nation-state." Moreover, "[w]ith one important modification—
the replacement of class by cultural identity—modern-day proponents
of globalization echo Marx's theories of transnational capital's [homog-
enizing] effects on states, cultures, and individuals" (Drezner 1998, 27).

Fukuyama himself has acknowledged that his own End of History
thesis is "a kind of Marxist interpretation of history that leads to a
completely non-Marxist conclusion" (Fukuyama 1992, 131). Fukuyama's
conjectural history is in fact very much like a paleo-Marxist narrative—
but one in which the Marxian value signs have been inverted. For
Fukuyama, the global-historical triumph of capitalism is not the transitional historical stage of class exploitation that Marx foretold; instead,
it is offered by Fukuyama and like-minded globalist colleagues as the
culmination of humankind's possibilities, as a veritable revelation of
humanity's redemption and self-transcendence at History's End.[4]

The Global Shock of the New:
Chronometries and Cartographies of Globalization
One of the most striking things about this millenarian "inevitability of
globalization" literature is what it takes to be news. It is commonly
asserted in passing that it was NASA's early satellite photos of Earth
published in *Life* magazine during the 1960s that first inspired humans
to view the planet as a discrete, precious, and lonely entity, a blue green
orb floating in the immense darkness of space, to see it as "spaceship
Earth."[5]

Of course, an Archimedean perspective had been conceptualized
as early as the third century B.C., when Archimedes himself reportedly
proposed that, if he were given a lever long enough and a place to stand,
he could move the earth itself. Another Greek of the third century B.C.,

Erastothenes of Cyrene, pictured the earth as a globe, proposed a geometric model of meridians of longitude and latitude, and made a (not very accurate) calculation of Earth's dimensions. This was the globe at the center of the Ptolemaic cosmology of concentric spheres that endured in the West until the time of emergence of the modern world-picture in the Renaissance of Copernicus, Bruno, Kepler, Columbus, and Galileo (Harvey 1989, 246).

The geographic and geometric project of the Renaissance and the Enlightenment did, of course, supersede the classical Ptolemaic cosmology, but this signified more than just a shift from a geocentric to a heliocentric model. Rather, the substitution of the secular optics of science for the gaze of the God looking down upon the earth marked the emergence of what Martin Heidegger called the "Age of the World-Picture." As Heidegger explained,

> world-picture . . . does not mean a picture of the world, but the world conceived and grasped as picture . . . The fact that whatever is comes into being in and through representedness transforms the age in which this occurs into a new age in contrast with the preceding one. The expressions "world-picture of the modern age" and "modern world-picture" both mean the same thing and assume something that could never have been before, namely, a medieval and an ancient world-picture. The world-picture does not change from an earlier medieval one into a modern one, but rather the fact that the world becomes a picture at all is what distinguishes the essence of the modern age . . . There begins a way of being human which means the realm of human capability as a domain given over to measuring and executing, for the purpose of gaining mastery over that which is as a whole . . . The fundamental event of the modern age is the conquest of the world as picture . . . In such producing, man contends for the position in which he can be that particular being who gives the measure and draws up the guidelines for everything that is. (Heidegger 1977, 129–34)

The age of the world-picture is most clearly exemplified in the Cartesian grid work of space-time and in the measurement of the earth and of the broader universe, most directly in the system of latitude and longitude conjoining space. With this infinite three-dimensional cellular topology, early European "explorers" could always know where they were, no matter how otherworldly were the wonders they encountered—all things had a place on the grid whose location was measured from Europe.[6] The infinite grid of earthly space was paralleled in the new, potentially infinite, sequence of secular linear temporality, exemplified in the development of mechanical clocks calibrated against the mechanics of the solar system. Indeed, the invention of the mechanical timepiece/chronometer provided the master metaphor for the new Newtonian clockwork mechanics of space, time, and motion, that is, for the modern cosmos in its totality and cognizability (Lovejoy 1936).

Any conceptual archaeology of globalization should not fail to acknowledge the foundations laid down by other, earlier, theocentric cosmologies. Classical Christendom and Islam's community of faithful were both global in their visions from their earliest histories, and each in its diverse sectarian forms continues to proselytize on a scale that is no less than planetary and that equally aspires to a universal community of the human species. It was the geographic expansion of the universalizing Abrahamic messianic religions of the Book—Judaism, Christianity, and Islam—that propagated the notion of "Time . . . as the medium of a sacred history," a history that came to supplant diverse, local, place-based seasonal and other cyclic temporalities (Fabian 1983, 2). This unilinear time—most especially the Christian trajectory of human perfectibility toward humanity's final redemption at the end of time—was a divinely foreordained progress toward an ultimate state of being (Auerbach 1957, 64; Anderson 1991, 22–24; Greenhouse 1996, 20–24, 89–91; Therborn 1995, 126–28).

This millennial Christian eschatology of redemption at the end time was subsequently reformulated as secular modern "progress," as "civilization," and as "development" in the European Enlightenment's conception of progressive time—a conception shared, in one version or another, by thinkers from Locke to Rousseau, Hegel, and Marx. Francis Fukuyama's schematic teleological history propelled by the "logic of natural science" closely follows this Enlightenment model of "natural history," just as his telos of historical progress, the convergence of capitalism and the liberal state in what he terms "inevitable globalization" now occupies the place of Christian salvation (Fabian 1983: 17; Escobar 1995, 25–26; Giddens 1990, 48; Perry 1996, 233–36). Jacques Derrida has also noted that Fukuyama's "[E]nd of History is essentially a Christian eschatology," an eschatology that follows the Hegelian vision, but for Fukuyama now it is the European Union and North America that are coming together in a "Christian state" (Derrida 1994, 211; cf. Hegel's description of the modern state as "the actualization of the ethical Idea," and "the march of God in the world" [Hegel 1952, sections 257, 258]).

Fukuyama's schema of progress explicitly retraces Hegel's "universal history" of human civilization and, following Hegel, Fukuyama's point of departure is Immanuel Kant's essay "An Idea for a Universal History." Kant proposed that human history would culminate in a final realization of individual human freedom, a moment from whose vantage point the whole of human history would be retrospectively legible as the unfolding progress of reason in the world. A generation after Kant, Hegel argued that the constitution of the modern liberal state from the immanent rationality of (Christian European) civil society would mark the actualization in world history of Kant's ideal of individual human freedom.

One commentary has suggested that "Fukuyama's contribution is . . . simply to shift the date at which the Liberal State is declared universally victorious—from 1806 and the Napoleonic conquest of Prussia (Hegel's chosen date) to 1989—with the collapse of Communism, and the 'victorious' emergence of the USA from the Cold War" (Morley and Robins 1995, 203). With the 1806 French defeat of the Prussian forces on the outskirts of Jena (where Hegel was then teaching; he could hear the sounds of battle and awaited the French victory), Napoleon Bonaparte (whom Hegel dubbed the Messenger of the World-Spirit) delivered the software of Universal Reason to Germany. The Spirit of the Age (Hegel's historical *Zeitgeist*) came bundled in the form of the metric system (whose prime unit, the meter, was itself calculated from the circumference of the globe), the prototype for the modern legal system in the *Code Napoléon*, and the most comprehensive system of finance and taxation, transport, resource management, population management and military conscription, and bureaucratic state administration then known in the West (on the notion of "cultural software," see Balkin 1998; for the metaphorical imagining of state-governmental rationalities as a DOS, a drive operating system, avowedly in the spirit of Fukuyama's account of Hegel, see Friedman 1999).

Hegel regarded Napoleon's arrival as the fulfillment and confirmation of his own dialectical stage theory of the progress of reason through history. Hegel's evolutionary model has served, speaking in broad terms, as the template for all subsequent theories of modernization and development. In order to locate Fukuyama and his kindred triumphal "inevitability of globalization" theorists in this Hegelian lineage, one might ask with a certain playfulness just who, at the present time, might stand in for Napoleon Bonaparte and what could be the contemporary global analogues of the metric system and the *Code Napoléon*?

Is our meter—the unit by which we quantify our world—to be a digital measure of information or bandwidth like the byte or the baud? Or, is the prime unit of globalization now the dollar, the yen, the euro, or the Nasdaq? Or could any of the various protocols for digital information transfer play the universal unifying and commensurating role of the metric system (http, html, URLs, or Microsoft DOS)? Is our counterpart of the *Code Napoléon* the General Agreement on Tariffs and Trade or the International Covenant on Human Rights? Who is today's Messenger of the Global-Spirit? Can we imagine Alan Greenspan, George Soros, Rupert Murdoch, or James Wolfensohn in the role of Bonaparte? Should the "flexible" nature of today's economic governance point us, at least in the short run, toward the wealthiest human being on the planet—Bill Gates and his *Business@thespeedofthought*?—or to some more widely recognized and enduring global figure, say, Mickey Mouse or Ronald McDonald? Fukuyama's grandiose claims for Western reason lend a certain "weird science" seriousness to such questions.

Globalization discourses have presupposed the standard "three lit-tle bears" modernization narrative: first the premodern, then the mod-ern, and then the postmodern. If, as I have suggested, the modern world order has always been as much metaphysical as actual, then it is not sur-prising that its actuality has not always conformed to its ideal—however difficult this may be for political theorists to recognize. The atavistic reappearance of "premodern" traits, the emergence of "postmodern" features: that both of these appear in the same frame (on the same his-torical screen/desktop) is consistent with the quote from Yeats (and Achebe) that recurs in globalization commentaries: "things fall apart; the center cannot hold, mere anarchy is loosed upon the world" (e.g., Barber 1995, 5). Less apocalyptically, it is also consistent with the asser-tion by Bruno Latour that "we have never been modern."[7]

Natural Geographic, the National Order of Things

No question is more central to globalization debates than the future of the nation-state as a "bordered power-container" (Giddens 1985). This question is typically framed as a binary choice: either the nation-state as power-container is alive and well, exercising its sovereign powers in an absolute and unconditioned fashion within its territorial borders, or, as one writer argues, "[a]t the close of the twentieth century, we are seeing the leaking away of sovereignty from the state both upwards, to supra-national institutions, and downwards, to sub-national ones" (Lipschutz 1992, 391).

The "Jihad versus McWorld" portrait of a looming "new world disorder," a "pandemonium" (in Senator Daniel Patrick Moynihan's Chicken Little alarmist terminology), is nowhere so evident as in the anxieties about the health of the nation-state form and the state-based international order (Barber 1995; Moynihan 1993). This volume's focus on the specific practices and effects of globalization (the effects of specific supra-, sub-, or parastatal governmental rationalities) enables us to approach the diverse contemporary transformations in nation-state governance in a manner less entrapped in this binary impasse (see Sassen 1995, xii; Ong, in this volume).

Globalization debates have called into question the nation-state and its sovereign powers of governance in a way that obliges us to recall that the nation-state must be regarded as one of the most successful inventions in human history. Indeed, the larger point is that the nation-state form has been so successful that the very fact that it is an invention, and one of relatively recent provenance, is generally forgotten. It is so taken for granted that it goes about its business tacitly bounding and structuring the lives and experiences of the greater part of humanity—it is taken as natural, as simply the national order of things (Malkki 1992).

Fukuyama's "inevitable" stage segmentation of universal linear history is iconically mirrored, mapped out, in the sectioned cartography of his global geographic schema. There now exists, he says, the "post-historical world," composed of those blessed nation-states where the convergence of capitalism and liberal democratic governance has brought an End to History. Then, left over in the residual "historical world" are all those regions where the logic of science has not yet switched off the motor of history.

It is instructive that Fukuyama's global mapping appears very like a photographic negative of Eric Wolf's celebrated study of "Europe and the People without History" (Wolf 1982). But, unlike Wolf's portrait, what is conspicuously absent from Fukuyama's global geography is any geohistorical understanding of how his map of a world segmented into "historical" and "posthistorical" territories reproduces almost exactly the geospatial order inscribed onto the earth's surface by the history of colonialisms, both classical and neo-. As Timothy Luke notes, Fukuyama's "strange but convenient division of all the world's nation-states . . . essentially reaffirms the old Cold War schemas of the First World nation-states setting the direction taken by the so-called Second, Third, and Fourth World countries" (Luke 1995, 91–92, citing Fukuyama 1992, xii–xiv; see also Goldberg 1993, 163–64).

Indeed, Fukuyama's 1989 End of History thesis (along with his more recent works, in which he has amplified and reiterated his original thesis) effectively assumes the nation-state and the post-Westphalian international order as a historical (even an ahistorical or natural) a priori (Fukuyama 1992). In this too, Fukuyama is representative of much of the writing on globalization, and on globalization's allegedly corrosive effects on the nation-state. This historical blindness of Fukuyama's End of History thesis is all the more embarrassing in that the last two decades have seen a flourishing of scholarship on the rise of the nation-state and its historical relation both to modernity and to European colonialism (Anderson 1991; Fitzpatrick 1992; Greenfield 1992; Goldberg 1993).

Memories Forgotten before the End of History

The epochal year 1492 not only marked the "discovery" of the Western hemisphere by Columbus in the name of the newly unified Spanish monarchy and of European Christendom; it also witnessed a parallel, internal self-conquest by Spain of itself. The year 1492 was the date of Spain's own *Reconquista*—the final expulsion of Muslims from Granada, as well as the forced conversion and/or expulsion of Spain's ancient Jewish community and a boom time for the Spanish Inquisition. The year 1492 was also the publication date of Antonio de Nebrija's Spanish grammar—the first grammar of a modern European language (Hobsbawm 1992; Todorov 1984, 50, 123; Morley and Robins 1995, 212–13). This is what Tzvetan Todorov has called the "double movement" of 1492—composed, on the one hand, of internal political "pacification" and homogenization of belief and language, and, on the other, of the simultaneous beginning of the conquest and colonization of the "New World." This double movement was foundational for the nation-state form and for the subsequent inter-national order. "No date," says Todorov, "is more suitable to mark the beginning of the modern era than the year 1492 . . . 'that time so new and like no other'" (1984, 5; quoting Bartolomeo de Las Casas).[8]

In the following year, 1493, Pope Alexander VI issued the bull *Inter Caetera Divinae*, which apportioned between the Catholic monarchs of Spain and Portugal the right to colonize the whole of the non-Christian world. Upon hearing of the pope's disposition, King François

I of France remarked that he would like to see that provision in Adam's will "wherein he divided the earth between Spain and Portugal" (quoted in Boal 1998, 6).

Fernand Braudel and others have exhaustively demonstrated that a global network of exchange had begun to take shape at least as early as the great expansion of the Portuguese and Spanish empires in the fifteenth century (Braudel 1984; Parker 1999). European colonial expansion from the time of Columbus to the first part of the twentieth century has been recognized by contemporary globalist writers as a "First Age of Globalization" (sometimes with more than a hint of nostalgic appreciation for the good old days; see especially Friedman 1999). The Portuguese and Spanish, and later the British, Dutch, and French empires, were circumplanetary structures of power, governance, transport, exchange, communication, language, and religion on which the sun never set.

These empires, of course, were not states, and still less nation-states. Rather, the imperial form was carved out by multiple institutional actors (military adventurers, religious proselytizers, religious refugees, regional expansionists, early mercantile entrepreneurs, chartered corporations) as networks of radically unequal exchange and flow that linked regions and peoples. Among the most original contributions of Benedict Anderson's celebrated study of the rise of the modern nation-state, *Imagined Communities* (1991), is his argument that the distinctive structures of modern nation-state governance did not, as the standard narrative has assumed, develop from the nationalist movements of Europe—pan-German, pan-Greek, pan-Slav, and so on. Anderson stands this familiar *Bildung*-story of the development of the nation-state on its head, arguing instead that what he calls the "modular" forms of the nation-state originated in the governmental practices of the European empires in the New World and elsewhere.

In particular, these were the practices of colonial censuses, cadastral surveys, and mappings, which constituted, Anderson says, the colonial state's "mode of imagining" (1991, 166). This mode of imagining created flexible managerial "identity categories" (especially of race, religion, language, social class) that exhibited "an extremely rapid, superficially arbitrary, series of changes, in which categories [were] continuously agglomerated, disaggregated, recombined, intermixed, and reordered" (ibid., 164; see also Merry, in this volume). These "modular" practices of the

> new demographic topography put down deep social and institutional roots as the colonial state multiplied its size and functions. Guided by its imagined map it organized the new educational, juridical, public health, police, and immigration bureaucracies it was building on the principle of ethno-racial hierarchies which were, however, always understood in terms of parallel series. The flow of subject populations through the mesh of differential schools, courts, clinics, police stations, and immigration offices created "traffic habits" which in time gave real social life to the state's earlier fantasies. (Anderson 1991, 169)

The fact that defining structures of the modern nation-state emerged not within the familiar nation-building narrative of European modernization, but rather in the context of the European empires' extension of control over non-European territories and populations, gives reason to reflect with a careful skepticism on the constant reports—whether triumphal or apocalyptic—that today's globalization marks the erosion, the disappearance, or the overcoming of the nation-state. Very much like the historical periodization of modernization theory, the neatly sectioned cartography of modernity's nation-state–based international order has always been more ideological than empirical—in Heidegger's phrase, "the planetary imperialism of technologically organized man" (1977, 152).

Nevertheless, the territorial nation-state–based patchwork map of the surface of the earth has, since the seventeenth century, come to be seen simply as part of the natural/national order of things according to which the seven seas, the five continents, the four Linnaean races of humankind (oriented to the four quadrants of the Cartesian grid coordinates of the compass: the North European white, the South

African black, the East Asian yellow, the West American red) all have their natural, geographically ordained place on the racial-spatial map of the earth (Goldberg 1993). Classical theorists of the nation-state and the "law of nations"—Bodin, Grotius, Montesquieu, Jefferson, and Hegel—all grounded their visions of the modern *Rechtstaat* in this natural order and its "natural law." These theorists' models have explicitly or implicitly undergirded the post-Westphalian international doctrine of territorially sovereign nation-states and its political theory.[9]

In a widely cited essay on national territorialization, Liisa Malkki offers a "schematic exploration of taken-for-granted ways of thinking about identity and territory that are reflected in ordinary language, in nationalist discourses, and in scholarly studies" (1992, 25). In the section titled "Maps and Soils," Malkki questions the "commonsense ideas of soils, roots, and territory built into everyday language and often also into scholarly work, . . . [ideas whose] very obviousness makes them elusive as objects of study" (ibid., 26). Malkki cites a passage from Ernest Gellner's 1983 book, *Nations and Nationalism*, in which Gellner describes two hypothetical maps, one drawn up before the rise of the nation-state form and the other after. As Gellner says, the "first map resembles a painting by Kokoschka . . . a riot of diverse points of color . . . such that no clear pattern can be discerned in any detail." Gellner's second map, an

> ethnographic and political map of an area of the modern world . . . resembles not Kokoschka, but, say, Modigliani. There is very little shading; neat flat surfaces are clearly separated from each other, it is generally plain where one begins and another ends, and there is little if any ambiguity or overlap. (Gellner 1983, 139–40, quoted in Malkki 1992, 26; see also the discussion of Gellner in Perry 1995)

Malkki observes that Gellner's second map is

> much like any school atlas with yellow, green, pink, orange and blue countries composing a truly global map with no vague or "fuzzy spaces" and no bleeding boundaries. The national order of things . . . also passes as the

normal or natural order of things. For it is self-evident that "real" nations are fixed in space and "recognizable" on a map. One country cannot at the same time be another country. The world of nations is thus conceived as a discrete spatial partitioning of territory; it is territorialized in the segmentary fashion of the multicolored school atlas. (Malkki 1992, 26)

Malkki illustrates the "naturalizing" effects of the characteristic deployment of "specifically botanical metaphors"—soil, roots, ethnic stocks, branches in the service of what she calls the "sedentarist metaphysics" of territorial nationalism.

Nation-states therefore are, and have always been, historically emergent constructs of their own ideological and practical efficacy. Yet, it is important to note that to acknowledge this fact is not at all the same thing as naively denying the actuality of states. Rather, it is to recognize the contingent and artifactual nature of state formations and to broaden the channels of investigation, to facilitate inquiry into the specific local effects of regulatory and managerial power and of their oppositional formations, and perhaps to enable ourselves to envision alternatives to the conceptual status quo. Further, to perceive the "sedentarist metaphysics" of nationalism may also help to bring to view the epistemic shifts implicit in the new metaphysics of flows.

Of Signs, Wonders, and Millenarian Portents of a New Age of Globalization

In the new millennium, "globalization," as noun, concept, and incantation, exercises a hold on the imagination of the global public media much like the specter that haunted old Europe a century and a half ago.[10] The goal of this essay is not to resolve the ultimate ontological question of what globalization is or is not. Instead, like others in this volume, it approaches globalization as a disparate array of practices and their effects, as discursive mediating structures of order and disorder, as effects of government and ungovernment. We are seeking to discern emerging patterns of governmentality in the disparateness of contemporary events.[11]

"Globalization" is less the name of a generally agreed-upon set of technological, economic, socio-cultural, or political developments than it is an ensemble of intersecting arguments about the history of the present, about contrasting world-pictures, and about the nature of the future that our present portends. "Globalization" is a cultural-discursive frame, a "window," a "screen" or "desktop," a "GUI" (graphical user interface) that displays rapidly shifting projections of an imagined futurama, a nightmare, or a Fantasyland, Adventureland, or Tomorrowland—that effectively reconstructs the present and mediates changing experience as a conceptual theme park.[12]

Globalization is a discursive space of hype and hope and horror; it is a debate, both popular and academic, that has emerged as the "successor to debates on modernity and post-modernity in the understanding of sociocultural change and as the central problematic for social theory" (Featherstone, Lash, and Robertson 1995, 1). Globalization is a debate about alternative visions of humankind's future—an imminent magic kingdom alternately imaged as utopian and dystopian.

Francis Fukuyama is not alone in proclaiming the "inevitability of globalization" at the post–Cold War moment that he has called the "End of History" (1992; see Fukuyama 1999a for his assertion that *New York Times* columnist Thomas Friedman's observations have confirmed Fukuyama's original thesis). Anthony Giddens (1990) has argued that globalization is a consequence of the "tendencies of modernity." Manuel Castells suggests that what distinguishes the new global order from the world systems of earlier eras is that it is driven by "an economy with the capacity to work in real time on a planetary scale" (Castells 1996, 92). This new economy, he says, is made possible by its "informational mode of production" that has created a new global "space of flows" (ibid.).[13] These are flows of capital, goods, services, "natural" resources and "extraction rights," atmospheric and water pollutants and "pollution rights," media images, and human beings (those privileged as tourists and transnational bearers of expertise, as well as rightless migrants who "flow" back and forth across borders as bodily units of flexible physical labor capacity; see Roberts, Merry, Coutin, Calavita, and Suárez-Navaz in this volume).[14] These flows are constantly represented as either emancipatory, frightening, or both, because of the sense that the nation-state, and indeed the entire modern order of governance, is "losing control" of them (the title of Sassen 1995). Globalization evokes a future history of the practices and politics and networks of such flows, on which both the hopes and fears of a unitary global civil society rest (Lash and Urry 1994; Appadurai 1996; Hannerz 1996; Basch, Schiller, and Szanton Blanc 1994).[15]

At the center of globalization debates are questions concerning the direction of shifts, their causation, and the locus of agency. Transnationally and translocally dispersed changes in social life are routinely attributed to the effects of new practices in economics and in technologies of communication and transport; yet there is little agreement on precisely which practices these are, nor on what their effects will be. Nor is there any certainty as to the directionality of causation. Therefore, rather than simply regarding these observed transformations in social relations as the inevitable consequences of new communications and economic practices, one might also inquire whether novel forms of human sociocultural interaction are driving technological innovation in particular directions.

Of Global Hype and Hope and Horror

Globalization theory is a discourse of contraries. Benjamin Barber's *Jihad vs. McWorld* is the best-known statement describing "tribalism and globalism" as two alternate and opposing futures presented by the "two axial principles of our time" (see also Robertson 1995). Even as there has been a proliferation of nativist and fundamentalist movements and other forms of resistance to the perceived homogenizing effects of globalization, and even as Ivy League economists are asking, "Has globalization gone too far?" (the title of a book by Dani Rodrik [1997], professor of international economics at Harvard's Kennedy School of Government), there has been no slowing in the rush of breathless proclamations that globalization heralds new utopian vistas of human reason and individual freedom (Friedman 1999; Fukuyama 1992).

This "cacophony" of "hyperbole and excessive generalizations" (Hannerz 1996, 18) has been called "global babble" (Abu-Lughod 1991) and "globaloney" (Krugman 1998). More than anything else, this cacophony testifies to the impossibility of distinguishing in any principled fashion a general "truth" of globalization from the "globaloney"; for one small but empirically observable "truth" about globalization is that "globaloney" appears to be integral to whatever it is that globalization might be. There is no more clarity to be found in denying globalization than there is in affirming it; the fact that there is no principled way to distinguish globaloney from the truth effects of "globalization" suggests that it is worthwhile to scrutinize the "global" sensibility itself. From this angle, globalization is ultimately as much a metaphysics, a new folk cosmology of the information classes, as it is an actuality; globalization is an effort at the most fundamental level of understanding to find or impose order, or even a "common sense," on rapid, aleatory shifts in collective experience.

Whether one is a true believer, an agnostic, or a critic of the discourses of globalization, even before September 11, 2001, there was no denying the visitation of a global millenarian anxiety about crashing planes, trains, ATMs, and currency markets under the sign "Y2K" of the digitized year 2000—a foreboding of what Neal Stephenson calls the "Infocalypse" (1992). It is fitting therefore—since globalization is commonly held to be a systemic consequence of these contemporary technologies of movement and exchange—that it is precisely these modes of communication and transport and their networks of flows that are both experiencing and generating panics of collapse.[16]

Beyond worries about malfunctions in transportation, communication, and banking, I suspect this anxiety points to a deeper unease, rather closer to the alienation or anomie of Max Weber's "Iron Cage of Reason," and other specters identified by classical social theory—call it a second-stage "disenchantment of the world." The Reverend Jerry Falwell asserted that in order for "God [to] get the attention of this mammoth superpower nation" (the United States) and of "our wicked leadership,"

God can send natural disasters that literally devastate us. God can send war. God can send economic collapse . . . overnight . . . instantly. God may use Y2K to crush us and prepare us for revival! (Quoted in Hilty 1999, 16)

Throughout 1999 and 2000, the government of Israel was busy arresting and deporting numbers of unruly millenarian Christians who had moved to Jerusalem to await the Second Coming. This disquiet recalls earlier movements that announced the end times at pivotal moments in the rise of modernity—from the radical dissenting sects of the seventeenth century (Ranters, Diggers, Levellers) to nineteenth- and early-twentieth-century Pentecostal and revival movements, the Church of Jesus Christ of Latter-day Saints, Jehovah's Witnesses, Seventh-Day Adventists, and so on.

Surely there was something iconic of our global millenarian sensibility in the 1997 mass suicide of the Heaven's Gate community of World Wide Web–page designers. From the moment the discovery of their ritually garbed bodies was announced by the media, a curious, cosmic connection was noted between the Heaven's Gate collective's professional engagement with the Internet, their faith that the passage of the Hale-Bopp comet would carry them away to a plane of existence beyond the burdens of human fleshy existence, and the globally familiar SWOOSH design on their identical new black Nike sneakers.[17]

For all its quirky technomysticism, indeed because of it, the Heaven's Gate community is exemplary of many other contemporary movements—geographically dispersed communities that disseminate charisma, and sometimes apocalyptic terror, through the informational channels of the Internet (see Poster 1997). Another example is Aum Shinrikyo, the Japanese sect whose release of nerve gas in the Tokyo subway was just the first phase of a more ambitious planned campaign. There are numerous other groups (e.g., Christian Identity, the Order, Posse Comitatus, and various other "militias," the World Trade Center bombers, Al-Qaeda, Falun Gong) that similarly seem to be resisting the homogenization of identity that allegedly follows from globalization even as they are making effective oppositional use of the digital communications and encryption technologies, offshore finance, transnational circuits of capital, arms, rumors, images, and techniques of terror that make up globalization's distinctive infrastructure.

"Modernity Falls Apart": Globalization, Disembedding, and the Disintegration of the Spatiotemporal Order of Modernity

Let us take the British sociologist Anthony Giddens, director of the London School of Economics and leading "third way" adviser to Britain's "New Labour" government, as a representative voice of liberal social thought at this global-transitional moment.[18] Giddens has defined *globalization* as "the intensification of worldwide social relations which link distinct localities in such a way that local happenings are shaped by events occurring many miles away and vice versa" (1990, 64). On the continuity/discontinuity of the "global" with the "modern," Giddens observes that "global markers—such as 'the year 2000' . . . shape our collective identity in a more integrated way than ever before; yet modernity consistently 'falls apart' as a disjointed series of contextual and material divisions" (1994, xiii). For Giddens, both the homogenization and the spatiotemporal dislocations associated with globalization are a consequence of the "tendencies of modernity," for modernity's "core," he proposes, "*is* precisely the transmutation of time and space" (ibid., xi–xii, emphasis in original).[19]

The global-millennial Y2K anxiety, when considered alongside many apocalyptic "particularist" passions and collectivities such as Heaven's Gate, betokens an underlying concern about contemporary "digitalized," "informationalized" modes of representation, calculation, commensuration of futures, securities, property rights, identities. These technologies exemplify what Giddens has called the distinctive "disembedding mechanisms" of modernity that enable human social relations to be "lifted out" of local contexts and restructured across infinite spans of time and space (Giddens 1990, 21).[20] For Giddens, this time-space distantiation and the disembedding mechanisms that make it possible are both central to the modern social order and, at the same time, key to its disintegration.[21] It is precisely this abstracting "disembedding effect" of modern practices of governance that relentlessly compels the modern order to transform itself from within, according to its own disruptive logic.

Giddens "distinguish[es] two types of disembedding mechanisms intrinsically involved in the development of modern social institutions"; these are the "creation of *symbolic tokens*" and the "establishment of *expert systems*" (ibid., 22; emphasis in original).

Money and Other Symbolic Tokens: Abstract Calculability and the Metaphysics of Equivalence

For Giddens, the paradigm case of *symbolic tokens* is money, as he draws on classical discussions by Marx, Georg Simmel, and John Maynard Keynes. His claim about money is, of course, neither very novel nor revealing of the present condition. Money has long been recognized, alongside writing, as a key coordinating medium that has for several thousand years enabled a number of social-cultural-political formations to be extended in space and time far beyond the immediacy of face-to-face interaction.

Giddens's point of departure is Marx's analysis of how money, as "pure commodity," generalizes exchange value and negates the substantive qualities of goods or services by substituting for them a universal, impersonal standard—it is by means of money magic/cash logic that the particularities of specific objects and actions are dissolved, held in solution, by the "liquidity" of currency (Giddens 1990, 22). Giddens borrows from Simmel the insight that money facilitates social relations of exchange across infinite distances; it functions "precisely as a means of bracketing time-space by coupling instantaneity and deferral, presence and absence" (ibid., 24–25). And, drawing on the work of Keynes, Giddens observes that modern money, what Keynes called "money proper," requires the state as "guarantor of value"; thus the modern nation-state coordinates private socio-economic relations through the medium of money by bringing "debt and credit into balance in respect of an indefinite number of transactions" (ibid., 24; see also Maurer in this volume).

It is this coordination of debt and credit that permits the "bracketing" of time by money, as finance "colonizes" the future by transforming it into a reserved and ordered "stream of obligations" (Giddens 1990, 24–27; see also Nigel Thrift's discussion of Giddens [1996, 216]). As Giddens concludes, "[t]oday, 'money proper' is independent of the means whereby it is represented, taking the form of pure information lodged as figures in a computer print-out" (1990, 25). Most instructive for my analysis here is to retrace Giddens's path of reasoning in the other direction, to note how what he too easily calls "pure information" is achieved on the model of "money proper" through the processes of disembedding human social relations from time and space, relying on informationalization and its "metaphysics of flows."[22] As Featherstone and Lash argue,

> it is the economy which is "determinant" . . . The abstract calculability and presumptions of formal equivalence involved in commercial transactions gives rise to what might be called a general metaphysics of equivalence . . . Hence "modernist identity" develops in "commercial civilizations." (In Featherstone, Lash, and Robertson 1995, 6).[23]

Coining Disembedded Knowledges: Expert Systems
In similar fashion, there at first appears nothing very illuminating about Giddens's description of the other disembedding mechanism that he argues distinguishes late modernity—*expert systems*. Giddens defines these as "systems of technical accomplishment that organize large areas of the material and social environments in which we live today" (1990, 27). These are organized as very general systems of abstracted and formalized knowledge/expertise of which laypeople have only a tenuous understanding, but in which they are obliged to place their trust as a condition of life in a complex modern state. Giddens gives examples of the architectural, aeronautical, and transport engineering systems that make much of contemporary life possible, yet that remain largely opaque to the majority of those who spend so much of their lives in large buildings, on airplanes, or in autos on motorways.

Giddens's description of expert systems could almost equally well characterize the building of the Egyptian or Mayan pyramids, Ankor Wat, Chartres cathedral, perhaps even Stonehenge. These were certainly all products of systematically organized and propagated esoteric knowledge formations. Yet, each of these knowledge formations was rooted in a historical and civilizational tradition—indeed, explicitly embedded in an entire regional or place-based cosmology (see Ponting 1991). What distinguishes contemporary expert systems from earlier knowledge formations is precisely their self-avowed disembeddedness (this fact also exposes a tautological aspect of Giddens's argument); for they define themselves by virtue of their portability and by the fact that they are decoupled from any cosmology beyond their own instrumental efficacy.

Yet, one might also say that this faith in their own decontextualized disembeddedness simply *is* the implicit cosmology or the metaphysics of modern expert systems. It embodies once again something like a fundamentalist faith in a metaphysics of globalizing flows.

Giddens observes that such disembedding mechanisms as symbolic tokens and expert systems "remove social relations from the immediacies of context," but they also "provid[e] 'guarantees' of expectations across distanciated time-space" (Giddens 1990, 28). The functioning of these disembedding mechanisms, he says, requires a specific "attitude of trust." This is, "in part an article of faith," but also a reliance on regulatory agencies, professional associations, and so on. The very notion of credit, on which any market exchange other than face to face depends, implies a sort of belief, or faith, if not necessarily in the other partner in the transaction, then in the sociolegal or other regulatory framework within which the exchange is taking place.

Giddens argues that the counterpart of trust is not risk but contingency. Risk is a profoundly modern notion, he notes, derived from early-modern maritime insurance usage. It refers to practices of calculating, distributing, and thereby institutionally managing the probabilistically projected costs and liabilities that may arise from the contingencies of any enterprise. The development of this risk-management system, and the trust it demanded, required both an organized market and a state-based system of legal-regulatory governance.

The Institutional Frames of Modernity: Capitalism and the State

Giddens has argued that the core of modernity is a transformation of time and space that marks a sharp disjuncture from all other "premodern" worldviews. He further argues that these transmutations of space-time are a consequence of characteristically modern disembedding mechanisms that enable human social relations to be "lifted out" and restructured across potentially infinite spans of time and space. What ultimately stabilizes the disembedding effects of modernity are its central institutional forms, "capitalism" and the "nation-state."[24]

The connection is evident between the "creation of symbolic tokens" (currency, securities, or other "money equivalents") and the structured forms and norms of market interaction that we know as capitalism. And, to the extent that Giddens and Keynes are correct that the state must serve as "guarantor of value" of money, then capitalism and the state are inseparably linked in the functioning of markets.

Less obvious is the connection between Giddens's "establishment of expert systems" and the nation-state. Yet, from the moment in early-modern Europe when the nascent postfeudal states succeeded the Christian church in their control of knowledge, education, research, and technology, until very recently, the nation-state was the undisputed proprietor of expertise. It is worth recalling that Max Weber argued as recently as the 1920s that rational expert state-bureaucratic administration was the essence of modernity. Indeed, the Frankfurt School thinkers, their followers, and some of their critics have maintained one or another version of this view until the present time (cf. Habermas 1987). What is most interesting therefore is that, at least since the Reagan–Thatcher years, it is increasingly taken as simple common sense that state-bureaucratic governance equals irrationality, backwardness, and inefficiency.

In his 1985 study *The Nation-State and Violence*, Giddens defined the nation-state as "a bordered power-container," as "the pre-eminent power-container of the modern era." The word *container* in Giddens's phrase indicates both that the practices of modern state governance are power effects whose intended domain is the population and territory of the nation-state and that the nation-state is a bordered vessel whose borders "contain," constrain, and delimit the legitimate field of efficacy of the state's sovereign powers. Even in the case of overt warfare or other interstate conflict, what we see is not simply a clash of raw, un-channeled forces, but rather a clash of "power containers" asserting themselves as such—seeking to advance their interests as discrete and bordered power-containers.

It is implicit in Giddens's 1990 account of expert systems that specialized knowledges are no longer assumed to be exclusively, or even primarily, the province of the state; rather, Giddens's account simply accepts the logic of disembedded knowledge systems on its own terms, a logic of decontextualized informational flows. In doing so, Giddens tacitly privatizes knowledge as units of intellectual/informational property available for circulation in a global market.

As Giddens declares, "[i]n circumstances of accelerating global-ization, the nation-state has become 'too small for the big problems of life, and too big for the small problems of life'" (Giddens 1990, 65, cit-ing Daniel Bell). In Giddens's own "third way" account of the processes of globalization, we see that the global market is unproblematically enthroned as the engine of global change in culture and politics, and that the nation-state has devolved to the role of just one among an array of regulatory structures. The state surfs the giddy ups and downs of global capital flows capable, at most, of steering the economy, or accel-erating or braking it a little, from time to time by shifting its political and institutional weight this way or that.

Since the seventeenth century, the emancipatory project of lib-eral modernity has striven for rights of property and for freedoms of belief and knowledge—these were rights against the repressive powers of state-regulatory governance, rights integral to the flourishing of civil society. In classical Hegelian terms, the liberal state emerged as a real-ization of the ethical-rational dimension of civil society and the market.

Giddens's account suggests that under the conditions of globalization the situation has been reversed; now the state has become handmaiden to the market in what might be likened to a striking instance of "regulatory capture."

It is not just disembedded flows of information, commodities, and people that are exceeding traditional state governance, but the contingencies, risk pools, and probabilities of global modernity that overflow state-territorial frontiers.[25] As Giddens quotes Ulrich Beck: "The most intimate—say, nursing a child—and the most general—say, a reactor accident in the Ukraine, energy politics—are now *directly* connected" (ibid., 121; empasis in original). In disembedded tokens and knowledges, the informational media representations of risk, questions of ontology, of nature, time, space, and contingency, are all held in solution by the metaphysics of flows. There is a fluid continuity between micro- and macrolevels of understanding, as these contingencies both subtend and supervene the governing capacities of the nation-state. Here, once again, Giddens argues that these risks and contingencies are distinctive of the modern order and very different from the threats of "premodern natural" disasters, plagues, and catastrophes:

> The contrast . . . is a very marked one. [Modern e]cological threats are the outcome of socially organized knowledge, mediated by the impact of industrialism on the material environment. They are part of what I call a new *risk profile* introduced by the advent of modernity. By a risk profile I mean the particular portmanteau of threats or dangers characteristic of modern life. (Ibid., 110; emphasis in original)

Waiting for a Screen Savior:
Flying Windows and God-Tricks for the End Times
No matter whether one regards globalization as the triumphal culmination of modernity's emancipatory Enlightenment project or as the apocalyptic fragmentation of modernity's world-picture, this plague of anxiety, this "Y2K problem," arises precisely to the extent that our digitized futures can no longer be enumerated in the same sequence as our

analog pasts. These "Y2K" crises mark the ending of an established order of sequential periodization, an end of history as it has been written, and the inception of a new temporality, one of stasis and catastrophe, of chance and risk management. Similarly, the viruslike simultaneous dispersion of the Y2K anxiety through global circuits of connection points to a compression or collapse of the modern global cartography of territorial distance and differentiation into today's "global positioning system," that is, into a new postgeographic, even postgeometric, ordering of spaces.

The "Y2K" plague is just one among many portents that our moment of globalization is rebooting the modern world-picture. It is redrawing the topography and rewriting the history of its uneasy present, busily imaging itself as a point of disjuncture, as the ending of things as they are known and a commencement of a new order of planetary governance. Could it be that globalization is itself a sort of abracadabra, a magical incantation to call up the zeitgeist of our moment, conjuring up a generalized historical agency whose locus cannot be identified nor even questioned? Instead of asking if it is the "invisible hand" of the "global economy" or the driving force of means–end technological logic, we might ask whether the "inevitability of globalization" is what Donna Haraway (1991) calls a "god-trick," a rhetorical naturalization of contingent events which lends to a quite specific set of possibilities an aura of necessity/inevitability?[26]

Something is definitely up with the familiar world-picture of modernity. No matter whether it is called high modernism, late or postmodernity, a growing sense of doubt is afflicting the ocular perspective, Cartesian spatial grid, and classical Newtonian mechanics of time and motion that have organized the cartography of modern territorial states and national regimes of knowledge, the familiar narratives of histories and civilizations. The quadratic screen of the world-picture is disaggregating into an oscillating array of pixilated icons and indexical point-and-click chronotopes that exceed our screens' enframing of time and space. With no screen savior yet at hand, there is a constant and heightening anxiety that the software will crash.[27]

Notes

This essay owes a great deal to close readings of it by Bill Maurer, Liisa Malkki, Laura Garcia-Moreno, and Kitty Calavita. All remaining errors and incoherences remain the private property of the author.

1. In this connection, see Donna Haraway's discussion of *National Geographic*'s history of popularizing globalist imagery. She cites in particular its January 1988 issue, which "featured on the front cover the holographic portrait of the endangered planet Earth at the dawn of the decade to save man's home world . . . [while a] holographic ad for McDonald's . . . the transnational fast-food chain . . . graced the back cover" (Haraway 1997, 165). Haraway notes that *National Geographic*'s readership has long numbered in the millions.

2. A close look at how the sentences in this excerpt have been selected and edited together suggests that *National Geographic* has appropriated Marx in a quite "postmodern" direction, inverting the primacy in Marx's theory of the "modes of production" in order to privilege instead the "magical" forces of what Marx called commodity fetishism, what many now regard as the creative power of consumption (Appadurai 1996, 41–42, 66–85), and to highlight the convergence of the "cultural" and the "economic" in the "new late-capitalist world-system" (Jameson 1998, 60).

3. *The Communist Manifesto*'s claim that "[n]ational differences and antagonism between peoples are daily more and more vanishing" is routinely quoted in support of the McWorld view that globalization is erasing the frontiers of nation-state political governance and homogenizing the world's diverse cultures into a uniform puree as an inevitable consequence of means–ends rationality and the drive for ever-greater efficiency embodied in innovation in economic and communications technologies (Marx and Engels 1998).

It seems that almost every recent text on contemporary global finance quotes Marx to the effect that quicksilver capital, as it relentlessly drives technological innovation, is accomplishing the "annihilation of space by time." However, Nigel Thrift tells us that this observation was not original to Marx, that it was in fact a "favorite meditation of Victorian writers" confronting the acceleration in human experience and social relations wrought by telegraphy and railway transport (Thrift 1996, 264, 309). For a contemporary variation on the "end of geography," see O'Brien (1992).

4. Fukuyama is quite literal-minded about this thesis. In his most recent work, he argues that, because of the changes in human nature brought about by

biotechnology, human history is indeed at an end and we are already embarked upon a future that is "posthuman" (Fukuyama 2001).

5. As Donna Haraway has observed, "NASA photographs of the blue, cloud-swathed whole Earth are icons for the emergence of global, national, and local struggles over a recent natural technical object of knowledge called the environment" (1997, 174). "The globalization of the world, of 'planet Earth,' is a semiotic-material production of some forms of life rather than others. Techno-science is the story of globalization; it is the travelogue of distributed, heterogenous, linked sociotechnical circulations that craft the world as a net called the global." (ibid., 12).

6. The Cartesian grid work of space, especially as exemplified by the lines of latitude and longitude projected onto an image map of the earth, is therefore the cardinal representation of the modern order of space and time (time, because longitude could not be definitively determined before the invention of a reliable chronometer; see, e.g., Landes 1983; Harvey 1989, 226–28).

The relation between this grid of "abstract space" and concrete concerns of military and commercial transport and communication is apparent in the fact that, from the seventeenth century to the present day, the zero point of the world grid of time and space has remained the site of the central timepiece of the British navy, the Royal Naval Observatory at Greenwich (also the site of the millenial celebratory Dome and Eye).

Similarly, an organized system of time zones was the product of the need for unified railway timetables across the great geographic expanse of the late-nineteenth-century United States. Organized by private American railway companies in 1883, the time-zone system was only made official during World War I, when Woodrow Wilson federalized control of rail transport for the war effort. (On the relation between the "social production" of the grid of "abstract space" and modern capitalism, see Lefebvre 1991; on chronometry and time zones, see Landes 1983.)

7. The title of Latour 1993. Indeed, the very fact that we expect premodernity, modernity, and postmodernity to manifest themselves as discrete stages that follow and supplant one another is itself the mark of a fundamentally modern conceptual scheme—that history should follow the stages that modernization theory has foreordained for it. Why, in fact, should "premodern customary" kinship-based societies *necessarily* be superseded by modern "rationalized" territorial nation-states that in turn *necessarily* give way to the advancing flows of

"hyperrational" globalization? Why should we be surprised to find what the studies in this volume have shown—that virtually all of these forms of governance can be identified, not in the theoretical imagination, but in actual practice, in diverse local and regional contexts today?

James Ferguson has pointed out that such evolutionary stage narratives were drawn upon Darwinian models (see here Marx's dedication of *Capital* to Charles Darwin), but they turn out not to work well even for biological history (as Stephen Jay Gould showed for years: dinosaurs and saber-toothed tigers are indeed no longer with us, but the most "primitive" early life forms such as bacteria might well be adjudged the most enduring and successful right down to the present moment, and we relatively recently arrived Homo sapiens ought not be overhasty in proclaiming ourselves the last and highest stage of life—the protozoans may very well write our eulogies). So why, Ferguson (1998) asks, should we expect that such evolutionary stage models will be adequate to describe developments in human sociopolitical history, such as globalization?

8. Calavita and Suárez-Navaz (in this volume) observe that, as Spain has "joined Europe," it has once again taken on a role as the southern rampart protecting the "European fortress" from invasion across the Straits of Gibraltar. A half millennium ago, Spain was the southern bulwark of Western Christendom, as it is once again now of a European Community or European Union that, interestingly, exhibits very nearly the same geographic silhouette as fifteenth-century Catholic Europe. Calavita and Suárez-Navaz also note that this new/old role for Spain is accompanied once again by an internal policing of ethnoracial identities, distinguishing Europeans from others. See also Calavita 1998.

9. It was Montesquieu who, in his 1751 *De l'Esprit des lois*, proposed a theory that connected social-ecological regions, natural/national reason, and the government of laws. Montesquieu argued that local geography and climate combined to produce different national characters and that there must therefore be laws appropriate to each nation's "nature." Temperate climes and island or mountainous geographies—like those of England and Switzerland—are conducive to democratic government; hot countries like India or flat lands like Poland are prone to despotism.

Montesquieu was far from an isolated eccentric; indeed, he was the most influential eighteenth-century proponent of constitutional government and the primary theorist of the tripartite separation of powers model that first achieved realization in the U.S. Constitution. Thomas Jefferson declared himself

Montesquieu's disciple and was the thinker who most effectively carried Montesquieu's ideas into practice, and not only in the U.S. Constitutional Convention of 1787.

Jefferson's 1798 work, *Notes on Virginia*, was a striking example of Montesquieu's political ecology. Jefferson observed that the different climates and land forms of the thirteen states produced distinct local characters—from hot-blooded Southerners to laconic New Englanders—and that each of the new states ought therefore have a set of laws appropriate to its character. Jefferson's exposition in *Notes on Virginia* proceeds somewhat in the manner of an incremental scientific proof. He began by describing the geographic formations of Virginia: the low-lying coastal wetlands of the Tidewater region, the elevations and watercourses of the Piedmont and the western mountains. He then described the flora and fauna of the regions, and then the three human races—the native tribes, the slaves of African descent, and the white citizens—and their patterns of settlement, forms of habitation, and their relations to one another. Finally, Jefferson proceeded to "derive" the Constitution and legal code of Virginia (much of which he had himself drafted according to this organic regionalist logic) from the specific "natural" facts of Virginia's land, climate, flora, fauna, and peoples.

10. And, much as under the nineteenth-century specter of capitalism, the great majority of human beings whose life circumstances are daily being reconfigured by the events gathered under the rubric of globalization have never heard the word, still less are they likely to join in celebration of its triumphal revelation. One remarkable feature of contemporary globalization discourse, more than a decade after the implosion of "actually existing socialism," is the resurrection of Marx and Engels as prophets of the twenty-first century. Virtually all of the most commonly heard versions of globalization treat it as a revival, or the culminating evolutionary stage of, the tendencies and elements of nineteenth-century capitalism that Marx and Engels spoke of: rapid advances in technologies of production, communications, transport, exploding urbanization, and the colonial-era organization of the world market. The major elements of this view are shared as least as much by those who regard globalization as the final triumph of human reason as by those who regard it as modernity's apocalypse.

11. On the notion of "governmentality," see Foucault and Gordon in Burchell, Gordon, and Miller 1991; on the notion of "ungovernment," derived by Pat O'Malley from the work of Foucault, see O'Malley 1994. As Aihwa Ong argues (in this volume), "globalization has induced governments to think up new ways

of governing and valuing different categories of their subject populations"; that is, globalization is emerging as new arts and rationalities of government, or governmentalities.

This is, in Foucault's words a government *omnes et singulatum*, of "all and each," which "manages populations in place" as an "economic pastorate," ultimately an "economic government" that is mobilized as "a government of the social" (Burchell, Gordon, and Miller 1991, 8–36). It is this line of inquiry in Foucault's later work on governmentality, and in the work of others who have followed his lead, that we are pursuing in this study of globalization. Rather than setting out either to bless globalization or to condemn it, our project is to explore the forms and practices and effects of governmentality that are integral to global modernity's architecture of flows and freedoms. We ask what are the rationalities of government implicit within global modernity's project of mobilizing space, time, and difference.

12. In what is probably the single most quoted book on globalization, Benjamin Barber's 1995 *Jihad vs. McWorld*, the author describes the global-homogenizing effects of American-style consumption-propelled capitalism as "McWorld." This is a "new world being *imagineered*," in the Walt Disney Corporation's copyrighted term (Barber 1995, 97). McWorld is a vision of the "future [painted] in shimmering pastels, a busy portrait of onrushing economic, technological, and ecological forces that demand integration and uniformity and that mesmerizes peoples everywhere with fast music, fast computers, and fast food—MTV, Macintosh, and McDonald's—pressing nations into one homogenous global theme park, one McWorld tied together by communications, information, entertainment, and commerce" (ibid., 4).

13. This intertwining of economic and information technologies, their metaphoric "on-line" imageries of flow and speed and connectivity, and their combined effects on the nation-state and other structures of sociopolitical governance is one of the key themes of globalization discourse. Thomas Friedman, the foreign affairs columnist of the *New York Times*, is at the forefront of globalization boosterism. Friedman offers a metaphor that wonderfully illustrates his imagining of governance, economic as much as, or more than, political, under globalization. He says that he "compare[s] countries to three parts of a computer." He likens the state institutions and economic infrastructure to "the actual machine, the 'hardware'"of a computer.

Friedman analogizes the "broad macroeconomic policies of any country" to the "operating system" of a computer. This permits him to rank different countries according to what he calls their "DOScapital"—on the model of the Microsoft DOS operating systems in 90 percent of personal computers—where, he says, the former Soviet bloc countries had a DOScapital level 0.0, Hungary and rural China are at DOScapital 1.0, Thailand and Indonesia are at DOScapital 3.0, Korea and Shanghai are at DOScapital 4.0, France, Germany, and Japan are at DOScapital 5.0, and the United States, Hong Kong, and the United Kingdom are at DOScapital 6.0. Finally, a country's "software," in Friedman's metaphor, composes "all the things that fall broadly in the category of the rule of law. Software is a measure of the quality of a country's legal and regulatory systems, and the degree to which its officials, bureaucrats, and citizens understand its laws, embrace them, and know how to make them work. Good software includes banking laws, commercial laws, bankruptcy rules, contract laws, business codes of conduct, a genuinely independent central bank, property rights that encourage risk-taking, processes for judicial review, international accounting standards, commercial courts, regulatory oversight agencies backed up by an impartial judiciary, law against conflicts of interest and insider trading by government officials, and officials and citizens ready to implement these rules in a reasonably consistent manner" (Friedman 1999, 128–29). Friedman's remarkable metaphor exemplifies several of the most distinctive features of millenarian triumphal globalization. His hardware–software divide reiterates the classic Marxian model of base and superstructure, reinforced by Friedman's not very subtle DOScapital–*Das Kapital* pun. His hierarchical ranking of countries from DOScapital 0.0 through 6.0, with the United States and Britain at the highest level, nicely recapitulates the crudest version of modernization theory and the "development" schema, wherein *Americanization* equals *modernization* equals *globalization*; and, finally, Friedman's very choice of computer architecture as a metaphor for the structure of global political economy offers a nice analogy to the way in which earlier cosmological views were metaphorically imagined as knowledge-representation media and technological devices of their age—just as seventeenth-century natural science deciphered the "Book of the World" and the eighteenth-century adherents of Newton's mechanics studied a "clockwork" universe.

14. Representative texts of the genre include *Blur: The Speed of Change in the Connected Economy* (Davis and Meyer 1998), *Faster: The Acceleration of Just about Everything* (Gleick 1999), and many other similar works.

15. Of course, the epochal hype of triumphal globalization claims too much. Globalization is routinely heard to describe everything from the World Trade Organization to what Jürgen Habermas (1987) has called modernity's "unfinished project" of Enlightenment. This is the modern vision of individual freedoms and the flows are made possible by their disembedding from traditions and localisms, by advances in technology that have enabled the organization of an around-the-clock and around-the-world market in securities and commodities and futures. This is the arrival of a regime of universal human rights and the formation of transnational alliances of modernity's outsiders: indigenous peoples, women, children, ethnoreligious and sexual minorities, oppressed classes, and endangered species, bioregional ecosystems, the rain forests, the seas, the ozone layer, and the totality of Nature on Earth.

This is the globalizing triumphalism sometimes termed "globaloney" (Krugman 1998). This sloganeering, periodizing rhetoric of globalization works to naturalize the current regime of planetary distribution of capital and resources and to claim for the status quo the status of a foreoredained evolutionary stage.

16. The *Wall Street Journal* reported that at least 15 percent of Americans believe that either Microsoft or the White House was "hiding the solution to the Y2K bug" (September 7, 1999).

17. On Nike and its imagery as representative of the new global corporation, see LaFeber 1999. News commentators pondered the fact that sexual relations among Heaven's Gate members were prohibited, very much as in earlier American Christian craft communities such as the Shakers. That its leader, Marshall Applewhite, and others of the group had undergone surgical removal of their testicles also resonated with a long Christian mystical-ascetic tradition of the mortification of the flesh.

18. Roland Robertson has divided globalization theorists into two camps: "homogenizers" and "heterogenizers." The former group, in which he places Giddens, regards globalization as a leveling of differences as a "consequence of modernity" (Giddens 1990). Robertson's "heterogenizers" include postcolonial theorists such as Edward Said, Stuart Hall, Homi K. Bhabha, and "reflexive" anthropolgists such as James Clifford and George Marcus. Robertson finds that Giddens's analytics of globalization—especially his attention to time-space distanciation and to disembedding mechanisms—are useful points of departure, but that Giddens's theorizing is characteristically too committed to an enterprise of generalization and abstraction to be of much help in specific cases

(Robertson 1995, 26–27). Ultimately, the argument is not between anthropology and sociology or political science, but between those committed to modernization theory and related universalizing evolutionary schemes, on the one hand, and their critics, on the other.

19. To quote Giddens again: "it is not sufficient merely to invent new terms, like post-modernity and the rest. Instead, we have to look again at the nature of modernity itself which, for certain fairly specific reasons, has been poorly grasped in the social sciences hitherto. Rather than entering a period of post-modernity, we are moving into one in which the consequences of modernity are becoming more radicalized and universalized than before. Beyond modernity, I shall claim, we can perceive the contours of a new and different order, which is 'post-modern'; but this is quite distinct from what is at the moment called by many 'post-modernity.'" (Giddens 1990, 2–3)

20. As Giddens explains: "The image evoked by disembedding is better able [than are classical evolutionary models of societal development] to capture the shifting alignments of time and space which are of elementary importance for social change in general and for the nature of modernity in particular" (ibid., 21–22).

21. Here, Giddens comes very close to Joseph Schumpeter's influential view of capitalism as a "creative destruction" that is necessarily integral to modern progress (Schumpeter 1939).

22. See Coombe, in this volume.

23. A quotation from Jonathan Friedman has been omitted here and the original order of sentences has been altered for clarity.

24. "If capitalism was one of the great institutional elements promoting the acceleration and expansion of modern institutions, the other was the nation-state" (Giddens 1990, 62).

25. These apparently countervailing tendencies toward increasing socioeconomic globalization, on the one hand, and intensifying localism, on the other, are captured as two facets of a single dynamic dialectical process in the concept of "glocalization" (see Roberts, in this volume). As Giddens observes: "This is a dialectical process . . . *Local transformation* is as much a part of globalization as [is] the lateral extension of social connections across time and space . . . The outcome [of factors such as world money and commodity markets] is not necessarily, or even usually, a generalized set of changes acting in a uniform direction, but consists in mutually opposed tendencies. The increasing prosperity of an

urban area in Singapore might be causally related, via a complicated network of global economic ties, to the impoverishment of a neighborhood in Pittsburgh whose local products are uncompetitive in world markets . . .

The development of globalized social relations probably serves to diminish some aspects of nationalist feeling linked to nation-states (or some states) but may be causally involved with the intensifying of more localized nationalist sentiments . . . At the same time as social relations become laterally stretched and as part of the same process, we see the strengthening of pressures for local autonomy and regional cultural identity" (Giddens 1990, 64–65; emphasis in original).

26. For Haraway, both poles of the usual epistemological opposition between the totalizing objectivity associated with modern science and subjectivist relativism are "god-tricks": "Relativism is a way of being nowhere while claiming to be everywhere equally. The 'equality' of positioning is a denial of responsibility and critical inquiry. Relativism is the perfect mirror twin of totalization in the ideologies of objectivity; both deny the stakes in location, embodiment, and partial perspective; both make it impossible to see well. Relativism and totalization are both 'god-tricks' promising vision from everywhere and nowhere equally and fully" (Haraway 1991, 191). In much the same way, globalization is consistently presented as either a unitary world system or an utter fragmentation—either radical totality or radical difference. What this binarism misses is the actuality of what Haraway calls "situated knowledges" and the positivity of their practices and their effects.

27. For an exploration of the analogy between the anxiety that the modern global political order is in crisis and a software crash, see Neal Stephenson's 1992 novel *Snow Crash*. In a book review of "political science fiction," Francis Fukuyama praises the novel. He says that Stephenson is "dealing with the moral breakdown of future societies" and that *Snow Crash* "presents an amusing picture of the post-nation-state world" (Fukuyama 1997, 153).

References

Abu-Lughod, Janet. 1991. "Going beyond Global Babble." In *Culture, Globalization, and the World-System*, ed. Anthony D. King. London: Macmillan.

Anderson, Benedict. 1991. *Imagined Communities: Reflections on the Origins and Spread of Nationalism.* 2d ed. New York: Verso.

Appadurai, Arjun. 1996. *Modernity at Large: Cultural Dimensions of Globalization.* Minneapolis: University of Minnesota Press.

Arquilla, John, and David Ronfeldt, eds. 2001. *Networks and Netwars: The Future of Terror, Crime, and Militancy*. Santa Monica, Calif.: RAND Publications.

Auerbach, Erich. 1957. *Mimesis: The Representation of Reality in Western Literature*. Trans. Willard Trask. Garden City, N.Y.: Doubleday.

Balkin, Jack M. 1998. *Cultural Software: A Theory of Ideology*. New Haven: Yale University Press.

Barber, Benjamin. 1995. *Jihad vs. McWorld*. New York: Random House.

Basch, Linda, Nina Glick Schiller, and Cristina Szanton Blanc. 1994. *Nations Unbound: Transnational Projects, Postcolonial Predicaments, and Deterritorialized Nation-States*. Langhorner, Pa.: Gordon and Breach.

Boal, Iain. 1995. "A Flow of Monsters." In *Resisting the Virtual Life: The Politics and Culture of Information*, ed. Iain Boal and James Brook. San Francisco: City Lights Press.

———. 1998. *Both Limbs and a Fork: Nature and Artifice on the West Coast*. San Francisco: Yerba Buena Center for the Arts Publication.

Bourdieu, Pierre. 1998. *Acts of Resistance: Against the New Myths of Our Time*. Trans. Richard Nice. Cambridge: Polity Press.

Braudel, Fernand. 1984. *Civilization and Capitalism: The Perspective of the World*. New York: Harper and Row.

Burchell, Graham, Colin Gordon, and Peter Miller, eds. 1991. *The Foucault Effect: Studies in Governmentality with Two Lectures and an Interview with Michel Foucault*. Chicago: University of Chicago Press.

Calavita, Kitty C. 1998. "Immigration, Law, and Marginalization in a Global Economy: Notes from Spain." *Law and Society Review* 32(3): 529–66.

Castells, Manuel. 1996. *The Rise of the Network Society*. Oxford and Malden, Mass.: Blackwell Publishers.

Cohn, Norman. 1961. *The Pursuit of the Millennium*. New York: Harper Books.

Davis, Mike. 1998. *Ecology of Fear: Los Angeles and the Imagination of Disaster*. New York: Metropolitan Books.

Davis, Stan, and Christopher Meyer. 1998. *Blur: The Speed of Change in the Connected Economy*. Reading, Mass.: Addison-Wesley.

Derrida, Jacques. 1994. *Specters of Marx: The State of the Debt, the Work of Mourning, and the New International*. London and New York: Routledge.

Drezner, Daniel. 1998. "Book Review of *The End of History and the Last Man*." *Current* 400: 26–34.

Escobar, Arturo. 1995. *Encountering Development: The Making and Unmaking of the Third World*. Princeton, N.J.: Princeton University Press.

Fabian, Johannes. 1983. *Time and the Other: How Anthropology Makes Its Object*. New York: Columbia University Press.

Featherstone, Mike, Scott Lash, and Roland Robertson, eds. 1995. *Global Modernities*. London: Sage Publications.

Ferguson, James. 1998. Remarks at the Association for Political and Legal Anthropology's invited roundtable titled "Globalization and Governmentalities," at the annual meeting of the American Anthropological Association, December 6, 1998. The roundtable was organized and chaired by Bill Maurer; other participants included Fernando Coronil, Ulf Hannerz, Emily Martin, Aihwa Ong, Richard Perry, Beth Povinelli, Sylvia Yanagisako, Mayfair Yang, and Barbara Yngvesson.

Fitzpatrick, Peter. 1992. *The Mythology of Modern Law*. New York: Routledge.

Friedman, Thomas L. 1999. *The Lexus and the Olive Tree: Understanding Globalization*. New York: Farrar, Straus and Giroux.

Fukuyama, Francis. 1992. *The End of History and the Last Man*. New York: Free Press.

———. 1997. "Review of Political Science Fiction." Ed. Donald M. Hassler and Clyde Wilcox. *Foreign Affairs* 76(6): 153.

———. 1999a. Review of Thomas Friedman's *The Lexus and the Olive Tree*. *New Statesman*, July 5, 53–54.

———. 1999a. *The Great Disruption: Human Nature and the Reconstitution of Social Order*. New York: Free Press.

———. 1999b. "Second Thoughts: The Last Man in a Bottle (Socialism at the End of Human Economy)." *National Interest* 56 (summer): 16.

———. 2001. *Our Posthuman Future: Consequences of the Biotechnology Revolution*. New York: Farrar, Straus and Giroux.

Gellner, Ernest. 1983. *Nations and Nationalism*. Oxford: Blackwell.

Giddens, Anthony. 1985. *A Contemporary Critique of Historical Materialism*, vol. 2, *The Nation-State and Violence*. Cambridge: Polity Press.

———. 1990. *The Consequences of Modernity*. Stanford, Calif.: Stanford University Press.

———. 1994. "Foreword." In *NowHere: Space, Time, and Modernity*, ed. Roger Friedland and Deidre Boden. Berkeley: University of California Press.

———. 1995. "Book Review of Francis Fukuyama's *Trust: The Social Virtues and the Creation of Prosperity*." *New Statesman and Society* 8(374) (October 13): 30.

Gleick, James. 1999. *Faster: The Acceleration of Just about Everything*. New York: Pantheon Books.

Goldberg, David Theo. 1993. *Racist Culture: Philosophy and the Politics of Meaning*. Oxford: Blackwell.

Greenfield, Liah. 1992. *Nationalism: Five Roads to Modernity*. Cambridge: Harvard University Press.

Greenhouse, Carol J. 1996. *A Moment's Notice: Time Politics across Cultures*. Ithaca, N.Y.: Cornell University Press.

Gupta, Akhil, and James Ferguson. 1992. "Beyond 'Culture': Space, Identity and the Politics of Difference." *Cultural Anthropology* 7(1) (February): 6–23.

Habermas, Jürgen. 1987. *The Philosophical Discourse of Modernity*. Cambridge: Polity Press.

Hannerz, Ulf. 1996. *Transnational Connections: Culture, People, Places*. New York: Routledge.

Haraway, Donna. 1991. *Simians, Cyborgs, and Women: The Reinvention of Women*. New York: Routledge.

———. 1997. *Modest_Witness@Second_Millennium. FemaleMan_Meets_Onco-Mouse*. New York: Routledge.

Harvey, David. 1989. *The Condition of Postmodernity: An Enquiry into the Origins of Cultural Change*. Cambridge: Blackwell Publishers.

Hegel, G. W. F. [1819] 1952. *Philosophy of Right*. Trans. T. M. Knox. Oxford: Clarendon Press.

Heidegger, Martin. [1952] 1977. "The Age of the World-Picture." In *The Question concerning Technology and Other Essays*. Trans. William Lovitt. New York: Harper and Row.

Hilty, Wyn. 1999. "Machine Age Y2K: Now with Fewer Cranky Christians!" *Orange County Weekly* 5(5) (October 8–14): 16.

Hobsbawm, Eric. 1992. "Goodbye Columbus." *London Review of Books*, September 7.

Huntington, Samuel. 1996. *The Clash of Civilizations and the Remaking of the World Order*. New York: Simon and Schuster.

Jameson, Fredric. 1998. "Globalization as a Philosophical Issue." in *The Cultures of Globalization*, ed. Fredric Jameson and Masao Miyoshi. Durham, N.C.: Duke University Press.

Krugman, Paul. 1998. "Globalization and Globaloney." In *The Accidental Tourist*. New York: W. W. Norton.

LaFeber, Walter. 1999. *Michael Jordan and the New Global Capitalism.* New York: W. W. Norton.

Landes, David S. 1983. *A Revolution in Time: Clocks and the Making of the Modern World.* Cambridge: Harvard University Press.

Lash, Scott, and John Urry. 1994. *Economies of Signs and Space.* London: Sage Publications.

Latour, Bruno. 1993. *We Have Never Been Modern.* Trans. Catherine Porter. Cambridge: Harvard University Press.

Lefebvre, Henri. 1991 (1974). *The Social Production of Space.* Trans. Donald Nicholson-Smith. Oxford: Blackwell.

Lipschutz, Ronnie. 1992. "Reconstructing World Politics: The Emergence of Global Civil Society." *Millennium: Journal of International Studies* 21(3): 399.

Lovejoy, Arthur O. 1936. *The Great Chain of Being: A Study of the History of an Idea.* Cambridge: Harvard University Press.

Luke, Timothy. 1995. "New World Order or Neo-world Orders: Power, Politics, and Ideology in Informationalizing Glocalities." In *Global Modernities,* ed. Mike Featherstone, Scott Lash, and Roland Robertson. London: Sage Publications.

Malkki, Liisa. 1992. "National Geographic: The Rooting of Peoples and the Territorialization of National Identity among Scholars and Refugees." *Cultural Anthropology* 7(1) (February): 24–43.

Marx, Karl, and Friedrich Engels. [1848] 1998. *The Communist Manifesto: A Modern Edition.* Introduction by Eric Hobsbawm. London: Verse.

Morley, David, and Kevin Robins. 1995. *Spaces of Identity: Global Media, Electronic Landscapes, and Cultural Boundaries.* New York: Routledge.

Moynihan, Daniel Patrick. 1993. *Pandemonium: Ethnicity in International Politics.* New York: Oxford University Press.

O'Brien, Richard. 1992. *Global Financial Integration: The End of Geography.* New York: Council on Foreign Relations Press.

Ohmae, Kenichi. 1990. *The Borderless World.* London: Collins.

O'Malley, Pat. 1994. "Gentle Genocide: The Government of Aboriginal Peoples in Central Australia." *Social Justice* 21(4) (winter): 46–66.

Parker, Geoffrey. 1999. *The Grand Strategy of Philip II.* New Haven: Yale University Press.

Perry, Richard Warren. 1995. "The Logic of the Modern Nation-State and the Legal Construction of Native American Tribal Identity." *Indiana Law Review* 28(3): 547–74.

————. 1996. "Rethinking the United Nations Right to Development: After the Critique of Development, after the Critique of Rights." *Law and Policy* 18(3/4): 225–50.

Ponting, Clive. 1991. *A Green History of the World: The Environment and the Collapse of Great Civilizations*. New York: Penguin Books.

Poster, Mark. 1997. "Nations, Identities, and Global Technologies." Unpublished manuscript.

Robertson, Roland. 1995. "Glocalization: Time-Space and Homogeneity-Heterogeneity." In *Global Modernities*, ed. Mike Featherstone, Scott Lash, and Roland Robertson. London: Sage Publications.

Rodrik, Dani. 1997. *Has Globalization Gone Too Far?* Washington, D.C.: Institute for International Economics.

Sassen, Saskia. 1995. *Losing Control: Sovereignty in an Age of Globalization*. New York: Columbia University Press.

Schumpeter, Joseph A. 1939. *Business Cycles: A Theoretical, Historical, and Statistical Analysis of the Capitalist Process*. New York and London: McGraw-Hill.

Stephenson, Neal. 1992. *Snow Crash*. New York: Bantam Books.

————. 1995. *The Diamond Age: A Young Lady's Primer*. New York: Bantam Books.

Therborn, Goran. 1995. "Routes to/through Modernity." In *Global Modernities*, ed. Mike Featherstone, Scott Lash, and Roland Robertson. London: Sage Publications.

Thrift, Nigel. 1996. *Spatial Formations*. London: Sage.

Todorov, Tzvetan. 1984. *The Conquest of America: The Question of the Other*. New York: Harper and Row.

Weber, Max. 1948. "The Nation." In *From Max Weber: Essays in Sociology*, trans. and ed. H. H. Gerth and C. Wright Mills. London: Routledge and Kegan Paul.

Wolf, Eric R. 1982. *Europe and the People without History*. Berkeley: University of California Press.

Zwingle, Erla. 1999. "A World Together." *National Geographic* 196(2) (August): 6–34.

Contributors

Kitty Calavita is professor of criminology, law, and society at the University of California, Irvine. Her research and teaching interests include sociolegal theory, immigration policy making, and white-collar crime. Her current research project is a comparative analysis of Spanish and Italian immigration policies.

Rosemary J. Coombe holds the Canada Research Chair in Law, Communication, and Cultural Studies in the Faculty of Arts at York University. She is the author of *The Cultural Life of Intellectual Properties*, as well as numerous articles in legal anthropology and the cultural studies of law. Her current research concerns the globalization of intellectual property norms and the ethics of exercising intellectual property rights in digital environments.

Susan Bibler Coutin is associate professor of criminology, law, and society at the University of California, Irvine. Her publications include *Legalizing Moves: Salvadoran Immigrants' Struggle for U.S. Residency* and *The Culture of Protest: Religious Activism and the U.S. Sanctuary Movement.* Her current research examines citizen-state relations within the Salvadoran diaspora.

Karen Leonard, a historian and anthropologist at the University of California, Irvine, has published on South Asian history and culture and

Asian American history and culture. Her books include *Social History of an Indian Caste: The Kayasths of Hyderabad*, *Making Ethnic Choices: California's Punjabi Mexican Americans*, and *South Asian Americans*. Her research interests now concern Muslim Americans and Hyderabadis working and living abroad.

Bill Maurer is associate professor of anthropology at the University of California, Irvine. He is the author of *Recharting the Caribbean: Land, Law, and Citizenship in the British Virgin Islands* and coeditor, with Alejandro Lugo, of *Gender Matters: Re-Reading Michelle Z. Rosaldo*.

Sally Engle Merry is professor of anthropology at Wellesley College. She is the author of *Colonizing Hawai'i: The Cultural Power of Law*, and her research focuses on colonialism and the anthropology of law.

Aihwa Ong is professor of anthropology and Southeast Asian studies at the University of California, Berkeley. Her interests are gender and Islam; Chinese transnationalism; and governmentality, migration, and citizenship. Her books include *Flexible Citizenship*; *Ungrounded Empires*; and *Buddha Is Hiding: Refugees, Citizenship, and the New America*. She is coeditor, with Stephen J. Collier, of *Global Assemblages: Oikas and Anthropos In-formation* (forthcoming).

Richard Warren Perry is associate professor and teaches law and society courses at San Jose State University. He was trained in law, linguistics, and philosophy, and he works in sociolegal theory and on cultural-anthropological studies of law, crime, and governmentality.

Susan Roberts is associate professor of geography at the University of Kentucky. Her interests in economic and political geography focus on the contemporary global economy and its regulation. She is coeditor of *An Unruly World? Globalization, Governance, and Geography*.

Lisa Sanchez is assistant professor of ethnic studies and critical gender studies at the University of California at San Diego. She has also taught at the State University of New York, Buffalo.

Liliana Suárez-Navaz is professor of anthropology at the Autónoma University in Madrid, where she coordinates a graduate program on migration and interethnic studies. She has conducted fieldwork in Latin America, southern Europe, and western Africa. She is the author of *The Rebordering of the Mediterranean: Boundaries and Citizenship in Southern Europe* and has written widely on migration, culture, and law.

Index